A Kabbalist in Montreal

The Life and Times of Rabbi Yudel Rosenberg

Touro University Press Books

Series Editor
MICHAEL A. SHMIDMAN, PhD (Touro College, New York)
SIMCHA FISHBANE, PhD (Touro College, New York)

TOURO UNIVERSITY PRESS

A Kabbalist in Montreal

The Life and Times of Rabbi Yudel Rosenberg

Ira Robinson

NEW YORK
2021

Library of Congress Cataloging-in-Publication Data

Names: Robinson, Ira, 1951- author.
Title: A Kabbalist in Montreal: the life and times of Rabbi Yudel Rosenberg/Ira Robinson.

Description: New York: Touro University Press, 2021. | Includes bibliographical references and index.
Identifiers: LCCN 2020034047 (print) | LCCN 2020034048 (ebook) | ISBN 9781644695036 (hardback) | ISBN 9781644695043 (adobe pdf) | ISBN 9781644695050 (epub)
Subjects: LCSH: Rozenberg, Yehudah Yudl, 1859-1935. | Rabbis--Poland--Tarłów Region--Biography. | Rabbis--Canada--Biography.
Classification: LCC BM755.R646 R63 2020 (print) | LCC BM755.R646 (ebook) | DDC 296.8/32092 [B]--dc23
LC record available at https://lccn.loc.gov/2020034047
LC ebook record available at https://lccn.loc.gov/2020034048

Published by Touro University Press and Academic Studies Press.
Typeset, printed and distributed by Academic Studies Press.
ISBN 9781644695036 (hardback)
ISBN 9781644695043 (adobe pdf)
ISBN 9781644695050 (epub)
ISBN 9798887194448

Touro University Press
Michael A. Shmidman and Simcha Fishbane, Editors
320 West 31st Street, Fourth Floor,
New York, NY 10001, USA
tcpress@touro.edu

Book design by PHi Business Solutions Limited.
Cover design by Ivan Grave.
On the cover: Photograph of Rabbi Rosenberg courtesy of Mr. Lionel Albert.
Manuscript by Rabbi Rosenberg courtesy of the Jewish Public Library of Montreal.

Academic Studies Press
1577 Beacon Street
Brookline, MA 02446, USA
press@academicstudiespress.com
wwwacademicstudiespress.com

To my young grandson, Ephraim Samuel Epstein

הבן יקיר לי אפרים

Jeremiah 31:20

Contents

Abbreviations ix
Preface xi

1. Introduction: Rabbi Yudel Rosenberg and the Paradigms of Jewish Modernity 1
2. On a Spiderweb Foundation: Yudel Rosenberg's Life in Small-Town Poland (1859–1889) 17
3. A Rabbi and Rebbe in Urban Poland (1890–1913) 38
4. "Allright! It's America!": A Rabbi in Toronto (1913–1918) 60
5. "The Rabbis Are for the Dollar": Rabbi Yudel Rosenberg and the Kosher Meat Wars of Montreal (1919–1935) 75
6. "Better to Be in Gehinnom": Yudel Rosenberg's Halakhic Voice 116
7. A "Folk Author": Yudel Rosenberg as Storyteller 142
8. "Almost Alone": Yudel Rosenberg as Preacher 173
9. Magic, Science, and Healing 190
10. "Those Who Understand Kabbala Are Extremely Rare in Our Generation": Yudel Rosenberg as Kabbalist 207
11. What Is Rabbi Yudel Rosenberg's Legacy? 242

A Chronological Bibliography of the Writings of Rabbi Yehuda Yudel Rosenberg 251
General Bibliography 267
Index 291

Abbreviations of Works by Rabbi Yudel Rosenberg

Ateret	*Sefer Ateret Tiferet* (1931)
Brivele	*A Brivele Fun di Zisse Mame Shabbes Malkesa* (1924)
Darsha	*Sefer Darsha Tsemer u-Fishtim* (1912)
Derekh Erets	*Derekh Erets*, unpublished manuscript, RFA, Savannah (written 1896)
Eliyahu	*Sefer Eliyahu ha-Navi'* (1910)
Goral	*Sefer Goral ha-'Assiriyot* (1904)
Greiditser	*Der Greiditser* (1913)
Haggada	*Haggada shel Pesaḥ 'im Perush R. Yehuda Liva'* (1905)
Haqqafot	*Seder Haqqafot le-Shmini Atseret ule-Simḥat Torah* (1909)
Homeopatia	*Homeopatia (1912)*
Ḥoshen	*Sefer Ḥoshen ha-Mishpat shel ha-Kohen ha-Gadol* (1913)
Qeri'ah	*Sefer ha-Qeri'ah ha-Qedosha* (1919)
Krizis	*Der Krizis fun Lodz Varsha* (1912)
KT	*Sefer Kol Torah* (1908)
Me'or	*Sefer Me'or ha Ḥashmal* (1924)
Miqveh	*Miqveh Yehuda* (1917–1919?)
Omer	*Omer va-Da'at* (page proofs, 1934; partial publication, 1996; full publication, 2007, 2020)
Nifla'ot	*Sefer Nifla'ot Maharal mi Prag 'im ha Golem* (1909)
NZ	*Nifla'ot ha-Zohar* (1927)
PY	*Peri Yehuda* (1935)
Prozbul	*Seder ha-Prozbul* (1910)
Refa'el	*Sefer Refa'el ha Mal'akh* (1911)
Refu'at	*Sefer Refu'at ha-Nefesh u-Refu'at ha-Guf* (1913)
Segulot	*Sefer Segulot u-Refu'ot* (1910)
Sha'arei	*Sefer Sha'arei Zohar Torah* (1905)

Shlomo	*Sefer Divrei ha Yamim le-Shlomo-ha Melekh* (1913)
Shpole	*Sefer Tif'eret Mahar'el mi-Shpole* (1912)
Yadot	*Sefer Yadot Nedarim* (1902)
ZK	*Sefer ha-Zohar ha-Qadosh* (two volumes, 1929–1930)
ZT	*Sefer Zohar Torah* (five volumes, 1924–1926)

OTHER ABBREVIATIONS

BMA	Ben-Meir Family Archive (Jerusalem)
KA	*Keneder Adler* (Montreal)
RFA	Rosenberg Family Archive (Savannah)
THJ	*Toronto Hebrew Journal* (Toronto)

Preface

I first came across the name of Rabbi Yehuda Yudel Rosenberg, the subject of this volume, quite by accident. In 1981, Library and Archives Canada in Ottawa put on an exhibition of rare Judaica and Hebraica from its then recently acquired Jacob Lowy collection. In this exhibition, the then curator, Brad Sabin Hill, presently Dean of the I. Edward Kiev Judaica Collection at George Washington University (who, I later discovered, was related through marriage with the Rosenberg family), inserted one volume of Rosenberg's Hasidic homilies entitled *Peri Yehuda,* of which you will hear later in this book. The exhibition catalogue called Yudel Rosenberg "Chief Rabbi of Montreal," and indicated that Rosenberg was "best known for his Hebrew edition of the *Zohar,* aside from several volumes of legends, folk-medicine and sorcery in Yiddish."[1]

This description piqued my curiosity. On the one hand, I was and am still interested in the history of Kabbala in general, and especially its popularization in modern times. I also maintain a scholarly interest in the development of Orthodox Judaism in North America. Rabbi Rosenberg, apparently, was a man who combined both areas of my scholarly interest in his career. Beyond that, he was also a Montrealer, for whom material might well be available in my own back yard.

I had no opportunity to pursue the matter further at that time, but Rabbi Yudel Rosenberg remained in my mind. A few years later, I began to follow up some of the leads I had acquired concerning him. These leads took me on an adventure of discovery, lasting more than three decades, which I share with you in this book.

Mi-kol melamdai hiskalti. I have learned from many people and benefited from the aid of many librarians and institutions in the course of researching and writing this book. I would like to acknowledge their help, however inadequately.

1 Brad Sabin Hill, ed., *Incunabula, Hebraica & Judaica* (Ottawa: National Library of Canada, 1981), 31.

I begin with my parents, Jacob and Hannah Robinson, who launched me at an early age on a voyage of discovery of Judaism and Jewish history that has lasted to this day. Their love and care never abated. Their personal intervention at a critical juncture of the research for this book is fondly remembered. The memory of my father, Jacob Robinson, who passed away in 1998, and of my mother, Hannah (Miller) Robinson, who died in 2007, remains a constant blessing to me.

The late David Rome, guide to generations of researchers into Canadian Jewry,[2] gave me my first solid information on Rosenberg. Though in many ways my research has tended to change the picture of Rosenberg he originally painted for me, without him, this book would likely not have even been attempted. Rosenberg's daughter Leah (Lilly), who was still among the living at the time I began my research, graciously gave me the benefit of her memories and her hospitality.[3] Other members of the extended Rosenberg family, including Lionel Albert, Yehoshua Ben Meir, Dr. Avrum Richler, Mordecai Richler, Baruch Rosenberg, and Dr. Lawrence Rosenberg have generously supplied me with information and documents over the years.

Yudel Rosenberg's surviving manuscripts and papers are to be found in several places. In Montreal, the Jewish Canadiana collection of the Jewish Public Library contains the largest single public collection of Rosenberg's works. The entire Jewish Public Library staff has helped me in one way or another. To single out the names of Claire Stern, Ronald Finegold, both now retired, Shannon Hodge, who has left the Library for another position, and Eiran Harris, who is still active, merely indicates that they maintained an interest in my work that went far beyond the call of duty. Janice Rosen of the Alex Dworkin Canadian Jewish Archives was equally helpful. During my research I had occasion to travel to Savannah, Georgia, where Rabbi Yudel Rosenberg's youngest son, Abraham Isaac, was rabbi for many years. Abraham Isaac Rosenberg had inherited his father's library and papers. Much of that library is now housed in the Ner Israel Yeshiva in Toronto. What remained of Rabbi Yudel Rosenberg's books, papers and manuscripts, however, were at that time to be found in Savannah, where Abraham Isaac's widow, Sylvia Mayta Sura Rosenberg generously allowed me access to examine them and photocopy extensively. Another

2 Ira Robinson, "David Rome as an Historian of Canadian Jewry," *Canadian Jewish Studies* 3 (1995): 1–10.

3 Leah Rosenberg's memoirs are published under the title *The Errand Runner: Reflections of a Rabbi's Daughter* (Toronto: Wiley, 1981).

important set of papers is found in Jerusalem, Israel where the descendants of Yudel Rosenberg's eldest son, Meir Joshua, reside. My thanks go to Rabbi Yehoshua Ben-Meir, who allowed these documents to be photocopied.

My search for Rosenberg publications and materials took me to the libraries of the Jewish Theological Seminary, the YIVO Institute (now part of the Center for Jewish History), the New York Public Library, Harvard University, the Jewish National and University Library (Jerusalem), the Schocken Library (Jerusalem), the Municipal Archives of Tel-Aviv, Library and Archives Canada (Ottawa), the Alex Dworkin Canadian Jewish Archives in Montreal, the Archives Municipales de Montréal, the Archives of the Quebec Ministry of Justice, (Montréal), and the Ontario Jewish Archives of Toronto. All of the librarians and archivists of these institutions were most helpful.

Aspects of this book have been seen and commented upon by my colleagues Morris Faierstein, Steven Lapidus, Sid Leiman, David Roskies, Marc Shapiro, Robert Shapiro, the late Stephen Speisman, and Eli Yassif. I received some important material and insights from Zanvil Klein, David Hoffman, and Marcin Wodziński of the University of Wrocław. Michael Stanislawski of Columbia University and Yakov Rabkin of l'Université de Montréal have helped me with some Russian language material. I am grateful to all of them for their time and effort. I have learned much from them, and particularly from Yassif's and Leiman's studies of Rosenberg. For part of this work, the late Henriette Kallus served as my research assistant. I am grateful for her help and fondly recall her friendship. I thank the Office of the Secretary of State for Multiculturalism of the Government of Canada for its partial funding of my research.

Special thanks go to my friend and colleague, Professor Simcha Fishbane of Touro College. While a doctoral student at Concordia, Fishbane took a personal interest in this project. He not only served as a sounding board for many of my ideas, but he also accompanied me on my research trip to Savannah, and was instrumental in obtaining material from the Ben Meir family in Jerusalem.

This book might have been completed well over a decade ago, save for my conviction that the documentary material relevant to Rabbi Rosenberg's career in Montreal had not yet been fully exploited and digested. Thus while I could say with certainty that I knew a great deal about Rabbi Rosenberg himself, I felt I still knew too little about the environment in which he functioned. Knowing, for instance, that he was preoccupied during much of his time in Montreal with his professional rivalry with Rabbi Hirsch Cohen, I could not responsibly write that chapter of the book without fully examining Rabbi Cohen himself, and the hundreds of letters Rabbi Cohen wrote which are extant in the Alex

Dworkin Canadian Jewish Archives in Montreal. Much of that time, therefore, was devoted to research on the Jewish community of Montreal in the early twentieth century, and particularly its immigrant Orthodox rabbinate. That research has now been published,[4] and its completion cleared the way for the fruition of this project.

Portions of the book have appeared in somewhat altered form in the journals *American Jewish Archives, Canadian Ethnic Studies, Canadian Jewish Studies, Jewish History, Journal of the Society of Rabbis in Academia, Judaism, Modern Jewish Studies,* and *Polin*. Their permission to republish the material is gratefully acknowledged. Special thanks to Stanley Diamond, Executive Director, Jewish Records Indexing–Poland, for sharing with me his discovery of Yudel Rosenberg's birth record.

My thanks go to my wife, Sandra Moskovitz Robinson and our children, Sara Libby and Yosef Dov, who managed to bear the inevitable strains that a project of this magnitude entail and, especially, my distractedness from everyday affairs while running down yet another lead. Whatever I have been able to achieve has been because of them. This book is theirs as well.

This book is dedicated to my young grandson, Ephraim Samuel Epstein. Every contact with him renews my faith in the future.

Montréal, Québec, Canada
January 3, 2020

4 Ira Robinson, *Rabbis and Their Community: Studies in the Immigrant Orthodox Rabbinate in Montreal, 1896–1930* (Calgary: University of Calgary Press, 2007).

CHAPTER ONE

Introduction: Rabbi Yudel Rosenberg and the Paradigms of Jewish Modernity

The modern era constitutes one of the great turning points in the course of Jewish history. Its coming presented Jews with unprecedented existential choices. It engendered a fundamental rethinking of the social, religious, and economic position of Jews who had hitherto lived separate, largely autonomous lives within Christian- or Muslim-dominated societies. Rethinking the position of Jews in society inevitably brought about a thorough reimagining of what Judaism and its traditional teachings might signify under radically new conditions. The many issues and movements that emanated from the turning point of Jewish modernity have significantly defined the directions Jews and Judaism have taken from early modern times to the present day. In the past, historians of the Jews and Judaism have most often considered the watershed of modernity through the prism of the dramatic and significant events, personalities, and movements mainly active in Western and Central Europe.[1] Gershon Hundert, however, has more recently argued that we should consider the importance of understanding Jewish modernity and all that it entailed from the perspective of the major Jewish population center of Eastern Europe that existed and functioned under significantly different conditions than obtained in Western Europe and that found its own path to modernity.[2] Eli Lederhandler and Arthur Green ably second Hundert's insight with respect to the nineteenth and early twentieth centuries.[3] More particularly, Glenn Dynner points out that:

---

1 For a statement of this position, see Michael Myer, "Where Does the Modern Period of Jewish History Begin?" *Judaism* 24, no. 3 (Summer 1975): 329–338.

2 Gershon David Hundert, *Jews in Poland-Lithuania in the Eighteenth Century: A Genealogy of Modernity* (Berkeley: University of California Press, 2004).

3 Eli Lederhandler, "Modernity without emancipation or assimilation? The case of Russian Jewry" in *Assimilation and Community: the Jews in Nineteenth-Century Europe*, ed. Jonathan Frankel and Steven J. Zipperstein (Cambridge: Cambridge University Press, 1992), 324,

> Theorists of modernity have begun to question historians' assumptions about the inexorable weakening of custom, tradition, and religious belief. ... Many now characterize modernity as a radically heterogeneous condition in which some individuals strive for ... freedom and autonomy while others opt instead for movements that privilege piety, humility, and self-denial.[4]

The scholarly interpretation of the complex processes that influenced the development of Judaism in the modern era thus tended to create narratives focussing on the decline, if not the actual fall, of traditional Jewish observance[5] as well as the emergence of other interpretations and restatements of Judaism, most notably Reform, which had its largest impact in Western Europe and North America.[6] Orthodoxy and its rabbis were all too often dismissed as a reactionary force, if not worse, echoing the sentiments of nineteenth-century advocates of Jewish westernization (*maskilim*) like Moses Leib Lilienblum who stated:

> Anyone acquainted with the spirit of our rabbis knows how ill-equipped they are to comprehend what is in the Jews' best interest; they do not know the suffering of their own people. ... I have no doubt whatsoever that the rabbis would be satisfied if the Jews did not win equal rights, just as long as every iota of the prayers inherited from our ancestors could be preserved.[7]

The firm conviction of Orthodoxy's opponents at that time was that the progress of nineteenth-century civilization was working decisively against Orthodoxy,

---

338; Arthur Green, "Three Warsaw Mystics," in *Kolot Rabbim: Essays in Memory of Rivka Shatz-Uffenheimer*, ed. Rachel Elior (Jerusalem: Magnes Press, 1997), 1–58.

4 Glenn Dynner, "Replenishing the "Fountain of Judaism": Traditionalist Jewish Education in Interwar Poland," *Jewish History* 31, nos. 3–4 (2018): 229–261.

5 Gershon Bacon, *The Politics of Tradition: Agudat Yisrael in Poland, 1916–1939* (Jerusalem: Magnes Press, 1996), 9–11; Cf. Glenn Dynner, "Jewish Traditionalism in Eastern Europe: The Historiographical Gadfly," *Polin* 29 (2017): 285–286.

6 Michael A. Meyer, *The Origins of the Modern Jew: Jewish Identity and European Culture in Germany, 1749–1824* (Detroit: Wayne State University Press, 1967, 1984); idem, *Response to Modernity: A History of the Reform Movement in Judaism* (New York: Oxford University Press, 1988). For the impact on Reform Judaism in nineteenth-century Eastern Europe, see Michael Stanislowski, *A Murder in Lemberg: Politics, Religion and Violence in Modern Jewish History* (Princeton: Princeton University Press, 2007), 34ff.

7 Cited in Antony Polonsky, *The Jews in Poland and Russia* (Oxford and Portland, OR: Littman Library of Jewish Civilization, 2009–2012), vol. 1, 438. Cf. Lederhandler, "Modernity without Emancipation or Assimilation?," 332.

or, in the words of Morris Winchevsky, writing to Perets Smolenskin in 1878: "Each new machine, each new railway station, each new telegraph, each new invention works against Hasidism."[8]

However, as Jay Berkovitz points out, this widespread scholarly preoccupation with the decline of Orthodox Judaism tends to obscure some important trends in cultural and intellectual Jewish history, especially those related to the role of Jewish law (halakha) and other aspects of Judaic religious life in this era.[9] These trends are among the matters that this book seeks to illuminate through its treatment of the life and times of Rabbi Yudel Rosenberg (1859–1935).

Certainly this book contends that there is a definite need to reconceptualise our understanding of these trends in the way suggested by Joshua Rothenberg:

> But the "modern" did not destroy or take over the "traditional". The "modern" galvanized the great mass of the hitherto inactive, and forced the traditional segment of the community to increase its efforts to compete with the new forms of Jewishness.[10]

This book also engages what Jack Wertheimer has called "Jewish continuity" as a factor in Jewish modernization:

> ... the persistence of tradition in modern Jewish life ... the Jews who have resisted change or managed to evade the powerful impress of modern culture in order to maintain a degree of fidelity to the traditions of the past ... emphasizing continuity rather than change.[11]

Likewise, we attempt in this book to understand in a more profound way the insight of David Biale, who points out that the Eastern European Jewish

---

8 David Assaf, "Hebetim Historiim ve-Ḥevratiyim be-Ḥeqer ha-Ḥasidut," in *Zaddik and Devotees: Historical and Sociological Aspects of Hasidism* [Hebrew], ed. David Assaf (Jerusalem: Zalman Shazar Center for Jewish History, 2001), 19–20.

9 Jay R. Berkovitz, "The Persona of a Poseq: Law and Self-Fashioning in Seventeenth-Century Ashkenaz," *Modern Judaism* 32, no. 3 (October 2012): 251–252.

10 Joshua Rothenberg, "Demythologizing the Shtetl," *Midstream* 27, no. 3 (March 1981): 30.

11 Jack Wertheimer, ed., *The Uses of Tradition: Jewish Continuity in the Modern Era* (New York and Jerusalem: Jewish Theological Seminary of America, 1992), x.

community of the nineteenth century created an "Orthodox Jewish culture which was every bit as 'modern'—in the sense of 'new'—as that of the modernizers."[12]

This book proceeds methodologically with the conviction that the insights of Langermann and Morrison are of prime importance in the sifting of historical evidence, particularly texts. As they state:

> The study of all ... themes in the production, preservation, and communication of knowledge begs for theoretical formulations, models that apply to a wide variety of historical instances. As in the natural and exact sciences, theory must be grounded in close observations of a sufficient number of cases. We are conscious of how, in the social sciences and humanities, theory sometimes must be reined in by the evidence, and influential theoretical models can cause scholars to overlook important evidence. Hence, as historians, we prefer weak versions of theories. We approach the data with theoretical considerations in mind, but do not allow existing theories to assert full hegemony over all of the data. Above all, we aim for insights about the nature of the texts themselves and of their transits. History is not an exact science; the available evidence must be read not only with philological rigor but also with imagination. Judiciously applying creative historical interpretation to new or forgotten texts, we hope to make a significant contribution to the history of texts, their contents, and their transits.[13]

Through its presentation of Rabbi Yudel Rosenberg's diverse rabbinic activities in Poland and North America, this book aims to join those studies that have sought to modify the previous narrative of nineteenth-century Eastern European Judaism[14] by showing that Eastern European Orthodoxy could itself serve as an agent of modernity no less than its religious and ideological opponents.[15]

---

12 Cited in Polonsky, *Jews in Poland and Russia*, vol. 2, 275.

13 Y. Tzvi Langermann and Robert G. Morrison, "Introduction," in *Texts in Transit in the Medieval Mediterranean*, ed. Y. Tzvi Langermann and Robert G. Morrison (University Park, PA: Penn State University Press, 2016), http://www.psupress.org/books/SampleChapters/978-0-271-07109-1sc.html, accessed October 30, 2016.

14 Cf. David E. Fishman, *Russia's First Modern Jews: the Jews of Shklov* (New York: New York University Press, 1995).

15 See Nahum Karlinsky, "The Dawn of Hasidic-Haredi Historiography" *Modern Judaism* 27, no. 1 (February 2007): 20–46; David Sorotzkin, *Orthodoxy and Modern Disciplination: The*

It will examine how an individual Eastern European Orthodox rabbi attempted to address contemporary issues through adapting new methods, forms and ideas in the service of the Orthodox message, in an atmosphere of perceived crisis, with the hope that they might resonate with his community's values.[16] In the eyes of many Orthodox Jews of that era, the solution to their perception of crisis could only be the coming of the messiah.[17] As we will see, messianic expectation played a key role in Rabbi Yudel Rosenberg's thought and writing and he often channelled his literary and publication efforts with the messiah in mind.

Through telling Rabbi Yudel Rosenberg's story, this book also attempts to better understand the complex role of the Orthodox rabbinate, a crucially important institution in an era in which modernity was both accommodated and resisted by Jews.[18] A comprehensive study of the Eastern European Orthodox rabbinate has not yet been written,[19] possibly because, as Ismar Schorsch has written in the context of the nineteenth-century German rabbinate, "the familiar is always difficult to define."[20] In fact there is not all that much scholarly literature on the institution of the rabbinate in Russia and Eastern Europe, considering its importance,[21] with the only study that attempted to define the institution in broader strokes, Simḥa Assaf's early monograph *Le-Kor'ot*

Production of the Jewish Tradition in Europe in Modern Times [Hebrew] (Tel-Aviv, Hakibbutz Hameuḥad, 2011), 15.

16 Cf. Berkovitz, "The Persona of a Poseq," 253.

17 Bacon, *The Politics of Tradition*, 64–67. Cf. Michael Stanislawski, "Reflections on the Russian Rabbinate" in *Jewish Religious Leadership: Image and Reality*, ed. Jack Wertheimer (New York: Jewish Theological Seminary, 2004), vol. 2, 440; Allan Nadler, "The War on Modernity of R. Hayyim Elazar Shapira of Munkacz," *Modern Judaism* 14 (1994): 236.

18 On accommodation and resistance as heuristic categories with respect to Orthodox rabbis in early twentieth-century North America, see Jeffrey Gurock, "Resisters and Accomodators: Varieties of Orthodox Rabbis in America, 1886–1983," *American Jewish Archives* 35 (1983): 100–187. Reprinted in *The American Rabbinate: A Century of Continuity and Change, 1883—1983*, ed. Jacob Rader Marcus and Abraham J. Peck (Hoboken, NJ: Ktav), 1985.

19 Simon Schwarzfuchs, *A Concise History of the Rabbinate* (Oxford: Blackwell, 1993), ix.; Haim Gertner, *The Rabbi and the City; the Rabbinate in Galicia and Its Encounter With Modernity, 1815–1867* [Hebrew] (Jerusalem: Zalman Shazar Center, 2013), 18; Mordechai Zalkin, *Rabbi and Community in the Pale* [Hebrew] (Jerusalem: Magnes Press, 2017), 1–2.

20 Ismar Schorsch, *From Text to Context: the Turn to History in Modern Judaism* (Hanover, NH: Brandeis University Press, 1994), 10.

21 Gershon Bacon, "Ha-Ḥevra ha-Mesoratit be-Temurot ha-'Itim: Hebetim be-Toldot ha-Yahadut ha-Ortodoqsit be-Polin uve-Rusya, 1850–1939," in *Qiyum va-Shever: Yehudei Polin le-Dorotehem*, ed. Israel Bartal and Yisrael Gutman (Jerusalem: Merkaz Zalman Shazar, 2001), vol. 2, 453 ff.

ha-Rabanut: be-Ashkenaz, Polinyah, ve-Lita' (Tel-Aviv, 1922), now nearly a century old.[22] Similarly, Eliahu Stern writes of:

> … the paucity of academic histories of modern rabbinics. … Over time what has come to pass for the academic study of modern rabbinic thought has been either the debunking of ultra-Orthodoxy's historical claims, showing the influences of "secular" ideas on the bearded and black hatted or, conversely, proving the endurance and so-called brilliance of Talmudic casuistry and exegesis.[23]

For Gershon Bacon as well the rabbinate is a subject scholars are only beginning to adequately investigate.[24]

In this connection, Michael Stanislawski has cogently pointed out that:

> … contrary to received stereotypes, traditional Jewish society in Russia, including the rabbinate, were hardly static in the imperial period, either ideationally or sociologically … rabbinic leaders were not relegated to the sidelines of life.[25]

Stanislawski has indeed presented a challenge to historians of the rabbinate with his interesting speculation that:

> The centuries-old system of Jewish self-government [in the Russian Empire] seems to have withered away slowly but substantially. To be sure, the Jewish community survived in law and in life, but it is not clear who was running the show. Perhaps some of the slack was taken up by rabbis and other religious functionaries; we can only speculate on the implications of such a radical change in Jewish self-rule. But we know even less about the role of rabbis in the administration of Jewish society in Russia than we do about the lay leadership. Put simply, traditional society in Eastern Europe has not yet been studied by secular historians, and history

---

22 Yedida Sharona Kanfer, "Lodz: Industry, Religion, and Nationalism in Russian Poland, 1880–1914" (PhD diss., Yale University, 2011), 139.

23 Eliyahu Stern, review of David B. Ruderman, *A Best-Selling Hebrew Book of the Modern Era: The Book of the Covenant of Pinḥas Hurwitz and Its Remarkable Legacy*, *AJS Review* 40, no. 2 (2016): 433.

24 Bacon, *Politics of Tradition*, 10–11.

25 Stanislawski, "Reflections on the Russian Rabbinate," 432.

> writing was not regarded as a suitable enterprise for the learned in traditional East European Jewish culture.[26]

This book is certainly indebted to the pioneering work of Gershon Bacon on the Eastern European rabbinate. Bacon has pointed out that:

> The fact that this most conservative of Jewish institutions underwent some degree of modernization and adaptation raises questions about the "master narrative" of Polish Jewish history. We customarily present the story of Polish Jewry as the slow but sure victory of the national approach to Judaism as the successor to both traditional Jewish society and to small but influential assimilationist minorities. At best, historians have widened the definition of "national" to take in movements such as Agudat Yisrael or the Bund, but the model remains the same. ... The traditional community suffered severe erosion, but its varied reactions to the challenges of the twentieth century have not received significant monographic treatment.[27]

Focussing on the rabbinic career of Rabbi Yudel Rosenberg, this book will attempt to arrive at a clearer and more nuanced understanding of the Eastern European rabbinate as a whole.

Along with Stanislawski and Bacon, this book will pay heed to other students of Jewish life in Imperial Russia, like Steven Zipperstein,[28] who have attempted to combat the common misconception that Jewish urbanization was a Western phenomenon and that Jews in Eastern Europe, until the convulsions of 1917, largely remained in culturally insulated small market towns

---

26 Michael Stanislawski, "The Transformation of Traditional Authority in Russian Jewry: the First Stage," in *The Legacy of Jewish Migration: 1881 and Its Impact*, ed. David Berger (New York, Brooklyn College Press, 1983), 28. For broader speculations on Russian Jewry in this era, see Michael Stanislawski, *For Whom Do I Toil?: Judah Leib Gordon and the Crisis of Russian Jewry* (New York: Oxford University Press, 1988); idem, "Reflections on the Russian Rabbinate," 432–433, 442.

27 Gershon Bacon, "Warsaw-Radom-Vilna: Three Disputes Over Rabbinic Posts in Interwar Poland," *Jewish History* 13 (1999), 122. Cf. idem., *The Politics of Tradition*, 9–11.

28 Steven Zipperstein, "Russian Maskilim and the City," in David Berger, ed., *The Legacy of Jewish Migration: 1881 and Its Impact* (New York: Brooklyn College Press, 1983), 32. Cf. Steven Zipperstein, *Imagining Russian Jewry: Memory, History, Identity* (Seattle: University of Washington Press, 1999).

[*shtetl*].[29] Up to the nineteenth century, the Jewish population of the Russian Empire had indeed been primarily rural in character. In the nineteenth century, however, partly due to economic factors and partly due to a conscious policy on the part of the Russian government, Jews became increasingly urbanized. Thus by the end of the nineteenth century, a majority of Jews in the Russian Empire lived in urban areas, many of them eking out a marginal existence.[30] The process of nineteenth-century Jewish urbanization in Eastern Europe was often painful, especially for the Orthodox, who in a sense had the most to lose with the increasing abandonment of the insulated, close-knit community and the social consensus of the small towns that had allowed their customs and lifestyle to prevail.

In the city, the Orthodox lifestyle was often challenged, in large measure because it was placed in competition with other Jewish lifestyles and religious choices that attracted numerous Jews. Furthermore, Orthodox Judaism in Eastern Europe in the nineteenth century was in the process of making a crucial and often painful transition from the premodern situation in which halakha and its lifestyle largely defined the Jewish community as a whole to the modern one in which adherence to halakha became essentially voluntary. This was an especially difficult transition since Orthodoxy could not constitutionally recognize the legitimacy of non-halakhic ideologies and lifestyles. This book will contend that halakha and the issues arising from it can usefully inform our understanding of the several alternative paths to Jewish modernity taken by Orthodox Jews and that the halakhic positions taken by Rabbi Yudel Rosenberg can help clarify our understanding of the nature of urban Orthodox Judaism and its halakhic issues. It will thus augment and nuance our still somewhat fragmentary picture of twentieth-century halakhic issues, in which Menahem Elon's magisterial treatment of Jewish law devotes only a few pages to twentieth-century developments in this area.[31] Though modern halakhic texts often need to be coaxed to tell their tales, it is as important to understand them as it is to understand the implications of halakhic texts for previous eras of Jewish

---

29 Antony Polonsky, *The Shtetl: Myth and Reality* (Oxford and Portland, OR: Littman Library of Jewish Civilization, 2004).

30 Sydney Stahl Weinberg, *The World of Our Mothers: the Lives of Jewish Immigrant Women* (Chapel Hill: University of North Carolina Press, 1988), 53.

31 Menachem Elon, *Jewish law: History, Sources, Principles. Ha-Mishpat ha-'Ivri* (Philadelphia: Jewish Publication Society of America, 1994), vol. 3, 1447–1451, 1495–1499.

history.[32] It is increasingly clear, from the work of Eliezer Schweid and others, that modern halakhic texts often bespeak important reconstructions of Judaism upon old foundations.[33]

In this book, we seek to better understand the phenomenon of Hasidism in the nineteenth century. From the perspective of the twenty-first century, Raphael Mahler's dismissal of Hasidism as a mere "blind alley in the historical path of the Jewish people" seems less and less cogent. [34] In the nineteenth century, Hasidism was in the process of evolving into a mass movement in which the differences with its opponents the *mitnagdim* at the beginnings of the Hasidic movement in the late eighteenth century were significantly mitigated as both Hasidim and *mitnagdim* faced a perceived common enemy in the form of "modernizers" in their various guises.[35] We still do not know enough about this process. As Kenneth Moss has stated:

> ... the paucity of properly social-historical research on orthodox Jewry in Warsaw renders it impossible at this stage to offer a full account. ... We need to know much more about the inner workings and the boundedness of the community (or, more likely, communities), the degree of social control exerted by various orthodox and Hasidic leaders in the city, and what various degrees of orthodoxy really entailed. Even the raw numerical strength of observant Jews in the city is unclear.[36]

Moss thus emphasizes that we "desperately" need research into what "being Hasidic" means for the period of the late nineteenth and early twentieth centuries. David Assaf reiterates this argument and states that we also need to know much more than we do about Hasidic biography in this era as well as about Hasidic emigration and the establishment of new courts in places like North America.[37] Assaf also observes that it is somewhat ironic that Hasidism in the

32 Jacob Katz, *Divine Law in Human Hands: Case Studies in Halakhic Flexibility* (Jerusalem: Magnes Press, 1998); idem, *The "Shabbes Goy": A Study in Halakhic Flexibility* (Philadelphia: Jewish Publication Society, 1989).

33 Eliezer Schweid, *Orthodoxy and Religious Humanism* [Hebrew] (Jerusalem: Van Leer Institute, 1977); idem, *Democracy and Halakha* (Lanham: University Press of America, 1994).

34 Raphael Mahler, cited in Assaf, "Hebetim Historiim ve-Ḥevratiyim," 31.

35 Polonsky, *Jews in Poland and Russia*, vol. 2, 281.

36 Kenneth B. Moss, "Negotiating Jewish nationalism in Interwar Warsaw," in *Warsaw. The Jewish Metropolis: Essays in Honor of the 75th Birthday of Professor Anony Polonsky*, ed. Glenn Dynner and François Guesnet (Leiden: Brill, 2015), 410.

37 Assaf, "Hebetim Historiim ve-Ḥevratiyim," 435.

nineteenth century, the very period of its greatest spread and influence, lacks a comprehensive scholarly treatment.[38] This gap is somewhat filled with the 2018 publication *Hasidism: A New History*, by David Biale, David Assaf, Benjamin Brown, Uriel Gellman, Samuel Heilman, Moshe Rosman, Gadi Sagiv, Marcin Wodziński, and Arthur Green. Yet that latest attempt at a comprehensive account of Hasidism still notes in its preface that Hasidism in the late nineteenth century is "poorly understood."[39]

Nahum Karlinsky signals a way in which the study of a Polish Hasidic rabbi, like Yudel Rosenberg, may serve yet another important purpose. He asserts that until now scholars have devoted far more effort and research to the "Orthodoxization" of non-Hasidic Jews than to Hasidic society itself and thus any further insight into the Hasidic society of this era would be of value.[40] In this book, we will take into consideration Karlinsky's idea that Hasidism created a "counter society":

> ... that, while drawing on and perpetuating the world of tradition has revised the prior scale of values and social order, and established a new order in their stead; the gist of the new order is the construction of a barrier against the permeation of modernity into tradition.[41]

As we examine Yudel Rosenberg's considerable literary output, we will also see how Jewish literature as it developed in the nineteenth and early twentieth centuries both divided and united Jews. We will learn among other things that the line between "modern" or "secular" and "traditional" literature was not always sharp and distinct. Indeed, as Steven Zipperstein has noted:

> For the literate traditional Jew, secular literature served an auxiliary function, a way of imposing clarity onto sacred texts which remained the sole source of truth. ... For the *maskil*, however, secular books represented in

---

38 Idem, "Ḥasidut Polin be Me'ah ha-19: Matsav ha-Meḥqar u-Sekira Bibliografit," in *Hasidism in Poland*, ed. Rahel Elior, Yisrael Bartal, and Chone Shmeruk (Jerusalem: Bialik Institute, 1994), 357.

39 David Biale, David Assaf, Benjamin Brown, Uriel Gellman, Samuel Heilman, Moshe Rosman, Gadi Sagiv, Marcin Wodziński, and Arthur Green, *Hasidism: A New History* (Princeton: Princeton University Press, 2018), ix.

40 Nahum Karlinsky, "The Dawn of Hasidic-Haredi Historiography," *Modern Judaism* 27, no. 1 (February 2007): 34.

41 Ibid., 34.

> themselves an alternative avenue to truth, a fundamental source of authority. Hence a conservative *maskil* … and a reasonably tolerant *mitnaged* had a good deal in common.[42]

In this book, we will see the ways in which Rabbi Yudel Rosenberg, from the Hasidic side, assimilated into his writing much that the *Haskala* had to offer.

Once Rabbi Yudel Rosenberg arrives in North America in 1913, the book will examine other salient issues that the once regnant narrative of American Jewish history largely neglected. In doing so, it will heed Paolo Bernardini's imperative that "European and American history should not be separated."[43] We will thus examine both the continuities and differences between Rabbi Rosenberg's European and North American experience.

Orthodox Judaism in the New World at the turn of the twentieth century has often been regarded in ways similar to the perspective turn-of-the-twentieth-century journalist Abraham Cahan placed in the mouth of his fictional character, David Levinsky:

> The Orthodox Jewish faith, as it is followed in the old Ghetto towns of Russia or Austria, has still to learn the art of trimming its sails to suit new winds. It is exactly the same as it was a thousand years ago. … It is absolutely inflexible. If … you attempt to bend your religion to the spirit of your new surroundings, it breaks. It falls to pieces.[44]

The considerable scholarly attention recently paid to contemporary North American Orthodox Judaism in general has caused a major reevaluation of the history of American Orthodoxy.[45] In particular, the role of the interwar Orthodox community in developing an institutional basis for the postwar development of American Orthodoxy has been increasingly noted.[46] This book aims

---

42 Steven Zipperstein, *Elusive Prophet: Ahad Ha'am and the Origins of Zionism* (Berkeley: University of California Press, 1993), 11–12.

43 Cited in Judah M. Cohen, "Trading Freedoms? Exploring Jewish Colonial Jewish Merchanthood between Europe and the Caribbean," in *American Jewry: Transcending the European Experience?*, ed. Christian Wiese and Cornelia Wilhelm (London: Bloomsbury, 2017), 59.

44 Abraham Cahan, *The Rise of David Levinsky* (New York: Grosset and Dunlap, 1917), 110.

45 See Adam Ferziger, *Beyond Sectarianism: the Realignment of American Orthodox Judaism* (Detroit: Wayne State University Press, 2015).

46 On Orthodox Judaism in North America during this period, see Jeffrey Gurock, "Resisters and Accomodators," *American Jewish Archives Journal* 35 (November 1983): 100–187; Jenna W. Joselit, *New York's Jewish Jews* (Bloomington: Indiana University Press, 1990). See also

to more fully illuminate the experience of Yiddish speaking Eastern European Orthodox rabbis in North America at the turn of the twentieth century, in whose number Rabbi Yudel Rosenberg found himself, their precarious search for a viable economic position in their new home, and the rabbinic turf wars this situation engendered.[47]

The significance of the immigrant Orthodox rabbinate at the turn of the twentieth century for the development of American Judaism has also been downplayed by those for whom the narrative of the development of the American Jewish community did not encompass traditional Orthodox Judaism. Thus the narrative of the development of the Eastern European Jewish immigrant community in North America in the late nineteenth and early twentieth centuries, as expressed classically in works like Moses Rischin's *The Promised City*,[48] attributes great importance to the development of the Jewish labor movement and its ethos, while often ignoring the immigrant Orthodox rabbinate.[49] This book will attempt to demonstrate how the two seemingly disparate social phenomena of the Orthodox rabbinate and Jewish labor shared many common values and were as often as not mutually reinforcing rather than antagonistic in their goals and strategies. Thus while much of the leadership of the North American Jewish labor movement may indeed have been religiously non-traditional, specifically anti-religious attitudes did not predominate in the North American Jewish labor movement in the way that they tended to do in the more doctrinaire political environments of Eastern Europe and Palestine. Many in the rank and file of Jewish labor tended to have positive attitudes toward much of the Judaic tradition and its practices. There is considerable evidence that prior to World War II many of the supporters of Jewish labor unions attended Orthodox synagogues,

---

Ira Robinson, *Rabbis and Their Community: Studies in the Immigrant Orthodox Rabbinate in Montreal, 1896–1930*. (Calgary: University of Calgary Press, 2007).

47 Marni Davis, *Jews and Booze: Becoming American in the Age of Prohibition* (New York: New York University Press, 2012), 83, 177. Cf. Arthur A. Goren, *New York Jews and the Quest for Community: the Kehillah Experiment 1908–1922* (New York: Columbia University Press, 1970), 77. Kimmy Caplan observes that in the nineteenth century there was a relative dearth of suitable rabbinic positions. "The Concerns of an Immigrant Rabbi: The Life and Sermons of Rabbi Moshe Shimon Sivitz," *Polin* 11 (1998): 195.

48 Moses Rischin, *The Promised City: New York's Jews, 1870–1914* (New York: Harper and Row, 1970). Cf. Irving Howe, *World of Our Fathers* (New York: Harcourt, Brace, Jovanovich, 1975).

49 Jenna Weissman Joselit, "What Happened to New York's 'Jewish Jews'?: Moses Rischin's *The Promised City* Revisited," *American Jewish History* 73 (1983): 163–172. On American Orthodoxy in general, see Jeffrey S. Gurock, *Orthodox Jews in America* (Bloomington: Indiana University Press, 2009).

purchased kosher meat, gave their children traditional Jewish educations, and did not always distinguish between what may seem to contemporary observers incompatible "religious" and "secularist" ideologies. The rabbis, for their part, often championed the cause of the Jewish labor movement, supported the organization of Jewish labor unions, and publicly sided with the workers in their labor disputes.[50] When circumstances were appropriate, rabbis, like Yudel Rosenberg, also engaged in actions influenced by the ethos of Jewish labor.

It is readily apparent, upon reflection, that the religious expression of the immigrant generation was largely guided by the model of Eastern European Orthodox Judaism. In my previous work on the immigrant Orthodox rabbinate in North America, particularly in my book *Rabbis and Their Community*,[51] I have asserted the importance of the immigrant Orthodox rabbinate in the development of North American Jewish communities in this era. I did so not because the majority of the immigrants were ideologically committed to the specific doctrines of Orthodox Judaism. That is certainly far from the case. It was rather because Orthodoxy, in its Eastern European guise, happened to be the Judaic religious model most easily and readily available to the Jewish immigrants as they moved to establish their new synagogues and communal institutions.[52] In any event, the religious institutions founded by the immigrants soon attracted immigrant Orthodox rabbis who, though often bewildered and dismayed at the many challenges to the religious observance of Jews in America,[53] doggedly began creating an institutional framework for rabbinic organization and supervision of kashrut and other areas of Jewish life.[54] Rabbi Yudel Rosenberg was highly implicated in this process.

---

50 Gurock, *Orthodox Jews*, 120.

51 Robinson, *Rabbis and Their Community*.

52 It is noteworthy that Reform Judaism at the turn of the twentieth century essentially gave up on influencing the immigrant generation religiously, hoping instead to attract their Americanized children. Conservative Judaism, significantly, got much of its impetus from the 1901 reorganization of the Jewish Theological Seminary of America supported by American Jews predominantly affiliated with the Reform movement who hoped to influence the Judaism of the immigrants' children. On the seminary reorganization, see Mel Scult, "Schechter's Seminary," in *Tradition Renewed: A History of the Jewish Theological Seminary*, vol. 1, ed. Jack Wertheimer (New York: Jewish Theological Seminary of America, 1997), 45–102. Cf. also Michael R. Cohen, *The Birth of Conservative Judaism: Solomon Schechter's Disciples and the Creation of an American Religious Movement* (New York: Columbia University Press, 2012).

53 An interesting expression of this bewilderment is Jonathan D. Sarna, trans., *People Walk on Their Heads: Moses Weinberger's Jews and Judaism in New York* (New York: Holmes and Meier, 1981).

54 Gurock, "Accommodators and Resisters."

The story of Rabbi Yudel Rosenberg in Canada may also serve as a counter-example to the often-expressed idea that among the myriads of Eastern European Jewish immigrants in North America at the turn of the twentieth century, Hasidism was essentially absent and exercised no significant influence on the development of American Judaism in this crucial era. Indeed the very prospect of the transplantation of Hasidic Judaism to North America greatly frightened many American Jews at the turn of the twentieth century.[55] Nearly one hundred years later, this transplantation is an accomplished fact. For many observers of the American Jewish scene, however, Hasidic settlement in North America appears basically to have been a post-World War II phenomenon. Though scholars acknowledged that a sizeable portion of the mass Eastern European Jewish emigration to North America from the 1880s to the 1920s came from areas where Hasidic Judaism was dominant, their regnant assumption was that organized Hasidic life as such did not exist. Thus one of the pioneers of the study of Hasidic life in America, Jerome Mintz, stated in his first book, published in 1968:

> Although Hasidic Jews had been part of the earlier waves of immigration to America in the last century, for the most part they had come as individuals, leaving behind their Rebbe and the majority of the court. As most Rebbes had remained in Europe during this earlier period, the focal point of Hasidic life had been missing.[56]

Thus, in the first place, there was a widespread idea that the European leaders of Hasidic Judaism did not go themselves to America before World War II and that they further discouraged their followers from going to a country which had a widespread reputation of not being supportive of maximal Judaic observance. Those Hasidic Jews who did somehow emigrate to North America did so, according to this assumption, bereft of spiritual leadership. On the surface, this assumption has much to recommend it. Within Eastern European Orthodox circles America certainly was considered an "impure" country to be

---

55 Ira Robinson, "The First Hasidic Rabbis in North America," *American Jewish Archives* 44 (1992): 501–515.

56 Jerome R. Mintz, *Legends of the Hasidim: An Introduction to Hasidic Culture and Oral Tradition in the New World* (Chicago and London: University of Chicago Press, 1968), 37. In Mintz's later book, *Hasidic People* (Cambridge, MA: Harvard University Press, 1993), there is some mention of prewar Hasidic rebbes in North America.

avoided if at all possible.[57] Many nineteenth-century Hasidic rebbes certainly did discourage their followers from emigrating. Thus, Rabbi David Shifrin, a follower of the Lubavicher Rebbe who emigrated to the United States at the turn of the twentieth century recalled his parting with his rebbe, Shalom Dov Baer Schneersohn:

> I did not come to ask whether to go. I had the ticket. I just did not want to be like a student who flees from the *ḥeder* [schoolroom] and does not tell the rebbe where he is going. Therefore I came to tell the rebbe that I am going to the United States.[58]

However the same hesitancy about America and its possible deleterious effects on Jews definitely existed within the mitnagdic rabbinic establishment as well. Thus it was the mitnagdic rabbi David Willowsky (Ridbas) who coined the phrase that, in America, "even the stones are *tref* [non-kosher]."[59] Likewise, the mitnagdic rabbi Israel Meir ha-Kohen (*Ḥafets Ḥayyim*) stated, in his book of well-meaning advice for emigrating Jews, *Nidḥe Yisra'el*, that emigration to America was ideally to be avoided, and. if this could not be prevented, then at least America was to be considered a temporary place of settlement with the emigrant having the clear intention of returning as soon as possible to a land where Judaism could be properly observed.[60] Despite this deep ambivalence on the part of the mitnagdic rabbinic establishment, prominent mitnagdic rabbis, like Rabbi Isaac Elḥanan Spector of Kovno, did begin sending rabbis to the United States and Canada as early as the 1880s to serve as religious leaders for the masses of Jewish immigrants.[61] We will see how Hasidic rabbis, somewhat later than their mitnagdic colleagues, also began coping with Judaism in the North American context, for it makes no sense that the Jewish immigrants from

57 Cf. Aaron Rothkoff, "The American Sojourns of Ridbaz: Religious Problems within the Immigrant Community," *American Jewish Historical Quarterly* 57 (1968): 557–572.

58 Shalom Duber Levin, *Toldois Chabad B'Artzois Ha'Bris* (Brooklyn: Kehot, 1988), 5. Cf. also another case reported on p. 7 of this book, where the rebbe was not asked since he would "almost certainly" advise against going.

59 Cf. Rothkoff, "American Sojourns," 560.

60 Israel Meir ha-Kohen, *Nidhei Yisra'el* (Warsaw, 1894), 288–293. On the phenomenon of Jewish immigrants returning to Europe, largely for "religious" reasons, see Jonathan Sarna, "The Myth of No Return: Jewish Return Migration to Eastern Europe, 1881–1914," *American Jewish History* (1981): 256–268.

61 Abraham Karp, "New York Chooses a Chief Rabbi," in *The Jewish Experience in America: Selected Studies From the Publications of the American Jewish Historical Society*, ed. Abraham Karp (Waltham and New York: American Jewish Historical Society, 1969), vol. 4, 130.

Hasidic areas of Eastern Europe should have emigrated in any great numbers without somebody attempting to fill the vacuum of Hasidic spiritual leadership. This book will pay special attention to the Hasidic aspects of Rabbi Yudel Rosenberg's North American rabbinate.

Of course, it is one thing to say that there were rabbis serving Hasidic congregations and propagating Hasidic doctrines and quite another thing to assert that there were Hasidic rebbes (spiritual leaders) in America in this early period. But in fact these existed as well, as long as we keep in mind that it was not merely descendants of established Hasidic dynasties who served as rebbes. To a limited extent at least, the field was open to men who could claim a distinguished Hasidic ancestry, and even to some who could not, whose charismatic qualities caused them to gain a following among Hasidim. It is inevitable that these spiritual leaders, whom Solomon Poll calls *shtikl rebbes* (minor spiritual leaders),[62] would be the first to go to North America given the prevalent conditions in the American Jewish community. Just as a distinguished figure like Rabbi Jacob Joseph would likely not have agreed to become chief rabbi of New York in the late nineteenth century had he not been in debt,[63] so those Hasidic spiritual leaders in Europe would have most likely not even considered emigration to the United States had there not been extenuating circumstances, especially dire poverty. Rabbi Yudel Rosenberg's North American experience as rabbi in Toronto and Montreal will be evaluated in this context and will sharpen our picture of how Hasidic life accommodated itself to early twentieth-century North America.

The book is divided into eleven chapters. The introductory chapter introduces some important issues in the interpretation of Jewish modernity and the varying ways in which Jews, especially in Eastern Europe and North America at the turn of the twentieth century, approached it. The next four chapters will deal with Rabbi Rosenberg's life on a chronological basis, divided into two chapters dealing with his life in Poland (1859–1913) and two chapters outlining his career in Canada (1913–1935). Following that, there will be five thematic chapters that will examine Rabbi Rosenberg's voluminous writings in the areas of Judaic law (halakha), sermons and stories, science, medicine, magic, and Kabbala. The book concludes with a chapter on Rabbi Yudel Rosenberg's legacy and what light it sheds on Jewish history and thought in the past century.

62 Solomon Poll, *The Hasidic Community of Williamsburg: A Study in the Sociology of Religion* (New York: Schocken, 1962), 63, 118, 121.

63 Karp, "New York," 141.

CHAPTER 2

On a Spiderweb Foundation: Yudel Rosenberg's Life in Small-Town Poland (1859–1889)

THE PRODIGY OF SKARYSZEW

On December 31, 1860 a birth was recorded in Radom, Poland, for "Judka Rozenberg," a son of Israel Isaac Rosenberg (1817?–1892) and his wife, Miriam Gitl (1829–1908). They named their red-headed son Yehuda Yudel at his circumcision.[1] The record lists the Rosenberg family living in Gębarzów, a village near Skaryszew, a small market town in Russian Poland approximately twelve kilometers south-southeast of

1 The birth was registered in Radom, image 897 B, 31 December, 1860, act 104, https://jri-poland.org/jriplweb.htm. There are many other candidates for Yudel Rosenberg's birth date. An undated family tree prepared by Rabbi Rosenberg himself, an original of which is in the possession of Mr. Lionel Albert of Montreal, gives his birth date as "New Moon [first of the month] of Ḥeshvan, 5620," corresponding to October 29, 1859 (Gregorian) and October 17 (Julian). In published works, Yudel Rosenberg's birth date is variously given as Ḥeshvan 1860 in Zvi Cohen, ed. *Sefer ha-Zikkaron le-Ḥag Yovel ha-Shiv'im shel ... R. Yehuda Rosenberg/ Souvenir Dedicated to Rabbi Jehuda Rosenberg ... on the Occasion of His Seventieth Anniversary Jubilee* (Montreal: Keneder Adler Drukerei, 1931), 5, or as the third of Kislev in ibid., 23, 25. Ben Zion Eisenstadt gives the year as 5620 (1859/60) in his *Dorot ha-Aḥaronim* (New York: Rosenberg, 1915) part 3, 319. Chaim Leib Fox, *100 Years of Hebrew and Yiddish Literature in Canada* [Yiddish] (Montreal: Adler, 1979), 273, states that his birth date is October 27, 1860. Zalman Reizin, in his *Leksikon fun der Yiddisher Literatur, Presse un Filologie* (Vilna: Kletzkin, 1929), vol. 4, col. 114, states that he was born in 1865. In Rosenberg's personal copy of Eisenstadt's *Dorot ha-Aḥaronim*, the year 5620 is changed to 5630 (1869/70). Why this was done I cannot explain. In any event, a birth date of either October 1859 or December 1860 is consistent with the one official document pertaining to Rosenberg that survives from his European career. It is presently in the archive of Mr. Lionel Albert. In the document, written on June 12, 1891, which attests to Rosenberg's competence in the Russian language, his age was listed as 31. The discrepancy between October 1859 and December 1860 may possibly be explained by a delay in the parents registering the birth in the provincial capital, some distance from their home. For the color of his hair, see Leah Rosenberg, *Errand Runner*, 21.

the provincial capital of Radom on the western fringes of the great Russian Empire then ruled by Tsar Alexander II.[2]

Skaryszew was a small place even by the standards of small-town Poland. In 1856, a mere 149 Jews and 840 Christians inhabited the town that would "officially" be closed to Jewish settlement until the reforms of 1862. Its population would increase dramatically in the ensuing decades so that in 1897 the Russian census counted 775 Jews in a total population of 1756.[3] In mid-nineteenth-century Skaryszew, many changes had come to the Jews through the persistent efforts of the Russian government to deal with its "Jewish problem."[4] Other changes were to come. Nonetheless, life for Jews in the small market towns of Poland in many ways still seemed in essential continuity with the rabbinic Jewish tradition as it had developed over centuries and millenia.

Yudel Rosenberg was born into a small-town Jewish society that was extremely class- and status-conscious. One's status within this society depended to a large extent on three factors: wealth, lineage, and possession of rabbinic learning for males, or marriage to the learned for females. The birth record lists Israel Isaac Rosenberg as a "*pachciarz krów*" meaning he made his living as a lessee of cattle in Gębarzów, not a particularly high-income occupation. The family was, however, sufficiently well-off to allow their son Yudel the opportunity to continue his religious studies after the age of thirteen, when most boys needed to stop their formal studies in order to earn a living. We also do not know much about Yudel's father's learning or lack thereof, though the family is described in one source as "a prominent rabbinic family."[5] We do know, however, that the Rosenbergs claimed what must have been one of the more distinguished pedigrees in town. Yudel Rosenberg in his many publications consistently claimed as his ancestor Rabbi Judah the Pietist [*he-Ḥasid*], leader of a major pietistic movement within thirteenth-century German Jewry, which

---

2 *Columbia-Lippincott Gazetteer of the World* (New York: Columbia University Press, 1962), 1779.

3 *Evreiskaia Entsiklopediia* (St. Petersburg: Brockhaus-Efron, 1906), s.v. "Skaryszew," 357, http://data.jewishgen.org/wconnect/wc.dll?jg~jgsys~community~-528179, accessed October 22, 2014.

4 For the history of the Jews in Poland, see Polonsky, *The Jews in Poland and Russia*. On the history of the Jews in the Russian Empire generally, see Simon Dubnow, *History of the Jews in Russia and Poland* (Philadelphia: Jewish Publication Society, 1916–1920). Cf. also Michael Stanislawski, *Tsar Nicholas I and the Jews: The Transformation of Jewish Society in Russia, 1825–1855* (Philadelphia: Jewish Publication Society, 1983).

5 Radom, image 897 B, 31 December, 1860, act 104, https://jri-poland.org/jriplweb.htm. Reizin, *Leksikon fun der Yiddisher Literatur, Presse un Filologia*, 114. Eisenstadt, *Dorot ha-Aḥaronim*, 319, refers to him as "the well-known, prominent benefactor, honest and whole." In nearby Radom, a Yitsḥak Rosenberg, possibly a relative, founded a House of Study [*Bet Midrash*]. Cf. A. Sh. Stein, ed., *Radom* (Tel-Aviv: n.p., 1961), 71.

had considerable religious and cultural influence on Polish Jewry,[6] and author of the well-known *Sefer Ḥasidim*.[7] Through Judah the Pietist, the Rosenbergs would have been able to trace their lineage all the way back to Rabbi Judah the Patriarch, the second-century editor of the first major document of Rabbinic Judaism, the *Mishnah*, a distinction he apparently shared with Maimonides.[8] However, despite the prominence Yudel Rosenberg gave to this ancestral relationship, he never quite made clear whether this ancestor was on his father's or mother's side, and other sources dealing with Rosenberg's ancestry are silent on this relationship.[9]

On his father's side, Yudel also proudly counted among his ancestors the early eighteenth-century Polish kabbalist, Jacob Koppel Lipschitz, author of the book *Sha'arei Gan Eden*, famed as a precursor of the Hasidic movement which largely dominated nineteenth-century Polish Judaism.[10] Jacob Koppel's likely adherence to the heretical messianic ideology of Sabbatianism, which would have made his name anathema to all right-thinking Jews in Skaryszew or elsewhere in Jewish Poland, was in Rosenberg's time completely unknown.[11] In any

---

6 Israel Ta-Shma, "*Le-Toledot ha-Yehudim be-Polin be Me'ot ha-12 veha-13*," *Zion* 53 (1988): 347–369; idem, "*Yedi'ot Ḥadashot le-Toledot ha-Yehudim be-Polin be Me'ot ha-12 veha-13*," *Zion* 54 (1989): 208; idem, "On the History of the Jews in Twelfth-Thirteenth Century Poland," *Polin* 10 (1997): 287–317.

7 See, *inter alia*, the title page of Yudel Rosenberg's *Zohar Torah* [hereafter ZT] (New York: Trio Press, 1926), where he describes himself as "from the stock of R. Judah the Hasid of blessed memory." Cf. Cohen, *Sefer ha-Zikkaron*, 5. Though Yosef Dan, *Ha-Sippur ha-Ḥasidi* (Jerusalem: Keter, 1975), 221, suggests that Rosenberg claimed descent from R. Judah Loewe (Maharal) of Prague, there is no evidence for this assertion other than that the Maharal was the hero of many of his tales. Cf. Shnayer Z. Leiman, "The Adventure of the Maharal of Prague in London: R. Yudl Rosenberg and the Golem of Prague," *Tradition* 36, no. 1 (2002): 26–58. Whether or not Yudel Rosenberg was actually descended from R. Judah the Pietist, it is clear that the sixteenth-century Polish rabbi Solomon Luria claimed such descent, and some contemporary scholars assert that groups of these pietists did indeed move from Germany to Poland in the thirteenth century. Hundert, *Jews in Poland-Lithuania*, 10.

8 Cf. Yudel Rosenberg, *Refa'el ha-Mal'aḥ* (Piotrków: Shlomo Belkhatovski, 5671/1911), 3.

9 Another modern Hasidic figure to claim descent from Judah the Pietist was the twentieth-century Rabbi Ḥannania Yom Tov Lippa Deutsch. Significantly, here too the genealogical connection is obscure. Cf. introductory material to Moses Gelernter, *Sefer Tehilim* (Brooklyn: n.p., 1980), unpaginated [between pages 4 and 5].

10 Eisenstadt, *Dorot ha-Rishonim*, 319.

11 Isaiah Tishby, "*Beyn Shabtaut le-Ḥassidut: Shabtauto shel ha-Mekubal R. Ya'aqov Koppel Lipschits mi-Mezrich*," in Isaiah Tishby, *Netivei Emuna u-Minut* (Ramat-Gan: Makor, 1964), 204–226; Shaul Magid, "The Metaphysics of Malkhut: *Malkhut* as *Eyn Sof* in the Writings of Ya'akov Koppel of Mezritch," *Kabbalah: Journal for the Study of Jewish Mystical Texts* 27

event, Yudel Rosenberg's grandfather, as well as his brother, were named Jacob Koppel after this ancestor.[12] On his mother's side, Yudel traced his descent from the early nineteenth-century Hasidic leader, Rabbi Meir of Opatów (Apt).[13]

The Rosenberg children were six siblings: Yehuda Yudel, Jacob Koppel (1858–1940), Reuben, Sara Perel (Perele) (b. 1863), and Eliezer (Lejzor, 1870–1940),[14] Armed with their distinguished lineage, the Rosenberg brothers began when quite small to acquire learning, the second of the three keys to success in the world of Eastern European Judaism. Yudel and his brothers (though most likely not his sister, Sara Perel)[15] would certainly have taken advantage of the traditional Jewish educational opportunities for boys offered by the town of Skaryszew. Yudel Rosenberg, by the evidence of his voluminous writings as an adult, would have studied and mastered the standard traditional Jewish curriculum and much else, as we will see.

The accounts we possess of Yudel's youth in Skaryszew, which probably all stem, in one way or another, from his own testimony, are unanimous in testifying to his excellence in the study of both Torah and *Ḥasidut*. This means that he excelled in the study of the Hebrew Bible, particularly the Pentateuch and its standard medieval commentaries. He also mastered the vast Talmudic literature that encompassed the *Mishnah* and *Gemara* with their standard commentaries as well as major collections of rabbinic *midrashim*. Since Skaryszew was located in a region where Hasidism was the dominant force in Judaism, he was also exposed to the major ideas and texts of Hasidic Judaism as well as most probably at least some portions of the kabbalistic literature upon which much of Hasidic ideology was based.[16] Yudel Rosenberg's later writings would eloquently testify to his expertise in all this material.

Whether it was because of his success in his studies or merely because of his family's social and financial position, at the age of thirteen, when most of his peers had to end their formal religious education and began their apprenticeships at one or another trade, Rosenberg was able to continue his Torah

---

(2012): 245–267. Tishby emphasizes that R. Jacob Koppel's alleged Sabbatian leanings were totally unknown in the nineteenth century.

12 For Rosenberg's grandfather's name, see Eisenstadt, *Dorot ha-Rishonim*, 319. Yudel Rosenberg's brother's name is mentioned in Cohen, *Sefer ha-Zikkaron*, 26.

13 Eisenstadt, *Dorot ha-Rishonim*, 319. Cf. Reizin, *Leksikon fun der Yiddisher Literatur*, 114.

14 Radom Register, 1858, act 72, 1869, act 2, 1871, act 26, 1876, act 9, https://jri-poland.org/jriplweb.htm. Cf. the genealogical chart of the Rosenberg family courtesy of Mr. Lionel Albert, Montreal.

15 Yudel Rosenberg's sister, Perele, is mentioned in Leah Rosenberg, *Errand Runner*, 17.

16 Eisenstadt, *Dorot ha-Rishonim*, 319.

education. It is a testimony to his promise as a scholar, to his parents' means, as well as to the paucity of suitable teachers in such a small town, that tutors were brought in from out of town to teach him. According to the accounts we have of his youth, he began to achieve a reputation as an up-and-coming Talmudic scholar—the "Prodigy" [*Ilui*] of Skaryszew.[17] Ultimately, Yudel Rosenberg joined a small group of boys who studied with the town's rabbi, Mordecai Ze'ev.[18] At the age of fifteen, he was reputed to be that rabbi's outstanding student [*talmid muvhak*] and at the age of sixteen, one source states that he was empowered by the rabbi to adjudicate questions of Jewish law in his teacher's absence.[19]

When we consider the foregoing description of Rosenberg's upbringing, there is much that sounds quite stereotypical for up-and-coming Torah students of Yudel Rosenberg's time and place. Indeed a student of this period, Heszel Klepfisz, comments:

> Upon reading the life story of a rabbi or spiritual leader of that period, one discovers that at five the subject had already displayed qualities of genius; at nine he had stunned everyone with his piercing questions; and of course at thirteen, when he was Bar Mitzvah, he had already thoroughly mastered the entire Talmud and commentaries, and his fame was spread all over the land.[20]

---

17 Ibid. Cf. Cohen, *Sefer ha-Zikkaron*, 5. Yudel Rosenberg was not the only distinguished Jew to stem from Skaryszew. For others, see Stein, *Radom*, 58, 60.

18 Rosenberg referred to an incident from that period of his education in Yehuda Yudel Rosenberg, *Yabi'a Omer: Ḥamishim Derushim 'al Kol ha-Mo'adim ve-Shabbatot ha-Meyuḥasin ve-'al Kol Me'orot ha-Mitragshot la-Vo' le-Kehillot Yisra'el* [hereafter *Omer*] (Jerusalem: *Hotsa'ah Meyuḥedet le-Nisu'e ben Nino*, 1996–2005), part 1, 56.

19 Rosenberg, in *Omer*, part 1, 56, recalls an incident that occurred in his youth when "we, some older boys, were studying with the town rabbi." Cf. Aaron Elimelech Rosenberg, *Liqqutei Beit Aharon* (Montreal: Friedman, 1954), 12; Eisenstadt, *Dorot ha-Rishonim*, 319; Stein, *Radom*, 116. Rosenberg mentions another rabbi of Skaryszew, Reb Joseph, who became the head of the rabbinic court of Lublin. See *Der Greiditser … vunderlikhe moftim vos hot bavizen ibergezetst oyf zhargon fun sefer Hadrat Eliyahu* [hereafter *Greiditser*] (Łódź and Piótrkow: Yitsḥaq Shlomovits and Shlomo Belkhatovsky, 1913), fasc. iii, 3. Stein, *Radom*, 116, mentions that Rosenberg studied in various yeshivot, without specifying their names. This is exceedingly doubtful given the paucity of yeshivot in Poland at this time. Cf. Mordecai Breuer, "Tradition and Change in European Yeshivot: 17th–19th Centuries," paper delivered at Harvard Conference on "Tradition and Crisis," 1988.

20 Heszel Klepfisz, *Culture of Compassion: the Spirit of Polish Jewry from Hasidism to the Holocaust*, trans. Curt Leviant (New York: Ktav, 1983), 16.

Though Klepfisz almost certainly did not have Yudel Rosenberg specifically in mind when he was writing, Klepfisz's description definitely seems to apply to him in full and serves to place us somewhat on our guard. In Yudel Rosenberg's description of his youth, we have been given a standard early intellectual biography of a nineteenth-century Polish rabbi. Since, as we have said, all the information we have on Rosenberg's early youth was most likely supplied by him, either directly or indirectly, it is not unlikely that the picture might have been rounded off at the corners to fit the pattern. Rosenberg, then, is another example of Isadore Twersky's insight that traditional Jewish conceptions tend to blur the individuality of Rabbinic scholars. All great rabbis, in a sense, partake of the characteristics of the basic paradigm of "the rabbi."[21]

Another aspect of Rosenberg's education that was equally part of the intellectual world of a Polish Hasidic boy growing up in the late nineteenth century was contact with the literature of the Jewish modernist movement known as *Haskala* [Enlightenment].[22] Some contact with the *Haskala* was practically inevitable for any intellectually curious Jewish boy of that era. For some, this contact ultimately led to their leaving the world of traditional Jewish learning and even the practice of traditional Judaism. Thus, the stereotypical biography of an Eastern European Jewish *maskil* [modernist intellectual] inevitably records both his prowess in traditional learning and his abandonment of the traditional Jewish ethos to embrace *Haskala*.[23] There is, however, another other side to this story, one that is not told as often: that of traditional Jews who encountered and were influenced by *Haskala* without abandoning tradition. This side of the story is well illustrated by Yudel Rosenberg's experience.

According to the primary account of Yudel Rosenberg's youth, which most likely was derived from an oral account Rosenberg gave to its author, he was once caught with five books in his possession which were considered *tref* [unfit] according to the standards of the Jewish society of Skaryszew and were therefore burned. They were: *Talmud L'shon 'Ivri*; *Sefer ha-Berit*; *la-Yesharim Tehilla*;

21 Isadore Twersky, *Introduction to the Code of Maimonides* (New Haven: Yale University Press, 1980), 92.

22 Arthur Green notes that the self-perception of Polish Hasidim was that they were "more sophisticated and less credulous" than their Ukrainian or Galician counterparts. Arthur Green, "Introduction" to Yehudah Leib Alter, *The Language of Truth: the Torah Commentary of the Sefat Emet* (Philadelphia: Jewish Publication Society, 1998), xvii.

23 Cf. Alan Mintz, "Guenzberg, Lilienblum and Haskala Autobiography," *AJS Review* 4 (1979): 71–110. On 73, Mintz remarks that the Maskilim, in writing their autobiographies, had a greater interest in stressing the typicality of their experience than its originality. *Mutatis mutandis*, this applies as well to rabbinic biography of the same period.

Melukhat Sha'ul; Ma'amarei Ḥokhma [by] Slonimsky."[24] A detailed examination of these books and their meaning for Rosenberg and his society will give us an important insight into Yudel Rosenberg's intellectual development and shed light on his later career.

The first book on Yudel Rosenberg's list, *Talmud L'shon 'Ivri* was written by Yehuda Leib Ben Ze'ev (1764–1811). It was a Hebrew grammar authored by a *maskil*. This popular Hebrew grammar was first published in 1796 and was reprinted not less than ten times during the nineteenth century.[25] The systematic study of the Hebrew language and its grammar, which had begun in the Middle Ages, was not necessarily heretical in itself. Nonetheless, its study was widely seen among traditional Eastern European Jews, and in particular in Hasidic circles, as indicating heretical proclivities that would likely find expression in other areas as well. An example of this attitude is the saying attributed to the eighteenth-century Hasidic leader, Menaḥem Mendel of Vitebsk: "Verily grammar is useful. I know that our great ones studied it. But what can we do, now that the godless have taken possession of it?"[26] Louis Ginzberg points out the deep ambivalence with which the study of Ben Ze'ev's Hebrew grammar would have been received in a town like Skaryszew: "for a century [Ben Ze'ev's] Hebrew grammar was the one that was liked best, while its author was in some circles the most hated of men."[27] The mere study of Hebrew grammar, of course, did not automatically make Yudel Rosenberg one of the "godless." It would, however, have served to differentiate him from a large proportion of Hasidim for whom expert knowledge of Hebrew grammar did smack of heresy. The grammar lessons Rosenberg studied in his youth and the love of the Hebrew language they bespeak remained with him in later life, and in his adult

---

24 Cohen, *Sefer ha-Zikkaron*, 5. In a variant on this list, N. Baumeil lists another play of Luzzatto, *Migdal 'Oz*, in place of *Melukhat Sha'ul*. "Ha-Rav R. Yehuda (Yudel) Rosenberg," in *Talmud Torah "Eitz Chaim" Jubilee Book* (Toronto: n.p., 1943), 104. On Rosenberg's eagerness for secular knowledge, see Leah Rosenberg, *Errand Runner*, 22, 65. Rosenberg explicitly claimed to possess knowledge of "economics and other worldly affairs" in his *Der Krizis fun Lodz Varshe* [hereafter Krizis] (Piotrków: Ḥanokh Henikh Folman, 1912), 1.

25 On Ben Ze'ev, see Yosef Klausner, *Historia shel ha-Sifrut ha-'Ivrit ha-Ḥadasha* (Jerusalem: Aḥiasaf, 1952), vol. 1, 178–190.

26 Cited in Harry M. Rabinowicz, *The World of Hasidism* (Hartford: Hartmore House, 1970), 190.

27 Louis Ginzberg, *Students, Scholars and Saints* (Philadelphia: Jewish Publication Society, 1928), 221.

publications grammatical observations are frequently made,[28] though, ironically, it is also true that these very publications were also made subject to criticism by non-Orthodox scholars as lacking in grammatical sense.[29] Stronger evidence for Rosenberg's belief in the value of correct Hebrew is a polemic he inserted in his work *Derekh Erets* against those Jews "devoid of good sense" [*ḥasrei da'at*] who wanted their children to study Talmud before getting a proper background in the Hebrew language or in history:

> There are those void of understanding who want a boy to study the entire Torah ... before he understands the holy language [Hebrew] and before he knows the Bible. ... How can they enter the innermost chambers of the Torah expounded in the Oral Torah if they do not have the keys to the gates which constitute the plain meaning of the Torah according to the grammar of the language and who also do not know the order of the days of old and previous generations. ... Now there is not one in a thousand who knows Hebrew properly and can understand the depth of the Torah. ... And we are guilty in this for this is something that can be corrected among the youth.[30]

The second questionable book in Rosenberg's list is *Sefer ha-Berit*, first published in 1797. The book is a Hebrew-language encyclopaedia of scientific and geographical information. It was written by a kabbalist, Pinḥas Elijah Hurwitz (1765–1821), who was continuing a tradition of harmonizing Kabbala and science that was at least as old as the sixteenth century. The book's stated aim was to prepare the reader to comprehend Ḥayyim Vital's treatise on Lurianic Kabbala, *Sha'ar ha-Qedusha*. Since Vital, in that book, makes a number of

28 Yudel Rosenberg, *Peri Yehuda* [hereafter PY] (Bilgoraj: Szloma Wajnberg, 1935), 134; ZT, vol. 4, 17, 29; ZT, vol. 5, 250. On Rosenberg's love of the Hebrew language, see Baumeil, "Rosenberg," 104.

29 It is fair to say that Yudel Rosenberg's secular critics, such as Gershom Scholem and Isaiah Tishby, found his essentially rabbinic Hebrew objectionable in that it did not adhere to the grammatical standards of the Modern Hebrew prose they espoused.

30 Rosenberg here cites as a source the writings of Rabbi Isaiah Horowitz (*Shlaḥ*), Rabbi Jonathan Eybeschutz, and Rabbi Jacob Emden (*Yavets*). *Derekh Erets*, 25–26. The original of this manuscript was in the Rosenberg Family Archive [hereafter RFA], Savannah. The author possesses a photocopy. It is the sole manuscript of substantial length Rosenberg is known to have written that was never published. It is evident, however, that Rosenberg intended on publishing it later in his life because he gave it an English title on the title page: "Etics [sic] and Moral from the Bible and Talmud."

references to the physical universe which might not be understood by a reader untutored in scientific fact,[31] knowledge of science was deemed by Hurwitz to be prerequisite to a study of this Lurianic work. Thus, scientific knowledge would lead the reader to the point where he could truly comprehend Lurianic kabbala and arrive at a higher level of holiness so as to receive the "holy spirit" [*ruaḥ ha-qodesh*]. *Sefer ha-Berit* was a book that was widely read by Eastern European Jews well into the twentieth century as a guide to the wide world of science and technology. Particularly for traditional Jews, the book adumbrated a wary acceptance of modern science and technology, coupled with a rejection of modern humanistic learning, which characterized their attitude toward modernity. Its creation of a nexus between science and Kabbala was also quite influential in accommodating traditional, Orthodox Judaism to the realities of the modern world.[32] *Sefer ha-Berit* is an important example of the interaction between philosophy, science, and Kabbala in the thought of early modern Jews, and it evidently influenced Yudel Rosenberg's later explorations in the areas of Kabbala and science.[33]

Also in the category of popular science are the writings of the Polish Jewish astronomer and mathematician, Ḥayyim Selig Slonimsky (1810–1904). Unlike the first two items on Rosenberg's list of "contraband" books, which had been published before he was born and were thus available to him, it would have been impossible for Rosenberg to have read the specific two-volume collection of articles by Slonimsky entitled *Ma'amarei Ḥokhma* in his home town, since they were only published in Warsaw in 1891–1894, long after Rosenberg left his birthplace. However, it would have been entirely possible for him to have access to some of the articles contained in *Ma'amarei Ḥokhma* that were originally published in the Warsaw periodical Slonimsky edited, *Ha-Tsefira*. Rosenberg might also have read others of Slonimsky's many books on astronomy, the

31 On Vital's scientific interests, see Gerrit Bos, "Hayyim Vital's Practical Kabbalah and Alchemy': A 17th-Century Book of Secrets," *The Journal of Jewish Thought and Philosophy* 4, no. 1 (1995): 55–112.

32 Cf. Dov Sadan, *A Vort Bashteit* (Tel-Aviv: Farlag Y. L. Perets, 1978). Cf. also Solomon Schechter, *Seminary Addresses and Other Papers* (Cincinnati: Ark, 1915), 2.

33 On *Sefer ha-Berit*, see Ira Robinson, "Kabbala and Science in *Sefer ha-Berit*: A Modernization Strategy for Orthodox Jews," *Modern Judaism* 9 (1989): 275–288; David B. Ruderman, *A Best-Selling Hebrew Book of the Modern Era: The Book of the Covenant of Pinḥas Hurwitz and its Remarkable Legacy* (Seattle: University of Washington Press, 2015). Cf. Raphael Mahler, *A History of the Jewish People in Modern Times* [Hebrew], vol. 1, book 4 (Merḥavia: Sifriat Po'alim, 1962), 45–52; Israel Zinberg, *A History of Jewish Literature*, ed. and trans. Bernard Martin (Cincinnati: Hebrew Union College, 1975), vol. 6, 260–269.

calendar, and other subjects. In this connection, it should be noted that Slonimsky, like Hurwitz before him, took care to present his scientific studies in a manner that did not necessarily conflict with the tenets of Orthodox Judaism.[34] As Klepfisz observed:

> Slonimsky was accepted by all strata of Jewish readers, religious and non-observant, because in him struggled the old and the new, the mind and the heart, and because he tied together scientific and maskilic content with old Jewish feelings, one could not sense the new and the strange in his writings. One might have thought that his works were a continuation of what was written in the holy texts.[35]

The last two of the five "unfit" works mentioned by Rosenberg were dramas written in the Hebrew language in the eighteenth century. As with the study of Hebrew grammar, the use of the Hebrew language for any purpose that was not manifestly liturgical or scholarly in the traditional sense would have been considered a dangerous sign of "modernist" tendencies which, in the small-town milieu of Rosenberg's youth, would tend to brand him a *maskil* and hence outside the consensus of traditional Hasidic society. In reality, of course, as we shall see, the line dividing the "holy" and "profane" in literature was not as clearly defined as those who burned Rosenberg's "unfit" books would have granted.

The first of the two literary works, *La-Yesharim Tehilla* [Praise for the Righteous] is one of the last works written by Moses Ḥayyim Luzzatto (1707–1746), an Italian poet and kabbalist of the early eighteenth century. Reflecting the author's persecution at the hand of Jewish society for his alleged messianic pretensions, *La-Yesharim Tehilla* also reflects Luzzatto's kabbalistic background.[36] It is perhaps significant that Rosenberg remembered this play in particular, for in his literary career he, too, would have a chance to transform kabbalistic material into "modern" literary forms.

---

34 On Slonimsky, see Ira Robinson, "Hayyim Selig Slonimski and the Diffusion of Science among Russian Jewry in the Nineteenth Century," in *The Interaction Between Scientific and Jewish Cultures*, ed. Yakov Rabkin and Ira Robinson (Lewiston, Queenston, and Lampeter: Edwin Mellen Press, 1994), 49–65. Cf. *Encylopedia Judaica* (Jerusalem: Keter, 1972), vol. 14, cols. 1674–1675, s.v. "Slonimsky, Hayyim Selig."

35 Klepfisz, *Culture of Compassion*, 179–180.

36 Cf. David Sclar, "Adoption and Acceptance: Moses Hayim Luzzatto's Sojourn in Amsterdam Among Portuguese Jews," *AJS Review* 40, no. 2 (2016): 351–352.

Melukhat Sha'ul [The Reign of Saul], the last item on Rosenberg's list, is another drama. This one was written by Yosef ha-Efrati of Tropplowitz (1770–1804) and has been called by David Roskies the *tref-posl* [unfit] book *par excellence*.[37] Based only loosely on the Biblical story of Saul and even less on traditional rabbinic interpretations of the first king of Israel, the play is a rendering into Hebrew of themes drawn from eighteenth-century European drama. Among other things, the author informs us that King David's concluding speech is a free rendition of a poem by the Swiss poet Albrecht von Haller.[38]

For a young man like Rosenberg, reading this *tref-posl* literature was an important influence, marking him as one who would not be completely satisfied with the intellectual fare offered by the Skaryszew House of Study. It did not, however, mean that he was going to burn the bridges connecting him with traditional Jewish life and learning. Others, growing up in Poland at the same time as Rosenberg and confronted with the same intellectual stimuli, did definitively leave the world of traditional Judaism. Not so Rosenberg. Though his encounter with the intellectual world of the *Haskala* changed him decisively, as we will see, his modernist tendencies played themselves out within the Hasidic community. His life would be that of a Hasid *and* a *maskil*.[39]

To be a Hasidic *maskil* in Poland in the late nineteenth century, with a foot in two intellectual worlds, was, to be sure, no easy task. It was not, however, inherently impossible, nor necessarily a binary opposition, nor was Yudel Rosenberg its only exemplar.[40] Raphael Mahler, commenting on Hasidism in nineteenth-century Poland, stated that "since the Haskala movement had no real social impact, the strong rationalist trends in Poland perforce attained some sort of expression within the most liberal wing of the devout."[41]

Writing toward the end of World War I, Yitzḥak Nissenboim detected "a new atmosphere in the Hasidic prayer houses" and concluded that Polish

37 David Roskies, "The Medium and the Message of the Maskilic Chapbook," *Jewish Social Studies* o.s. 41 (1979): 279.

38 Ibid., 279–280. Cf. Gershon Shaked, introduction to *Melukhat Sha'ul* (Jerusalem, 1968).

39 On the Hasid-Maskil concept see Jonatan Meir, "The Image of Habad among Maskilim: Kabbalah, Christianity and Reform" [Hebrew], in *Habad Hasidism: History, Thought, Image*, ed. Jonatan Meir and Gadi Sagiv (Jerusalem: Zalman Shazar Center, 2016), 190, 193.

40 Biale et al., *Hasidism: A New History* (Princeton: Princeton University Press, 2018), 466, 477.

41 Raphael Mahler, *Hasidism and the Jewish Enlightenment: Their Confrontation in Galicia and Poland in the First Half of the Nineteenth Century* (Philadelphia: Jewish Publication Society, 1985), 282. Cf. also ibid., 243.

Orthodoxy wanted to be a part of the modern world.[42] As well, Norman Solomon cogently comments: "the barrier which the traditionalists would have liked to exist and even imagined to exist between them and the *maskilim* was unreal."[43] It is as a member of the "maskilic" wing of Polish Hasidism that Yudel Rosenberg would mature and attempt to make his mark.

As Yudel Rosenberg grew to young manhood, he, like all young Jews, expected to marry, and his family sought a worthy bride for him. Just as his well-publicized intellectual prowess and his evident economic means meant that teachers would be sought for him outside Skaryszew, so his position as an up-and-coming rabbinic scholar meant that a suitable match would be found for him beyond the confines of his town. In 1877, at the age of seventeen, he was married. His relatively young age at the time of his first marriage may be an indication of his family's higher economic status since marital age was often closely correlated with economic ability to bear the expenses that marriage required.[44]

Like her groom, Yudel Rosenberg's bride Ḥaya Ḥava could point to a suitably impressive lineage, including Reb Leibush Zucker, rabbi of Ostrowiec (Ostrowiec Świętokrzyski) and his father, Reb Meirl son of Hertskes.[45] After his wedding with Ḥaya Ḥava, Yudel Rosenberg followed the widespread custom which dictated that he move to the home of his father-in-law, Shlomo Elimelekh. His new residence was the town of Tarłów, approximately sixty kilometers distance from Skaryszew, which was situated in the province of Kielce southwest of Lublin. Tarłów was a town slightly larger than Skaryszew, boasting a population of 663 Jews and 566 Christians in 1856, which increased to 1210 Jews and 714 Christians by 1897.[46]

42 *Ha-Tsefira*, August 15, 1918. Cited in Ezra Mendelsohn, *Zionism in Poland: the Formative Years, 1915–1926* (New Haven: Yale University Press, 1981), 72.

43 Norman Solomon, "The Analytic Movement in Rabbinic Jurisprudence: A Study of One Aspect of the Counter Emancipation in Lithuanian and White Russian Jewry from 1873 Onwards" (PhD diss., University of Manchester, 1966), 43.

44 On age of marriage as a status indicator, see Steven Lowenstein, "Ashkenazic Jewry and the European Marriage Pattern: A Preliminary Survey of Jewish Marriage Age," *Jewish History* 8, nos.1–2 (1994): 155–175. Cf. Shaul Stampfer, *Families, Rabbis and Education: Traditional Jewish Society in Nineteenth-Century Eastern Europe* (Oxford: Littman Library of Jewish Civilization, 2010).

45 Aaron Rosenberg, *Liqqutei Beit Aharon*, 263; Reizin, *Leksikon fun der Yiddisher Literatur*, 115; Cohen, *Sefer ha-Zikkaron*, 5; Eisenstadt, *Dorot ha-Rishonim*, 319.

46 *Evreiskaia Entsiklopediia*, vol. 14, col. 759.

THE RABBI OF TARŁÓW

As was customary in Polish Jewish society of that era, the marriage of a budding scholar such as Yudel Rosenberg did not mean the end of his studies. On the contrary, in the normal course of events, such a prodigy was promised, as part of the marriage agreement, a certain period of financial support by his father-in-law during which he was to continue his studies. Apparently, this was the case with Rosenberg as well. One account of his early life states that he applied himself to continuing his studies in Tarłów "with great dedication"[47] and it is reported that he received a rabbinic ordination there at age twenty.[48] This account signifies that he would likely have been able to devote fully three years to study while receiving financial support. His ordination would normally have meant the end of this period.

What was he to do now in order to make a living? He had learned no trade. His rabbinic learning, while distinguishing him from a majority of the town's Jews, was not considered by the people of his society to be a truly legitimate means to earn a livelihood. In nineteenth century Eastern Europe, in fact, the rabbinate was considered far from an ideal career for a scholarly Jew. Emmanuel Etkes has demonstrated that reluctance to enter upon a rabbinic career was a constant theme in the biographies of nineteenth-century Lithuanian rabbis.[49] The same phenomenon is discernible in the Hasidic world of Polish Jewry. The Polish rabbinate was widely felt to be in decline, surrounded by intrigue and factional quarrels. Often, middle-class traditional Jews discouraged their sons from studying halakhic codes because they feared that they might, in a pinch, be tempted to enter the rabbinate.[50] The reason for this reluctance may

47 Nachman Shemen, "Ortodoxie," *Der 'Idisher Journal* [Toronto]: *Yubiley Oisgabe* (1950): 10.

48 Reizin, *Leksikon fun der Yiddisher Literatur*, 115; Fox, *100 Years of Yiddish and Hebrew Literature*, 273. Baumeil, "Rosenberg," 104, mentions the fact of his ordination in Tarłów but does not record the year. It should be noted that he had already, supposedly, served as substitute halakhic decisor in his hometown of Skaryszew.

49 Immanuel Etkes, "Between Torah Scholarship and Rabbinate in Nineteenth-Century Lithuania," [Hebrew], *Zion* 53 (1988): 386.

50 Efraim Urbach, "The History of Polish Jews After World War I As Reflected in the Traditional Literature," in *The Jews of Poland between Two World Wars*, ed. Yisrael Gutman, Ezra Mendelsohn, Jehuda Reinharz, and Chone Shmeruk (Hanover, NH: Brandeis University Press, 1989), 242. See also another article in this volume, Ben-Zion Gold, "Religious Education in Poland: A Personal Perspective," 275. Cf. Jiri Langer, *Nine Gates to the Hasidic Mysteries* (New York: David McKay, 1961), 34. Indeed, the problem of attracting candidates for the rabbinate was quite widespread even in the West. Thus, Michael Meyer, in his "History of Hebrew Union College," notes that in the nineteenth century it was difficult to attract

be found, as Etkes suggests, in the low salaries paid to town rabbis as well as the low prestige of the rabbinic position relative to that of the Head of Yeshiva in Lithuania and of the Hasidic Rebbe in Poland.[51]

Thus for a young man like Yudel Rosenberg, without any special marketable skill, the only recourse was to try to set himself up in business using the capital provided by his dowry. Accordingly, he tried several business ventures. He first became a leather merchant and then attempted to run a hardware store.[52] These were both occupations that he may well have been exposed to in his hometown, as the Radom district was known in this period both for the manufacture of leather and metalwork.[53] In this case, as in numerous cases of scholarly Jews setting up businesses, his wife might have normally kept shop, enabling her husband, as far as possible, to continue studying. This, in any event, is a conclusion that may be drawn from a reminiscence of Ḥaya Ḥava by her son Aaron Elimelech, who stated:

> She attempted with all [her] means to give the ability to my father—his righteous memory for a blessing—to spend all his time in Torah [study] and [divine] service. She did not mind the difficult conditions of life.[54]

In any event, the effort was seemingly for nought; his last business attempt failed in 1885 when his store was destroyed in a fire and his capital literally went up in smoke.[55] At this point, Yudel Rosenberg had a wife and four children to support: Hessel (b. 1880), Aaron (1882–1960), Meir Joshua (1884–1938), and Sarah (1885–1954),[56] and he was thus forced by circumstances to utilize his rabbinic learning for worldly gain.[57] As the town of Tarłów happened to need a

---

rabbinic students from middle- and upper-class homes. Samuel E. Karff, ed., *Hebrew Union College-Jewish Institute of Religion at One Hundred Years* (Cincinnati: Hebrew Union College Press 1976), 26.

51 Etkes, "Between Torah Scholarship," 392, 398.

52 Baumeil, "Rosenberg," 105; Cohen, *Sefer ha-Zikkaron*, 5.

53 Stein, *Radom*, 179, 185.

54 Aaron Rosenberg, *Liqqutei Beit Aharon*, 263. On this phenomenon, see Sydney Stahl Weinberg, *The World of Our Mothers: the Lives of Jewish Immigrant Women* (Chapel Hill: University of North Carolina Press, 1988), 5–6.

55 Cohen, *Sefer ha-Zikkaron*, 5.

56 Genealogical chart in the private archive of Mr. Lionel Albert.

57 For another instance of bankruptcy in business leading to a rabbinic career in Poland, see Marcin Wodziński, *Hasidism and Politics: The Kingdom of Poland 1815–1864* (Oxford: Littman Library, 2013), 238.

rabbi at that point, he took the job; he was then twenty-five years old.[58] As he looked back on that period toward the end of his career, in 1931, he stated, "In my youth I tried very hard not to accept upon myself the responsibility of the rabbinate … but from heaven they fought against me and I did not succeed in anything I undertook and all my businesses went up in smoke."[59]

The loss of his capital was not the worst of Yudel Rosenberg's troubles at that point. Either shortly before or shortly after he accepted the rabbinate of Tarłów, his wife Ḥaya Ḥavva died on 7 Kislev 5646 (November 15, 1885).[60] According to one account, after she died Yudel Rosenberg sent his four children to live temporarily with his sister.[61]

In the nature of things in that society, a man left with small children to care for was not expected to delay finding a new wife and, indeed, we find that Yudel Rosenberg wasted no time in remarrying. The marriage contract with his second wife, Sara Gitl, indicates that the wedding took place barely two months after his first wife's death, on 9 Shvat 5646 (January 15, 1886), in a place called Yar Shtshekriev.[62] According to one account, Sara Gitl's father, Isaac ha-Levi Greenberg, was an employee of a timber merchant. This might indicate that the Greenberg family was far from wealthy and would hence be unlikely to attract a learned groom for a daughter unless he were a widower. Indeed, one account states that Sara Gitl had already been engaged to a laborer. If so, then Yudel Rosenberg definitely represented a step up in marital status for her. Not to be completely outdone in the matter of descent, however, Sara Gitl was able to bring to the marriage a proper Hasidic geneology, claiming descent from the famous Hasidic rebbe Israel Friedman of Ruzhyn.[63]

---

58 Reizin, *Leksikon fun Der Yiddisher Literatur,* 115; Fox, *100 Years of Hebrew and Yiddish Literature in Canada,* 273.

59 *Omer,* part 2, 5.

60 Aaron Rosenberg, *Liqqutei Beit Aharon,* 260, 263–264; Leah Rosenberg, *Errand Runner,* 17, 25–26; Meir Joshua Rosenberg (Yudel Rosenberg's son), *Kur ha-Mivḥan* (Jerusalem, 1968), introduction.

61 Leah Rosenberg, *Errand Runner,* 17.

62 The original *ketuba* is in the private archive of Mr. Lionel Albert of Montreal. A photocopy is in the possession of the author. On the contrary, Baumeil, "Rosenberg," 105, states that "some time" [*a shtikl tsayt*] elapsed prior to his remarriage. This is echoed in Stein, *Radom,* 116.

63 Baumeil, "Rosenberg," 105. Cf. Aaron Rosenberg, *Liqqutei Beit Aharon,* 263. In the introduction to Meir Joshua Rosenberg, *Kur ha-Mivḥan,* the editor states that Ḥaya Ḥava was descended from the eighteenth-century rabbi Joshua Falk ha-Kohen, author of the well-known work *Pnei Yehoshua.* There is no early attestation for this, however. It may be that

Rosenberg's lot at this point could not have been a happy one. At home there was strife in the family because Ḥaya Ḥava's four small children would not fully accept Sara Gitl as their mother.[64] Added to that were the troubles which came to him from his new rabbinic position. First and foremost among these troubles was making ends meet. As mentioned above, rabbinic salaries were generally not enough to support a family, even if they were paid as promised. At times, rabbis were forced to beg the community for their salaries and, in at least one case from interwar Poland, a rabbi was forced to run a stall in the marketplace.[65] As was often the case, the community of Tarłów attempted to supplement the rabbi's salary by granting Rosenberg's wife a monopoly on the sale of certain domestic items such as candles, salt, and yeast.[66] However, even with this supplement making ends meet was problematic. Moreover Rabbi Rosenberg experienced other problems with his community. Toward the end of his life, Rosenberg looked back on his early career in the rabbinate and commented:

> Almost all my days until I reached the days of old age and hoary head I did not know rest or peace. Rather I was always full of trial and tribulation stemming from poverty and pain, persecution and suffering. In my youth I greatly endeavored to be able to avoid taking upon myself the burden of the rabbinate ... for instead of being the head [*ro'sh*], [the rabbi] finds gall and wormwood [*le'ana va-rosh*]. However, opposition from heaven prevented me and I did not succeed in whatever I did.[67]

All accounts of Yudel Rosenberg's life agree that as rabbi of Tarłów, he had opponents who made his life miserable and who, according to one account, ultimately drove him out of town.[68] What were the specific causes of opposition

---

this error stemmed from the fact that Joshua Falk was supposed to have been at one time rabbi of Tarłów. Cf. Cohen, 5.

64 Leah Rosenberg, *Errand Runner*, 17.

65 Samuel D. Kassow, "Community and Identity in the Interwar Shtetl," in *The Jews of Poland Between Two Wars*, ed. Yisrael Gutman, Ezra Mendelsohn, Jehuda Reinharz, and Chone Shmeruk (Hanover, NH: Brandeis University Press, 1989), 205.

66 Cohen, *Sefer ha-Zikkaron*, 5; Stein, *Radom*, 116. Cf. Emanuel Etkes, "Family and Torah Study in the Circles of *Lomdim* in Nineteenth-Century Lithuania" [Hebrew], *Zion* 51 (1989): 87–106.

67 *Omer*, part 1, 5. Cf. Biale et al., *Hasidism: A New History*, 432, 537.

68 Cohen, *Sefer ha-Zikkaron*, 5; Baumeil, "Rosenberg," 105; Shemen, "Ortodoxie," 10; Cf. *Omer*, part 1, 5.

to Yudel Rosenberg as rabbi of Tarłów? His writings from his later years contain hints that enable us to discern what some of the problems may have been.

In one of his responsa, Yudel Rosenberg deals with a case that, as he indicated, occurred during his rabbinate in Tarłów. Tarłów, like many other Eastern European towns with a sizeable Jewish population, maintained an *'eruv*, a legal "boundary," which rendered the entire enclosed area one "domain," thus allowing Sabbath-observant Jews to carry necessary items on the Sabbath day.[69] Certifying and maintaining the town's *'eruv* was normally the province of the town rabbi. However, according to Rosenberg's responsum, this responsibility continued to be in the hands of another rabbinic decisor [*moreh tsedeq*],[70] who had exercised it for a number of years.[71] Thus, Rabbi Rosenberg did not have an effective monopoly over halakhic decision-making in his town. In a small town that possessed at least two halakhic authorities, therefore, young Rabbi Rosenberg's authority likely came into question and it needs little imagination to assume that factionalism within the Jewish community would tend to make his life miserable.

Then again, there is the question of Rabbi Yudel Rosenberg's general compatibility with small-town Jewish life. Previously we have seen that Yudel Rosenberg was exposed as a youth to the modernist writings of the *Haskala*, which often severely criticized the perceived "backwardness" of traditional Jewish life.[72] Though there is no direct evidence from his period in Tarłów that Yudel Rosenberg had internalized the *Haskala* critique of Jewish customs, one of his books, published in 1913, contains a number of passages severely critical of small-town Jewish life. In this work, for instance, Rabbi Rosenberg complained of the terrible conditions found in small-town Jewish bathhouses. This is how he described them:

> The condition of the Jewish bathhouse in small towns is very bad. Most of them are dark and dirty. The ceiling is spattered with mould and mildew,

69 Adam Mintz, "Halakhah in America: The History of City Eruvin, 1894–1962" (PhD diss., New York University, 2011), http://www.rabbimintz.com/wp-content/uploads/Mintz-Dissertation-Final.pdf, accessed May 18, 2015, 147–151, 156–163.

70 *Moreh tsedeq* is a title that was given to individuals who fulfilled rabbinic functions but were of lesser status than a rabbi. Rachel Manekin, "Gaming the System: The Jewish Community Council, the Temple, and the Struggle over the Rabbinate in Mid-Nineteenth-Century Lemberg," *Jewish Quarterly Review* 106, no. 3 (2016): 355.

71 *Omer*, part 2, 27, responsum 6.

72 Cf. Zinberg, *A History of Jewish Literature*, vol. 6, 12–13.

> from which filthy drops continuously drip. On the eve of the Sabbath and holidays, there is terrible crowding and congestion. At times the temperature reaches 40–50 degrees [Celsius]. Many people wash their dirty laundry there and clean out their various scabies, haemorrhoids, and ulcers. Under the benches it is terribly filthy, full of all sorts of dirt. Such bathhouses often do more harm than good.[73]

Equally intense is Rosenberg's criticism, from the same work, of the custom of early marriages among Jews without adequate preparation for making a living; a situation, as we have seen, that fit his own experience:

> The great disaster for the Jews in Exile stems from the foolish custom of marrying off boys at a young age. This is practically the greatest cause of thousands of paupers and of thousands of families whose life is ruined, destroyed, and embittered all their days. Let us merely cast a glance at provincial life, where this insane custom is carried on more strongly than in the big cities,[74] [and see] what destruction and unhappiness result. First of all the young man is still a child lacking in understanding. He still has no comprehension of what making a living means. Then he will have several children ... and the young man must eat "bread of shame" which is called "keep" [*kest*].[75] Meanwhile he must scrounge a bit from his father and a bit from his father-in-law. As is normal, this scrounging is not lacking in quarrels. The draft comes up. If the young man becomes a soldier, the wife remains at home with three or four small children, poor souls, out of which comes ruin. When the young man comes home from being a soldier, he has nothing to do. On his shoulders is the support of a weak and emaciated wife, and of weak children who are barely alive. The young man cannot bear to look at their distress, because he has nothing with which to support them.

Having presented this devastating critique of the marital mores of the shtetl society, which would have done credit to a convinced *maskil* like Moses Leib

---

73 Yudel Rosenberg, *Refu'at ha-Nefesh u-Refu'at ha-Guf* [hereafter *Refu'at*] (Warsaw, 1913), 38.

74 Cf. Shaul Stampfer, "Marital Patterns in Interwar Poland," in *The Jews of Poland Between Two Wars*, ed. Yisrael Gutman, Ezra Mendelsohn, Jehuda Reinharz, and Chone Shmeruk (Hanover, NH: Brandeis University Press, 1989), 173–197.

75 This refers to the arrangement, which Yudel Rosenberg experienced, whereby the father-in-law agrees to support his new son in law's studies for a specified period.

Lilienblum,[76] Rosenberg went on to attempt to put the problem in an historical perspective, once again unusual from the pen of a rabbi writing for a traditional audience:

> Such things are everyday occurrences. … These troubles are found mostly in the Polish small towns, where the Jews think like they did one hundred years ago, when their ancestors behaved like that, making a wedding for their son when he was still young. But how misguided they are! For they do not consider that one hundred years ago, when Poland was a separate kingdom, the nobles ruled all the land. The lords loved to have a good time and gave over their business affairs to Jews, in whose hands all the business lay...For business in the old days you didn't have to be terribly smart. … Therefore in those days it was quite easy and entirely Jewish to marry off sons at an early age. Even today, among wealthy families, this custom is not bizarre. But that this custom should exist other than among great rich families is crazy and the cause of many troubles. It is against what the Torah states and it is against common sense. … The time has certainly come when people should take care not to build any houses on foundations of spiderwebs.[77]

Rabbi Rosenberg in this 1913 work has further words for pious small-town Jews who recite their Psalms devotedly but consider tale-bearing, slander, falsehood, and mockery to be no sins.[78]

If, as is entirely likely, these anti-*shtetl* outbursts represent Rosenberg's opinion of small-town Jewish life when he was actually living it, it stands to reason that he would be considered a *maskil* by at least some of the townspeople and would thus be opposed as one who sought to destroy the bastion of traditional Judaism. This would be especially so for critics who might have gotten wind of his encounter with "forbidden" literature in his hometown that we have

76 Eliyahu Stern, *Jewish Materialism: the Intellectual Revolution of the 1870s* (New Haven: Yale University Press, 2018), 74–79. On this thrust of maskilic literature, see David Roskies, "S. Ansky and the Paradigm of Return" in *The Uses of Tradition: Jewish Continuity in the Modern Era*, ed. Jack Wertheimer (New York and Jerusalem: Jewish Theological Seminary of America, 1992), 2118. Eli Yassif discerns maskilic sensibilities in his stories as well. Eli Yassif, ed., *The Golem of Prague and Other Tales of Wonder* [Hebrew] (Jerusalem: Mossad Bialik, 1991), 56.

77 *Refu'at*, 52–54.

78 *Refu'at*, 63.

previously described. Such traditionalist opposition, which would dog him at a later point in his rabbinic career,[79] would be an additional reason for him to feel less than comfortable as rabbi of Tarłów.

The final problem Rosenberg would have faced during his tenure as rabbi of Tarłów was the necessity of obtaining a governmental license to function as rabbi. In Poland, this required demonstrating one's literacy in Russian as well as familiarity with the Russian laws relative to the rabbinate.[80] Earlier in the century, the number of rabbis who possessed the requisite linguistic skills was apparently small and the custom arose of appointing "official" rabbis—often with not the slightest pretension to rabbinic learning—to satisfy the government's requirements. By the late nineteenth century, however, there is considerable anecdotal evidence that the study of Russian by Polish rabbis of the younger generation was becoming common and, as we shall see, Yudel Rosenberg became one of their number, though not for several years after he had left Tarłów.[81] It may indeed have been possible, by dint of judicious bribery, to get away without knowledge of Russian in small, remote settlements.[82] In any larger settlement, however, that was becoming nearly impossible.

During his tenure in the Tarłów rabbinate, some sources claim that Yudel Rosenberg headed a yeshiva, an academy for rabbinic learning. He is said to have conducted classes [*shi'urim*] in this academy twice daily.[83] It is unclear what, exactly, the nature of this academy was. All indications are, however, that this was at best a local institution, perhaps attracting older boys from Tarłów in the same way that Yudel Rosenberg had studied with the town rabbi of Skaryszew as a youth, "together with some older boys."[84] In Hasidic areas of Eastern Europe in the nineteenth century, the idea of conducting a *yeshiva* along the lines of those in existence among Mitnagdic Jews was not yet widely accepted. Indeed the first Hasidic *yeshiva*, under the auspices of the rebbe of Vishnitz, had

79 Letter of Yudel Rosenberg to Meir Joshua Rosenberg, dated Lodz, Wednesday, weekly Torah portion *va-Yiggash*. The year is uncertain but is from the period 1910–1913. Original in possession of Rabbi Yehoshua Ben-Meir of Jerusalem. Photocopy in possession of the author.

80 Azriel Schochat, *The "Crown Rabbinate" in Russia: A Chapter in the Cultural Struggle between Orthodox Jews and Maskilim* [Hebrew] (Haifa: University of Haifa Press, 1975), 119.

81 The details of Rosenberg's study of Russian and his examination will be found in the next chapter.

82 An example of this phenomenon is Rabbi Pinḥas Mendel Singer, father of the Yiddish writers Israel Joshua and Isaac Bashevis. Cf. Israel Joshua Singer, *Of a World That Is No More* (New York: Vanguard Press, 1970), 16, 139.

83 Cohen, *Sefer ha-Zikkaron*, 5; Shemen, "Ortodoxie," 10; Baumeil, "Rosenberg," 104.

84 Cf. especially Cohen, *Sefer ha-Zikkaron*, 5 and Baumeil, "Rosenberg," 104.

been founded only in 1880.[85] It is most likely that the term *yeshiva* was given to the group Rosenberg headed in Tarłów only retroactively, when the concept had gained ground among Hasidim and heading such an institution would, therefore, be counted to one's credit.

Yudel Rosenberg, as we have seen, had his reasons to be dissatisfied with his lot as a small town rabbi. However, by this time he had no real alternative to the rabbinate. Evidently, he had made his decision not to rebel against his traditional Jewish weltanschauung. The only way for him to broaden his horizons intellectually and financially was for him to move to a bigger city. The only way for him to function as a rabbi in a bigger city was for him to learn Russian and pass the government examination. It did not take him long to make his move. The last evidence placing him in the town of Tarłów comes from the manuscript of a sermon preached there on Rosh ha-Shana of 5650 (September 26–27, 1889).[86] When exactly he left Tarłów for good is unclear. What is certain, however, is that by 1890 he was to be found in the city of Lublin, engaged in the study of Russian, and hoping to obtain a post in the rabbinic establishment of that city, as we will see in the next chapter.

Yudel Rosenberg had good reason to look back on his trials in the town of Tarłów with great bitterness. However, for his later rabbinic career, Tarłów represented an important beginning. He could henceforth claim that he had been the rabbi somewhere. When he began publishing books, he would invariably bill himself as "former rabbi of Tarłów" on the title page.[87] He likewise became known by the name of Tarłów when he settled in larger cities in Poland, going by the name "Reb Yudel Tarler" [of Tarłów] in preference to either his surname, Rosenberg, or his birthplace, Skaryszew.[88]

85 Breuer, "Tradition and Change in European Yeshivot," 10, 15.

86 Aaron Rosenberg, *Liqqutei Beit Aharon*, 45.

87 The title pages of Yudel Rosenberg's works inevitably called him "Rabbi of Tarłów."

88 Thus, he was referred to as Reb Yudel Tarler in the ordination document from Rabbi Samuel Zanvil Klepfisz of Warsaw, published at the beginning of Rosenberg's first book, *Yadot Nedarim: Ve-Hu Be'ur Maspiq 'al Kol ke-Lomar asher be-Ferush Rashi uva-Ran … uvi-She'ar Meqomot … shebe-Masekhet Nedarim* [hereafter *Yadot*] (Warsaw: Ephraim Baumritter, 5663/1902).

CHAPTER 3

A Rabbi and Rebbe in Urban Poland (1890–1913)

RABBINIC POLITICS IN THE CITY OF LUBLIN

When Rabbi Yudel Rosenberg decided he had enough of small-town rabbinic life, he became a tiny part of a massive population movement that was dramatically changing the demographic character of Eastern European Jewry. The cities of the Russian empire offered Jews wider opportunities, both economic and cultural.[1] Yudel Rosenberg, as we have seen, was an individual who had been prepared by his *Haskala* readings to look critically upon small-town Jewish life, and was likely considered suspect because of this by some of his fellow townsmen. He was likely prepared to see city life as both opportunity and liberation.

Rosenberg chose to move to Lublin, an industrial and manufacturing center with the third greatest population in Russian Poland. In the 1897 census, it boasted a population of 48,758, of which almost half (23,788) was Jewish.[2] Lublin was a natural choice for Rosenberg, given that it was the nearest big city to Tarłów, a distance of sixty-five kilometers. However, there may have been more to his decision. The accounts of Yudel Rosenberg's life emphasize the fact that he was connected to two prominent Hasidic rebbes of Lublin, Rabbis Yehuda Leib Eger (1817–1888) and Tsadoq ha-Kohen (1823–1900), both of them disciples of Rabbi Mordechai Yosef Leiner of Izbica.[3] Rosenberg directly mentions having visited Rabbi Eger in 1886.[4] Moreover, there is evidence that one of the officials of the Lublin Rabbinic Court, a Rabbi Joseph, had at one

1 Steven Zipperstein, *The Jews of Odessa: A Cultural History, 1794–1881* (Stanford, CA: Stanford University Press, 1985), 116–117.

2 *Jewish Encyclopedia* (New York: Funk and Wagnalls, 1901–1906), vol. 8, 199, 201, s.v. "Lublin."

3 On Tsadoq ha-Kohen, see Alan Brill, *Thinking God: The Mysticism of Rabbi Zadok HaKohen of Lublin* (Hoboken: Ktav and Yeshiva University Press, 2002). Cf. Aaron Ze'ev Aescoly, *Hasidism in Poland* [Hebrew] (Jerusalem: Magnes Press, 1998), 117–118. On Eger, see Biale et al., *Hasidism: A New History*, 356–357.

4 Meir Joshua Rosenberg, *Kur ha-Mivḥan*, introduction; Stein, *Radom*, 116. Rosenberg mentions his 1886 visit in *Sha'arei Zion* 1, no. 11 (1903): 356. Cf. PY, 92.

time been rabbi of Skaryszew, Rosenberg's hometown.[5] In the tricky process of getting one's foot on the slippery ladder of rabbinic advancement, an acquaintance from one's hometown [*landsman*] in a position of authority might make all the difference.

Everything we know about Rabbi Yudel Rosenberg indicates that he wished to pursue a rabbinic career in Lublin. But how? To gain such a position in Lublin, Rosenberg needed both rabbinic ordination from a prominent rabbi as well as a permit to exercise rabbinic functions from the Russian government. Though, at this point, Rosenberg had possessed the title of rabbi for at least a decade, and had served as rabbi of the town of Tarłów, he needed something more, an ordination that emanated from a rabbi with more than a local reputation. This was an important consideration since Orthodox rabbinic ordination [*semikha*] was granted not by institutions but by individuals. The reputation of the individual rabbi doing the ordaining was therefore crucial to the public acceptance of his certificate. Moreover, even if one received ordination by a reputable rabbi, acceptance of that ordination was not necessarily automatic, for it was possible that the rabbi doing the ordaining had no real intention of certifying that the ordained "rabbi" was actually capable of deciding questions of halakha. Thus one of the most prominent Lithuanian rabbis of the late nineteenth century, Jacob David Wilowsky, known as the Slutsker Rav, stated:

> No reliance should be placed on such [ordination] certificates granted in recent years. It was given to any young man who desired it, in order to encourage him to continue his studies ... every young man who studied some *Yoreh De'ah* was granted ordination. I have done so myself.[6]

It was just such a pitfall that Rosenberg hoped to avoid as he approached two very prominent rabbis for their certification of his rabbinic competence.

5 *Greiditser*, iii, 3.

6 Cited in Abraham Karp, "The Ridwas: Rabbi Jacob David Wilowsky, 1845–1913," in *Perspectives on Jews and Judaism: Essays in Honor of Wolfe Kelman*, ed. Arthur Abraham Chiel (New York, Rabbinic Assembly, 1978), 228. Cf. the citation for Rabbi Eliezer Gordon of Telz in Emanuel Etkes, "Talmudic Scholarship and the Rabbinate in Lithuanian Jewry," in *Scholars and Scholarship: The Interaction between Judaism and Other Cultures*, ed. Leo Landman (New York: Yeshiva University Press, 1990), 124. Cf. also Kimmy Caplan, "Rabbi Isaac Margolis: From Eastern Europe to America" [Hebrew], *Zion* 58 (1993), 219.

The first of them was Rabbi Meir Yeḥiel ha-Levi Halstok, the Ostrovtser Rebbe (1852–1928).[7] Rabbi Halstok, whose ascetic piety and prodigious learning were considered the more remarkable because he was the son of a baker and thus did not stem from the Jewish upper classes, was at first rabbi in the town of Skierniewice, serving there from 1878 to 1888. After that, he moved to Ostrowiec Świętokrzyski and gained a Hasidic following as the Ostrovtser Rebbe.[8] Possibly Yudel Rosenberg went to the Ostrovtser for an ordination certificate because he had family connections in that town through his first wife. Possibly, he was one of the many Torah scholars and Hasidim in Poland attracted to Rabbi Halstok.[9] In any event, he received an ordination certificate [*semikha*] from Rabbi Halstok on Wednesday, weekly Torah portion *be-Shalaḥ*, 5650 (February 5, 1890).[10] The certificate, which indicated that Yudel Rosenberg had been tested on his knowledge of practical rabbinic law by satisfactorily answering "numerous questions" which had arisen in Ostrowiec and were presumably directed to the town rabbi, hint at the possibility that he may have been "trying out" for a position on the Ostrowiec rabbinic court, but there is no evidence that he lived for any appreciable time in Ostrowiec.

The second rabbi to whom Rosenberg went, and by far the more important, was Rabbi Shneur Zalman Fradkin (1830–1902), who was popularly called Liader after his Belorussian birthplace. Rabbi Fradkin was a Lubavitcher Hasid who had served as rabbi of Lublin since 1868.[11] Rosenberg presented himself before Rabbi Shneur Zalman on Sunday, 2 Iyar 5651 (May 10, 1891) along with his previous ordination certificates. He was duly presented with a second major rabbinic approbation.[12] With these two ordination certificates in hand, it must have seemed to Rosenberg that there was a good chance for him to gain a position in the rabbinate of Lublin under Rabbi Shneur Zalman as well as to participate in the vibrant rabbinic and Hasidic life of Lublin, led by Rabbi Abraham Eger (1847–1914), the son and successor of Yehuda Leib Eger, and

---

7 Isser Frankel, *Rabi Meir Yeḥiel mi-Ostrovtsa: Ḥayyav, Shitato, ve-Torato* (Tel-Aviv: Netsaḥ, 1953).

8 Rabinowicz, *The World of Hasidism*, 161; idem, *Hasidism: The Movement and Its Masters* (Northvale, NJ, and London: Jason Aronson, 1988), 260; idem, *Chassidic Rebbes: From the Baal Shem Tov to Modern Times* (Southfield, MI, and Spring Valley, NY: Feldheim, 1989), 262–266. Cf. Urbach, "The History of Polish Jews After World War I," 245.

9 Aescoly, *Hasidism in Poland*, 118.

10 *Yadot*, 41.

11 Naḥman Shemen, *Lublin: City of Torah, Rabbinism, and Piety* [Yiddish] (Toronto: Gershon Pomerantz, 1951), 89.

12 *Yadot*, 41.

Tsadoq ha-Kohen. As late as 1931, Abraham Eger's son David, who had in his turn succeeded his father as rebbe in Lublin, fondly recalled Yudel Rosenberg's presence at his father's court.[13]

There was, however, one remaining hurdle for Yudel Rosenberg to overcome: the Russian language. For centuries, men aspiring to the rabbinate in Eastern Europe had been expected to demonstrate their expertise in the sort of law that counted within the Jewish community—halakha. Whether or not they had any acquaintance with the laws and culture of their non-Jewish neighbors was a matter of little formal importance. While it was always important for the Jewish community to have people able to communicate with non-Jewish officials in their language and to have familiarity with the country's legal system, such men were seldom rabbis. In Yudel Rosenberg's era, however, this situation had changed.

In Russia, as in all European lands, the legal autonomy of the Jewish community was formally a thing of the past.[14] Rabbis in the Russian Empire, who were legally responsible to the government for keeping official records of vital statistics, were expected to have a sufficient command of the Russian language in which, according to the law, these records had to be kept. This Russian language education, moreover, carried with it an expectation that the rabbis would ultimately exercise an acculturating influence upon their coreligionists.[15] They were, in a word, to become instruments for the prosecution of state policy with regard to the Jews.

When the Russian government initially promulgated the law concerning the rabbinate, most Jewish communities were forced to appoint "official" rabbis with the requisite literacy and educational attainments in Russian, while maintaining "unofficial" rabbis who continued to engage in the time-honored rabbinic pursuits of legal adjudication and education. By the late nineteenth century, however, the combination of a rabbinic education and literacy in Russian was becoming less and less rare. In the 1897 Russian census, nearly one-quarter of the Jews of Russia were recorded as literate in Russian[16] and rabbis were no exception to this growing literacy. Russian-speaking rabbis seem to have been quite prevalent in Poland which, juridically separate from the rest of the Empire, had promulgated somewhat different standards of rabbinic literacy.

---

13 Cohen, *Sefer ha-Zikkaron*, 26.

14 Cf. Stanislavski, *Tsar Nicholas*.

15 Cf. Schochat, *"Crown Rabbinate"*; Stanislawski, *Tsar Nicholas*, 133–137.

16 Zipperstein, *Jews of Odessa*, 15; idem, *Elusive Prophet: Ahad Ha'am and the Origins of Zionism* (Berkeley: University of California Press, 1993), 107.

Whereas in the rest of the Empire, the person desiring a government license to practise the rabbinate was required to possess the equivalent of a gymnasium education, in Poland the candidate needed only to demonstrate his literacy in Russian and his knowledge of the government's laws regarding the rabbinate.[17]

In the late nineteenth century, there is evidence that the Russian government requirements were actually being enforced, at least in the larger centers. In 1887, for instance, Jacob David Wilowsky was the rabbi of Vilkomir, Lithuania. Because of the enforcement of the regulation that rabbis master the Russian language, he was forced to leave Vilkomir to take on a rabbinic position in Slutsk in Belorussia.[18] Though many of the older rabbis in Poland did not master Russian, many of the younger generation of rabbis were doing so almost as a matter of course. Among those reputed to have learned Russian were Judah Leib Gordon, rabbi of Lomza,[19] Leizer Itche, grandson of the rabbi of Łódź, Eliyahu Ḥaim Meisels,[20] the Ostrovtser Rebbe[21] and his son Yeḥezkel.[22] A careful survey of rabbinic biographies of this era would doubtless increase this number.

Detailed evidence of this process at work with one Polish rabbi is to be found in the case of Rabbi Pinḥas Mendel Singer, father of the Yiddish novelists Israel Joshua and Isaac Bashevis Singer. Rabbi Singer married Batsheva, daughter of the rabbi of Biłgoraj. Batsheva's brothers, Itche and Joseph, had both mastered Russian, and Itche had been placed by his father in charge of keeping the town's official records and birth register.[23]

---

17 Schochat, *"Crown Rabbinate,"* 119; ChaeRan Y. Freeze, *Jewish Marriage and Divorce in Imperial Russia* (Hanover: University Press of New England, 2002), 95ff. Cf. Jacob J. Schacter, "Haskalah, Secular Studies and the Close of the Yeshiva in Volozhin in 1892," *Torah u-Madda Journal* 2 (1990): 102. In that same article (109), Schacter reports that the influential Rabbi Naftali Zvi Yehuda Berlin stated that learning the Russian language was important for at least some of his students. There was also opposition to this decree. Thus the Gerer Rebbe, Yehuda Aryeh Leib Alter, asked by a student whether he should study Russian to comply with the decree, is said to have responded, "I would envy you much more if you became a shoemaker." Max A. Lipschitz, *The Faith of a Hassid* (New York: Jonathan David, 1967), 135.

18 Rothkoff, "The American Sojourns of Ridbaz," 558.

19 Oscar Z. Fasman, "Trends in the American Yeshiva Today," in *Dimensions of Orthodox Judaism*, ed. Reuven Bulka (New York: Ktav Publishing, 1983), 317.

20 P. Minc (Alexander), *Lodz in Mayn Zikoron* (Buenos Aires: IDBUJ, 1958), 210.

21 Gershon Silberberg, Meir Shimon Geshuri, eds., *Ostrowiec: A Monument on the Ruins of an Annihilated Jewish Community*, English Section, 123, https://www.jewishgen.org/yizkor/ostrowiec/oste111.html, accessed February 14, 2019.

22 Meir Amsel, *Encyclopedia Hamaor* (Brooklyn, NY: Hamaor, 1986), 39–40.

23 Israel Joshua Singer, *Of a World That Is No More* (New York: Vanguard Press, 1970), 99, 105.

When Rabbi Singer married, one of the formal conditions in the articles of engagement [*tena'im*] stated that Pinḥas Mendel was to learn the Russian language and pass the government examination for a rabbinic license. Unfortunately, Rabbi Singer was unable to fulfil this condition despite money spent on tutors and self-teaching texts.[24] His failure to learn Russian barred him from any official rabbinic position and condemned him to rabbinic positions in very small towns, where, by dint of bribery, it was possible to be a rabbi without a license, or, in large cities like Warsaw where he seems to have led an "illegal" hand-to-mouth existence as a rabbinic decisor.[25]

Yudel Rosenberg did not have the problem with learning Russian that Rabbi Singer had. Possibly this was because he was influenced by the maskilic openness to the acquisition of non-Jewish languages. Without doubt it was driven by his desire to get ahead in the rabbinate, the only profession which promised him a living. In any event, Rabbi Rosenberg plunged into the study of the Russian language and other secular books. Despite his ostensibly worthy purpose, Yudel Rosenberg's Russian studies nonetheless rendered him suspect to the pious. A story is told that while Rosenberg was cramming for his government examination, he fell asleep in the House of Study [*Bet Midrash*] of Lublin with a Russian book in his hand. The discovery that he had brought an "impure" book into the *Bet Midrash* created a hullabaloo that was not quieted by his protests that he was studying Russian only because of the government's decree.[26]

Yudel Rosenberg took his Russian language examination in Radom on March 31, 1891, at the age of thirty-one. The Examination Committee of the Radom Provincial Government, in accordance with the Imperial decree requiring rabbis to demonstrate competence in the Russian language and the laws regarding the rabbinate, certified that Yudel Rosenberg had demonstrated his capacity in the Russian language and the pertinent laws. The document was issued by the Ministry of Internal Affairs, Radom Provincial Government on June 12, 1891.[27]

---

24 Ibid., 16, 139.

25 Isaac Bashevis Singer, *Love and Exile: A Memoir* (Garden City, NY: Doubleday, 1984). Such unlicensed rabbis were popularly called *vinkl rebbes* ["corner rabbis"]. See Robert M. Shapiro, "Jewish Self-Government in Lodz, 1914–1939" (PhD diss., Columbia University, 1987), 307.

26 Stein, *Radom*, 116–117; Baumeil, "Rosenberg," 105.

27 The original of the certificate is in the private archive of Mr. Lionel Albert of Montreal. A photocopy is in the author's possession.

One curious aspect of this examination was the fact that Rosenberg submitted to the examination not in Lublin, where he was apparently living at the time, but in his native province of Radom. The reason for the choice of Radom is made clear in a letter Rosenberg wrote approximately a year later to another rabbi, Moshe Naḥum Yerusalimsky of Kamenka, Kiev Province[28] in the course of urging him to take the examination:

> Of all the places in Poland, the city of Radom is to be preferred to pass the examination easily with the addition of the working of money [bribery]. Moreover I have acquaintances there. ... The chief rabbi of Radom, R. Abraham Zvi Perlmutter, the son of R. Leizerke Ḥazan of Łódź, is able to do good with the authorities in this matter.[29]

It was well known that government licenses and permits in the Russian Empire and, especially in Poland, often required bribes.[30] In his letter to Yerusalimsky, Rabbi Rosenberg remarked that the process had cost him nearly 200 rubles, a considerable sum.

The regulations for the examination were numerous and precise. As Rosenberg described the process:

> A petition addressed to the governor of Radom is necessary as well as a small photograph of the head and most [of the body]. The photograph must be included in the petition. In the photograph, you should not show the *pe'ot* [sidelocks] of your head. ... Two 80-kopeck stamps need to be included in the petition. ...
>
> In the petition one needs to write briefly and clearly that the petitioner requests the governor to accept him for the examination for the rabbinate. ... You also need to include in the petition attestation ... that you are a Russian subject and of excellent conduct.

---

28 For Yerusalimsky's biography, see Eli Lederhandler, *Jewish Responses to Modernity: New Voices in America and Eastern Europe* (New York: New York University Press, 1994), 76–77.

29 Rosenberg's letters to Yerusalimsky are found in the Yerusalimsky collection, Schocken Archives, Jerusalem. The first is dated Sunday, weekly Torah portion *Devarim*, 5652 (July 24, 1892) and the second, Tuesday, weekly Torah portion *Ki Tetse'*, 5652 (August 30, 1892). On Rabbi Perlmutter, see Gershon Bacon, "Perlmutter, Abraham Tsevi," *YIVO Encyclopedia of Jews in Eastern Europe*, http://www.yivoencyclopedia.org/article.aspx/Perlmutter_Avraham_Tsevi, accessed May 19, 2015.

30 On the prevalence of bribery in the Russian Empire, see Shabtai Teveth, *Ben-Gurion: the Burning Ground, 1886–1948* (Boston: Houghton Mifflin, 1987), 7.

Once the petition had been accepted, the candidate could advance to the examination stage. As Rosenberg wrote:

> This is the order of the examination. It takes place in the government building [*gubernie*] in a session of notables. ... In the beginning they will order [you] to write a dictation of approximately fifteen sentences. Afterwards you need to write on some topic and include at least fifteen sentences.[31] ... Afterwards, if they see that [the candidate] has [the equivalent] of three grades, they allow him to finish the second part of the examination. ... This consists of reading about six to ten sentences in some book. You need to explain the difficult words thoroughly. You also need to analyse two or three sentences with respect to grammar. ... Afterwards you need to answer orally one question on a law of theirs, such as maintenance of a register of births and deaths, choice of a rabbi, burying the dead, administering oaths, divorce, marriage, and similar things.

However he had managed it, Rosenberg had passed his examination and was thus one of a relatively small number of Polish Jews in possession of a government certificate enabling him to take up an official rabbinic position.[32] He could now hope to be appointed a judge of a rabbinic court [*moreh tsedeq*] in the Lublin rabbinate or elsewhere. Indeed, the date of his ordination certificate signed by the Chief Rabbi of Lublin, coming barely a month after he passed his government examination, makes it entirely likely that the ordination document was accompanied by at least the hope for such a position. According to some accounts of Yudel Rosenberg's career, he did become an official of the Lublin rabbinic court.[33] However, in the two letters he wrote Rabbi Yerusalimsky from Lublin in the summer of 1892, he described himself as merely "rabbi of Tarłów now dwelling [*mitgorrer*] in Lublin."[34] Had he been officially appointed in a rabbinic position in the city, he would not have failed to mention that fact.

---

31 In the letter, Rosenberg gave sample topics that might appear on the examination. They include "How Does One Make Bread?," "What is the Difference Between Town and Country?," "Fall, Winter, Spring, Summer," "Uses of Domestic Animals," "Uses of a Horse," "Field Work," and "Jewish Holiday—New Year."

32 As late as 1910 there were no more than fourteen licensed rabbis in Warsaw. Piotr Wrobel, "Jewish Warsaw Before the First World War," in *The Jews in Warsaw: A History*, ed. Wladyslaw Bartoszewski and Antony Polonsky (Oxford: Blackwell, 1991), 250.

33 Eisenstadt, *Dorot ha-Aḥaronim*, vol. 1, part 3, 320; Reizin, *Leksikon fun der Yiddisher Literatur*, 115.

34 Yerusalimsky collection, Schocken Archives.

Furthermore, his letters to Rabbi Yerusalimsky make prominent mention of his poverty-stricken state. Had he actually received the sort of position he was aiming for, his financial condition would likely not have been quite that bad.

If Yudel Rosenberg was counting on acquiring a rabbinic position in Lublin, he was to be disappointed, though he could not have known it at the time he took his examination. Rabbinic politics intervened. Scarcely a year after Rosenberg passed his examination, the rabbi of Lublin, who had given him *semikha*, left his rabbinate to live in the Land of Israel. In 1892, therefore, the prestigious rabbinate of Lublin was up for grabs. It would only be natural for someone like Rabbi Rosenberg to be vitally interested in the election of the new chief rabbi. As we will see, Rosenberg plunged himself into the thick of the politicking.

Our main evidence for his role in the rabbinic election comes from the two letters Yudel Rosenberg wrote to Rabbi Yerusalimsky in the summer of 1892. One of the two major candidates for the position was Rabbi Halstok, the Ostrovtser Rebbe, with whom, as we have seen, Rosenberg had connections and, perhaps, obligations. Rabbi Halstok's candidacy was supported by the Hasidim and was opposed by the Maskilim, who wished to appoint a more "enlightened" rabbi in the city. However, despite the fact that Rabbi Halstok gained the greater number of votes in the rabbinic election held on 17 Tammuz 5652 (July 12, 1892), political reality demanded that the rabbi elected be acceptable to both sides and Rabbi Halstok was persona non grata to the maskilic faction. Thus he lost his bid for the Lublin rabbinate.[35]

It is not farfetched to assume that Rosenberg was a partisan of Rabbi Halstok, who had granted him a *semikha* certificate, in the politicking prior to the decision. However, the need to find a compromise candidate acceptable to both sides may have indicated to Rosenberg that he had a chance to play a role, and perhaps obtain some advantage for himself, in the election of the rabbi of Lublin. The candidate for the Lublin rabbinate he supported was Rabbi Moshe Naḥum Yerusalimsky.

Yudel Rosenberg did not approach Rabbi Yerusalimsky completely on his own. He did so with the knowledge of, and on behalf of Rabbi Abraham Eger, one of the two most powerful Hasidic leaders in the city.[36] Rosenberg thus wrote to Yerusalimsky offering himself as a sort of "campaign manager" in order

35 Shemen, *Lublin*, 89–90.

36 This is confirmed in a letter of Rabbi Abraham Eger to Yerusalimsky, Yerusalimsky Papers, Schocken Library.

to get him elected to the chief rabbinate of Lublin.[37] His two letters to Yerusalimsky from this period, which we have already utilized for their description of the process of passing the Russian examination, contain news of the twists and turns of the election, encouragement of Yerusalimsky's candidacy, advice on how to approach the community as well as the issue of Rabbi Yerusalimsky passing the Russian examination to be able to legally function in the Lublin rabbinic position.[38] That there might be a quid pro quo for Yudel Rosenberg's advice and support for Rabbi Yerusalimsky's candidacy was obvious, though it went unstated in the letters. Despite Rosenberg's best efforts, however, Rabbi Yerusalimsky did not win the rabbinic election. In a 1908 letter to Rabbi Yerusalimsky recalling the matter, Yudel Rosenberg blamed Yerusalimsky's failure to gain the Lublin rabbinate on opposition to him by the Gerer Hasidim.[39]

It is not unlikely that Rabbi Rosenberg's support for the losing candidate in the Lublin rabbinate election of 1892 would make his relationship with the newly elected rabbi somewhat difficult. Thus if he had ever expected a rabbinic appointment in Lublin, Yudel Rosenberg could realistically expect it no longer. Moreover, we may speculate that Rabbi Rosenberg could have had a falling out with Rabbi Abraham Eger, because we would otherwise expect that Rabbi Eger would supply a letter of approbation for Rabbi Rosenberg's first book, published in 1902. But Rabbi Eger's approbation is conspicuously missing from the book. What we do know is that relatively soon after the Lublin rabbinic election Yudel Rosenberg left the city to try his luck in the metropolis of Polish Jewry some 100 kilometers away—Warsaw.

REB YUDEL TARLER GOES TO WARSAW

Warsaw was far and away the metropolis of Polish Jewry. According to the 1897 Russian census, 219,141 Jews lived in that city—fully 20% of the Jews in Congress Poland.[40] By 1910, 39.2 percent of the total population of the city, approximately 350,000 Jews lived in Warsaw.[41] There, surely, Yudel Rosenberg

37 It was not unusual for rabbis vying for positions to have local agents agitating on their behalf. See Etkes, "Talmudic Scholarship," 121. A circular on behalf of R. Ḥayyim Mendel Landau, a candidate for the Łódź rabbinate in 1912, is preserved in the YIVO Archives, RG28-Lodz#19.

38 Rosenberg to Yerusalimsky, Yerusalimsky Papers, Schocken Library.

39 Rosenberg to Yerusalimsky, 1908, Yerusalimsky Papers, Schocken Library.

40 Zipperstein, *The Jews of Odessa*, 15.

41 Biale et al., *Hasidism: A New History*, 537.

hoped he would find a rabbinic position commensurate with his abilities and ambitions. The trouble was, of course, that he was not alone. Rabbis no less than other Jews were flocking to Warsaw in the late nineteenth century in great numbers, creating what must have been a major glut of rabbinic talent, whereas the official Warsaw Jewish community as such supported only fifteen rabbis.[42] Rosenberg, despite his experience and expertise would most likely have been seen by Warsaw Jews as merely another small town rabbi who had arrived in the city. He would have to struggle to make his mark there.[43]

Without doubt, one of the first things Rosenberg, who was so proud of his former rabbinate in Tarłów that he called himself "Reb Yudel Tarler,"[44] should have done upon arriving in Warsaw was to present his credentials to the person whose approval he most needed to operate "officially" in his chosen profession: the chief rabbi of the rabbinic council which controlled the Warsaw rabbinate, Rabbi Samuel Zanvil Klepfisz.[45] This, however, he did not do for several years. Klepfisz examined Yudel Rosenberg and his credentials and issued a document attesting this only on 25 Sivan 5658 (June 15, 1898).[46] Prior to this, however, Rosenberg had been living in Warsaw for at least four years, since he records at the beginning of his first published book, *Yadot Nedarim* [Monuments of Vows], that he began writing it in Warsaw on Sunday, May 6, 1894.[47]

Whether or not Yudel Rosenberg's departure from Lublin was of such a nature as to make him hesitate to approach Rabbi Klepfisz immediately, it is reasonable to assume that, at least for his first years in Warsaw, Rosenberg operated as a rabbi outside the auspices of the official chief rabbinate, a situation that was

---

42 Scott Ury, *Barricades and Banners: the Revolution of 1905 and the Transformation of Warsaw Jewry* (Stanford: Stanford University Press, 2012), 48.

43 On the experiences of another small-town rabbi, Pinḥas Mendel Singer, who came to Warsaw shortly after Rosenberg, see Isaac Bashevis Singer, *In My Father's Court*, and Israel Joshua Singer, *Of a World That Is No More.*

44 *Yadot*, 41.

45 On Warsaw rabbinic politics in the nineteenth century, see Shaul Stampfer, "An Unhappy Community and an Even Unhappier Rabbi," in *Warsaw. The Jewish Metropolis: Essays in Honor of the 75th Birthday of Professor Antony Polonsky*, ed. Glenn Dynner and François Guesnet (Leiden: Brill, 2015), 154, 179. On the Warsaw rabbinate in the twentieth century, see Gershon Bacon, "Enduring Prestige, Eroding Authority: the Warsaw Rabbinate in the Interwar Period," in *Warsaw. The Jewish Metropolis: Essays in Honor of the 75th Birthday of Professor Antony Polonsky*, ed. Glenn Dynner and François Guesnet (Leiden: Brill, 2015), 347–369.

46 *Yadot*, 41. Though Klepfisz did not have the official title of chief rabbi of Warsaw, he acted in that capacity in all but name as chair of a committee of rabbis that ran the Warsaw rabbinate. See *Encyclopedia Judaica*, s.v. "Klepfish, Samuel Zanvil."

47 *Yadot*, 7.

not at all uncommon.[48] Possibly through the patronage of the Rabbi Halstok, the Ostrovtser Rebbe, whose partisan he was back in Lublin, Rabbi Rosenberg obtained the position of rabbi of the synagogue of the Skierniewice Hasidim in Warsaw.[49] Nonetheless, though this position doubtless helped, it was insufficient to keep him and his family from starvation and want. Yudel Rosenberg's poor financial situation was compounded by the increase in his family; four children from his first marriage and no less than fourteen with his second wife, of whom only seven survived to adulthood.[50] The seven children who survived were Benjamin (Baruch, 1887–1919), Hannah (1890–1955), Israel Mordecai (1892–1958), Bracha (Elsie, 1895–1962), Rivka (Ruth, b. 1902), Leah (Lily, 1903–1997), and Abraham Isaac (1912–1985).[51] Without doubt, the extremely high mortality rate of Rosenberg children, not unusual among contemporary Eastern European Jews, was influenced by the family's poverty and the resulting poor living conditions. Another indication of the straits the Rosenberg family found itself involves the marriage of one of Yudel Rosenberg's daughters. According to the story told by his daughter Leah, a prospective son-in-law was promised a dowry of 500 rubles. As the Rosenberg family had at that time only five rubles in its bank account, Sara Gitl Rosenberg is said to have added two zeros to the five in the bankbook to indicate the required sum so that the marriage could proceed.[52]

Rabbi Yudel Rosenberg and his family clearly needed more than the Skierniewice Hasidim of Warsaw could give them. According to one source, he obtained occasional speaking engagements at the *shtibls* of other Warsaw

---

48 On the status of "unofficial" rabbis in Warsaw, see Isaac Bashevis Singer, *In My Father's Court,* 248–252.

49 Baumeil, "Rosenberg," 105. There is a possibility that Rosenberg's initial contact with the Skierniewice Hasidism could have come earlier since Skierniewice Hasidim were to be found in Radom. See Stein, *Radom*, 68. Over twenty years after Rosenberg had left Warsaw, he was still remembered fondly by the members of the Skieniewice Shtibl in Warsaw. See Cohen, *Sefer ha Zikkaron*, 25–26.

50 Leah Rosenberg, *Errand Runner*, 18.

51 Genealogical chart in the private archive of Mr. Lionel Albert. Among those children who died, Jacob was born c. 1897. See genealogical records, https://www.geni.com/people/Lily-Richler-Rosenberg/6000000002623235491; https://www.thebreman.org/Research/Cuba-Family-Archives/Finding-Aids/ID/708/Mss-338-Abraham-I-Rosenberg-Papers, accessed February 14, 2019.

52 Leah Rosenberg, *Errand Runner*, 24. On the often poor living conditions of Eastern European Jews at the time, see Andrew R. Heinze, *Adopting to Abundance: Jewish Immigrants, Mass Consumption, and the Search for American Identity* (New York: Columbia University Press, 1990), 36.

Hasidic groups.[53] The money he gained through his free-lance preaching efforts, however, could hardly be expected to make a real dent in his poverty. An obvious way out of his poverty would be to gain an official position in the Warsaw rabbinate. But to succeed in the overcrowded and highly competitive rabbinic world of Warsaw at the turn of the century, Rosenberg needed a reputation. To gain such a reputation, the letters of approbation he had at hand, even if they were from two rabbis with large reputations, were clearly insufficient. There were many rabbis who claimed to possess even more approbations "from the great ones of our generation."[54] If Yudel Rosenberg was going to make it in the big city, he would have to write and publish a book. It is to this task that he set himself.

There were many types of books Rosenberg could have attempted: Biblical commentary, *mussar* [moral exhortation], sermons, halakha. However, he evidently decided that the most effective way of gaining the sort of reputation he sought in Warsaw rabbinic circles was to write a book commenting on the basic text of Rabbinic Judaism, the Babylonian Talmud. Thus though he completed a manuscript in 1896 on the popular theme of moral exhortation, entitled *Derekh Erets*, he left it unpublished.[55] He presumably did not have the financial resources to spend on such a publication that would not necessarily redound to his rabbinic credit. The work he did publish first was a super-commentary on Tractate *Nedarim* of the Babylonian Talmud, which deals with the subject of formal oaths and their halakhic consequences.

This super-commentary, which he entitled *Yadot Nedarim*, was meant to be an aid to the study of that tractate and may well have originated in his experience teaching Talmud to young students. It was certainly considered by his family, when they republished the book in the 1950s to have been an effort designed for young students.[56] As a general rule, Jews who studied the Talmudic tractate *Nedarim* did so with the help of two standard commentaries, written by the eleventh-century Rabbi Solomon ben Isaac, or Rashi, and the fourteenth-century Rabbi Nissim ben Reuben Gerondi, also known as Ran. However, these commentaries were themselves often obscure to Talmud

53 Thus he spoke before the Minsker Hasidim of Warsaw on Shabbat Shuva, 1901. Aaron Rosenberg, *Liqqutei Beit Aharon*, 46.

54 Such a claim was made by Rabbi Joshua ha-Levi Herschorn of Montreal. He announced that he possessed no less than eight such approbations. *Keneder Adler* [hereafter *KA*], November 11, 1921.

55 *Derekh Erets*, 3.

56 *Yadot* (New York, Glass, 1956), preface.

students. Rosenberg therefore set himself the task of clarifying the many obscurities in these commentaries and providing a clear and succinct explanation each time the commentators used the term *kelomar* ["that is to say"], which indicated that there was a difficulty that required further clarification.

Yadot Nedarim, which Rosenberg began in 1894, was published in the fall of 1902 by the Warsaw printer F. Baumritter.[57] That Rosenberg took so long to publish the book is likely because it would have taken him considerable time to collect the money necessary to finance the printing. There may possibly have been an additional dynamic at work, however. It may only be coincidence that Rosenberg published his first work shortly after attaining the age of forty-three. On the other hand, rabbinic tradition looked upon the age of forty as the age at which one could commence public teaching [*hora'a*] even if there was a greater rabbinic authority in the city. According to the interpretation of the *Tosafot*, the forty years were not to be counted from birth but rather from the time one began one's studies. As it was the custom of Jewish boys in that era to begin their education at the age of three, the year 1902 would mark the beginning of Rosenberg's period of *hora'a*.[58]

As was the custom in rabbinic works, Rosenberg prefaced his book with a number of letters of approbation [*haskamot*] from various rabbis. In this case, there were seven such letters. The first and most prominent was from his patron, Rabbi Yeḥiel Halstok, the Ostrovtser Rebbe. Others were received from Rabbis Hillel Aryeh Leib Livshits (1844–1907) of Lublin, Jacob Orner (1866–1916) of Nasielsk, Isaac ha-Kohen Feigenbaum (1826–1911), Petaḥia Hornblass, Tuvia ha-Kohen Rotlev, and Solomon David Kahana (1869–1953), all of Warsaw. Of the four Warsaw rabbis, three at least, Feigenbaum, Hornblass, and Kahana, were connected with the chief rabbinate council.[59] The absence of Rabbi Abraham Eger of Lublin, with whom Rosenberg had been in close

57 *Yadot*, title page. The year is given as 5663 according to the Jewish calendar and as 1902 in Arabic numerals. This means that it was published sometime between Rosh ha-Shana 5663 (October 2, 1902) and the end of that year. On Hebrew printing in Warsaw and elsewhere in Poland, see Ḥayyim Dov Friedberg, *Toledot ha-Defus ha-'Ivri be-Polania*, second edition (Tel-Aviv: Barukh Friedberg, 1950).

58 Cf. R. Shabbetai b. Meir (Shakh) on *Yoreh De'ah* 242:31, note 49.

59 On the relationship of Feigenbaum, a Gerer Hasid, with Klepfisz, see Jacob Marshak, *Sefer Divrei Moshe* (Warsaw, 1885), [4], in which they jointly signed a letter of approbation as "heads of the rabbinic court." On Kahana's relationship with Klepfisz, see *Jewish Encyclopedia*, s.v. "Kahana, Solomon David." On Hornblass (1844–1914), see the obituary which appeared in *KA*, August 14, 1914, "Der Varshaver Rov Geshtorben"; Yitshak Alfasi, *Jewish Glimpses of Warsaw*, trans. and ed. A. Y. Finkel (New York: CIS, 1992), 37.

contact during his Lublin period, is striking. Rabbi Klepfisz, who might have also been expected to write a letter of approbation, had died in 1902.

At this point, in 1902, neither Rosenberg nor any of the seven rabbis who wrote letters on his behalf mentioned any official rabbinic post held by him in Warsaw, though none of them failed to mention his rabbinate in Tarłów and the fact that he was now sojourning in Warsaw. This practically precludes the possibility that Rosenberg was part of any "official" Warsaw rabbinate at this point, despite his government license and the 1898 approbation of the chief rabbi of Warsaw.

Rabbi Yudel Rosenberg's *Yadot Nedarim* is primarily a technical work, which fully fulfilled its promise of usefulness as a study-aid to students attempting to master tractate *Nedarim.*[60] It was not, however, as Rosenberg made clear in his introduction, a book likely to be of use to advanced Talmud scholars. In the first place, as he took pains to point out, it did not seek to innovate [*miḥadesh*] but simply to explain the comments of the commentators to "a generation of small intellect and inferior knowledge like our own."[61] Thus, in addition to supplying a useful work for Talmud students, he may still have felt the need to make his reputation as a brilliant Talmudist.

In order to demonstrate his brilliance and full mastery of Talmudic literature, he added, as part two of his book, a collection of Talmudic disquisitions [*pilpul*] clarifying obscurities in and reconciling perceived differences between various Talmudic passages.[62] Such disquisitions had once been *de rigeur* for any Polish rabbi seeking recognition by his peers, though they were beginning to go out of favor in certain yeshivot of Lithuania, and even in Warsaw Rosenberg felt it necessary in his introduction to part two to justify the publication of yet another collection of *pilpulim.*[63]

---

60 Baumeil, "Rosenberg," 105; Meir Joshua Rosenberg, *Kur ha-Mivḥan*, introduction, 7. B. Schwartz, *Artsot ha-Ḥayyim* (Brooklyn: published by the author, 1992), 30b, claims that the book "is studied in all the yeshivot."

61 *Yadot*, introduction. This theme is repeated several times in the course of the introduction. It is a typical instance of the classic as well as rabbinic notion that the generations have been continually in decline.

62 For an early modern definition of *pilpul*, see Elchanan Reiner, "Transformations in the Polish and Ashkenazic Yeshivot during the Sixteenth and Seventeenth Centires and the Dispute over *Pilpul*" [Hebrew], in *Ke-Minhag Ashkenaz ve-Polin: Sefer Yovel le Khone Shmeruk*, ed. Israel Bartal, Chava Turniansky, and Ezra Mendelsohn (Jerusalem: Merkaz Zalman Shazar, 1989), 9–80. Cf. William Kolbrener, *The Last Rabbi: Joseph Soloveitchik and Talmudic Tradition* (Bloomington: Indiana University Press, 2016), 61.

63 *Yadot*, 37, introduction to part 2. On the breakup of the hold of *pilpul* on some Eastern European Jews, see Solomon, "The Analytic Movement in Rabbinic Jurisprudence." Cf. Chaim

Included at the end of part one of *Yadot Nedarim* was a sermon which Rosenberg stated was originally delivered at a ceremony marking the end of studying tractate *Nedarim*, entitled "The Power of Speech and Thought."[64] This sermon is interesting because it adumbrates a theme that was to be of major significance in the later development of his thought: the relationship of Judaism to the natural sciences through the medium of the Jewish mystical tradition of Kabbala.

It was Rosenberg's thesis in this sermon that a fruitful analogy may be made between the kabbalistic concept of a cause and effect relationship between man and *Eyn Sof* (God's aspect of absolute transcendence) and the cause and effect relationship of the natural sciences. In referring to human prayer ascending aloft on wings of thought, he utilized the analogies of electricity and balloons. He similarly introduced analogies with other scientific discoveries and recent technological innovations such as the speed of light, magnetism, the telephone, and the phonograph.

The publication of a successful rabbinic book could not but stand Rosenberg in good stead. Indeed, the difference the publication of his *Yadot Nedarim* made with respect to his position in Warsaw became obvious in a relatively short period. By the summer of 1904, Rosenberg was signing his letters to Rabbi Yerusalimski as "religious judge [*dayyan*] of the aforementioned holy community [Warsaw]."[65] In the year 1907, Rabbi Halstok, the Ostrovtser Rebbe, writing the salutation in a letter to Rosenberg, described him, in the language of Judges 5, 10, as "sitting on rich cloths," a phrase which rabbinic exegesis had connected with the position of judges.[66] This seems to indicate that he had achieved his goal of becoming an official part of the Warsaw rabbinate. Certainly by the year 1908, he would begin calling himself, on the title pages of his books, *dayyan u-moreh tsedeq* ["judge and rabbinic decisor"], indicating a position on a rabbinic court in Warsaw.[67]

Zalman Dimitrovsky, "On the Pilpulistic Method," in *Salo Wittmayer Baron Jubilee Volume*, ed. Saul Lieberman and Arthur Hyman (New York: American Academy for Jewish Research, 1974), Hebrew Section, 111–182.

64 *Yadot*, 37–38.

65 Yerusalimsky Papers, Schocken Library, Jerusalem. Cf. Chaim I. Waxman, "Toward a Sociology of Psak," *Tradition* 25, no. 3 (1991): 20–21.

66 The letter is dated 10 Adar, 5667 (February 24, 1907). ZT, vol. 1, 5. On the rabbinic interpretation, see Targum Jonathan and Rashi to Judges 5, 10.

67 *Sefer Kol Torah. Hu Qovets Ḥiddushei Torah. ...* [hereafter KT] (Warsaw: n.p., 1908), title page; *Sefer Nifla'ot ha-Zohar* [hereafter NZ] (Montreal, 1927), title page. Cf. *KA*, October 24, 1935.

The publishing of *Yadot Nedarim* launched a publishing career that would last until Rabbi Rosenberg's death in 1935. Yudel Rosenberg would not, however, return to the sort of rabbinic *pilpul* that marked his first publication, though he did publish some short pieces of this sort in various rabbinic periodicals in Warsaw[68] and toward the end of his life he also included some of his Talmudic novellae at the end of his collected responsa, *Yeḥeveḥ Da'at.*[69] Instead, his mastery of Talmudic literature having been established, he perhaps felt able to branch out into other areas. First of all, he began publishing a number of books designed for a popular market. These popular books would both bring him fame and also embroil him in controversy. These books and their implications will be fully described in chapter seven. Another major scholarly project he commenced at this time, a Hebrew translation and re-edition of the classic work of Kabbala, the *Zohar,*[70] will be discussed in detail in chapter ten.

By 1908, Rabbi Rosenberg, who had apparently succeeded in obtaining a position as *dayyan* in Warsaw, was clearly a person to be reckoned with on the Warsaw rabbinic scene. As if to signal this fact, to consolidate his professional position, and hopefully to increase his fame and influence, he launched yet another major literary project—a rabbinic journal, which will be fully discussed in chapter six.

THE TARLER REBBE OF ŁÓDŹ

Apparently dissatisfied with Warsaw, Rabbi Rosenberg was looking for opportunity elsewhere. A 1906 letter to Joseph Levy in London as well as a 1908 letter to Rabbi Moshe Naḥum Yerusalimsky broaching the possibility of securing for him the rabbinate of Lublin in return for a post in the rabbinate demonstrate this.[71] Though

68 *Sha'arei Zion* 1, no. 11 (1903–4), 356 on *Yoreh De'ah, Hilkhot Melikha,* chapter 69; *Sha'arei Torah* 2, no. 4, 130–132, on *Gittin* 24a and Baba Kama 16b.

69 *Kovets Ḥidushim be-Shas u-Poskim, Omer,* part 2, 128–139.

70 The first volume, entitled *Sha'arei Zohar Torah,* perhaps an intended compliment to Rabbi Isaac ha-Levi Feigenbaum, editor of *Sha'arei Torah,* was published in Warsaw by J. Edelstein in 5666/1905. An expanded edition of *Sha'arei,* ZT, covering the Book of Genesis as well as volumes covering the rest of the Pentateuch were only published in 1924. The several volumes of *Sha'arei Zohar Ktuvim* [hereafter ZK] on Psalms, Song of Songs, Proverbs, and Ecclesiastes were published between 1929 and 1931. A companion volume, NZ, consisting of tales concerning Rabbi Simeon bar Yoḥai, the purported author of the *Zohar,* was a further attempt to spur the popularization process.

71 Rosenberg to Joseph Levy, April 18, 1906, BMA; to Yerusalimsky, 1908. Yerusalimsky Papers, Schocken Library, Jerusalem.

nothing came of that, the letter indicates that Yudel Rosenberg was in some way dissatisfied with his position in Warsaw and sought to improve it by moving elsewhere. Possibly as early as 1909, but at the latest by 1910, Rabbi Rosenberg left Warsaw and moved to Łódź, the second largest city of Poland.[72] Why did he decide to make such a move? The best explanation seems to be that he saw possibilities of self-advancement in Łódź that would have been next to impossible had he remained in in Warsaw. Łódź, which possessed a rapidly growing Jewish population of 166,628 in 1910 (up from 98,677 in 1897)[73] attracted Jews from all over the Russian Empire. It was a city with no home-grown intelligentsia and which hence tended to look to the outside for its intellectual and religious leadership.[74] Its rabbinate, under the leadership of its chief rabbi, Elijah Ḥayyim Meisel was well-organized and powerful.[75] Rosenberg, his reputation enhanced by his numerous and varied publications, had the idea that he would be able to set himself up in Łódź as a Hasidic rebbe.[76] He stated as much in a letter he wrote in 1934: "I lived for five years in the city of Łódź as a rebbe of Hasidim."[77]

Such an ambition would certainly be difficult to achieve but was not inherently unattainable in early twentieth-century Poland.[78] While in the interwar period, Łódź housed no less than thirteen Hasidic rebbes, most, if not all of them, had come to the city due to the exigencies of World War I. Prior to the war there would have been few resident rebbes as rivals.[79] Also, newly urbanized

---

72 Both NZ, published in 1909, and *Seder Haqqafot le-Shmini Atseret ule-Simḥat Torah. ... Kemo she-Ne'emru be-Veyt Midrasho shel ... Pinḥas mi-Korets* [hereafter *Haqqafot*] (Piotrków: Ḥanokh Henikh Folman, 1909) state on the title page that Rosenberg was a resident of Warsaw. *Seder ha Prozbul* [hereafter *Prozbul*] (Piotrków: Mordecai Tsederboym, 1910), states that Rosenberg was a resident of Łódź.

73 The figures are cited in Deborah Dwork, "Immigrant Jews on the Lower East Side of New York, 1880–1914," in *The American Jewish Experience*, ed. Jonathan D. Sarna (New York and London: Holmes and Meier, 1986), 102.

74 P. Minc, *Lodz in Mayn Zikoron*, 209

75 Ibid., 206.

76 Meir Joshua Rosenberg, *Kur ha-Mivḥan*, introduction, refers to Yudel Rosenberg as an *admor*. Cf. n.a., "Memorandum [on the Rosenberg Family]," Jewish Canadiana Collection, Jewish Public Library, Montreal.

77 Letter from Rosenberg to Moshe Blistreich, Hanukkah, 5695, RFA, Savannah.

78 Aescoly, *Hasidism in Poland*, 117–118. This position is contradicted by Biale et al., who state that unlike Hungarian Hasidism, the formation of a new Hasidic court in which the rebbe is not related to an older dynasty was "practically impossible" in Galicia or Poland. Biale et al., *Hasidism: A New History*, 391.

79 Marcin Wodziński, "War and Religion; or, How the First World War Changed Hasidism," *Jewish Quarterly Review* 106, no. 3 (2016): 296; Biale et al., *Hasidism: A New History*, 538–539.

Hasidim, whose rebbes remained in their home towns, might have felt enough of a weakening of their bonds with their rebbe such that they might be willing to accept a new local spiritual leader as well.[80] Though by the early twentieth century the Hasidic scene was dominated by major institutionalized dynasties such as Ger, Lubavich, Alexander, and Belz, there was still a possibility for new rebbes to find their place. Solomon Poll, in his analysis of Hasidic life in post-World War II Brooklyn, calls this sort of person a *shtikl rebbe* ["partial rebbe"].[81] As Poll describes him, such a person is not usually in direct line of descent from the well-known Hasidic rebbes, though invariably he will claim descent from some well-known rabbi. He sets up a synagogue or house of study and attracts followers, though often he must supplement his income from other sources. Poll's description of the *shtikl rebbe* fits Rosenberg's experience in Łódź very well.

When Rabbi Yudel Rosenberg arrived in Łódź, he became one of nearly one hundred "unofficial" rabbis known as *vinkl rabbonim* ["corner rabbis"] in the city and began calling himself "The Tarler Rebbe of Łódź,"[82] continuing to play upon the name of the town whose rabbi he had been over twenty years previously.

Someone who knew Rabbi Rosenberg during his sojourn in Łódź, Chaim Leib Fox (1897–1984), wrote the following poetic reminiscence of Rosenberg during this period:

> I see my Rebbe, the kabbalist Reb Yidel Talner [sic],
> And I perceive with youthful eagerness
> His wonder stories and compositions,
> Every one of which I feel contains a [divine] name....
> Reb Yidl, my rebbe, I see you in my Łódź,
> In the dark room on Polnocna Street,
> Lit only by a "five" [?] bulb,
> Since it has no windows.
> But you did not resent this,
> For your home was like a Holy Temple,

---

80 Wodziński, "War and Religion," 297; Biale et al., *Hasidism: A New History*, 537.

81 Solomon Poll, *The Hasidic Community of Williamsburg: A Study in the Sociology of Religion* (New York: Schocken, 1962), 63, 118, 121.

82 This title is utilized on the title pages of Rosenberg's books *Sefer Segulot u-Refu'ot* (Piotrków: Yitsḥaq Shlomovits, 1910) and *Greiditser*. On the phenomenon of *vinkl rabbonim*, see Shapiro, "Jewish Self-Government in Lodz," 379, note 143.

> Like God's own temple.
> I study your books, your works fashioned in hunger,
> Which give me light to this day.[83]

As is evident from Fox's description, Rosenberg did not have an easy time as the Tarler Rebbe of Łódź. Indeed, opposition to him in Łódź seems to have sprung up from several sources. In a letter to his son, Meir Joshua, by then married and living in Warsaw, Yudel Rosenberg wrote concerning a man called Yekl of Opoczno. Yekl came to Łódź and made the accusation against Rabbi Rosenberg:

> that I am not a rebbe, but only a Maskil, an unbeliever [*apikoros*], and a bit of a doctor, that I have an in-law in Warsaw who is a tailor and a bankrupt, that my son shaves his beard, and that I have explicitly commanded my daughter-in-law to go about with [uncovered] hair.[84]

Indeed, there were aspects of Rosenberg's personal and family life which would likely have been an embarrassment to one who aspired to the mantle of a rebbe. He *did* have a maskilic educational experience and demonstrated the internalization of certain maskilic values in his criticism of small-town Jewish life, as we have seen.[85] Then, too, there were his children, some of whom were already adults. His eldest son, Meir Joshua, had married Shaindel Wachsman, the daughter of a wealthy Hasidic merchant in Warsaw. Meir Joshua wrote Hebrew poetry, which he published, anonymously, in the journal *Ha-Tsefirah*. He was also involved in the politics of the Religious Zionist party, Mizraḥi.[86] Neither of these activities would have elicited accolades from a Hasidic audience. Among Yudel Rosenberg's other children, one son, Benjamin, was a student of agronomy at the University of Kharkov and was apparently involved in revolutionary activities. Yet another son, Israel, was a budding Yiddish actor and playwright.[87] These "non-kosher" activities on the part of his children would have certainly provided ammunition to his detractors, some of whom may have been other

83 Chaim Leib Fox, "From the Poem 'Montreal,'" *Idisher Kempfer* (Pesaḥ 5740), 8. Cf. idem, *100 Years of Yiddish and Hebrew Literature in Canada*, 276.

84 Letter from Yudel Rosenberg to Mayer Joshua Rosenberg, undated, Ben-Meir Family Archive [hereafter BMA] (Jerusalem).

85 *Refu'at*, 38, 52, 54, 63.

86 Meir Joshua Rosenberg, *Kur ha-Mivḥan*, introduction.

87 Cf. Leah Rosenberg, *Errand Runner*, 27–28.

shtikl rebbes in Łódź, engaged in a fierce competition for followers and income.[88] Indeed, it is entirely likely that several condemnations of "false" rabbis found in Rabbi Rosenberg's works emanating from his Łódź period reflect this competitive situation and were returned in kind.[89]

Yudel Rosenberg made numerous attempts during his four-year sojourn in Łódź, to assert his public presence. One of the most interesting is his practice as a homeopathic healer, which will be discussed in detail in chapter six. These years also saw some of his most successful and lasting literary efforts as well as some publications which, though less significant ultimately, point to some of the interesting directions in which his mind was developing. His Łódź publications can be classified under three headings: halakha, medicine, and stories that will be analysed in detail in chapters six, seven, and nine.

However, despite Rosenberg's best efforts to succeed at the various tasks he had set himself, there is no evidence that he achieved much success either in attracting supporters and followers as a Hasidic rebbe or in securing a sufficient income as an author to support his family. Whatever evidence exists is all on the other side. In a letter he wrote his son, Mayer Joshua, from Łódź, he spoke of his daughter, Hessl Glass, who was about to emigrate to Canada to join her husband, who was then in Toronto. She had the ticket [*shiffskart*] that had been sent to her but had no way of paying the expenses of the journey to the port city. Rosenberg commented:

> She [Hessl] has no [money for] expenses. If she keeps living with me, what shall she live on? As for me, I have nothing to give her, because want and pressure on livelihood is very, very great here. It is plain as can be that people are dying of hunger.[90]

Given his condition of poverty and the failure to make himself a prominent place in the religious life of Łódź, Rosenberg was open to yet another move. When, in 1913, a congregation of Polish Jews in Toronto needed a rabbi, Rosenberg's son-in-law, Shlomo Ze'ev Yosef Glass (1879–1953), recommended his

88 See letter to Yudel Rosenberg from Rabbi Petaḥia Hornblass of Warsaw, published in Rosenberg's *Miqveh Yehuda* [hereafter *Miqveh*] (Toronto, n.d.), unpaginated. Cf. also the letter from Yudel Rosenberg to Moshe Naḥum Yerusalimsky, 1913, Yerusalimsky Papers, Schocken Library.

89 Cf. *Refa'el*, 4, 6, 58; *ZT*, vol. 2, 86.

90 Rosenberg to Mayer Joshua Rosenberg, dated Łódź, Wednesday, weekly Torah portion *va-Yiggash*, no year stated, BMA.

father-in-law for the post. Rosenberg jumped at the chance and accepted the position offered to him.[91]

Numerous Eastern European rabbis, who had been forced by economic circumstances to cross the ocean and seek their fortune in a North America widely reputed to be inimical to Orthodox obsevance, recorded their regrets at their departure from Orthodox Judaism's secure home in Europe.[92] Yudel Rosenberg, if he felt any such regrets, never expressed them in his subsequent voluminous writings. He would now experience a new beginning, trying to make his mark in the burgeoning Jewish communities of the New World.

---

91 Cohen, *Sefer ha-Zikkaron*, 6. Zalman Reizin records an assertion that Rabbi Rosenberg travelled to North America as a representative of the Polish rabbinate. Yassif rightly dismisses this as farfetched. Yassif, *The Golem of Prague*, 63.

92 Kimmy Caplan, "Rabbi Isaac Margolis," 235–236.

CHAPTER 4

"Allright! It's America!": A Rabbi in Toronto (1913–1918)

A POLISH RABBI IN TORONTO

On Saturday, July 26, 1913, the Cunard Line Steamship Andania arrived at Quebec City, Canada, from Southampton, England after a crossing that lasted ten days. One of its 1,398 passengers was Rabbi Yudel Rosenberg. At immigration inspection, he declared his age to be fifty-two; his occupation: rabbi. He further declared that he had $60.00 in cash, that his destination was Toronto, and that he did not intend to reside permanently in Canada. The document noted that Rabbi Rosenberg would travel to Toronto on the Grand Trunk Railway.[1] Having thus satisfied the demands of the Canadian Immigration Act of 1910, which specified that adult immigrants had to be in possession of a minimum of $25.00 in cash and a railway ticket to their destination,[2] Rosenberg left Quebec City at 11:00 P.M. on a special train and, presumably, arrived in Toronto the next day.[3] So began Yudel Rosenberg's career in the New World, as one of its pioneer Hasidic rabbis. He was one of over 18,000 Jews to immigrate to Canada in that year, the last full year of immigration prior to the onset of World War I.[4]

He was leaving the world of Polish Hasidism, having made a farewell visit to his patron, Rabbi Meir Yeḥiel Halstok, the Ostrovtser Rebbe, before

---

1 Microfilm Reel T-4801, 16, National Archives of Canada, Ottawa. The person who recorded the information rendered Rosenberg's unfamiliar first name, Yudel, as "Yondra." His family would arrive in North America that autumn. See Library and Archives Canada, Passenger Lists, 1865–1922, File 5, http://www.bac-lac.gc.ca/eng/discover/immigration/immigration-records/passenger-lists/passenger-lists-1865–1922/Pages/item.aspx?IdNumber=6302&, accessed April 29, 2020.

2 Valerie Knowles, *Strangers at Our Gates: Canadian Immigration and Immigration Policy, 1540–1997* (Toronto: Dundurn Press, 1997), 85–86.

3 See note 1 above.

4 Gerald Tulchinsky, *Taking Root: The Origins of the Canadian Jewish Community* (Toronto: Lester Publishing, 1992), xxiv.

leaving for Canada.[5] He was entering a North American Jewish world in which Orthodox rabbis counted for little and Hasidic rabbis counted for even less. Yudel Rosenberg began his North American experience in the Jewish community of Toronto.[6] He was to be the rabbi of Beth Jacob, a congregation founded in 1899 with sixty-five members. The synagogue was then housed at 17–19 Elm Street, in a building that had been built as a church in 1870. The congregation had purchased the building in 1905.[7] According to one account, hundreds of Polish Jews worshipped there and participated in Hasidic ceremonies such as the discourse at the "third meal" of the Sabbath, on Saturday afternoons, at which Rabbi Rosenberg presided.[8] This account is consistent with the large increase in the Jewish population of Toronto and of Canada as a whole in the immediate pre-war period. The Jewish population of Canada, which stood at approximately 16,000 in 1901, jumped to 75,681 in the 1911 Dominion census. The Jewish population of Toronto itself increased from approximately 18,000 in 1911 (out of a total population of 381,383) to over 30,000 by 1913.[9] Many of these immigrants were Polish Jews; prime candidates for membership in the Polish congregation Beth Jacob, which needed to expand and which built a large synagogue building on Henry Street in the early 1920s costing $156,000.[10] However, the Beth Jacob congregants' recent migration militated against their having either the time or the resources to devote themselves to adequately supporting either their synagogue or its rabbi even in the most ideal of circumstances.

As it turns out, in fact, circumstances in Toronto were far from ideal. Rabbi Yudel Rosenberg had come to serve a congregation for whose leaders he had not been the first choice.[11] This fact clearly spelled trouble. Even worse was the almost inevitable factionalism within the congregation, to which Rosenberg openly alluded in his inaugural sermon, delivered on Saturday, September 16,

---

5 *Omer*, part 1, 6.

6 On the Jewish community of Toronto in this era, see Shmuel Meyer Shapiro, *The Rise of the Toronto Jewish Community* (Toronto: Now and Then Books, 2010).

7 Bill, Gladstone, "History Scrapbook: Beth Jacob Congregation," December 15, 2011, http://www.billgladstone.ca/?p=3890, accessed January 19, 2016.

8 PY, 4. Cf. N. Shemen, "Ortodoksia," 10.

9 Stephen A. Speisman, *The Jews of Toronto: A History to 1937* (Toronto: McClelland and Stewart, 1979), 71.

10 I am indebted for this information on the synagogue to Dr. Arthur E. Zimmerman of Toronto (email to author, March 14, 2006).

11 Speisman, *The Jews of Toronto*, 154, 166–167, 173. Cf. Cohen, *Sefer ha-Zikkaron*, 6.

1913.[12] Rabbi Rosenberg's reference to these facts during his sermons to the congregation did not help the situation.[13]

In the Toronto Jewish community, within a context of rivalry at times bordering on enmity between Polish and Lithuanian Jews, Rabbi Rosenberg was definitely on one side. He became known as the Poilisher Rebbe.[14] This was a time when Hasidic rebbes and those with connections to Hasidic rebbes were only beginning to come to North America either as visitors[15] or settlers. Settling in the heavily immigrant Jewish district of "the Ward" on Elizabeth Street,[16] Rabbi Rosenberg continued to look the part of a Hasidic rabbi, with his long beard and *pe'ot* [earlocks], *shtreiml* [fur hat] and *bekeshe* [long coat]. However, his appearance in this guise meant that he was subject to harassment when he appeared on the street, so he went out infrequently.[17] Though he had learned the Russian language in his native Poland, he never became truly comfortable with the English language, though soon enough English words and phrases began appearing in his speech and writings.[18]

There were things that had changed in the way Rabbi Rosenberg did things once he crossed the Atlantic. Though there is evidence that he continued to write amulets for those who desired them, as he had done in his role as Hasidic rebbe in Łódź,[19] he ceased the open practice of homeopathic medicine in Canada, with which he had been engaged in Łódź, and is described in detail in chapter 9. It is likely he abandoned homeopathy because the practice of medicine was more stringently regulated in North America. As he wrote in a 1935 letter:

---

12 *Omer*, part 1, 98.

13 *Omer*, part 1, 101–102. Cf. Shemen, "Ortodoksie," 11.

14 "Hoda'a fun Poylishn Rov," *The Hebrew Journal* [hereafter *THJ*], January 1, 1915; "Vegn der Kashrus Frage," *THJ*, January 3, 1915. As Rosenberg later wrote: "The Jews of Lithuania have a baseless hatred [*sin'at ḥinam*] of Polish Jews and Poles do not like the Lithuanian Jews even if both sides are pious [*Ḥaredim*] and observers of Torah." *Sefer 'Ateret Tiferet* (New York: Reznick Menshil, 1931), 199. Cf. Leah Rosenberg, *The Errand Runner*, 41. Cf. also Caplan, "Rabbi Isaac Margolis," 231.

15 Thus *KA*, August 27, 1913, 1, reported that the son of the Tulchiner Rebbe was in America.

16 *THJ*, October 29 and 31, 1915. Another source claims he made his home on "Dundas Street, near Centre Avenue." "The Rebbe's Progeny," *Jewish Standard*, January 15–31, 1983, 5.

17 Leah Rosenberg, *Errand Runner*, 50. On such incidents, see Ira Robinson, *A History of Antisemitism in Canada* (Waterloo: Wilfrid Laurier University Press, 2015), 59–60. Cf. Moses Rischin, *The Promised City* (New York: Harper and Row, 1970), 91. Cf. also Weinberg, *The World of Our Mothers*, 95. On the rarity of Hasidic appearance in North America in that era, see Mintz, *Hasidic People*, 19.

18 Yudel Rosenberg to Meir Joshua Rosenberg, 5695 (1934/5), RFA.

19 Undated examples of amulet texts in Rosenberg's handwriting are found in the BMA.

> When I accepted the rabbinate in Canada I was forced to cease dealing in cures and I sold all [my] books on medicine [*sifrei refu'ot*] for I have no time to deal with this.[20]

Rabbi Rosenberg's prudence was eminently reasonable. Though evidently not all North American Hasidic rabbis completely cut their ties with their European healing practices, those who continued them ran the risk of legal difficulties. Thus in New York in the 1920s, the Hasidic rabbi Yeraḥmiel Gedalia Tsuker advertised a patent medicine and was summoned to court to answer charges stemming from his healing practices, though he was ultimately acquitted.[21]

Moving to Canada, unfortunately, did not solve the financial problems that drove Rabbi Rosenberg from Łódź. Toronto, no less than Łódź, was suffering from a serious economic recession in the winter of 1913–1914,[22] and Rosenberg's congregants in the Polish-Jewish community, having arrived in the city the most recently, were relatively less in a position to support a rabbi than other sectors of Toronto's immigrant Jewish community.[23] The relative economic situation of Polish Jews in Toronto, incidentally, was hardly unique. Hasia Diner notes that in general Jews from Lithuanian areas of Eastern Europe [*Litvaks*] got to North America earlier and in stronger numbers than Jews from other areas, including Poland.[24] George Kranzler, in his account of the Jewish community of Williamsburg, Brooklyn in the early twentieth century, also remarks that its Hasidic community at the turn of the twentieth century was economically less well off than the Mitnagdic (Lithuanian) Orthodox community.[25]

---

20 Yudel Rosenberg to Moshe Blistreich dated Ḥanukkah, 5695 (1934), Jewish Canadian Collection, Yudel Rosenberg, Jewish Public Library, Montreal. A photocopy is in the possession of the author. Rosenberg's descendants in Toronto preserve jars of *materia medica* that, it is claimed, were used by Rosenberg, presumably in North America. Personal communication from Mr. Baruch Rosenberg.

21 "Ha-Rav Yeraḥmiel Gedalia Zucker zts"l," in *Me-'Asifat ha-Moreshet, me-Otzaro she moreshet Ḥakhmei Amerika, le-Ḥeqer ha-Rabanim ha-Qedumim me-Arha"b*, no. 7, *parshat va-Yishlaḥ*, 5776.

22 Tulchinsky, *Taking Root*, 135.

23 Stephen A. Speisman, "St. John's Shtetl: The Ward in 1911," in Robert F. Harney, *Gathering Place: Peoples and Neighbourhoods of Toronto, 1834–1945* (Toronto: Multicultural History Society of Ontario, 1985), 108.

24 Hasia Diner, *Roads Taken: The Great Jewish Migrations to the New World and the Peddlers Who Forged the Way* (New Haven: Yale University Press, 2015), 29, 38.

25 George Kranzler, *Williamsburg: A Jewish Community in Transition* (New York: Feldheim, 1961), 18.

In order to make ends meet, Yudel Rosenberg engaged in a variety of activities. He served as a *mohel* [ritual circumciser];[26] adjudicated disputes brought to him;[27] and travelled outside Toronto to serve on rabbinic courts when called upon.[28] Despite all these attempts, the accounts we have of Yudel Rosenberg's rabbinate in Toronto testify that, as in Łódź, he suffered from economic want to the point, at times, of actually having no bread to put on the table.[29]

As he had done in Europe, Rabbi Rosenberg also turned to the written word to attempt to assert his authority as well as to supplement his income. In Toronto, however, as opposed to Poland, he managed to publish relatively little. One reason for this is that the major market for the sort of works he wrote was in Europe. As well, facilities for Hebrew or Yiddish publishing, as distinct from the Yiddish press, were relatively restricted in Canada at that time.[30] Most importantly, Rosenberg did not have immediate access to New York—the only place in North America where such publishing facilities were more readily available.

Other reasons for the diminution of Rabbi Rosenberg's literary output may include the culture shock inherent in his emigration as well as the rather different demands made upon his time as an Orthodox rabbi in North America, as we will see. In his Toronto period, Rosenberg published only two substantial items,[31] the first of which at least had been conceived, if not actually written, in Łódź.[32] Both books were on halakhic subjects that were of consequence to local Jews. Writing on these subjects were also useful in creating for Rosenberg the image of a rabbi who recognized and was able to cope with the crisis Orthodox Judaism was facing in the cities of North America.

Rabbi Rosenberg's first publication was a relatively small pamphlet entitled *Miqveh Yehuda*. It is undated but was likely published during Rabbi

---

26 Leah Rosenberg, *Errand Runner*, 49–50.

27 Undated draft business agreements from Yudel Rosenberg's Toronto period are preserved in RFA, Savannah.

28 Leah Rosenberg, *Errand Runner*, 59.

29 Shemen, "Ortodoksia," 11. Cf. Baumeil, "Rosenberg," 105.

30 On the limited publishing facilities at that time, see Brad Sabin Hill, "Early Hebrew Printing in Canada," *Studia Rosenthaliana* 38/39 (2005/2006): 306–347.

31 Rosenberg also sketched out an anthology of *midrashim* that would be called *Midrash Zuta*, referring to himself as Rabbi in the city of Toronto. RFA, Savannah.

32 *Miqveh* was at least researched in Łódź, as evidenced by the letter to Yudel Rosenberg from Rabbi Petaḥia Hornblass addressed to him in Łódź and published in facsimile in the booklet on p. 2, as well as a letter from Yudel Rosenberg in Łódź to Moshe Naḥum Yerusalimsky from 1913 preserved in the Yerusalimsky Papers, Schocken Library, in which Rosenberg apparently sought information on this subject from Yerusalimsky as well. Rosenberg's publication *Keri'ah* was listed as one of his books on the title page of *Miqveh*.

Rosenberg's stay in Toronto.[33] It deals with the problematic situation of the contemporary observance of the Judaic laws of menstrual purification. It has been described by bibliographer Brad Sabin Hill as the "launch of Canadian rabbinic literature" though it was not quite the first Hebrew book published in Toronto.[34] Yudel Rosenberg's second Toronto publication was a much more ambitious book entitled *ha-Qeri'ah ha-Qedosha* [The Holy Reading], which had likely been ready for the printer earlier but which was not published until 1919. The delay in publication undoubtedly stemmed from lack of funds and the book was finally published due to an anonymous donation of $200.00 by a childless couple.[35] It was published in New York, which is no doubt a commentary on the paucity of adequate Hebrew printing facilities in Toronto. The book concerned itself with the etiquette of one of the central ceremonies of the synagogue–the public reading of the Torah. Both publications will be discussed in detail in chapter four.

Given the contemporary halakhic situation of North American Jewry, Rabbi Rosenberg probably hoped he had best sellers on his hands, works on topics of immediate relevance to many Orthodox Jews in Toronto and elsewhere. He clearly connected his publishing efforts and his financial wellbeing: at the beginning of his *Qeri'ah ha-Qedosha* he inserted a prayer to be able to publish his other works and that "I will not know any more [financial] pressure and want."[36] However, neither of these publications seems to have made much of a splash, and certainly neither yielded Rosenberg a sufficient income to raise him from his poverty.[37]

An interesting perspective on the relative lack of means in the Rosenberg household is an invitation to the wedding of Rabbi Rosenberg's daughter Ḥana to Moshe Hadler on 1 Adar I 5676 (February 5, 1916) at his home, 176 Agnes

---

33 A short article published in *THJ* on November 27, 1916, entitled "Miqveh fir Kontri 'Iden," gives the gist of the book and advises people interested to contact Rabbi Rosenberg but does not specify the existence of the book. If the book were in print, it would surely have been mentioned. So at the earliest it might have been published sometime in 1917.

34 Hill, "Early Hebrew Printing in Canada," 334. Yosef Goldman mistakenly stated that this book was the first Hebrew imprint in Toronto. See his *Hebrew Printing in America: a History and Annotated Bibliography* (Brooklyn: YG Books, 2006), entry 631, 558. The book is undated but its Toronto imprint definitely puts it in Rosenberg's Toronto period, 1913–1918.

35 *Keri'ah*, 128.

36 *Keri'ah*, 5.

37 On rabbinic poverty in North America, cf. David Zohar, *Jewish Commitment in a Modern World: Rabbi Hayyim Hirschenson and His Attitude to Modernity* [Hebrew] (Jerusalem: Shalom Hartman Institute, 2003), 321, note 67.

Street (now Dundas). The wedding was held at 3:00 PM on a short Friday afternoon, so that the wedding feast would take place after the beginning of Shabbat. Such Friday afternoon weddings among Eastern European Jews tended to indicate a household too poor to afford both a wedding feast and a Shabbat meal.[38]

On the other hand, Rosenberg's reputation in the Toronto Jewish community was certainly growing. When the prominent Yiddish novelist Sholom Asch came to Toronto for a speaking engagement in 1915, he was brought to meet Rosenberg. According to the *Hebrew Journal*'s account, Asch felt quite at home at Rosenberg's table and later commented, "It is simply a delight to visit and converse with him."[39] Similarly, when the Toronto Yiddish newspaper received a letter from a Jewish family in Welland, Ontario, asking a halakhic question often discussed in that era,[40] whether a ritual circumcision could be deferred from a Friday to a Sunday because of the convenience of out-of-town guests, the paper turned the letter over to Rosenberg and published his response. In reply to the query, Rosenberg forbade the deferral of the circumcision from the baby's eighth day for any other than health reasons. He further denounced the circumciser [*mohel*] who had reportedly asserted the opposite to the family as a mere "businessman" doing his "job."[41] He exclaimed: "The one and only excuse which answers almost all the [halakhic] problems of America is: 'Allright! It's America, isn't it?'"[42]

In 1916, Rabbi Rosenberg also made a public pronouncement in a letter to the Montreal Yiddish newspaper, *Keneder Adler*, on a project to unite all Orthodox Jews in Canada. In it he reflected on his perception of the immigrant experience of Jews in the United States and Canada. In previous years, he stated. Jews had come to North America with the purpose of making money and returning to their European homes. These who remained became a sort of "mixed multitude" that assimilated. However in more recent years, since the Kishinev Pogrom (1903) and the anti-Jewish pogroms of 1905, decidedly different Jewish immigrants were arriving who had come to stay. These newer Jewish

38 A photograph of the wedding invitation was posted on Facebook by Mizrahi Bookstore, judaicaused.com, on December 19, 2019 at 7:51 PM. I am grateful to Professor Steven Fine for bringing this item to my attention.

39 *THJ*, March 5, 1915. Leah Rosenberg recalls that Asch visited the Rosenbergs several times and that the Yiddish writer, Peretz Hirschbein also visited him. *Errand Runner*, 42.

40 Heinze, *Adapting to Abundance*, 63.

41 On the "businesslike" attitude of religious functionaries in North America, cf. Jonathan Sarna, *People Walk on Their Heads: Moses Weinberger's Jews and Judaism in New York* (New York: 1982), 16–17.

42 *THJ*, March 23, 1916.

immigrants brought with them their traditions and spiritual ideals. Moreover, they brought rabbis and founded synagogues, Talmud Torahs, newspapers, etc. It was thus apparent that North America would take on a greater profile in the Jewish world. However, Orthodox Jews in North America were still in a bad way, and therefore Yudel Rosenberg fully supported the founding of this new organization and looked forward to its founding meeting in Montreal.[43]

In North America at the turn of the twentieth century, the only hope of making a decent living for any immigrant Orthodox rabbi—Hasidic or not—was through the supervision of the kosher meat industry, with all its drawbacks. As Yudel Rosenberg put it in a later responsum:

> Because of our many sins, rabbis have no source of livelihood other than [kosher] slaughtering. [But] if the rabbi decides that for the sake of kashrut it is necessary to add *shoḥtim,* and the Association of Shoḥtim is not happy with this, the rabbi must be silent in order not to lose his right [to supervise]—for that is his livelihood.[44]

In Toronto, as in all the Jewish communities set up by Eastern European immigrants in this era, kosher meat meant many things. The purchase and consumption of kosher meat was one of the only Judaic customs followed by nearly all immigrant Jews in this era, whether otherwise religiously observant or not.[45] It thus served as an important unifying factor in an otherwise disparate community. Furthermore, the demand for a constant supply of kosher meat gave rise to a major industrial enterprise in all major North American Jewish communities which employed hundreds of Jews in various capacities. Because the kosher meat industry required certification that its products were prepared according to halakha, it afforded immigrant Orthodox rabbis with practically their only

43 "Fun ha-Rav Rosenberg Toronto," *KA*, April 1, 1915. On the project, see "Leaders of Orthodox Jews Visit Montreal," *Canadian Jewish Chronicle*, March 12, 1915, 3. "To Establish a Union of Orthodox Jewish Congregations in Montreal," *Canadian Jewish Chronicle*, March 19, 1915, 1; "A Union of Orthodox Jewish Congregations," *Canadian Jewish Chronicle*, March 19, 1915, 8; "Conference for Orthodox Union on April 4," *Canadian Jewish Chronicle*, March 26, 1915, 11; "The Preliminary Conference for an Orthodox Union," *Canadian Jewish Chronicle*, April 2, 1915, 4; "The Conference for an Orthodox Union," *Canadian Jewish Chronicle*, April 9, 1915, 6; "The Meeting for a Union of Religious Forces," *Canadian Jewish Chronicle*, April 9, 1915, 7.

44 *Omer*, part 2, 99.

45 *THJ*, June 15, 1916. For a similar report with regard to Montreal, cf. Israel Medres, *Tsvishn Tsvei Velt Milkhomes* (Montreal: Keneder Adler, 1964), 32.

opportunity to acquire a well-paid livelihood and real power within their community. Rabbi Rosenberg inevitably turned to this field as well.

The problem was that at the point Rabbi Yudel Rosenberg arrived in Toronto, the supervision of kosher meat was already controlled by other, already established rabbis, with whom he would have to compete for his livelihood. Since the microfilm issues of Toronto's Yiddish daily newspaper, *Hebrew Journal* are not extant prior to January 1915, we do not have sources that testify with any exactitude to the manner in which Rabbi Rosenberg was received and interacted with the three other significant Orthodox rabbis of the city during his first year or so in the city. The most prominent of these already established rabbis was Jacob Gordon (1877–1934),[46] a graduate of the well-known Volozhin yeshiva and rabbi of the Goel Tzedec synagogue on University Avenue. He had come to Canada to serve Toronto's Lithuanian Jewish community.[47] A second was Rabbi Meir Tsvi Levy (1872–1956), another Lithuanian graduate of the Volozhin Yeshiva who had served as rabbi in Toronto since 1906.[48] Yosef Weinryb (1869–1943) was the third. He was known as the "Galitsianer Rov" and had come to Toronto as early as approximately 1900 to serve in the Shomrei Shabbat Maḥziqei ha-Dat congregation.[49]

At the point at which we are able to obtain data from the *Hebrew Journal*, January 1, 1915, we find Rabbi Rosenberg announcing that three kosher butcher shops were under his supervision, presumably patronized by the Polish Jewish community whose rabbi he was.[50] He also announced that he was supervising the kashrut of a brand of cooking oil,[51] as well as Passover macaroons.[52] At about this time, attempts were being made to establish a unified system of

46 Gordon's prominence among Toronto's rabbis is evidenced by the fact that in 1916 Proctor and Gamble contracted with him along with Rabbi Hirsch Cohen of Montreal to supervise and attest to the kashrut of Crisco. The contract, dated August 31, 1916, is extant in the Alex Dworkin Canadian Jewish Archives, Montreal, fond P0073, Gordon, Rabbi Jacob. On Gordon, see Kimmy Caplan, "There is No Interest in Precious Stones in a Vegetable Market: The Life and Sermons of Rabbi Jacob Gordon of Toronto," *Jewish History* 23, no. 2 (2009): 149–167.

47 Tulchinsky, *Taking Root*, 57.

48 Mayer S. Abramowitz, "Toronto Sages: Prominent Rabbis of Blessed Memory," http://www.billgladstone.ca/?p=10027, accessed February 19, 2019, 13, 38.

49 Ibid., 7, 36.

50 *THJ*, January 1, 1915. Cf. "A Brif fun Poylishn Rob Vegn di Basar Kosher Frage," *THJ*, January 3, 1915.

51 "Hekhsher 'al Shemen," *THJ*, January 11, 1915. This product was in competition with Crisco, which had made its own kashrut claims. *THJ*, February 2, 1915.

52 "Shifs Pesaḥdike Makaronen," *THJ*, February 26, 1915.

kashrut supervision in Toronto in order to stop the existing situation of internecine quarrels and competition that rendered the situation of kashrut supervision in the city highly problematic.[53] There were four Toronto rabbis heavily involved in kashrut supervision, including Rosenberg, but the *Hebrew Journal* pointed to Rosenberg as being the hardest to get to cooperate.[54] However, on January 3, 1915, the newspaper announced that Rabbi Rosenberg was prepared to affiliate with the other three rabbis in Toronto's Va'ad ha-Kashrut [Kashrut Committee]. It published a letter from Rosenberg asserting that he was ready to unite with the other rabbis for truly kosher kashrut supervision as in Europe.[55] He also asserted, on January 23, 1915, that the Canadian government in Ottawa should be addressed by the Jewish community in order to promulgate a law criminalizing false claims of kashrut.[56]

However, things did not go smoothly at all for the unification of kashrut supervision in Toronto. On the contrary there were evidently forces within the Jewish community that did not wish to accept such a unification of kashrut supervision in Toronto with equanimity. In fact, matters came to blows in late October 1915, when Rabbi Rosenberg was assailed both on the street and in his Elizabeth Street home by four young men on issues regarding kashrut.[57]

Things were not much quieter in 1916. With conflicting claims concerning kashrut rife within the Toronto Jewish community,[58] Rabbi Rosenberg announced that he had withdrawn his supervision of several butcher shops.[59] By May 1916 it had become clear to Toronto Jews that the local rabbis still had their differences and that the city's kashrut system was in urgent need of repair.[60] In light of this situation, it probably surprised no one that in July, Rabbi Rosenberg

---

53 One complicating factor was undoubtedly a 1914 case brought in the Ontario Court system between Rabbi Weinryb and Toronto *shoḥet* Marcus (Mordecai) Dickman. JPL Archives, Reuben Brainin Papers, Group 2, Box C, file 8. For a parallel example of divided kashrut supervision in England, see Miri J. Freud-Kandel, *Orthodox Judaism in Britain Since 1913: An Ideology Forgotten* (London: Valentine Mitchell, 2006), 19–21.

54 *THJ*, January 3, 1915.

55 Ibid. In Montreal there also existed a *Va'ad ha-Kashrut*. Cf. its announcement in *KA*, July 18, 1913, 9.

56 "Etlikhe Verter fun Rabi Rosenberg vegn Toronter Kashrus," *THJ*, January 23, 1915, 2

57 *THJ*, October 29 and 31, 1915. "Toronter Hefkerus," *THJ* October 31, 1915. Cf. "Azhara Gedola," *THJ*, October 29, 1915.

58 "Le-Harim Mikhshol," *THJ*, April 13, 1916, 5.

59 "Keyn Hashgaha oif Basar Kosher," *THJ*, May 10, 1916.

60 "Unzer Entfer," *THJ*, May 12, 1916; "Vifill Koshere Butshers Zaynen Faran in Toronto?," *THJ*, May 21, 1916; "Drei Sent in Funt Flaysh Muz der Butsher Ferdinen," *THJ*, May 23, 1916, 1; "Ver Vil Esn Kosher Flaysh?," *THJ*, May 31, 1916, 1; "Ver Is Shuldig?," *THJ*, June 15, 1916.

decided to break away from the unified rabbinate and reorganize his own system of kashrut supervision, employing the very ritual slaughterers who had refused to affiliate with the united Toronto *Va'ad ha-Kashrut* and whose meat had therefore been banned by Rosenberg along with the other three rabbis. Thus, Rabbi Rosenberg was attacking the very legitimacy of the *Va'ad.*[61] As the *Hebrew Journal* editorialized, it was not up to the newspaper to say which of the four major Orthodox rabbis of the city, Gordon, Levy, Rosenberg, or Weinryb, was most responsible for the situation. All of them, however, had stooped to the level of merchants, the newspaper asserted.[62] In trying to go it alone against his rabbinic colleagues, Rabbi Rosenberg was certainly counting on the patronage of his own Polish Jewish community for the butcher shops under his supervision. But he was also accused by Rabbi Gordon of attempting to pirate other Jewish consumers and "create a Polish Kashrut Board with Lithuanian customers."[63] However, perhaps due to the smaller economic power of the Polish Jewish community of Toronto, Rabbi Rosenberg's independent efforts ultimately came to naught. Thus by late August 1916 he had rejoined Rabbis Gordon and Weinreb in publishing a unified directory of Kosher establishments.[64] The three rabbis also cooperated in giving approbation to the Passover kashrut of certain liquors,[65] to the 1917 drive for the 'Ezrat Torah fund on behalf of impoverished rabbinic scholars,[66] and for the Canada Liberty Bonds drive in Toronto.[67]

The year 1917 saw the promulgation of the Balfour Declaration by the British government, causing no end of excitement in Jewish communities worldwide. Yudel Rosenberg, though he tended to be critical of political Zionism, nonetheless viewed the Balfour Declaration in a positive light.[68] He

61 "Rabonim un Ba'alei Batim vern Gerufen zu a Din Torah," *THJ*, July 28, 1916; "Vos Rabi Gordon Hot zu Zogen vegn dem Nayem Tumel mit di Fleysh," *THJ*, July 28, 1916. Cf. Stephen Speisman, *The Jews of Toronto*, 281.

62 *THJ*, May 12 and June 15, 1916.

63 Y. Gordon, "Vos Rabi Gordon Zogt Vegn ha-Rav Rosenbergs Staytment," *THJ*, August 4, 1916; Yudel Rosenberg, "Hodo'ah vegn Basar Kosher," *THJ*, August 17, 1916, appealed to all Toronto Jews, and especially the Polish Jews, not to believe adverse reports concerning him.

64 This directory began being published in *THJ* in August 1916. At that time (August 22), Rabbi Levy published a separate list of butcher shops under his supervision. Cf. "Zu di Rabonim," *THJ*, August 22, 1916.

65 *THJ*, February 25, 1917.

66 *THJ*, March 2, 1917.

67 *THJ*, November 19, 1917.

68 ZT, vol. 5, 52, 152–153, 195–196. Cf. David Ellenson, "Rabbi Haim Hirschensohn: An Orthodox Rabbi Reponds to the Balfour Declaration," *American Jewish History* 101, no. 3 (July 2017): 247–269.

definitely approved of Jews purchasing land and settling in Palestine. As we will see, Rabbi Rosenberg expressed a desire to go to live in Palestine as early as 1923,[69] and later in the 1920s he bought land in Palestine.

His approval of Jewish settlement in the Land of Israel, however, was on the proviso that those Jews setting there not pretend that the Balfour Declaration heralded the biblically foretold messianic redemption.[70] As Rabbi Rosenberg later put it, the Balfour Declaration has no equivalence to the ancient Decree of Cyrus that allowed the return of the Babylonian Exiles to Jerusalem. It nonetheless had the potential to be a spark [*hitnotsetsut*] of the "beginning of Redemption." He envisaged a situation in which "proper people" [*kesherim*] would go to the Land. If these Jewish settlers in the Land of Israel would conduct themselves according to the Torah, then the Balfour Declaration would indeed constitute an "arousal from below" that will cause an "arousal from above"[71] and thus the true redemption will come about in a "natural" manner. In that kabbalistic spirit, Rosenberg put forward a suggestion that the flag of the Jewish nation should be established in a manner consistent with the kabbala's color symbolism: "a white stripe above, a red stripe below and a green stripe in the middle ... and they can also make the form of a star of David on the green stripe in the middle of the flag."[72] However, Rosenberg observed, Satan is at work to populate the Land of Israel with Jews who do not obey the Torah.[73] Creating a Jewish state by such people, who do not obey God, would be foolhardy [*ma'ase shotim*]. [74] Rabbi Rosenberg further stated: "These unbelievers [*apikorsim*] rebelliously build up the Land of Israel on the basis of nationalism without belief [in God], Torah and the commandments."[75]

Furthermore, Rabbi Rosenberg heartily disapproved of the speaking of Hebrew in Palestine with the "Sephardic" pronunciation, as the Zionists did, which he considered to be a form of "jargon" that derived from the holy tongue

69 ZT, vol. 5, 256. This desire continued. In 1932, Rabbi Benzion Uziel wrote Yudel Rosenberg, hoping that his dream to come to Palestine would be fulfilled. Uziel to Rosenberg, 15 Sivan 5692 (June 19, 1932), Arkhion Histori, Iriyat Tel-Aviv-Yaffo, Rabbi Benzion Uziel papers, 92/1505.

70 *Omer*, part 1, 15.

71 For similar terminology on the part of contemporary kabbalists, see Jonatan Meir, *Kabbalistic Circles in Jerusalem (1896–1948)* (Leiden and Boston: Brill, 2016), 45

72 ZT, vol. 2, 35; ZK Tehilim, 257.

73 ZK Tehilim, 257. Cf. ZK Shir ha-Shirim, 84; PY, 139; *Omer*, part 1, 25–26, 32–33.

74 ZT, vol. 5, 195.

75 *Omer*, part 1, 32.

(Hebrew) and could not be used for prayer and blessings.[76] Rabbi Rosenberg was, then, something of an exception to the observation of Michael Brown that within the Canadian Jewish community in the early twentieth century there was virtually no Orthodox opposition to Zionism.[77]

Another one of Yudel Rosenberg's initiatives in Toronto proved considerably more successful than his forays into kashrut. As leader of the Polish Jewish community in Toronto, he was dissatisfied with the existing school for the religious instruction of children in the immigrant Jewish community, the Simcoe Street Talmud Torah. The Talmud Torah had been founded by Rabbi Gordon in 1907 and reflected his Lithuanian Jewish heritage.[78] Rabbi Rosenberg therefore initiated the organization of another Jewish school, located on D'Arcy Street, which was at first called simply the "Polish Talmud Torah" and was soon renamed 'Ets Ḥayyim. The original organization of the school took place at a meeting held in Rosenberg's house in the summer of 1915.[79] However, the school was not opened until the next year, possibly because of communal pressure to keep a united Talmud Torah.[80] In July 1916, Rabbi Rosenberg addressed a meeting of more than one hundred people at his synagogue at which approximately $100 was raised for the school.[81] In October 1916 the school was actually opened.[82] Rabbi Rosenberg was largely responsible for the spiritual direction of the school, which soon boasted four teachers and some 120 students. He made sure that the Jewish education offered in the 'Ets Ḥayyim Talmud Torah would be free of "secular" tendencies and be as close as possible to the elementary Jewish education offered in Poland.[83] Thus, when one of the teachers brought to the school pencils bearing the picture of a "radical" (Yiddishist) Jewish writer,

76 *Derekh Erets*, 28. In a radicalized form, this idea was expressed by the fiercely anti-Zionist Satmar Rebbe, Yoilish Teitelbaum. See Basil Mitchell, *Language Politics and Language Survival: Yiddish among the Haredim in Post-War Britain* (Louvain: Peeters, 2006), 59.

77 Michael Brown, *Jew or Juif? Jews, French Canadians, and Anglo-Canadians, 1759–1914* (Philadelphia: Jewish Publication Society, 1987), 217. It was generally understood that American Orthodox rabbis were adherents of Mizraḥi. See Dafna Schreiber, "Melekh Yisrael: R. Avraham Mordecai mi-Gur, ha-'Imrei Emet,'" in *The Gedoilim: Leaders Who Shaped the Israeli Haredi Society*, ed. Binyamin Brown and Nissim Leon (Jerusalem: Magnes Press, 2017), 254.

78 Speisman, "St. John's Shtetl," 114.

79 Speisman, *Jews of Toronto*, 173–174.

80 This communal pressure is reflected in a THJ editorial, "Eyn Torah un Eyn Talmud Torah!," *THJ*, February 24, 1915.

81 *THJ*, July 18, 1916.

82 Speisman, *Jews of Toronto*, 173–174.

83 Ibid.

Rosenberg ordered the pencils burned, and the teacher, who persisted in using these pencils, was fired.[84]

Within a few years of his move to Toronto, it had become clear to Yudel Rosenberg that he would be unable to make ends meet in his present home, and so he began looking for a rabbinic post elsewhere in North America. His efforts eventually bore fruit. In January 1918, the Jewish community of Toronto heard the news that Rosenberg had been invited by the Jews of Detroit, Michigan, to establish himself there as a rabbi.[85] He had likely visited that community, not too far from Toronto, to serve as one of the judges in a rabbinic hearing [*Din Torah*], for which purpose he travelled extensively.[86] In response to the prospective loss of their spiritual leader, Toronto's Polish Jews called a mass meeting, at which Rabbi Rosenberg was urged to stay.[87] In his response to the meeting, Yudel Rosenberg reiterated to his supporters that the prospect of his leaving Toronto was no mere idle threat. He was looking for a position elsewhere not because he did not like Toronto, but rather because he had no prospect of a secure livelihood in that city. A rabbi, he stated, could not live in the hand-to-mouth fashion in which he had been living for several years.[88] The response by his community was a project to unite all the Polish Jews in the city into one congregation, to be called Kehillat Yisra'el, of which Rosenberg was to be appointed rabbi.[89]

The crisis passed, Rabbi Rosenberg did not move to Detroit, and his life in Toronto in the ensuing months continued quietly to all outward appearances. In August 1918, to mark the second anniversary of the 'Ets Ḥayyim Talmud Torah, Rosenberg gave an address and, as the reporter for the *Hebrew Journal* wrote: "As always, Rabbi Rosenberg mixed into his speech beautiful parables and tales which made a big hit."[90]

Despite these outward appearances, however, Rosenberg evidently remained dissatisfied with his economic conditions in Toronto and was determined to move at the first opportunity. The next serious invitation he received

84 N. Shemen and Y. Y. Wohlgelernter, "Entstehung un Antwicklung fun Talmud Torah 'Ets Ḥayyim,'" in *Talmud Torah "Eitz Chaim" Jubilee Book* (Toronto: n.p., 1943), 132–133. On Yudel Rosenberg's opposition to modern methods of Hebrew instruction, see ZT, vol. 5, 27.

85 "Elektrisitet bey 'Iden," *THJ*, January 22, 1918.

86 Leah Rosenberg, *Errand Runner*, 59.

87 "Poilishe 'Iden Khapn zikh," *THJ*, January 24, 1918.

88 "An Erklerung fun Rabi Rosenberg," *THJ*, February 3, 1918.

89 "Poilisher Rov Farblaybt in Toronto," *THJ*, February 4, 1918.

90 *THJ*, August 13, 1918.

was from Montreal, the largest city and the largest Jewish community in the Dominion of Canada. Rabbi Rosenberg had visited Montreal from Toronto as early as January 1916.[91] By January 1919, Rabbi Rosenberg shifted his base of operations to Montreal, where he had been invited by a faction of butchers and slaughterers to become their "chief rabbi" and, not incidentally, to serve as a counterweight to the authority of Rabbi Hirsch Cohen (1860–1950), a Lithuanian rabbi who had been in Montreal since the 1890s and who was generally acknowledged by the established Jewish community of that city as its "chief rabbi."[92] This time, the news of his Montreal invitation was not leaked to the Toronto Jewish community. There would be no publicity and fanfare in Toronto concerning his departure. He simply left Toronto by himself, and only after he settled in Montreal did he send for his family.[93]

Previous accounts of Rabbi Rosenberg's sojourn in Toronto from 1913 to 1918, while emphasizing his poverty and inability to make a decent living, also spoke of his difficulties with his congregation and the fact that he "could not conceive of the necessity of actively seeking to make himself popular with his congregation."[94] His community's response to his threat of leaving for Detroit, however, seems to indicate a more complex situation. While surely not every Polish Jew in Toronto loved Rabbi Rosenberg, there seems to have been a genuine outpouring of communal support for him when he initially told them he was leaving. It is much more likely that it was his community's inadequate ability to support him properly as well as his failure to make a successful breakthrough in kashrut supervision in Toronto that ultimately drove him to Montreal. There, his greatest challenge would be to make a place for himself as rabbi and supervisor of kosher meat in that city in competition with Montreal's established immigrant rabbinate.

---

91 *KA*, January 12, 1916

92 See *KA*, January 16 and 23, 1919. Coincidentally, in Cleveland in 1918 twenty-four Orthodox congregations came together to form a council that intended to invite Rabbi Maier Jung of London as chief rabbi. Lloyd Gartner, *History of the Jews of Cleveland* (Cleveland: Western Reserve Historical Society and the Jewish Theological Seminary of America, 1978), 178.

93 Rosenberg, *Errand Runner*, 59.

94 Speisman, *Jews of Toronto*, 167.

CHAPTER 5

"The Rabbis Are for the Dollar": Rabbi Yudel Rosenberg and the Kosher Meat Wars of Montreal (1919–1935)

As we have seen, Rabbi Yudel Rosenberg was heavily involved in the controversies surrounding kashrut supervision during his sojourn in Toronto. He was brought to Montreal by that very same issue, one that resonated in all major Jewish communities in North America in this era. Rabbi Rosenberg's daughter Leah records the circumstances of her father's move to Montreal in her memoir:

> Father had originally come to Montreal for a Din Torah ... between a powerful rabbi and a group of shoychtim [ritual slaughterers]. The upshot was that the shoychtim were divided into two camps. ... After the Din Torah, father became rabbi of those shoychtim he thought had been maligned.[1]

What Leah Rosenberg did not specify in her narrative is that Rabbi Yudel Rosenberg had come to Montreal to succeed Simon Glazer, a rabbi who had for over a decade contended with Rabbi Hirsch Cohen for primacy among Montreal Orthodox rabbis. Glazer had recently given up the fight and left Montreal for a rabbinic position in Seattle, Washington, as far away as you can get from Montreal while remaining in North America.[2] However, the Montreal kashrut situation went far beyond rabbinic personality conflicts. There was, in fact, a rivalry between two rabbinic and community coalitions that lasted for well-nigh two decades. In the first phase of this conflict (1907–1918), the struggle

1 Leah Rosenberg, *Errand Runner*, 64.

2 On Rabbis Cohen, Glazer, and their rivalry, see Robinson, *Rabbis and Their Community*, 21–55.

took place between rabbis Hirsch Cohen and Simon Glazer and their respective partisans. This phase of the struggle for control of Montreal kashrut ended with Rabbi Cohen having largely prevailed and Rabbi Glazer leaving Montreal. Rabbi Glazer's partisans hoped that a new rabbinic champion like Yudel Rosenberg would revive their fortunes. This becomes clear from an examination of Rabbi Rosenberg's early Montreal letterhead. In a letter he wrote in 1920 to Rabbi Glazer, his letterhead refers to him in English as "Rabbi of the United Hebrew Community of Montreal, Canada," and calls his organization Adat Yisra'el de-Montreal [Community of Israel of Montreal] in Hebrew [3] This was the very same name that had been used by Rabbi Glazer's group. It is thus clear that Rabbi Rosenberg inherited the departed Rabbi Glazer's communal structure. At the same time, he also inherited the enmity of Rabbi Cohen and his powerful supporters.[4]

The response of Rabbi Cohen to Yudel Rosenberg's appearance in Montreal was not long in coming. Rabbi Rosenberg settled in Montreal in January 1919. His inaugural sermon took place on February 8, 1919.[5] His arrival took place in an atmosphere of strife evidenced by the printing of anti-Rosenberg handbills and vitriolic accusations appearing in Montreal's Yiddish newspaper, the *Keneder Adler*.[6] This charged atmosphere is fully reflected in Yudel Rosenberg's inaugural sermon whose main theme is factionalism within Jewish communities.[7] Rabbi Rosenberg published a handbill related to this strife in late February. Though it has not survived, we know of it because on February 24 the *Keneder Adler* published a refutation of its arguments written by Rabbi Cohen in the name of his rabbinic court [*Bet Din Tsedeq*].[8] In this refutation, Hirsch Cohen sharply attacked Yudel Rosenberg, dismissing his pretensions to rabbinic leadership in Montreal and calling him an

3 American Jewish Archives, Simon Glazer Papers. Cf. "Adas Yisra'el de-Montreal," *KA*, January 29, 1919.

4 Zvi ha-Kohen, "Ver Zenen di Adas Yisra'el de-Montreal?," *KA*, February 3, 1919.

5 *Omer*, part 1, 102.

6 "Der Kaos in Higer 'Idisher Kehile" and "A Ḥilul Hashem vos Tor Nit Farshvigen vern," *KA*, January 16, 1919; "Erklerung fun B.D.Ts. vegn Higer Sheḥite Lage," *KA*, January 23, 1919; "Ha-Rav Cohens Tsveyter Staytment vegn der Kashrus Frage in Montreal," *KA*, January 29, 1919.

7 *Omer*, part 1, 102, 107–108.

8 As of February 22, 1918, the three members of Rabbi Cohen's *Bet Din Tsedeq* were Rabbis Hirsch Cohen, Simcha Garber, and Moshe Gedaliah Blitz. "Azhara mi-Bet Din Tsedeq de-Po," *KA*, February 22, 1918, 5.

ignoramus whose learning did not measure up to that of a rabbinic student [*yeshiva baḥur*].[9]

Rabbi Rosenberg responded to Rabbi Cohen's attack in a letter addressed to Hirsch Wolofsky (1878–1949), publisher of the *Keneder Adler*, which was dated February 26 and printed the next day in facsimile, strongly protesting the newspaper's blatant partisanship:

> In your newspaper of February 24 you printed a great deal of dirt and mockery against me from the local *Bet Din Tsedeq*. If they wish to fight with me, that's fine. But I ask you on what grounds do you stand on one side [of the issue]? You should know that in a public newspaper one may not libel people. ... Do not think that you are dealing with a kid or an out of touch scholar [*batlan*]. I am a Canadian citizen just like you.[10]

Thus, Montreal did not turn out to be a peaceful home for Rabbi Yudel Rosenberg. There was, nonetheless, a certain change for the better in his general situation. Whereas in Toronto, Rabbi Rosenberg's scanty income seems to have come primarily from fees paid to him for performing rabbinic functions such as marriages, divorces, and circumcisions, in Montreal the bulk of his income was apparently from the outset derived from the regulation of kashrut and much of his time was spent in the supervision of kosher slaughtering.[11] In the *Keneder Adler* for March 7, 1919, he advertised that his rabbinic office was open at 761 Cadieux Street, and later that month he advertised that a certain brand of coffee, tea, and spices was kosher for Passover under his supervision.[12] Some months later he added "Butter-Ol," a brand of vegetable oil,[13] and the

9 "Erklerung fun Bet Din Tsedeq," *KA*, February 24, 1919. The Yeshiva student comparison may have been an assertion of the superiority of Lithuanian Jewish yeshiva system as opposed to the educational system of Polish Jewry. It was also part of Rabbi Cohen's rhetorical style, for he characterized the eight *shoḥtim* he opposed as "assistant [*unter*] *shoḥtim*" "A Ḥilul Hashem Vos Tor Nit Farshvigen vern," *KA*, January 16, 1919.

10 "A Briv mit an Antwort," KA, February 27, 1919, 5. Rabbi Rosenberg's claim to Canadian citizenship was only partially true at the time. He had received his prior naturalization papers at the General Session of the Peace, Toronto, Ontario, October 24, 1917. His final naturalization papers were issued on October 21, 1920. See the list on the website of Library and Archive Canada, http://central.bac-lac.gc.ca/.item/?id=P20-21_541&op=pdf&app=naturalization19151936.

11 Robinson, *Rabbis and Their Community*, 39, 65–66; Speisman, *The Jews of Toronto*, 166–167, 173–174.

12 *KA*, March 7 and 12, 1919; *KA*, March 14, 1920.

13 *KA*, December 29, 1919; *KA*, March 12, 1920.

Parisian Wine Company[14] to the list of his kosher supervised products. In 1922, Rabbi Rosenberg added a milk company to his kashrut supervision for Passover.[15] There were other sources of peripheral income. In 1921 he advertised that he sold *etrogim* [citrons] for use in the rituals of the festival of Sukkot like other Montreal rabbis, including Rabbi Cohen.[16] He continued to sell *etrogim* through the 1930s.[17]

As Rabbi Rosenberg began to take stock of his new community, he expressed his dissatisfaction with the nature of Shabbat observance in the Montreal and began attempting to improve the situation. One such attempt was to advocate for Jewish bakeries that did not operate on the Sabbath, which did not then exist in Montreal.[18] Rabbi Rosenberg added to his 1924 publication on electricity a warning against eating bread baked on the Sabbath. He observed that even somewhat learned people [*lomdim ha-kalim*] habitually made mistakes in this area.[19] He thus urged patronage of bakers who carried his Shabbat-observant label.[20]

Similarly in 1921, he published in the *Keneder Adler* a protest against open fundraising for the Yiddishist schools [*shules*] on the Sabbath.[21] In pursuit of his goal of making Sabbath observance more prominent in the Montreal community, Rabbi Rosenberg saw fit in 1922 to publicly disagree with a pair of distinguished Lithuanian rabbis, Israel Meir ha-Kohen Kagan (*Ḥafets Ḥayyim*, 1839–1933) and Ḥayyim Ozer Grodzinsky (1863–1940), who had proclaimed a public fast day on behalf of Soviet Jewry, a call that had been seconded by the premier Orthodox rabbinic association in North America, Agudat ha-Rabbanim. While Rabbi Rosenberg did not disagree with calling on

14 *KA*, February 22, 1920; *KA*, April 13, 1921.

15 "Milkh Kosher le-Pesaḥ," *KA*, April 7, 1922.

16 *KA*, October 11, 13, 14, 16, 1921, 2. Cf. "Etrogim," *KA*, September 5, 1920. On Rabbi Cohen's sale of *etrogim*, see Robinson, *Rabbis and Their Community*, 30–31. Rabbis Hershorn, Zalmanovitz, and Dubitzsky also sold them. See *KA*, October 6, 1922.

17 Emanuel Friedmann & Co. to Yudel Rosenberg, 2 Nissan 5692 (April 8, 1932), RFA, Savannah.

18 "Kosher Gebeks," *KA*, May 13, 1921; *A Brivele Fun di Zisse Mame Shabbes Malkesa zu Ihre Zin und Tehter fun Idishn Folk* [hereafter *Brivele*] (Montreal, City Printing Co., 1924), 12–14. On the situation of Jewish bakeries in Montreal in this era, see Eve Lerner, "Making and breaking bread in Jewish Montreal, 1920–1940" (MA thesis, Concordia University, 2002).

19 *Me'or ha Ḥashmal She'ela u-Teshuva 'al Dvar Me'or ha-Elektrin be-Shabat ve-Yom Tov* [hereafter *Me'or*] (Montreal: Rapid Printing Co., 1924), 13.

20 *KA*, June 5, 1921, 2; *KA*, August 28, 1921, 2; *KA*, September 4 and 11, 1921. Cf. *Me'or*, 13.

21 "A Sharfer Protest gegn Ḥillul Shabbat in Montreal fun Rabbi Rosenberg," *KA*, November 6, 1921.

Jews to gather in their synagogues and pray for Soviet Jewry, he doubted the ability of most North American Jews to fast, and he thought that the focus of any organized Jewish action ought rather to be charity and the strengthening of Sabbath observance. In this connection, he expressed the opinion that a recent tragedy in Montreal in which eight young people had died in a fire was the result of the sin of Sabbath desecration on the part of Montreal Jews.[22]

Rabbi Rosenberg attempted to assert his own communal leadership by calling for a mass meeting on May 28, 1919 to protest anti-Jewish pogroms in the Ukraine. At this meeting, he enlisted as speakers local Jewish community notables such as Zionist leader Clarence de Sola (1858–1920),[23] Montreal Alderman Leon V. Jacobs, and Peter Bercovitch (1879–1942), a member of the Legislative Assembly of Quebec.[24] In March 1920, Rabbi Rosenberg transmitted to the *Keneder Adler* two letters he had received from Polish rabbinic organizations asking for help from American Jews, and publicly appealed to Montreal Jews on behalf of the 'Ezrat Torah Fund for indigent rabbinic scholars. All this indicated that he was becoming known as a Montreal rabbi to contact by international Jewish charities.[25] In 1921, Yudel Rosenberg gave a speech on behalf of the Montreal Talmud Torah campaign that was printed in the *Keneder Adler*, indicating that he was also becoming known as a speaker on behalf of local Jewish charities.[26]

At the same time that he was attempting to establish himself financially and communally in Canada, Yudel Rosenberg also faced the task of putting various adult children who showed up at his doorstep on a solid footing. This began in Toronto. In 1917 his son, Israel, an actor in the Yiddish stage then in his mid-twenties, arrived in Canada together with his wife. Upon arriving in Canada, however, Israel Rosenberg's biography states: "due to family reasons, he avoided acting in the theatre and became a prompter."[27] It is likely that the "family reasons" involved Rabbi Rosenberg's objections to his son appearing on

22 "Yom Kippur Qaton," *KA*, August 20, 1922. Cf. the *KA* editorial of that day, "A Protest tsum Himel un Erd," which distanced itself from Yudel Rosenberg's opinion.

23 On de Sola, see Gerald Tulchinsky, "de Sola, Clarence," in *Dictionary of Canadian Biography*, http://www.biographi.ca/en/bio/de_sola_clarence_isaac_14E.html, accessed August 21, 2016.

24 "Tsum Montrealer 'Identum," *KA*, May 28, 1919.

25 "Di Troyredige Lage fun di Rabonim in Poylin," *KA*, March 1, 1920; "Helft di 'Ezrat Torah Fond," *KA*, March 4, 1920.

26 "Matamim tsum Talmud Torah Kampyn," *KA*, February 22, 1921.

27 "Israel Rosenberg II," in "Lives in the Yiddish Theatre: Short Biographies of Those Involved in The Yiddish Theatre as Described In Zalmen Zylbercweig's 'Leksikon Fun Yidishn Teater':

the Yiddish stage as an actor. The next relatives needing help appeared in Montreal in 1920. Yudel Rosenberg's radical son Benjamin had died in 1919, fighting for the Red Army on the Ukrainian front. The next year Helen, Benjamin's widow, arrived in Montreal along with her daughter Suzanne (Shoshana) and son Shurri. Helen, a convinced communist like her husband, lived with Rabbi Rosenberg's family for a time until she quarreled with Rabbi Rosenberg and left his home.[28] That same year saw Yudel Rosenberg's son, Meir Joshua, arrive from Poland. Though Meir Joshua originally intended to come to Montreal only for a visit before he and his family settled in Palestine, the collapse of the German currency he held effectively bankrupted him and forced him to stay in North America. Rabbi Rosenberg wasted no time in acquainting the Montreal Jewish community with his son and Meir Joshua's article on the Jewish holiday of Shavu'ot appeared in the *Keneder Adler* on June 1, 1920.[29] Ultimately Meir Joshua obtained a rabbinic position in Holyoke, Massachusetts[30] and his father sent him numerous letters giving detailed advice on how to function as an Orthodox rabbi in North America.[31] Yudel Rosenberg succeeded the next year, 1921, in having yet another son settle in Montreal. Aaron Elimelekh Rosenberg was installed as a poultry *shoḥet* in a shop in Rachel Market.[32] The fact that the new *shoḥet* was Yudel Rosenberg's son was prominently displayed in the shop's newspaper ad.[33]

In August 1919, Rabbi Jacob Gordon of Toronto came to Montreal for a rabbinic hearing concerning kashrut.[34] This was a sign that Rabbi Cohen had not succeeded in his campaign against Rabbi Rosenberg and was faced with the necessity to somehow compromise with his rival. Rabbi Gordon was the first of a long series of distinguished out-of-town rabbis who tried unsuccessfully to

---

1931–1969," http://www.museumoffamilyhistory.com/yt/lex/R/rosenberg-israel-II.htm, accessed February 20, 2019.

28 Reinhold Kramer, *Mordecai Richler: Leaving St Urbain* (Montreal and Kingston: McGill-Queen's University Press, 2008), 227. Cf. Suzanne Rosenberg, *A Soviet Odyssey* (Toronto: Oxford University Press, 1988).

29 Meir Joshua Rosenberg, "Be-Taḥtit ha-Har: Shavu'os Gedanken," *KA*, June 1, 1920. Cf. "Der Ongekumener Rav fun Poyln vet Redn iber Mizraḥi," KA, June 29, 1921.

30 "Rabbi Meir Yehoshua Rosenberg Oyfgenumen als Rav in Holyoke," *KA*, November 7, 1920.

31 Ira Robinson, "The Education of an American Orthodox Rabbi: Mayer Joshua Rosenberg Comes to Holyoke, Massachusetts," *Judaism* 40 (1991): 543–551.

32 "Azhara," *KA*, February 9, 1921.

33 *KA*, November 27, 1921; December 18, 1921, 8.

34 "Ha-Rav Gordon fun Toronto a Gast in Montreal," *KA*, August 1, 1919. Cf. "Vegn Shoḥet Singer," *KA*, August 6, 1919; "Ofener Briv zu Rabbi Garber," KA, August 8, 1919; "Teshuva la-Rabbim meha-Rav Garber," *KA*, August 10, 1919.

resolve the kashrut dispute in Montreal between Rabbis Rosenberg and Cohen. But was Rabbi Rosenberg going to stay in Montreal given the constant opposition he faced from Rabbi Cohen and his partisans or try his luck elsewhere? In February 1921 he reported in a letter to his son Meir Joshua that there was a financial crisis in Montreal which adversely affected the rabbis.[35] This crisis is reflected in a story published in the *Keneder Adler* on March 3, 1921 portraying the dire situation of kashrut in Montreal in which 50% of "kosher" meat did not come from kosher-slaughtered animals and in which the rabbis had lost all control.[36] In March 1921 Rosenberg visited New York where he reported to Meir Joshua he met with Hasidim "spotted, speckled and striped."[37] This may indicate that he was contemplating another move for economic reasons.

In the end, however, Rabbi Rosenberg stayed. What had become clear in his first two years in Montreal was that Rabbi Rosenberg had been able to stand his ground against Rabbi Cohen and in the spring of 1921 the two sides were clearly exploring ways in which they could cooperate. As a result, in May 1921 Montreal kosher butcher shops began advertising the cooperative kashrut supervision of a "local rabbinate."[38] Rabbis Cohen, Simcha Garber (1860–1924), and Rosenberg had united to present to the public a joint list of kosher butchers and to cooperate in inspecting butcher shops.[39]All this cooperation on the part of the rival rabbis was apparently in response to the appearance of a new rabbi in Montreal. Rabbi Sheea (Joshua ha-Levi) Herschorn (1894–1969) arrived in Montreal in 1921 and immediately began to carve his own niche in Montreal kashrut supervision.[40] Much ink was spilt in the failed attempt of the newly united rabbis to supress Rabbi Herschorn's venture into kashrut.[41] However, this cooperation with the other rabbis in Montreal did not prevent Rabbi Rosenberg from publishing in his own name a list of reliable

35 Yudel Rosenberg to Meir Joshua Rosenberg 2 Adar I 5681 (February 10, 1921), BMA, Jerusalem.

36 "Hige Hefkerus in Basar Kosher Ibershtaygt Ale Grenitsen," *KA*, March 3, 1921.

37 Yudel Rosenberg to Meir Joshua Rosenberg, Thursday, weekly Torah portion *va-Yakhel*, 5681 (March 3, 1921), BMA, Jerusalem.

38 *KA*, May 30, 1921, 6; *Canadian Jewish Chronicle*, August 26, 1921.

39 They called themselves *di hige shtot rabbonim*. "Kashrut Direktori," *KA*, July 21, 1921; "Moda'a Raba," *KA*, January 3, 1922.

40 Thus, on November 9, 1921, KA advertised that a kosher butcher, M. Pesner, was under Rabbi Herschorn's supervision. Cf. "Moda'a," *KA*, February 12, 1922.

41 "Briv in Redaksia," *KA*, February 17, 1922. This letter was jointly signed by Rabbis Cohen Zalmanovitz, Garber, and Rosenberg.

poultry slaughterers,[42] or from authorizing a kosher butcher in Ste. Agathe, outside Montreal proper.[43]

The joint rabbinic initiative ultimately led, in February 1922, to plans for the founding of the Religious Community Council of Montreal [Va'ad ha-'Ir ha-Dati], designed in large part to regulate kashrut on a more rational and sustainable basis.[44] While this was going on, there was continuing strife in the kosher meat industry, which culminated in a strike in September 1922. Strike activities included women picketing butcher shops and Jews coming to blows over perceptions of price-gouging on the part of the butchers, while exposing tensions between rabbis, *shoḥtim*, butchers, and consumers.[45] Eventually, community meetings designed to resolve the issues of the strike[46] engendered a plan for what became the Jewish Community Council [Va'ad ha-'Ir] of Montreal.[47] Supported by *Keneder Adler* publisher Hirsch Wolofsky,[48] the organizational meeting of this Council took place on October 29, 1922.[49] Its first election was on December 17.[50]

A Montreal Rabbinic Council [Va'ad ha-Rabbanim] was established under the Jewish Community Council with Rabbi Cohen as its chair and Rabbi

42 "Direktori fun ha-Rav Yudel Rosenberg," *KA*, January 12, 1922. Cf. "Statement vegn di Montrealer oyfes Shoḥtim," *KA*, February 6, 1922.

43 *KA*, June 12, 1922.

44 "Di Geflonte Enderung un der Sheḥite Frage," *KA*, February 24, 1922; "Va'ad ha-'Ir ha-Dati Gegrundet in Montreal," *KA*, February 28, 1922.

45 "Shturm in Shtot tsuleyv Nayem Butsher Trost," *KA*, September 6, 1922; "Geshlegen Lebn di Butsher Sheper ven Froyen Derolzn nit Koyfn Keyn Fleysh," *KA*, September 7, 1922; "Blut Gist zikh in Groysen Kampf gegen Butshers," *KA*, September 8, 1922; "The 'Kosher' Meat Agitation," *Canadian Jewish Chronicle*, September 8, 1922;"Shtot Oyfgeshturmt tsuleyv dem Fleysh Strik," *KA*, September 10, 1922; "Gut Morgen," *KA*, September 10, 1922.

46 "Shturmisher Riziger Miting Protestirt gegn Fleysh Yakrus," *KA*, September 11, 1922; "Orthodoksishe 'Iden Bashlisn zu Helfen gegen Fleysh Trost," *KA*, September 11, 1922; "Riziger Masmiting fun Hige 'Iden Bashlist zu Shteyn Fest biz der Butsher Trost vet Gebrochen vern," *KA*, September 13, 1922.

47 "Groyse Konferents Heist Gut Plan far a Kehile," *KA*, September 18, 1922, 1; "Der Kehile Grindung Plan in Montreal," *KA*, September 20, 1922; Abraham Shmuel Dubitsky, "Oyf Velkhen Ofen Zol Organizirt veren di 'Idishe Kehile?," *KA*, September 25, 1922

48 Hirsch Wolofsky, "Ḥeshbon ha-Nefesh far der Higer Gemeynde," *KA*, October 1, 1922; idem, "Der Rikhtiger Moment far Grinden a 'Idisher Kehile?," *KA*, October 1, 1922

49 "Groyser Organizatsions Miting far a Fareynigten Yudentum Zuntag dem 29-ten Oktober," *KA*, October 10, 1922; "A Kehillah for Montreal," *Canadian Jewish Chronicle*, October 13, 1922;"Vegn der Kehile Frage," *KA*, October 23, 1922; "Kehile Konferents Legt Grundstayn far an Organizirten 'Identum," *KA*, October 30, 1922

50 "Yeder 'Id Muz Haynt Kumen Shtimen in di Vahlen farn Va'ad ha-'Ir," *KA*, December 17, 1922.

Rosenberg as vice chair.[51] Whereas up to that point payment for kashrut supervisors had come from the butchers themselves—creating an obvious conflict of interest—now the salaries would come from a disinterested communal organization, the Council. The Council would receive its funds from a levy on the slaughter of kosher animals and distribute this income not merely for the salaries of rabbinic supervisors and *shoḥtim* but also to support local Jewish educational institutions.[52]

Since the regulation of the kosher meat industry was a major goal of the Council, the institution of this new system necessitated the cooperation of the rabbis, the slaughterers and the butchers.[53] As we have seen with Rabbi Rosenberg's experience in Toronto, such cooperation was by no means easy to obtain in an industry that suffered from nearly constant strife. Rabbi Rosenberg, in particular, was probably somewhat reluctant to cooperate with a Rabbinic Council headed by his rival, Hirsch Cohen. Indeed, as early as January 1923, allegations were published in a handbill by dissident butchers claiming that the Jewish Community Council was not unified on the kosher meat issue.[54] For about three months, however, the coalition that Wolofsky and others had brought together to create this new institution held, if only by a thread, despite fault lines within the Rabbinic Council.

One of these fault lines was between the two leading rabbis of the Rabbinic Council, who undoubtedly retained vivid memories of mutual insults and accusations from previous years. As Yudel Rosenberg, writing to his son, Meir Joshua on December 12, 1921, stated: "There is no Orthodox rabbi who does not have enemies and opponents."[55] Another fault line was between the other rabbis and Rabbi Sheea Herschorn, who had attempted to carve his own niche in the kosher meat supervision scene in Montreal.[56] There were

51 "Beys Din Fareynigt untern Va'ad ha-'Ir, Nominatsies far Ekzekutive Dizen Monat," *KA*, November 12, 1922; Hirsch Wolofsky, "Der Va'ad ha-Rabonim un di Talmudei Torah," *KA*, November 17, 1922, 1

52 Leah Rosenberg, *Errand Runner*, 67. Cf. Ira Robinson, "The Kosher Meat War and the Jewish Community Council of Montreal, 1922–1925," *Canadian Ethnic Studies* 22, no. 2 (1990): 41–53.

53 "Va'ad ha-'Ir Nemt Shtake Shtelung in der Fleysh Frage," *KA*, January 16, 1923; "Riziger Mass-Miting Dizen Zuntag Beytog vegen der Fleysh Frage," *KA*, January 19, 1923.

54 "Riziger Mass-Miting Bashlist zu Shteyen Fest mitn Va'ad ha-'Ir," *KA*, January 22, 1923, 1.

55 Yudel Rosenberg to Meir Joshua Rosenberg, 11 Kislev 5682 (12 December, 1921), BMA.

56 See note 134 above.

further fault lines among the *shoḥtim,* whose leader was Getsel Laxer,[57] and who were often loath to take orders from the Rabbinic Council because many of them felt themselves to be equals with the supervising rabbis and therefore, did not particularly like the hierarchy that was being imposed upon them by the Jewish Community Council.

The butchers also had reservations concerning the Council. Most Jewish butchers in Montreal in the early 1920s ran small, marginal businesses. Their problems began, first of all, with competition. In the 1920s, there were over eighty Jewish butchers serving the Jewish community, which meant one butcher shop for approximately every 500 Jews. They organized in a group known as the Association of Jewish Butchers of Montreal[58] in order to advance their own interests. From the point of view of the consumers they served, the Association constituted a cartel, a veritable Butcher Trust,[59] and thus the public distrusted them. The butchers themselves distrusted the Jewish Community Council, fearing strict supervision standards according to which many of them might not pass muster.

Therefore after an initial period of affiliation with the Jewish Community Council lasting only a few months, in late February 1923, Rabbis Rosenberg and Herschorn, and seven *shoḥtim,* led by Getsel Laxer, left the Jewish Community Council and formed an organization called the Kashrut Council [Va'ad ha-Kashrut] of Montreal.[60] In essence they had reformed the organization founded by Rabbi Glaser, and led after him by Rabbi Rosenberg. Thus kashrut supervision in Montreal was once again divided between the forces of the Jewish Community Council, led by Hirsch Cohen, and the Kashrut Council, led by Yudel Rosenberg.

Rabbi Rosenberg gave a number of reasons for his actions. However, he and his supporters were unable to address the public directly through the

---

57 "Eynige Shoḥtim Zukhen Vider Tsoros," *KA,* February 25, 1923. On Laxer, see Robinson, *Rabbis and Their Community,* 69–81.

58 It is important to note that they were called "Jewish" and not "kosher" butchers. Regardless of the greater or lesser strictness of the kashrut of their establishments, in the literature of the era, Jews went to "Jewish" butchers.

59 For American examples of the same phenomenon, see Hasia Diner, *Hungering for America: Italian, Irish, and Jewish Foodways in the Age of Migration* (Cambridge: Harvard University Press, 2002), 206. It is worth noting that even though there is a perfectly good Hebrew/Yiddish word for butcher, *katsev,* practically the only term ever employed in the *KA* stories from this era I have examined is *butsher.*

60 "7 Shoḥtim un 2 'Rabonim' Farraten di Shtot," *KA,* February 27, 1923.

Keneder Adler newspaper that heavily favored his opponents.[61] They could publish their positions only by means of handbills, relatively few of which have been preserved. Yudel Rosenberg's statements are thus largely not extant, but a great deal can be discerned from the rebuttal to his arguments published in the *Keneder Adler*, for which Rabbi Rosenberg and his partisans were "traitors" [*fareter*]. The newspaper also "defrocked" Rabbis Rosenberg and Herschorn, calling them "former rabbis," "Purim rabbis," and "Torah peddlers."[62]

One hostile review of Yudel Rosenberg's arguments was published in the *Keneder Adler* on March 5, 1923. It reported that Rabbi Rosenberg had stated on Shabbat in the Galician synagogue that people from the Jewish Community Council had threatened him with bodily harm and threatened that would be kicked out of Montreal as he had been kicked out of Toronto. The *Keneder Adler* denounced this accusation as a lie.[63]

One of Rabbi Rosenberg's few extant undated circulars gives us an example of his rhetoric:

> It is now clear to everyone that if Rabbi Cohen knew his prohibition to be substantial ... he would come to a *Din Torah* and prove that the *shoḥtim* are forbidden. Why has he not done so? This is the best demonstration that his prohibitions are false ... and that the *shoḥtim* [Rabbi Cohen forbade] are really kosher.[64]

One of Rabbi Rosenberg's arguments in opposition to Rabbi Cohen and the Jewish Community Council was technical. He objected to the inadequate number of inspectors [*mashgiḥim*] on the job and errors in slaughtering on the part of Jewish Community Council *shoḥtim*.[65] Secondly, Rabbi Rosenberg was

61 "An Erkelrung vegen unzer Poylishen 'Rabi'" *KA*, March 5, 1923. Rosenberg sent a lawyer to the *Keneder Adler* who attempted to discuss the newspaper's prejudice against his client. "Yudel Rosenberg vert Bodeks Tsif Rabi," KA, March 25, 1923.

62 "Mass-Miting Git Heylige Shvue nit zu Koyfen Flaysh bay Trefe Butshers," *KA*, March 1, 1923; "Redner fun Va'ad ha-'Ir hoben Geredt in Ale Shuln," *KA*, March 4, 1923.

63 "An Erklerung vegen unzer Poylishen 'Rabi.'"

64 "Aroysgetsaygt der Emes ohn dem Din Toyre," Jewish Public Library, Jewish Canadiana Collection: Yehuda Rosenberg, Circular in the name of "The Rabbis and *Shoḥtim* of the Kashrut Council" (1924).

65 "Jewish Housewives in Quandary While Kosher Butchers Lock in War," *Montreal Star*, March 12, 1923. Cf. "Entfer fun di Agudas ha-Shoḥtim zu Rabi Rosenberg," *KA*, March 25, 192; "A Brif vegen Rabi Rosenberg un di Iberige vos hoben Farraten di Shtot," *KA*, May 27, 1923.

dissatisfied with his salary. Under the Jewish Community Council, Rabbi Cohen was receiving $60.00 a week, whereas Rabbi Rosenberg's salary was only $45.00 a week.[66] Yudel Rosenberg obviously did not relish playing second fiddle to his rival financially.

Finally, the coalition of Montreal Jews that founded the Jewish Community Council comprised both religious and non-religious Jews, and the Community Council's founders took care to ensure that both elements would cooperate to make the organization a success. This meant that the educational institutions supported by the Council included not only Orthodox schools like the Talmud Torah, but also the Yiddishist Folks Shule, Peretz Shule, and Arbeiter Ring Shule. Rabbi Rosenberg, who in Toronto had insisted on strict standards for religious education, obviously felt uncomfortable with non-religious elements sharing control of the Jewish Community Council, especially with having money raised through the production and sale of kosher meat go to non- and even anti-religious education.[67]

The kosher meat war of Montreal was not only fought with newspaper articles and handbills. The Adat Yeshurun synagogue formally forbade Rabbis Rosenberg and Herschorn from entering its building.[68] There was violence among butchers and threats of violence among *shoḥtim*. Rabbi Cohen and his supporters accused their opponents of using violence to enforce the closing of certain butcher shops, or to make sure that others remained open.[69] Leah Rosenberg recalls violence directed against her father that likely occurred at this time:

> We became victims. Just before Yom Kippur a crowd gathered outside our home and threw stones. Father finally went out and faced the people. He told them their behaviour was unforgivable and not to be taken lightly a day before Yom Kippur. The people were petrified and left.[70]

Newspaper reports from March 1923 indicate that Rabbi Rosenberg was assaulted on the street and that, moreover, any bearded Jew, who by his attire

66 "A Brif vegen Rabi Rozenberg un di Iberige vos hoben Farraten di Shtot."

67 "Varum der Rabonim Delegatsie iz nit Gelungen zu Brengen Sholom" *KA*, May 11, 1924.

68 "Adas Yeshurun Shul Farbot de 'Rabis' Rosenberg un Hershorn Araynzukumen in Shul" *KA*, March 5, 1923.

69 "Arrest Butchers in Assault Case," *Montreal Star*, March 10, 1923; "Butshers Nemen zikh zu Teror Mitlen tsu Tsubrekhen dem Va'ad ha-'Ir," *KA*, March 8, 1923, 1.

70 Leah Rosenberg, *The Errand Runner*, 68.

might have been suspected as belonging to Rabbi Rosenberg's group, could not show his face on the street with impunity.[71]

Violence was attributed to Rabbi Rosenberg's side as well. On March 8, 1923, the *Keneder Adler* reported that a Mr. H. Cohen, who managed the butcher shop of the Consumers' League on 25 Roy Street loyal to Rabbi Cohen and the Council,[72] had been assaulted on Main Street (St. Laurent Boulevard) near Pine Avenue. Witnesses said that the assault was perpetrated by a butcher. The *Montreal Star* added that the victim had been hit on the head from behind and left unconscious, and was still confined to bed several days later. Three of the officers of the Jewish Butchers' Association were arraigned in this case on a charge of attempted murder.[73]

The *Keneder Adler* reported one week later that threats were received by *shoḥtim* loyal to the Council, warning them to desist from slaughtering or else harm would come to them. All had received the following letter, delivered to their home addresses:

> Mr._______
> If you will go and slaughter for the Canadian Packing Company, you will be shorter by a head.
> Signature Unclear

Those who received the threat were reported to be certain that this was the work of Getsel Laxer, the leading *shoḥet* on the opposing side, who had threatened them in the slaughterhouse.[74] On April 9, the *Keneder Adler* further reported that a Jewish Community Council butcher shop on 33 Ontario Street, East had been broken into and vandalized.[75]

---

71 *KA*, March 1, 1923. Cf. *Canadian Jewish Chronicle*, March 2, 1923. This, of course, goes beyond the normal harassment that bearded Jews faced from non-Jews on the street, particularly from children. Cf. Leah Rosenberg, *The Errand Runner*, 50; Rischin, *The Promised City*, 91; Weinberg, *The World of Our Mothers*, 95.

72 On the Jewish Community Council, see Ira Robinson, "The Foundation Documents of the Jewish Community Council of Montreal," *Jewish Political Studies Review* 8, nos. 3–4 (1996): 69–86.

73 "Arrest Butchers in Assault Case," *Montreal Star*, March 10, 1923.

74 "Community Council News," *Canadian Jewish Chronicle*, March 16, 1923; "Shoḥtim fun Va'ad ha-'Ir Geshtrashet mitn Toyt oyv tse Veln Shekhten farn Va'ad ha-'Ir," *KA*, March 15, 1923, 1.

75 "Va'ad ha-'Ir Butsher Stor oyf Ontario Strit Ayngebrokhen," *KA*, April 9, 1923.

The charged nature of the situation can also be ascertained from the minutes of a conference held by the Jewish Community Council in Prince Arthur Hall on April 5, 1923.[76] During that meeting, the leaders of the Consumers' League offered to picket the opposition's butcher shops and a Mr. Lachavitsky felt impelled to adjure them that the picketing must be peaceful in nature and that "anyone bringing in violence shall be held personally responsible."[77]

On April 29, 1923, a headline in *Keneder Adler* proclaimed that the opponents of the Council had hired gangsters to intimidate their opponents.[78] More threatening letters, similar to those that had been sent to *shoḥtim* in previous weeks, had been received by members of the Council. These letters were handed to a private investigation agency for further action. In an open letter, Rabbi Cohen accused his opponents of hiring gangsters to enforce closing of certain butcher shops, or to make sure that others remained open. As he stated:

> Horrible things [concerning] those who call themselves butchers have reached our ears, which no fantasy could eclipse. Hear and be amazed:
>
> A group of butchers and *shoḥtim* with rabbinic approval have hired gangsters. They have given them a $100.00 deposit and have promised a further $200.00 so that the gangsters should drive away the other *shoḥtim*. They have justified[79] [their action] with a permission [*heter*] since "blood has a double meaning"[80] and since they [their opponents] cause them loss of money, they could spill blood. [It is] only through a miracle that other *shoḥtim* threatened to reveal [the plot] and that they stood guard at

76 "Riziger Miting Heist Gut di Arbeit fun Va'ad ha-'Ir," *KA*, April 5, 1923; "Konferents Bashlist Ontsunemen Shtrenge Mitlen gegen di Butshers vos Kempfen gegen Va'ad ha-'Ir," *KA*, April 6, 1923.

77 Jewish Community Council of Montreal Papers, Alex Dworkin Canadian Jewish Archives, Montreal, box 23.

78 "Zogen az Butshers un Shoḥtim hoben Gedungen Gengsters zu Opramen fun veg Zeyere Gegner," *KA*, April 29, 1923, 1. On the infiltration of underworld elements in the kosher meat industry of New York City at this time, see Goren, *New York Jews and the Quest for Community*, 79; Harold Gastwirth, *Fraud, Corruption and Holiness: The Controversy Over the Supervision of the Jewish Dietary Practice in New York* (Port Washington, NY: Kennikat, 1974), 44–54. Joseph Belsky, *I the Union: Being the Personalized Trade Union Story of the Hebrew Butcher Workers of America* (New York: Raddock & Brothers, 1952), 48.

79 Literally, "greased."

80 The reference is to the rabbinic usage, in which the Hebrew word *damim* can signify either "blood" or "money."

> night that this should not take place, [otherwise] the murder would have come to pass.[81]

While all this was going on, a sympathetic rabbi in New York, Gavriel Ze'ev Margolis (1847–1935), wrote Yudel Rosenberg on March 13, 1923:

> I have seen your letter concerning the men who have arisen against you ... and truly their intention is to harm your Torahship monetarily and Rabbi Cohen has gone together with the editor [Wolofsky] and with other wicked people to publicly state not to rely on your *hekhsherim* [kashrut certifications] and to place your honor in the dirt.

Rabbi Margolis went on to offer to write letters to Montreal Jews on Rosenberg's behalf,[82] and he subsequently appointed Yudel Rosenberg vice president of the rabbinic organization he headed, Knesset ha-Rabbanim.[83] Also in the midst of this crisis, amazingly enough, Rabbi Rosenberg found the time to complete the manuscript of his masterwork on the *Zohar*, to be discussed in chapter 7, on Purim 5683 (March 2, 1923).[84]

By the beginning of May 1923, Montreal Jews understood that they were in for a long and bitter fight.[85] At the outbreak of this kosher meat war, the Jewish Community Council, in its public statements, asserted that from sixty to seventy percent of the kosher meat trade in Montreal was in its hands, and its statements of income from late 1922 and early 1923 show that this estimate was more or less accurate. However as the struggle continued and the Council continued losing income, painful economies had to be made. The first thing that went was the Council subsidy to Jewish schools. After that the Jewish Community Council began cutting salaries so that Rabbi Cohen's paycheck went from sixty to forty-eight dollars per week. They fired the secretary, who was getting fifteen dollars per week, and replaced her with a "girl" to simply answer the telephone at three dollars a week, so that the office would remain "open." The Council was also forced to obtain a bank loan for $800.00, and received

---

81 "A Brif fun Va'ad ha-Rabonim zum Va'ad ha-'Ir" *KA*, April 29, 1923, 5.

82 G. Wolf Margolis to Yudel Rosenberg, 25 Adar 5683 (March 13, 1923), RFA, Savannah.

83 G. Wolf Margolis to Yudel Rosenberg, 1925, RFA, Savannah.

84 *ZT*, vol. 5, 256.

85 "Riziger Massmiting Haynt Batog vet Bashlisn Kamfs-Mitlen gegn dem Butsher-Trost," *KA*, May 6, 1923, 1; "Groyser Massmiting Git zu Nayem Mut zum Kampf gegen Farreter fun Shtot," *KA*, May 7, 1923, 1.

interest-free loans from various synagogues and benefit societies, which were an important factor in keeping the enterprise afloat.

When the benefit societies ultimately demanded payment, the Council was in no position to pay its debts. We read in the Council finance committee's minutes for February 21, 1924: "Madame Boucher has taken action to recover rent for January to May 1, 1924 amounting to $240.00. It was decided in order to gain time that we hand this to our lawyer. Carried." At the next meeting, February 28, 1924, there was a follow-up: "Mr Nadler[86] reports having given the case of Madame Boucher to Mr Louis Fitch [1888–1956][87] who promised to try to drag the case for about two weeks." Ultimately, the Council succeeded in compromising on the rent with Madame Boucher for $150.00, $50.00 of which was to be paid in cash, with two further monthly payments of the same amount.

Most of the Jewish butchers of Montreal originally sided with Rabbi Rosenberg. They obviously saw freedom from the Community Council's control as advantageous. The first butcher shop adhering to the Council only opened its doors on March 2, 1923. However, though the butchers themselves were initially with Rabbi Rosenberg and his colleagues, the *Keneder Adler* was wholeheartedly on the side of the Council, which thus possessed a built-in advantage. Pressing its advantage, the Community Council proclaimed a boycott against butchers selling meat certified by Rabbis Rosenberg and Herschorn, which, it declared, was not kosher.

In response to this move, Rabbi Rosenberg's butchers began a price war. Kosher meat was then selling in Council-loyal butcher shops for 14 cents per pound. The Association of Jewish Butchers began selling meat at 8–10 cents per pound, but apparently with little effect. On March 20, the Council claimed to control fourteen butcher shops (of approximately eighty). On March 22, it claimed twenty-four. On March 25, it claimed twenty-seven. It was advertising in the *Keneder Adler* practically on a daily basis giving the names and locations of Council-affiliated butcher shops. The public clearly seemed on the Council's side, and was apparently not buying meat from the other butchers, even at bargain prices. The public's goal was to break the Butcher Trust, and even though Butcher Trust prices were currently low, the public sensed that the Trust could not be trusted not to jack up prices if the conflict were decided in its favor.

86 The Executive Secretary of the Jewish Community Council.

87 Mr. Fitch, the Council's lawyer, was later elected to the Quebec Legislative Assembly on the Union Nationale ticket.

Eventually most butchers concluded that the right side of the issue was the side their customers were on.

By this time, it was obvious that the conflict was going against the Association of Jewish Butchers, which began sending out peace feelers to the Jewish Community Council in late March.[88] However, at this point the Council felt it had the upper hand and in its minutes there are very harsh words against the opposing *shoḥtim*, referred to as "Laxer and his gang," a possible indication that the Community Council felt it might be able to separate Rabbi Rosenberg from the rest of his group.[89] In April 1923, though, *Keneder Adler* reported that hopes for peace were in vain.[90]

In the weeks, months, and years that followed, there were numerous attempts to mediate between the two sides on the part of some Jewish mutual-benefit societies with the *Keneder Adler* blaming Rabbi Rosenberg's side for the failure of these attempts while nonetheless not completely blaming Rabbi Rosenberg himself, asserting that he was under the control of the Herschorn-Laxer-Temkin cabal.[91] In any event, a meeting held by the Jewish Community Council on April 25, 1923 put an end to the peace feelers for the moment.[92]

There were also attempts to get eminent rabbis from outside Montreal to mediate the dispute. Rabbi Bernard Levinthal of Philadelphia (1864–1952), acknowledged by many as the dean of the immigrant Orthodox rabbinate in North America, was invited by the Jewish Community Council but did not come. In his place, he sent Rabbi Ḥayyim Fishel Epstein of St. Louis (1874–1942). Rosenberg, commenting on this attempt in a letter to his son, stated that, as was normal in such a *Din Torah*, each side had appointed its own arbitrator, that his choice had been Rabbi Yehuda Leib Graubart (1862–1937) of Toronto, while the Council's choice was Rabbi Epstein.[93] In the end, Rabbi Rosenberg

---

88 "Butsher Trost Tut op Nayem Shpitsel der Shtot," *KA*, March 28, 1923; "Butshers shrayen Sholom un Riren zikh nit fun Ort," *KA*, April 3, 1923.

89 A letter to the editor of the *Keneder Adler* described Rabbi Rosenberg as weak and under the influence of a troublemaking *shoḥet*, clearly Laxer. "Vegn der Fleysh Frage," *KA*, April 20, 1923.

90 "Frisher Butsher Blof Fardamnt," *KA*, April 11, 1923; "Butshers-Rabomin-Shoḥtim Trost Brekht op Sholom Farhandlungen," *KA*, April 23, 1923.

91 "Farreterishe Shoḥtim un Rabonim Layben ois Zeyer Mishpkohe Als Umpareyeshe," *KA*, April 15, 1923.

92 "Keyn Sholom mit Butsher Trost Bashlist Rizige Konferenz," *KA*, April 26, 1923, 1.

93 "Barimter Rov Kumt Morgen zu Fartreten Va'ad ha-'Ir in Zayn Sikhsukh mit Farretishe 'Kley Koydesh,'" *KA*, July 8, 1923.

stated, they went home without having the *Din Torah* "and the obstacle [*meni'a*] was not from our side but from theirs."[94] When Rabbi Abraham Isaac Kook (1865–1935), chief Ashkenazic rabbi of Palestine came to North America in 1924, he also visited Montreal to attempt mediation and he, too, failed, stating that "the disputes are complex and cannot be solved in a short time."[95]

There was, however, a certain tide in this conflict. The Council claimed the loyalty of more and more butchers in the summer of 1923. On June 20, the Council listed seventy-two butchers on its side. On July 25, it was able to produce a list of holdout butcher shops still affiliated with the other side, which contained only eleven names.[96] It is thus clear that the Community Council had gained a decisive advantage in the conflict. It was nonetheless hurting very badly. It could not make ends meet on its reduced income and was certainly in no position to subsidize Jewish education. Moreover, because of the overwhelming nature of the kosher meat war, the Jewish Community Council had no time or attention to spare for other critical issues facing the Montreal Jewish community of this era, most particularly the School Question.[97] There were thus voices within the leadership of the Council, which advocated abandonment of the struggle. For them, the really important issue was not kosher meat, but rather the question of the legal basis for the schooling of Jewish children in the Province of Quebec, and they expressed the opinion that perhaps the answer was for the Council to get out of the kosher supervision business entirely. Their sentiment was actually brought to a vote at a meeting of the Council. It was defeated by a vote of fourteen for the resolution, and forty-four opposed. Nonetheless, the fact that this idea was brought to a formal vote at all shows that, even though the Council had an advantage over its opponents, it was seriously hurting.

---

94 Yudel Rosenberg to Meir Joshua Rosenberg, Sunday, weekly Torah portion *'Eqev*, 5683 (July 29, 1923), BMA. This claim was hotly denied by the Community Council: "Nayer Shvindel fun Farretisher Klike Klor Gemakht farn Oylam," *KA*, June 14, 1923; "Vemens Shuld vet Es Yetst Zayn," *KA*, July 12, 1923; "Aroysgetrotene Rabonim hoben Nit Gevolt Keyn Din Toyre, Zogt Rabi Epstein," *KA*, July 13, 1923. Cf. the undated handbill "Aroysgezaygt der Emes on dem Din Torah," extant in the Alex Dworkin Canadian Jewish Archives, which characterizes the *KA* version of events as "a damn lie."

95 "Rabonim Delegatsie Opgefaren Nekhten Ovent; Shtendiger Mosad Torah Gegrundet," *KA*, May 8, 1924.

96 "Butshers vos Zenen gegen dem Va'ad ha-'Ir," *KA*, July 25, 1923.

97 On the School Question, see David Fraser, *Honorary Protestants: The Jewish School Question in Montreal, 1867–1997* (Toronto: University of Toronto Press, 2015).

Rabbi Rosenberg's side was obviously hurting much worse, but it too carried on with the fight on all fronts. Beyond kosher meat, there was a conflict over kosher milk. Every Spring, the three major Montreal dairies, Guaranteed, Borden's, and J. J. Joubert, got together and hired rabbis to certify the kashrut of a batch of milk for Passover, which has especially stringent kashrut rules.[98] In one meeting of the Finance Committee of the Community Council, Mr. Nadler reported that the best deal he was able to reach with the dairies was $600.00, which barely covered the Council's costs including supervisors' salaries, printing of labels, and so forth. However, he reported, we cannot do any better because Rabbi Rosenberg had also approached these companies and offered to do the job gratis.

The butchers were a fickle lot. The Council had gone from zero to seventy affiliated butchers in only a few months. Not all of these butchers had affiliated with the Council because they particularly wanted to. As someone in a Finance Committee meeting stated succinctly, "In America, the butchers are for the dollar. The rabbis are for the dollar." Montreal's Jewish butchers wanted to make a profit and moved from side to side when they sensed an advantage. The Council was acutely aware that there were many butchers affiliating for opportunistic reasons who were neither religiously nor morally "reliable." Thus, by Fall 1923, the number of butchers claimed by the Council fell from a high of seventy-three in midsummer to fifty-eight, and the number of butchers listed as against the Council increased.[99] This counter tide was noted by the *Keneder Adler*. Through its articles and editorials, readers were strongly exhorted that those who bought meat from "traitor" butcher shops were rebelling against God, their community, and its schoolchildren. Women were warned not to sell their souls to the devil before the high holidays by buying non-kosher meat from the "traitors."[100]

An additional example of this rhetoric pertains to yet another aspect of the conflict—poultry, a trade that was considerably harder to organize and control than kosher meat. In 1922, when he was still in partnership with the other rabbis, Rabbi Rosenberg formulated a plan for the City of Montreal to establish municipal kosher poultry abbatoirs. As he stated in a communication to the Montreal City Council's Committee on Health, his only extant communication in the

98 Rabbi Cohen advertised kosher milk for Passover in *Canadian Jewish Chronicle*, March 16, 1923; *KA*, March 30, 1922.

99 Sixteen butchers are listed, up from eleven in July. "Butshers vos Zenen gegen Va'ad ha-'Ir," *KA*, August 23, 1923.

100 "Farzikhtig 'Idishe Froyen, Farkoyft nit Ayere Neshomes far Ro'sh ha-Shana," *KA*, September 7, 1923.

English language, "I beg that you take into consideration that Montreal should, in the Hygienic aspect, not be lower than all large cities in Canada."[101] Yudel Rosenberg's initiative ultimately spurred the creation of Montreal bylaw 828 that limited licensed kosher poultry abattoirs in Montreal to eight. This measure was passed by the Montreal City Council in 1923, after the conflict between Rabbis Rosenberg and Cohen had commenced. Immediately the Community Council moved to get the licenses for all eight abbatoirs in its own hands. Rabbis Rosenberg and Herschorn, having been shut out of the kosher poultry market, protested to Montreal Mayor Médéric Martin (1869–1946) that this infringed their freedom of religion.[102] On September 16, 1923, *Keneder Adler* reported that:

> The renegades who have sought to destroy all that is holy and dear to Montreal Jews seek now also to aid the chicken dealers in their struggle against order. Former rabbis Yudel Rosenberg and [Sheea] Herschorn have sent to the city's mayor a protest against the decision that the eight slaughter rooms be under the control of the Jewish Community Council. It is interesting that in Yudel Rosenberg and Herschorn's protest, they say that they represent three-quarters of Montreal Jewry. This was between Rosh ha-Shana and Yom Kippur, when ordinary flesh-and-blood people guard themselves from telling a lie. However, it seems that former rabbis are not plain flesh-and-blood people, and what others cannot do, they may.[103]

By December 1923, the beleaguered Community Council was being urged not to give up its fight.[104] Rabbi Rosenberg's partisans continued the struggle and the other side accused them of creating a "pogrom" against Council-affiliated butcher shops.[105] The ongoing struggle for the loyalty of butchers continued.[106]

---

101 "Vegn Sheḥitas 'Oyfes," *KA*, June 18, 1922. Cf. "Kol Qore," *KA*, July 4, 1922; "Ver iz Shuldig in dem vos di Shtot hot Eyngefirt Sheḥite Shiblekh?," *KA*, December 5, 1923. Cf. Ira Robinson, "Toward a History of Kashrut in Montreal: The Fight Over Municipal Bylaw 828 (1922–1924)," in *Renewing Our Days: Montreal Jews in the Twentieth Century*, ed. Ira Robinson and Mervin Butovsky (Montreal: Véhicule Press, 1995), 30–41.

102 "Sheḥitas 'Oyfes unter Kontrol fun Va'ad ha-Rabonim Durkhgegangen in Siti Hol," *KA*, August 14, 1923. Ira Robinson, "Toward a History of Kashrut in Montreal," 30–41.

103 *KA*, September 16, 1923, 1.

104 "Rizige Folks-Konferents Fodert oyf Va'ad ha-'Ir nit Oyfzugeben Basar Kosher Kampf," *KA*, December 4, 1923.

105 "Ofitsiele Meldung fun Va'ad ha-Rabonim," *KA*, February 24, 1924.

106 "Ofitsiele Meldung fun di Kashrus un Religieze Komiteten fun Va'ad ha-'Ir," *KA*, February 15, 1924; "Hodo'o mi-Va'ad ha-Rabonim" *KA*, July 3, 1924.

As of Spring 1924, the conflict had come to a relative standstill. The Council was certainly hurting badly, its opponents were almost certainly worse off, but both sides continued with the struggle, though calls for peace were still made.[107] Butchers wound up roughly evenly divided, with only a slight advantage to the Council. The *Keneder Adler* estimated the number of butcher shops on the side of the Council at this point as between forty-five and fifty. Considering that there were approximately eighty to eighty-five Jewish butcher shops in Montreal,[108] the other side must have held the allegiance of some thirty to forty butchers. Thus neither side was ultimately strong enough to decisively defeat the other. What in fact ultimately succeeded in ending the kosher meat war was the Quebec Superior Court.[109] Judicial decisions in two cases relevant to the conflict were handed down that brought about the necessary conditions for the final denouement. One of these cases involved kosher beef; the other involved kosher poultry.

First in chronological order is the kosher poultry case. Because, as we have mentioned, the Community Council gained control of the licenses for the eight chicken abattoirs in Montreal, Rabbi Rosenberg and his associates went to court in September 1923. The case was heard by Quebec Superior Court Judge Louis Coderre (1865–1935). The suit was brought by poultry dealer Hattie Vineberg and poultry *shoḥet* Leib Simon Woloz. The plaintiffs charged that the City of Montreal, by limiting the number of kosher poultry abattoirs to eight while allowing other poultry abattoirs to operate freely, was discriminating against Jews. Thus, bylaw 828 was unconstitutional, "particularly as creating class and religious distinctions to the prejudice of the Jewish citizens," and would result in "great and irreparable injury insofar as it affects the trade of Jewish poultry dealers within the City of Montreal."[110] On April 11, 1924, Judge Coderre found for the plaintiffs, declared the article limiting the amount of kosher slaughtering establishments for poultry to be unconstitutional, and awarded the plaintiffs court costs, which amounted to $272.85. The City of Montreal did not appeal this decision and the bylaw was suitably amended in May 1924. That decision

107 "Nayer Va'ad ha-'Ir Instalirt by a Prakhtfulen Miting Nekhten Bay-Tog," *KA*, Febrauary 25, 1924, 1.

108 Deposition of M. Katz, Quebec Ministry of Justice Archives, Montreal. S. C. Montreal 3312, Getzel Laxer et al. vs. Jewish Butchers Society of Montreal et al., 6.

109 On the use of secular courts to solve issues of kashrut in the United States, see Bernard J. Meislin, *Jewish Law in American Tribunals* (New York: Ktav, 1976), 175–214.

110 "Tshiken Dilers Kempfen gegen Sheḥita Shtiblekh," *KA*, November 11, 1923.

was an important blow against the Jewish Community Council's claim of a monopoly on kosher poultry slaughter in Montreal.

The other case was of even greater importance for the resolution of the conflict. Its plaintiffs were *shoḥet* Getsel Laxer and other "renegade" *shoḥtim* vs. the Association of Jewish Butchers of Montreal.[111] The plaintiffs argued that the Association, most of whose members were now on the Council's side, had reneged on its contract with Laxer and the others to supply them with kosher meat on the grounds that the Council had declared the meat they had slaughtered non-kosher. This case was brought before Quebec Superior Court Judge Maclennan. In this case as well, the court found for the plaintiffs.[112] Thus the Council found itself unable to legally enforce its control of either the kosher meat industry or the kosher poultry industry of Montreal. Its legal defeats largely negated its other advantages over the opposing side.

The end of the conflict came on December 2, 1925, when the *Keneder Adler* carried an extremely brief notice to the effect that the kosher meat question in Montreal had been solved.[113] There was no comment in the *Keneder Adler* on the terms of the settlement, either at that time or at any later date. Editor Israel Rabinovitch (1894–1964) only expressed the hope that the settlement of the kosher meat strife would enable the Council to concentrate on matters he considered more important, particularly the School Question.[114]

The minutes of the Community Council for this period have disappeared.[35] The minutes of the Council's Finance Committee, which are extant, simply state: "Mr. Nadler related how *sholom* [peace] was achieved." After fully two years of bitter conflict, essentially nothing had changed. Starting in December 1925, Rabbis Rosenberg and Herschorn[115] went back on the payroll of the Council, with Rabbi Rosenberg resuming his role as vice-chairman of the Rabbinic Council.[116] The "renegade" slaughterers went back to work together

111 S. C. Montreal, 3312, Getsel Laxeer et al. vs. The Jewish Butchers Society of Montreal et al. For the beginning of this legal tactic, see "Aroysgetrotene Shoḥtim Strashen Va'ad Butshers mit Loyers Brif," *KA*, August 29, 1923.

112 "Butshers Muzen Tsohlen Shadenratz zu 6 Shoḥtim," *KA*, March 19, 1925. Compared with all the space the KA had given in condemnation of the other side in the past two years, the story on their complete vindication was exceedingly brief.

113 "Basar Kosher Frage in Shtot Geschlikhtet," *KA*, December 2, 1925.

114 "Di Naye Gelegenhayt farn Va'ad ha-'Ir," KA, December 3, 1925, 1.

115 Nonetheless, Rabbi Herschorn was called a "minor rabbi" [*reb'l*] in a story regarding his testimony in a Toronto kashrut case. "Der Basar Kosher Skandal in Toronto," KA, July 2, 1926, 5.

116 He is listed immediately after Rabbi Cohen in "Der Va'ad ha-Rabonim vegen Talmud Toyreh Kampayn," KA, March 21, 1926, 9

with their erstwhile foes. The butchers resumed their pursuit of the consumer's dollar, and the number of butchers supervised by the Council still fluctuated greatly.[117] Problems of butchers selling non-kosher products to their customers continued,[118] and the public was still being warned of butchers who did not have the Council's supervision.[119]

Rabbi Yudel Rosenberg continued his communal activities, presiding over student examinations at the Montreal yeshiva,[120] participating, with rabbinic colleagues Yehuda Leib Zlotnick (1887–1962) and Abraham Samuel Dubitsky (d. 1954), in a reception for visiting European rabbi Baruch Epstein (1860–1941),[121] and speaking on behalf of the Keren ha-Yesod.[122] By mid-1927, relations between Rabbis Rosenberg and Cohen, at least on the surface, had normalized. Thus, Yudel Rosenberg gave a witty and well-received speech at a banquet honoring Rabbi Cohen[123] and spoke on behalf of the Rabbinic Council in Rabbi Cohen's absence.[124]

Through all this, unrest in the kosher meat industry continued. The most important influence for continued unrest was the group of slaughterers, who established a volatile union, Agudat ha-Shoḥtim.[125] In 1927–1928, Getsel Laxer along with fellow *shoḥtim* Temkin and Eisenberg led yet another secession movement of *shoḥtim*, wholesalers and butchers.[126] While Rabbi Rosenberg continued with the Council in this dispute, Rabbis Moshe Yom Tov Wachtfogel (d. 1951) and Sheea Herschorn were noted for their absence from

---

117 Thus, the Council's directory of kosher butchers published in *KA*, January 6, 1926, listed thirty-six butchers. The directory of January 17, 1926 included sixty-nine, that of January 31, 1926, seventy-one, and that of August 15, eighty-one.

118 "Kaved Lev Paro'," *KA*, February 13, 1927.

119 "Azhara Gedola fun Va'ad ha-Rabonim de-Po," *KA*, December 22, 1925.

120 "Di Ekzamens in der Higer Yeshive," *KA*, March 26, 1926.

121 "Hartsiger Kabalas Ponim far ha-Rov Barukh Epstein Nekhten Ovent," *KA*, October 4, 1926.

122 "Oyfruf fun Rabi Rosenberg," *KA*, March 14, 1927, 6.

123 "Montreal Ehrt Rabi Cohen bay an Opsheds Banket," *KA*, June 25, 1927.

124 Yudel Rosenberg, "Meshulakh fun Yeshivas Ohel Moshe Yerushalyim a Gast in Montreal," *KA*, November 23, 1928.

125 Robinson, *Rabbis and Their Community*, 69–86.

126 Cf. "Strenge Varnung fun Va'ad ha-Rabonim," *KA*, January 4, 1928; "Koshere Butshers Laykenen Teyl fun dem Nekhtigen Barikht vegen Oyfgeben Hashgokhe," *KA*, January 4, 1928; "Keyn Koshere Fleysh in Montreal Zayt Nekhten in der Fri," *KA*, August 21, 1928; "Va'ad ha-'Ir Refarat," *KA*, August 23, 1928; "Basar Kosher Sikhsukh Geshlikhtet," *KA*, September 5, 1928; "Va'ad ha-'Ir Shlikhtet Sikhsuskh mit Holseyl Butshers; Shoḥet Temkin Makht a Basunder Kleyzl," *KA*, September 7, 1928; "Trefa Fleysh Gefunen mit Gefelshten Stemp in Higen Butsher Shop," *KA*, October 17, 1928.

the ranks of the Rabbinic Council on this issue.[127] In October 1928 Rabbis Wachtfogel and Herschorn seceded from the Community Council.[128] During this struggle, Rabbi Rosenberg's overcoat was torn by an opposing butcher.[129] Again in 1929, Getsel Laxer led a strike of *shoḥtim* that lasted nearly five months and caused no end of bitterness and recriminations.[130] The difference between this and previous incidents was that previously Laxer had been allied with various rabbis whereas now only *shoḥtim* led by Laxer seceded. Rabbi Rosenberg maintained his solidarity with the *Va'ad* in 1929 at the cost of his relationship with Getsel Laxer. They had been allies, partners and neighbors, but from the late 1920s until Rabbi Rosenberg's death in 1935 they did not speak to each other. In the aftermath of that strike, the Agudat ha-Shoḥtim signed a contract with the Jewish Community Council that stipulated that the *shoḥtim* would receive 62% of the gross income from slaughtering and an income of $53.00 per week.[131]

There was a brief moment of prosperity for Rabbi Yudel Rosenberg in October 1929, prior to the Depression. At that time, he bought several plots of land in Palestine,[132] hoping that he would be able to go there to live.[133] He also became a subscriber to the annual campaign of Montreal's Federation of Jewish Philanthropies.[134] But the moment of prosperity soon passed and neither Yudel Rosenberg nor the Community Council were on completely firm ground when the Depression hit. It adversely affected Montreal's Jewish community and institutions, including the Community Council, which was reorganized in 1933[135] and continued to survive by the skin of its teeth. Among the cattle

127 "Trefos durkh Aygene Gemakhte Kosher Stemps," *KA*, October 18, 1928, 1.

128 "Montrealer Ba'aley Batim Nemen on Shrit zu Brengen Ordnung in der Higer Basar Kosher Situatsie," *KA*, October 31, 1928.

129 "Rabonim un Va'ad ha-'Ir Forshteyer Balaydigt un Mashgiaḥ Geshologen fun Butshers," *KA*, November 30, 1928.

130 Robinson, *Rabbis and Their Community*, 78–81.

131 *KA*, February 27, 1935.

132 There were as many as three plots of land, in the Jerusalem, Tel-Aviv, and Haifa areas. The Jerusalem plot, in the district of Sanhedria, was purchased for 185 Palestine pounds. Leah Rosenberg, *The Errand Runner*, 114; interview with Leah Rosenberg, January 28, 1987.

133 In 1931 he expressed his wish to live in Palestine. *Omer*, part 1, 5.

134 He is listed among the subscribers in the 12–15th Annual Reports of the Federation of Jewish Philanthropies (1928–1931) with a subscription of $5.00.

135 *Vaad Hoir Bulletins* 1, March 9, 1933, and 2, April 28, 1933. Alex Dworkin Canadian Jewish Archives, Jewish Community Council of Montreal, file 17.

shoḥtim as well as the poultry slaughterers there continued to be great restiveness and latent opposition.[136]

1930 saw a grand communal celebration of Rabbi Hirsch Cohen's seventieth birthday, culminating in a banquet held on September 14, which was marked by numerous laudatory articles in the *Keneder Adler*.[137] Shortly afterward, Rabbi Rosenberg, who had been born some months previous to Rabbi Cohen, let it be known that he, too, was to celebrate his seventieth birthday.[138] Rabbi Yudel Rosenberg's seventieth jubilee was celebrated on February 18, 1931, and his many writings and accomplishments were praised not merely in Montreal,[139] but also in New York's *Morgen Journal*.[140] As was the case with Rabbi Cohen, several of the laudatory articles published in the *Keneder Adler* were collected and printed in a souvenir book.

During the celebration there was an exchange between Rabbis Cohen and Rosenberg that illustrates both their surface cordiality and the undercurrent of rivalry between them. Yudel Rosenberg remarked that "Rabbi Cohen resolves all rabbinic questions alone. But when a Jewish woman comes to him with a dream, he sends her to Rabbi Rosenberg to decipher it." Rabbi Cohen replied praising dreams and dream interpretation in the Jewish tradition but did not deny Rosenberg's assertion.[141] In a sermon delivered on the Sabbath of Ḥanukkah, 5691 (December 20, 1930) in honor of his seventieth birthday celebration, Rabbi Rosenberg also dealt with the latent hostility he felt with Rabbi Cohen by making his theme a citation from the Babylonian Talmud (Sotah 49a): "If two disciples of the sages reside in the same city and do not support one another in halakha, one dies and the other is exiled." Rosenberg did not have to give the names for his audience to catch the drift of his remarks.[142] In a thank-you letter published in the *Keneder Adler* a few days later, Rabbi Rosenberg thanked the

136 The arrangements of chicken slaughtering continued to plague the Community Council in 1933. *KA*, December 28, 1933.

137 "Ha-Rav Zvi ha-Kohens 70 Yoriger Yubelium vet Gefayert veren oyf a Zeyer Shenem Oyfn," *KA*, August 29, 1930; "Haynt Ovent Groyser Banket zu Fayeren 70 Yoriger Yubelium fun ha-Rav Zvi ha-Kohen" *KA*, September 14, 1930.

138 "Ha-Rav Yudel Rosenberg Zibtsig Yor Alt," *KA*, November 12, 1930. His celebration was announced for January.

139 "Ha-Rav Rosenbergs Yubilee Feyerung in der Ḥevra Kadisha Shul," *KA*, February 10, 1931; "Rabbi J. Rosenberg's Seventieth Anniversary," *Canadian Jewish Chronicle*, February 13, 1931.

140 "Montreal Ehrt Rabi Rosenberg," *Jewish Morning Journal*, February 6, 1931.

141 "Der Groyser Banket le-Khavod ha-Rav Rosenbergs 70 Yorigen Yubileum," *KA*, February 20, 1931.

142 *Omer*, part 1, 70–71.

community but also reminded it that it needed to do better in the key areas of kashrut, Sabbath observance, Jewish education, and family purity.[143]

Jewish butchers in the 1930s were no more amenable to rabbinic supervision than they had been in previous decades and there were numerous reports of individual butchers caught in flagrant violation of kashrut rules.[144] The consumers themselves were often restive and were often suspicious of the motives and tactics of rabbis, slaughterers and butchers. They continued the tactic of boycotting butchers who were thought to be constantly plotting to raise the price of meat.[145]

1931 saw a move to essentially replace the Community Council with a Council of Orthodox Synagogues, but the underlying problems facing the community remained unsolved.[146] In February 1932 both Rabbis Cohen and Rosenberg published articles warning consumers against the still vexed problem of poultry slaughtering,[147] and the Rabbinic Council continued to publicize butchers who infringed kashrut rules.[148]

By 1932 the Depression was hitting the Montreal Jewish community hard.[149] It damaged the ability of the Community Council to fulfill its financial obligations.[150] The rabbis of the Vaad ha-Rabonim were growing restive as can be seen in a report Rabbi Rosenberg made to the Council in April 1932 in place of Rabbi Cohen, who was out of the city. In his report, he did not mince words, accusing the Council of taking from the rabbis' salaries in order to support the

---

143 "Vending tsum Montrealer 'Identum fun Rabi Rosenberg," *KA*, February 24, 1931. For Rosenberg's support of the Talmud Torah campaigns see his articles "Kol Qore' vegen dem Envelop Kampayn be-Yeme ha-Nora'im far di Fareynigte T"t," *KA*, September 7, 1931, and "Vegen dem Talmud Torah Kampayn" KA March 14, 1932.

144 "Ofitsiele Bakantmakhung fun Va'ad ha-Rabonim," *KA*, March 16, 1932; "Religion and Profits" *Canadian Jewish Chronicle*, March 16, 1932.

145 On a similar phenomenon in New York City, see Paula Hyman, "Immigrant Women and Consumer Protest: The New York City Kosher Meat Boycott of 1902," *American Jewish History* 69 (1980): 91–105. Cf. also Hasia Diner, *Hungering for America*, 206.

146 "The Council of Orthodox Synagogues," *Canadian Jewish Chronicle*, October 20, 1931; "Va'ad ha-Kehilos Nemt zikh unter tsu Shafn Mitlen far 'Idishe Erziung," *KA*, October 19, 1931; M. Ginzberg, "Der Va'ad ha-Kehilos," *KA*, November 6, 1931, 4, 10.

147 Zvi ha-Kohen, "Kashrut," *KA*, February 3, 1932; Yudel Rosenberg, "Azhara Gedola vegen Sheḥitas 'Oyfes," *KA*, February 17, 1932.

148 "Gevezener Falshe Stempl-Makher Tut Vider Trefene Biznes," handbill stamped August 16, 1932, Alex Dworkin Canadian Jewish Archives.

149 Aharon Zalmanovitz, "Kol Qore' le-'Ezra!," *KA*, September 2, 1932.

150 Yudel Rosenberg, "Der Va'ad ha-'Ir," *KA*, October 21, 1932, 1.

Talmud Torahs, which were on the verge of financial collapse.[151] Yudel Rosenberg bluntly warned the Council of possible consequences:

> I say to you in the name of the *Va'ad ha-Rabanim*. ... You should not think that the rabbis are children in *ḥeder* [primary school] and that you are going to hit them with a strap. You should also not think that the rabbis are as weak as the *shoḥtim* and that you can deal with them as you like, with no regard to their feelings. If you think so, you are making a great error. You must understand that if you handle the rabbis so roughly they could unite with the *shoḥtim* or they could take some *shoḥtim* and wholesalers and do for themselves and the Community Council would be completely destroyed. You must also understand that the entire foundation of the Council ... is solely kashrut. ... Therefore I say to you that if you want the Council to exist you must try to make sure that there is no division between the Community Council and the Rabbinic Council.

Rabbi Rosenberg concluded his blunt message with a calculation that the Community Council owed the rabbis $2070.00 in back wages.[152] It is around this time that Yudel Rosenberg put into writing a "covenant of love, brotherhood and peace" with Rabbi Moshe Wachtfogel according to which they agreed to support each other on the Rabbinic Council and in other matters.[153]

The imminent financial collapse of the United Talmud Torahs spurred the *Vaad ha-'Ir* to reorganize itself at its annual meeting on November 6, 1932, and attempt to assert its control of the income from kosher slaughtering to provide funds for the city's educational institutions.[154] The complete financial collapse of the United Talmud Torahs in January 1933 was marked by the teachers, who had not been paid in six months, going out on strike.[155] This event plunged the Community Council into yet another crisis in which it accused the *shoḥtim*,

---

151 Samuel J. Browsky, "On the Verge of Collapse," *Canadian Jewish Chronicle*, November 24, 1932; "Ladies' Auxiliary of the United Talmud Torahs Challenges Vaad Ho'Ir," *Canadian Jewish Chronicle*, December 9, 1932; "Hebrew Teachers on Strike!," *Canadian Jewish Chronicle* January 13, 1933.

152 Yudel Rosenberg, "A Refarat," *Der Shtern*, April 8, 1932, 3.

153 Moshe Wachtfogel to Yudel Rosenberg, 22 Tevet 5692 (January 1, 1932), RFA, Savannah.

154 *Vaad Hoir Bulletin*, no. 1, March 9, 1933, 1, Alex Dworkin Canadian Jewish Archives, Jewish Community Council of Montreal, File 17; "Va'ad ha-'Ir Nemt Zikh unter zu Retten 'Idishe Erziungs Anshtalten," *KA*, November 7, 1932.

155 "Hebrew Teachers on Strike!," *Canadian Jewish Chronicle*, January 13, 1933.

whom the *Canadian Jewish Chronicle* called "racketeers,"[156] of intransigence in their wage demands and threatened to hire a new set of *shoḥtim*.[157] The Council made good its threat. The old *shoḥtim* were "dismissed" and a new set of *shoḥ tim* began work on March 10.[158] Thus another chapter of Montreal's kosher meat strife began. This episode included price wars between the Council-affiliated and non-affiliated butchers as had happened in the past.[159] The public was able to peruse lists of butchers on one side or another.[160] The Agudat ha-Shoḥtim issued handbills calling the rabbis of the Community Council's "Hitler's students."[161]

An example of violent behaviour in connection with the kosher meat strife in Montreal in this period is a handbill whose language is suffused throughout with the rhetoric of the militant labour movement, which was a potent force within the immigrant Jewish community of Montreal.[162] The handbill states:

> DO NOT EAT ANY MEAT!
>
> THE MEAT IS DRIPPING WITH HUMAN BLOOD!
>
> On Saturday night, the butchers struck and wounded several women and men who had peacefully crowded into the butcher shops. One woman and two men lie wounded in hospital. One of them, Mr. Klein, received a [blow from a] butcher's file in the head and is in critical condition.
>
> JEWISH WOMEN AND MEN: DO NOT PURCHASE ANY MEAT DRIPPING WITH HUMAN BLOOD, WITH THE BLOOD OF THOSE WHO ARE FIGHTING FOR CHEAPER MEAT.
>
> DO NOT SCAB, AND DO NOT BETRAY [EITHER] YOURSELVES OR THE JEWISH MASSES OF MONTREAL.
>
> Strike for cheap meat. Do not buy any meat until the strike will be won.
>
> Come in masses to a protest

---

156 "Stand by the Vaad Ho'ir," *Canadian Jewish Chronicle*, February 10, 1933, 1.

157 "Vaad Ho'Ir Advertises for New Shohtim," *Canadian Jewish Chronicle*, February 10, 1933, 8; "Va'ad ha-'Ir Bashlist Optsubrekhen Batsiungen mit Zayne Shoḥtim," *KA*, February 6, 1933; "Rabonim Velen Ekzaminiren Naye Shoḥtim," *KA*, March 1, 1933. Cf. H. Wolofsky, "Di Talmud Torahs un der Va'ad ha-'Ir," *KA*, February 7, 1933.

158 "Va'ad ha-'Ir Vert Folshtendiger Balebos iber sheḥita sistem" *KA*, March 10, 1933; "Va'ad ha-'Ir Ekzekutive Barikhtet vegen dem Kontrakt vos Tsi hot Geshlosen mit Naye Shoḥtim," KA March 13, 1933.

159 "Ershte Tseykhens fun Basar-Kosher Kampf Vayzen zikh oyf Mayn Strit," *KA*, March 23, 1933.

160 "Folshtendiger List fun di Va'ad ha-'Ir Butsher Sheper," *KA*, April 5, 1933.

161 "Paskvil fun 'Agudas ha-Shoḥtim' Ruft Aroys Greste Oyfregung in Shtot," *KA*, May 26, 1933.

162 See Tulchinsky, *Taking Root*, 204–230.

MASS MEETING
MONDAY, NOVEMBER 20
8:30 P.M.
IN CARMEN SILVA HALL
Protest against the gangster methods of the butchers and of those who stand behind them.[163]

In July 1933 kosher butcher shops went on a "stoppage" that lasted several weeks until August 1.[164] In August, the dispute went to arbitration which did not, however produce a unified recommendation.[165] It was not until September 17, 1933 that the complex dispute between the Community Council and the Agudat ha-Shoḥtim was finally sorted out, a new contract signed, and the erstwhile opponents began working together again, but not for long.[166]

When the wages of the *shoḥtim* were reduced,[167] Agudat ha-Shoḥtim called a strike that was to last from March to September 1934.[168] One of the reasons for the strike by Agudat ha-Shoḥtim, beyond the obvious wage issue, was that the administration of the Jewish Community Council was under increasing pressure to fulfill its promise to help fund Montreal Jewish educational institutions and had given significant amounts of money (over $31,000 between April 1933 and May 1935) to these institutions.[169] The strike action of the Agudat ha-Shoḥtim was publicly condemned. *Canadian Jewish Chronicle* editorialized that the "uncompromising Agudath ha-Shochtim," which had "let loose a torrent of abuse" directed at the Jewish Community Council, "stands today discredited and unmasked before the entire community."[170]

163 Alex Dworkin Canadian Jewish Archives, Jewish Community Council of Montreal, file 19b. The handbill is undated. It is in a file of newspaper clippings from late 1933 and early 1934. The date of the mass meeting is Monday, November 20. In 1933, November 20 fell on a Monday, so the incident most likely occurred in that year. Cf. "Drey 'Idishe Butshers Velen Darfen Durkhmaken Protses oyf Klage fun Angrif," *KA*, December 1, 1933.

164 "Basar Kosher 'Stopazh' vet Haynt Nokh nit Ge'endikt veren," *KA*, July 24, 1933; "Basar Kosher "Stopazh" Ge'endikt," *KA*, August 1, 1933.

165 "Di Tzvey Bazundere Refarats fun der Arbitratsion Komitee iber dem Sikhsukh tsvishen Va'ad ha-'Ir un di Alte Shoḥtim," *KA*, August 18, 1933.

166 "Sholom tsvishen Va'ad ha-'Ir un Shoḥtim Geshlosen," *KA*, September 17, 1933; "Vos Hert zikh in Va'ad ha-'Ir?," *KA*, October 21, 1933.

167 "Va'ad ha-Kashrus vert Formirt in Opozitsie tsum Va'ad ha-'Ir," *KA*, March 11, 1935.

168 *KA*, September 28, 1934.

169 *Keneder 'Id*, August 23, 1935.

170 *Canadian Jewish Chronicle*, June 2, 1933.

Given the kashrut situation in Montreal, it is no wonder that Toronto's *Hebrew Journal*, looking at the state of kashrut in Canada as a whole in 1934, could state: "the kosher meat question has brought disgrace [*shande*] on the name of the Jew in several communities. The rabbis are dragged into gentile courts and the kosher meat industry is widely considered a 'racket.'"[171] In March 1934 the problem of *trefa* [non-Council] butcher shops was described as a demoralizing plague that needed to be tackled head on by the Community Council.[172] A follow-up article on April 4 with the title "Are the *trefa* butchers really *tref*?" demonstrates that the Council still needed to educate a large segment of the public if it wished to truly control the kashrut of the city's kosher consumers.[173] This article was followed by a house-to-house campaign in which twenty canvassers promoted both the Jewish schools and the Council's kashrut.[174] At the same time the wholesale and retail butchers were given warnings to follow the Council's rules.[175] In June Justice Surveilleur of the Quebec Superior Court recognized the Council's authority to regulate kashrut in a case brought by a *shoḥet*, Uri Schwartz, whose slaughtering was certified by rabbis outside Montreal, but who was not certified by the Council and was therefore not allowed to practice as a *shoḥet* in Montreal.[176] Within weeks, the Jewish Community Council's authority would be challenged once again in court, this time by *shoḥet* Itamar Brenner who contested the Council's preliminary injunction against his slaughtering kosher meat.[177] When the Council went to court in September to make the injunction against Brenner permanent, it was opposed by Getsel Laxer and three other *shoḥtim* who contested the Council's monopoly on kashrut certification. In this case, Rabbi Rosenberg was called as a witness, because he had previously certified Brenner as a slaughterer for the Jewish community of Glace Bay, Nova Scotia.[178]

When Brenner moved to Montreal and attempted to establish himself as a *shoḥet* there, the Jewish Community Council claimed that he was not qualified

171 THJ, January 30, 1934. On issues of kashrut before American courts in this era, see Bernard J. Meislin, *Jewish Law in American Tribunals* (Hoboken, NJ: Ktav, 1976), 175–188.

172 "A Kampf gegen der Hefkerus in der Montrealer 'Idisher Kehile," *KA*, March 23, 1934.

173 "Tsi Zenen di Trefa Butshers Virklikh Tref?," *KA*, April 4, 1934.

174 "Va'ad ha-'Ir Firt durkh Hoyz-zu-Hoyz Kenves far Kashrus," *KA*, April 27, 1934.

175 "In Kampf gegen Tarfus," *KA*, May 27, 1934.

176 "Va'ad ha-'Ir Oytoritet Onerkent fun Gerikht," *KA*, June 15, 1934.

177 "Va'ad ha-'Ir Krigt aroys Tseitviligen Indjunktion tsu Farboten a Melamed fun Shekhten Behaymos far Basar Kosher," *KA*, July 4, 1934.

178 "Mitglider fun Agudas ha-Shoḥtim Treten aroys gegen Rabinat baym Va'ad ha-'Ir Indjonktion Farher," *KA*, September 28, 1934, 1.

to slaughter in the eyes of the Montreal rabbinate and had refused the rabbis' summons to appear before them.[179] The issue, then, was the authority of the Community Council and its Rabbinic Council to be the sole authority for kashrut in Montreal.[180] Getsel Laxer, in his testimony, denied that the Community Council had the sole authority to certify slaughterers. Rabbi Rosenberg's testimony affirmed that he certified Brenner to slaughter only poultry, not cattle. When Brenner was called to the stand, however, he testified that Rabbi Rosenberg had indeed asked him to slaughter cattle for the Jewish Community Council during the 1933 Agudat ha-Shoḥtim strike but that he had refused to betray his colleagues and become a scab.[181] The contentiousness of the hearing caused one of the lawyers to comment facetiously that this dispute should be brought before the League of Nations for resolution.[182] The emotions engendered by the Brenner dispute were high. In a poster evidently from this period, Rabbi Rosenberg came in for a savage attack from the Brenner-inspired dissidents in which he was described as a women's [*vaybersher*] tsaddiq with his earlocks [*pe'ot*] and with his check for $50.00, for which he declares food kosher.[183]

It was reported that the meatpacking companies of Montreal, for whom the kosher trade was a significant part of their business, had an interest in the results of this dispute and favored the dissident slaughterers over the Community Council.[184] Rumor had it that the dissident *shoḥtim* were plotting to make a separate deal with the wholesalers in order to circumvent the Council's control.[185] On November 15, the *Keneder Adler* reported that Justice Wilson had denied the Council a renewal of its temporary injunction against Brenner, a blow against its control of kashrut in Montreal.[186]

Entering the year 1935, it was clear that tensions between the Jewish Community Council and the Agudat ha-Shoḥtim had not been resolved by the Brenner trial. For Getsel Laxer and his partisans, it seemed clear that the best way to deal with the Jewish Community Council was to bring further court

---

179 *KA*, September 27, 1934.

180 "Use of Word 'Kosher' is Held Unwarranted," *Montreal Daily Star*, September 26, 1934, 1.

181 *KA*, September 30, 1934.

182 *KA*, September 28, 1934.

183 Alex Dworkin Canadian Jewish Archives.

184 *KA*, October 9, 1934.

185 "Va'ad ha-'Ir Konsil iz Entristet Herendig Barikht fun Shoḥtim Intriges," *KA*, October 8, 1934.

186 "Va'ad ha-'Ir Farlang far Tseitviligen Injunktsion gagen Brennern vert nit Baviligt," *KA*, November 15, 1934. Cf. "'Kosher' Meat Case Petition Dismissed," *Montreal Gazette*, November 15, 1934, 6.

cases in which the dissident *shoḥtim* could assert their independence from the Rabbinic Council.[187]

Meanwhile the Depression continued taking its financial toll. In December 1934, the annual meeting of the Jewish Community Council reported expenses of $83,741.72 and income of $73,737.99.[188] There was, in other words, a significant deficit of some $10,000 that needed to be dealt with. This resulted in pressure to reduce Council expenditures. There were two possible areas of reduction, each with its own pitfalls. One was to cut salaries and risk the renewed wrath of the *shoḥtim*, which would not be advisable in the aftermath of the Brenner decision. The other, no less risky, was to cut the financial subsidies it had been paying to Montreal Jewish educational and cultural institutions. But how could these already penniless institutions, already in a desperate state, absorb a further cut in their meager income?[189]

Thus the first challenge for the Community Council at the beginning of 1935 was financial. To help meet this challenge, on January 22, the Council presented its financial state to the rabbis, and proposed a 15–20% reduction in rabbinic salaries.[190] The fallout was not long in coming. On February 7, the Rabbinic Council issued a statement to the Community Council calling its statement "unheard-of and shameless effrontery [*ḥutzpah*]" and warned that in two weeks it would cut off its relationship with kosher meat supervision in the city.[191]

On February 19, the *Keneder Adler* reported that the Agudat ha-Shoḥtim, under the leadership of the ever militant Getsel Laxer, had broken its contract with the Jewish Commuity Council.[192] For its part, the Rabbinic Council tried to arrange a compromise in an attempt to attempt to placate the Agudat ha-Shoḥtim, while still keeping faith with the schools, which, under this compromise, would continue to get at least $5,000–10,000 annually.[193] But once the issue of pay cuts for the rabbis was broached, the situation deteriorated rapidly. On February 25, the *Keneder Adler* reported that the Community Council, in order to continue financial support to the schools, would have to reduce the

187 "Shohatim," *KA*, April 12, 1935.

188 "Va'ad ha-'Ir Endigt Yor mit Defizit fun $10,000; Nayer Rat fun 45 Erveylt," *KA*, December 10, 1934.

189 The Community Council's annual meeting reported that over $15,000 had been allocated to four schools and the Jewish People's Library. *KA*, December 10, 1934.

190 *KA*, March 13, 1935.

191 Copy of letter dated Thursday, Torah weekly portion *Terumah*, 5695 (February 7, 1935), RFA, Savannah.

192 "Agudas ha-Shoḥtim Brekht op Kontrakt mit Va'ad ha-'Ir," *KA*, February 19, 1935.

193 *KA*, February 24, 1935.

salaries of the supervising rabbis, which ranged from $25.00 to $65.00 weekly, by 15–20%. For the rabbis, confronted with this new and disturbing reality, enough was enough. The *Keneder Adler* reported that in response to the proposal to cut their wages, the majority of the members of the Rabbinic Council staged a walkout and joined the Agudat ha-Shoḥtim in their strike against the Council.[194] This created what Rabbi Hirsch Cohen somewhat facetiously described as "a strike in heaven" [*a strayk in himmel*].[195]

The Jewish Community Council, for its part, claimed that the kosher slaughtering it supervised was ongoing with well-known, qualified slaughterers and the supervision of rabbis Moshe Yom Tov Wachtfogel and Yitzḥak Shternberg.[196] This meant that only one of the eight rabbinic members of the Rabbinic Council, Rabbi Wachtfogel, was still on the job. The seven others walked out, including the chair and vice chair, rabbis Cohen and Rosenberg. Others participating in the walkout were Rabbis Aaron Zalmanovitz,[197] Abraham Samuel Dubitsky, Sheea Herschorn, Yosef David Berger, and Nathan Nata Aframovitz. These rabbis continued to regard themselves as constituting the Rabbinic Council, and in this guise they published a statement in the *Keneder Adler* that in Jewish Community Council slaughterhouses where five *shoḥtim* were normally stationed, there were now only three, and that the possibility for non-kosher meat to be marked as kosher under these conditions was very likely.[198]

The *Keneder Adler*, as in the past, firmly sided with the Community Council in its struggle against dissidents, and the editor Israel Rabinowitz stated on February 26 in his front page column: "The Community Council is, after all, the elected Kehilla corporation of Montreal Jewry. Any attempt to attack it, from whatever side, attacks the will of the majority."[199]

The Canadian Jewish Chronicle, which often commented on Jewish labor issues, used standard labor terms to describe this development, and spoke of

194 "Teyl fun Agudas ha-Rabonim Fareynigt zikh mit Oysgetretene Shoḥtim," *KA*, February 25, 1935.

195 This was the title of an essay written by Rabbi Hirsch Cohen and published in *KA*, April 12, 1935. On the reticence of rabbis to call their organization a trade union, see Asher Cohen and Aaron Kampinsky, "Religious Leadership in Israel's Religious Zionism: The Board of Rabbis," *Jewish Political Studies Review* 18, nos. 3–4 (2006): 129.

196 "Teyl fun agudas ha-rabonim fareynigt zikh mit oysgetretene shoḥtim" KA February 25, 1935.

197 On Rabbi Zalmanovitz as a Rosenberg supporter, see *Omer*, part 2, 60, 112.

198 *KA*, February 27, 1935.

199 *KA*, February 26, 1935.

the rabbis as having "downed their tools."[200] The Community Council charged the rabbis with having walked out for no reason and with no warning.[201] Other charges were hurled back and forth. The *Keneder Adler* reported on March 4 that Rabbi Cohen had stated in a meeting of leaders of congregations that the rabbis had walked out because the Community Council was concerned only with issues of kosher meat and not with other communal questions. Not so, retorted the Council, on the contrary, it had for years wanted the rabbis to fulfill functions other than kashrut, including visiting hospitals and schools, but that it was the rabbis who balked at such extra work.[202] Moreover, the Council charged, the rabbis had walked out because the Council continued to support the schools at the expense of their own salaries.[203]

In a response, published in the *Keneder Adler* on March 6, Rabbi Cohen quoted the "gentile Shakespeare" [*der 'orel Shekspir*], asserting that "the devil can quote scripture."[204] He pleaded for a nonpartisan committee to hear the rabbis' complaints.[205] The very next day, Israel Rabinowitz in his daily column replied to Rabbi Cohen, asking openly and pointedly who was at fault in this kashrut dispute.[206]

On March 11, the rhetoric ratcheted up a notch. The Jewish Community Council placed an advertisement in the *Keneder Adler*, claiming to employ eleven *shoḥtim* and ten *mashgiḥim* [supervisors], and to have oversight in sixty-seven butcher shops. More significantly, the advertisement claimed that rabbis Wachtfogel and Shternberg constituted the legitimate Rabbinic Council.[207] For their part, the dissident rabbis formed their own organization, the Kashrut Council. At a meeting held in the Chevra Kadisha synagogue, the Kashrut Council rabbis promised $10,000 yearly to support the Talmud Torah.[208]

---

200 *Canadian Jewish Chronicle*, March 1, 1935.

201 KA, March 3, 1935.

202 "Konferenz Drikt oys Tsutroy tsum Va'ad ha-'Ir," *KA*, March 4, 1935. *KA*, March 15, 1935, quoted Rabbi Herschorn who stated, in response to a request that the rabbis visit hospitals, that this was for priests who were there to "kidnap souls."

203 *KA*, March 4, 1935.

204 William Shakespeare, "Merchant of Venice," act 1, scene 3; "'Al Tagidu be-Gat," *KA*, March 6, 1935.

205 *KA*, March 6, 1935.

206 *KA*, March 7, 1935 This position was repeated in the next day's *Canadian Jewish Chronicle*, March 8, 1935.

207 "A Bisel Kashrus Statistik," *KA*, March 11, 1935.

208 "Va'ad ha-Kashrus vet Formirt in Opozitsie tsum Va'ad ha-'Ir," *KA*, March 11, 1935.

It is noteworthy that the dissident rabbis, organized as the Kashrut Council, referred to themselves as a specifically Orthodox body, as opposed to the Jewish Community Council, which was inclusive of elements in the Jewish community that were not strictly Orthodox. It is at this point that one of the major fault lines in the rabbinic walkout became publicly visible. In its inception, the Community Council was purposefully inclusive of elements of the "radical" Jewish community and undertook to financially support financially not merely the religiously oriented education of the Talmud Torah, but also the "radical" educational institutions of the Folks and Perets Shules. The fact that Rabbi Cohen offered the Kashrut Council's financial support only to the Talmud Torah indicates that he and his rabbinic colleagues wished to have no part in this inclusive coalition. Rabbi Cohen further charged that "radical" elements had gained control of the Community Council, and that the opponents of the rabbis and their Kashrut Council came from people who possessed neither *tefillin* [phylacteries] nor separate meat and dairy utensils at home.[209] This meant, of course, that Rabbi Cohen and his striking colleagues probably saw in this crisis an opportunity to create a strictly Orthodox institution and to put an end to communal subsidies of non-Orthodox Jewish schooling. As Israel Rabinovitch commented, this strike had now taken on the aspect of a "holy war." As far as he was concerned the key issue was money, though the rabbis wished people to believe that there were other issues.[210]

A handbill dated April 6, 1935[211] gives the rabbis' side of the affair. It is entitled "Why Change the Community Council?" [Farvos Darf Men Tshengen dem Va'ad ha-'Ir?]. It accused the Jewish Community Council of misallocation of funds: "The Community Council supports 'radical' educational institutions that teach Jewish children to become 'complete nonbelievers' [*apikorsim*]; and it further pays $25.00 weekly to a man unacceptable to the religious community, who was characterized as a 'black sinner' [*shvartsen ba'al avera*]." In general, the handbill portrayed the rabbis' battle against the Community Council as a fight for Torah and Judaism and against antireligious radicals. Furthermore, the rabbis reiterated their charges that the Community Council's kashrut supervision was inadequate. The Community Council, it was charged, places only three

209 Ibid. An article that appeared in the *KA* on March 15, 1935, "Nayer Va'ad ha-Kashrus vet fun keynem nit Geshitzt, Erklert Va'ad ha-'Ir," refuted this charge, saying that of 55 representatives to the Community Council, only 9 represented the "radical" institutions.

210 "Heyliger Krieg," *KA*, March 11, 1935, 1.

211 April 6 is a handwritten note on the handbill, the original of which is in the possession of the author. *KA*, April 9, 1935 reacts to this circular.

shoḥtim where the rabbis say there is a need for five. There is, furthermore, no rabbinic supervision of the Community Council's butcher shops, which thus operate in a state of anarchy [*hefker*]. Kashrut supervision for the upcoming Passover season, during which the rules are more complex than in the rest of the year, is now the hands of people who are as competent to do this job "as a Cossack knows [the intricate Aramaic liturgical hymn] *aqdamut*."

However partisan the message of this handbill was, it was signed "The new committee for peace." By April, in other words, while strong recriminations still flew back and forth between the two sides, each side was looking for a way out of the mess the rabbis' walkout had caused. The Community Council could not see dispensing with the services of the most important Orthodox rabbis of the city. The rabbis, for their part, had hoped to form a Kashrut Council as a communal institution that worked specifically for their religious interests in a way that the Community Council did not. However, their hope was disappointed because they failed to attract a recognized communal leader to become the head of the Kashrut Council. They had hoped to persuade Mr. A. Drazin, a vice-president of the *Va'ad ha-'Ir*, to become the Kashrut Council's president and it was reported in the *Keneder Adler* on March 15 that he had accepted this post.[212] The very next day, however, the newspaper reported Drazin's claim that he had not in fact accepted the post.[213] In retrospect, it was likely the Kashrut Council's failure to attract viable lay leadership that ultimately doomed the rabbis' walkout to failure.

Israel Rabinovitch commented on April 21, "One day this [dispute] will be settled and we will have to look each other in the face."[214] Two days later, a meeting held at the Nusaḥ Ari Synagogue called for a peace conference between both sides of the conflict.[215]

A key break in the conflict came about a month later, when rabbis Rosenberg, Aframovitz, and Berger petitioned to return to the Jewish Community Council and were reinstated. They were accepted back into the Rabbinic Council, joining with rabbis Wachtfogel and Shternberg. According to the *Keneder Adler*, the three rabbis had seen the error of their ways and had written letters to the Community Council expressing regret for their actions. Due to the extenuating circumstances, the Jewish Community Council had decided to take

212 *KA*, March 11, 1935.

213 Yudel Rosenberg, "Kazov va-Sheker," *KA*, March 15, 1935, 1. Cf. also *KA*, March 17, 1935.

214 *KA*, April 21, 1935.

215 *KA*, April 23, 1935.

them back.[216] What the newspaper reportage did not say was that on May 10, Rosenberg's youngest son, Rabbi Abraham Isaac Rosenberg, came before the Community Council and pleaded with it to take his father back since he was now seriously ill and could not take any more of this aggravation. The request was granted on May 16.[217]

This turn of events constituted a cruel blow to the hopes of the dissident rabbis, and received an immediate response from the remaining dissidents. A handbill was issued entitled "Appeal to All Shuls and Orthodox Jews in Montreal." It was signed by Rabbi Zalmanovitz the most prominent dissident then in the city (Rabbi Cohen was at that point in the United States) proclaiming that the founding of communal organizations [*kehillot*] in cities such as Winnipeg, Toronto, and Montreal had been unmitigated disasters for Orthodoxy. The Jewish Community Council continued to support the radical schools where students were taught not to believe in the Torah of Moses and whose leaders had no need for either the rabbis or the Talmud Torahs.[218] Rabbi Rosenberg responded on the next day on behalf of the Rabbinic Council that he had recently rejoined with a call for the remaining dissident rabbis to rejoin as well. Resignedly he stated that from this sort of communal division, no one profited except Satan, whose purpose it is to increase senseless hatred in Israel.[219]

Through the summer of 1935, the newly reconstituted Rabbinic Council functioned with five members: rabbis Rosenberg, Wachtfogel, Aframovitz, Berger, and Shternberg.[220] Remaining for the moment outside the new consensus were rabbis Cohen, Zalmanovitch, Dubitsky, and Herschorn. This continuing division within the Montreal Orthodox rabbinate is symbolized by the fact that, when Rabbi Abraham Isaac ha-Kohen Kook, Ashkenazic chief rabbi of Palestine under the British Mandate, died in early September, an official Montreal eulogy was delivered by rabbis Berger and Afromovitz of the Community Council.[221]

216 *KA*, May 24, 1935.

217 Jewish Community Council Protocol Book 1934–1935, May 10 and May 16, Alex Dworkin Canadian Jewish Archives Jewish Community Council of Montreal.

218 Handbill dated 22 Iyar 5695 (May 25, 1935), in possession of the author.

219 Yudel Rosenberg, "Hodo'a me-ha-Rav Yudel Rosenberg," *KA*, May 26, 1935.

220 These five rabbis signed a pronouncement of the Montreal Rabbinic Court. *KA*, July 3, 1935.

221 *KA*, September 9, 1935. Leah Rosenberg (*Errand Runner*, 114) asserts that Rabbi Rosenberg was a candidate to replace Rabbi Kook.

A few days later, however, the leading holdout rabbi, Hirsch Cohen, returned to Montreal after what the *Keneder Adler* described as "a lengthy vacation" and visited the newspaper's offices.[222] Cohen immediately began reasserting his presence in the city and, on September 23, the *Keneder Adler* reported that he and Rabbi Zalmanovitz had publicly eulogized Rabbi Kook a second time.[223] The division between the rabbinic Council and the holdout dissident rabbis was still apparent in early October, when a *Keneder Adler* report presented Rabbi Wachtfogel as spokesman for the Rabbinic Council.[224] However, on October 17, when the Rabbinic Council appealed for funds for the Rabbi Isaac Elchanan Yeshiva in New York, Rabbi Hirsch Cohen was once again listed as chair of the Rabbinic Council, taking his former place.[225] By the annual meeting of the Jewish Community Council in December of that year, things had returned to at least a semblance of normalcy and it was reported that the Community Council was once again in control of "96%" of the kosher slaughter in Montreal.[226]

So did the "strike in heaven" result in anything meaningful? On the one hand, the rabbinic personalities and the financial situation that brought about the crisis of February to October 1935 remained almost exactly the same. On the other hand, the crisis did bring about some important structural changes in the way the rabbis and *shoḥtim* did their business.

One of these changes involved the payment of rabbis and slaughterers. The Jewish Community Council's income was truly insufficient to support eight rabbis and twenty-four *shoḥtim*. Rabbis' salaries were thus cut still further so that in the Community Council budget presented in October 1936,[227] the salary of the chair of the Rabbinic Council, Rabbi Hirsch Cohen, was set at $40.00 per week, the vice-chair got $35.00 weekly, two other rabbis got $25.00 a week, and four others received $50–75 monthly. For their part, the *shoḥtim* were divided into three categories in terms of their work and remuneration: able-bodied people with large families, able-bodied people with small families or other sources of income, and older men with limited physical strength.

These measures were unpopular with the rabbis and *shoḥtim*, but served to mitigate the budgetary crisis by trimming what had been an inflated payroll. In

222 *KA*, September 13, 1935.
223 *KA*, September 23, 1935.
224 *KA*, October 2, 1935.
225 *KA*, October 17, 1935.
226 *KA*, December 16, 1935.
227 *KA*, October 30, 1936.

fact, many of the men on the payroll were rabbis who came to Montreal from the ruined Jewish communities of Eastern Europe after World War I and had been given jobs in the Community Council even though they were not fully able to work.[228]

The rabbinic walkout of 1935 also clearly exposed the changing role of the Orthodox rabbinate, as well as new expectations that rabbis ought to be performing pastoral duties like other clergymen, such as visiting the sick. It further delineated the tension within the immigrant Jewish community of Montreal between Orthodox and "radical" Jews that would ultimately result in the Jewish Community Council becoming a decidedly Orthodox institution with hardly a memory of its initial "radical" presence.[229]

In the 1930s Rabbi Yudel Rosenberg had an ambition, fated to be unfulfilled, to go to the Land of Israel to live. In 1931 he spoke of his hope that he would soon be able to go to live in the Holy Land with his family.[230] He corresponded on this topic with his friend, Rabbi Benzion Uziel (1880–1953), then Chief Rabbi of Tel-Aviv. On March 5, 1935 Rabbi Uziel wrote him from Palestine concerning the difficulties Rosenberg had encountered in getting an immigration certificate and regretfully told him he could be of no help.[231] Possibly as a result of this disappointing news, on March 10, 1935, Rabbi Rosenberg, who was also undoubtedly feeling financially pressed by the strike, attempted to sell his one asset other than his books, the plots of land he had purchased in Palestine.[232] Ironically, on the third day of mourning [*shiva*] for his death, in October 1935 a Palestine Immigration Certificate in his name arrived. He had apparently applied for it without his children's' knowledge.[233]

On September 3, 1935, Rabbi Rosenberg made his will. His assets were few. He gave his son, Abraham Isaac all his books except the copies of his *Zohar* edition that were for sale. These copies, housed in Montreal, New York, and Warsaw, as well as his land in Palestine he bequeathed to Sarah Greenberg.

---

228 *KA*, April 21, 1935. On Rosenberg's reaction to the massacres of Jews in the Ukraine in the years 1919–1921, see ZT, vol. 5, 52, 152–153.

229 On the later history of the Community Council, see Steven Lapidus, "Orthodoxy in Transition: The Vaad Ha'ir of Montreal in the Twentieth Century" (PhD diss., Concordia University, 2011).

230 *Omer*, part 2, 5.

231 Benzion Uziel to Yudel Rosenberg, 30 Adar I 5695 (March 5, 1935), Arkhion Histori, Iriyat Tel-Aviv-Yaffo, 2016/95.

232 Letter, March 10, 1935, RFA, Savannah.

233 Yehuda Rosenberg, "Memorandum [on the Rosenberg Family]," 3. Leah Rosenberg, *The Errand Runner*, 115, say it happened six weeks after he died.

Yudel Rosenberg's last extant letter, dated 3 Tishrei 5696 (September 30, 1935), speaks to his terrible financial situation. It was addressed to his physician, Dr. A. Stillman, explaining why he could not pay a $5.00 doctor's bill: "Surely you know that it has already been a year that the Community Council has ceased paying wages to the Rabbinic Council, and to a part of them it pays only a third [of their salary]." Because of this he was unable to go to the country in the past summer for fresh air and was unable to pay his bill.[234]

Yudel Rosenberg had a history of heart trouble and had experienced a heart attack in the late 1920s. In a letter to his son, Meir Joshua, of December 1934 he complained of ill health.[235] On Simḥat Torah of 5696 (October 20, 1935), while speaking in the synagogue, Rabbi Rosenberg suffered a major stroke and died three days later on October 23, 1935.[236]

His funeral procession began at his home on 4587 Jeanne Mance and proceeded to the Hadras Kodesh Shul on Ste. Dominique and from there to the Adas Yeshurun Shul. At Hadras Kodesh the first to speak was Rabbi Sheea Herschorn, who alluded to the many controversies surrounding Rabbi Rosenberg in Montreal and spoke of them as "controversy for the sake of Heaven [*le-shem shamayim*]." His eulogy was followed by that of Rabbi Hirsch Cohen. At Adas Yeshurun the first to speak and master of ceremonies was *Keneder Adler* publisher Hirsch Wolofsky, who spoke of Rabbi Rosenberg's great spiritual bequest. Yudel Rosenberg's two rabbinic sons, Meir Joshua and Abraham Isaac also spoke. Meir Joshua in his eulogy asked the community to support his widow and to build a shelter [*ohel*] over his grave.[237]

An anonymous obituary published in the *Keneder Adler* spoke of Rosenberg's love of spiritual matters and how his writing provided him a retreat from the conflicts that beset him. The obituary also spoke of Rosenberg as one of the interesting, old-fashioned rabbis whose fate took them from the places where

234 Yudel Rosenberg to A. Stillman, Jewish Public Library, Jewish Canadiana Collection: Yehuda Rosenberg.

235 Yudel Rosenberg to Meir Joshua Rosenberg, 3, Ḥanukkah 5695 (December 3, 1934), BMA, Jerusalem.

236 "Ha-Rav Yudel Rosenberg Ernst Krank," *KA*, October 23, 1935; "Ha-Rav Yudel Rosenberg Niftar gevoren," *KA*, October 24, 1935. Leah Rosenberg, *The Errand Runner*, 114, 117–118.

237 "Groyser Olam Bagleyt ha-Rav Rosenberg zu Eybiger Ru," *KA*, October 25, 1935. On May 10, 1937 the Community Council agreed to raise the amount it was paying to Rabbi Rosenberg's widow from $10.00 to 25.00 weekly. Leah Rosenberg, *The Errand Runner*, 121.

they belonged and threw them into a new world where they were not understood.[238]

Despite all the struggles and tribulation Rabbi Yudel Rosenberg found during his years in Montreal, it would seem that, on balance, he was at least somewhat happy there. In 1934, Rabbi Rosenberg summed up his career by saying:

> For nearly all my days until I reached old age I did not know rest and peace. I was always full of tribulation from the troubles of poverty and the pain of persecution and suffering. ... But thank God when I came to old age I rested and was somewhat at peace in this city of Montreal.[239]

---

238 "Ha-Rav Yudel Rosenberg A"h," *KA*, October 25, 1935.

239 *Omer*, part 2, 5.

CHAPTER 6

"Better to be in Gehinnom": Yudel Rosenberg's Halakhic Voice

From the moment Rabbi Yudel Rosenberg determined to make his way in the world as a rabbi in a crowded and competitive field, he set about gaining the credentials necessary to be seen not merely as an authentic rabbi, but as a leader among rabbis. We have seen how he worked to obtain rabbinic ordinations from several prominent Polish rabbis in chapter 3. As we have also seen in that chapter, his Talmudic commentary, *Yadot Nedarim,* which was published in 1902, during his Warsaw period, was one forceful way to assert his rabbinic credentials.

Other publications designed to attract the attention of his rabbinic colleagues were to follow. Yudel Rosenberg had entered an Orthodox rabbinate in the midst of great change in the ways rabbis expressed themselves and communicated with each other. One of the ways in which that change was expressed was the appearance of rabbinic journals designed to present the current work of contemporary Orthodox rabbis and in general to foster greater professional communication among rabbis. At the beginning of the twentieth century, when Rabbi Rosenberg began to publish, rabbinic journals constituted a relatively new phenomenon, though Hebrew-language periodicals, mostly sponsored by *maskilim,* had been established for over a century.[1] The first rabbinic journal in Eastern Europe was founded and edited by Rabbi Israel Lipkin (Salanter, 1810–1883). Its title was *Tevuna,* and it was first published in Memel in 1860/1.[2]

1 On these periodicals, see Menuḥah Gilbo'a, *Leksikon ha-'Itonut ha-'Ivrit ba-Me'ot ha-Shemoneh 'Esreh veha-Tesha' 'Esreh* (Tel Aviv: Mossad Bialik, 1992).

2 Salanter's periodical *Tevuna* is available online: http://www.hebrewbooks.org/pdfpager.aspx?sits=1&req=44040&st=%u05EA%u05E8%22%u05DB. On its significance, see Norman Solomon, *The Analytic Movement: Hayyim Soloveitchik and His Circle* (Atlanta: Scholars Press, 1993), 48. Cf. Immanuel Etkes, *Rabbi Israel Salanter and the Mussar Movement: Seeking the Torah of Truth* (Philadelphia: Jewish Publication Society, 1993).

By the turn of the twentieth century, the number of rabbinic journals was increasing.[3] In Warsaw at that time there existed such a journal, *Sha'arei Torah*, to which Rabbi Rosenberg contributed three short articles, published in 1903 and 1904.[4] This journal was edited by Rabbi Isaac ha-Kohen Feigenbaum, who as we have seen was well acquainted with Yudel Rosenberg.

Clearly, Rabbi Yudel Rosenberg saw potential in rabbinic periodicals and determined to publish one of his own in his quest for rabbinic recognition. A successful journal would translate into influence and prestige for its editor. If really successful, it might even gain him some needed additional income. Rabbi Rosenberg took the plunge and founded his own rabbinic journal in 1908. He named it *Kol Torah* [The Voice of Torah]. As he stated in the prospectus that was to be posted in synagogues and houses of study, the journal was primarily directed toward practicing rabbis. It was meant to come out three times a year. As Yudel Rosenberg conceptualized it, in each issue, there were going to be three sections. The first, entitled "The Four Cubits of Halakha," was designed to showcase rabbinic solutions to halakhic questions and its contributors were to be restricted to those actually practicing as rabbis and religious judges. The second section, entitled "Sprouts and Flowers for the Torah" was to consist of *pilpul* and explications of passages in the Talmud and the codes of halakha. The third, "Words of Aggada," was meant to include "pleasant explanations of the verses of the Bible, the aggada of the Talmud and the Midrashim in the purity of holiness according to the spirit of eternal Judaism."[5] The latter two sections were to be open to "non-professional rabbis"—and even rabbinic students—so long as their contributions were judged by the editor (Rosenberg) to be of a proper standard.

Yudel Rosenberg's *Kol Torah* saw the light of day and in all, three numbers of the journal appeared (with consecutive pagination). As might have been expected, Rabbi Rosenberg's writings were prominently featured in this journal and he wrote numerous contributions in all three issues.[6] *Kol Torah*, however, was far from a one-man show. The great majority of the contributions

---

3 Menahem Slae, "Halakhic Periodicals," in *Encyclopaedia Judaica*, second edition, vol. 8, ed. Michael Berenbaum and Fred Skolnik (Detroit: Macmillan Reference USA, 2007), 258–259.

4 "Number 118," *Sha'arei Torah* 1, no. 11 (1903): 356; "Number 40," *Sha'arei Torah* 2, no. 4 (1904): 130–132; "Number 79," *Sha'arei Torah* 2, no. 9 (1904): 280–285.

5 KT, title page.

6 Of the fifty-seven pieces that appeared in the three numbers of KT, Yudel Rosenberg wrote fourteen.

to *Kol Torah* came from rabbis throughout the Russian Empire as well as from Germany, Romania and South Africa.[7]

Kol Torah gave Rabbi Rosenberg an editorial platform from which to make known his opinion on halakhic issues current within the Jewish community. Thus in the second issue, he wrote an editorial condemning the current scandal in Warsaw Jewish community: Jews buying cheaply priced *tefillin* were finding that they housed no proper parchment.[8] More importantly, the journal gave him an outlet to publish a number of responsa on contemporary halakhic questions, such as the kashrut of cream of tartar, a byproduct of non-kosher wine, and the propriety of wearing shoes meant to make noise at each step on the Sabbath.[9] These contributions enabled him to present himself as a professional halakhist, whose reputation could spread far beyond the confines of Warsaw.

Rosenberg's rabbinic journal folded after its first year. It is not known whether the demise of *Kol Torah* was due to financial difficulties, such as lack of a sufficient number of subscribers, or whether a dearth of material sent in by other rabbis played a role. In all probability, it was a combination of these two factors.[10]

When Rabbi Yudel Rosenberg moved from Warsaw to Łódź, shortly after the demise of his journal, he was still seeking recognition as a rabbinic authority, and among his prodigious literary output in his years in Łódź, one prominent category was that of halakhic guides. Toward the end of his career, in 1931, a reviewer of one of his books stated that Rabbi Rosenberg had a talent for creating useful books.[11] This talent certainly is evident with respect to his halakhic output in Łódź, as we will see.

The nineteenth and twentieth centuries witnessed the creation of a new format for the presentation of halakha, a major example of which is the book *Ḥafetz Ḥayyim* (1873), written by Rabbi Israel Meir Kagan (1838–1933). As Justin Lewis states, Rabbi Kagan "compiled and synthesized for the first time the many scattered teachings of Jewish texts regarding *lashon hara* ... effectively

---

7 Contributors to KT came from numerous places in the Russian Empire, including Warsaw, Łódź, Riga, Boisk, Kishinev, Kharkov, Berdichev, and Radom. In addition there were contributions from Ştefăneşti, Romania; Würzberg, Germany; and Ladysmith, South Africa.

8 KT, 20.

9 KT, 43–44; *Yadot*, 38.

10 In several places in KT, Yudel Rosenberg appealed both for contributions and subscriptions. See KT, title page, 20.

11 Ḥaim Kruger, "'Ateret Tif'eret," *KA*, May 8, 1931.

building them into a new category of Jewish law."[12] Precisely this sort of innovation may be seen in the halakhic guides compiled in Łódź in the early twentieth century by Rabbi Yudel Rosenberg.

These halakhic guides were generally responses to Rabbi Rosenberg's perception of what the public needed. The first of them, entitled *Sefer ha-Prozbul* (1910), was a small pamphlet explaining *prozbul,* the custom, enjoined in rabbinic literature, of circumventing the abolition of debts decreed by the Torah in the sabbatical year by officially giving the debt to a rabbinic court for collection. It is interesting to note that this custom had been largely abandoned by Ashkenazic Jews because of the prevalence of the opinion among medieval rabbinic authorities that *prozbul* was only valid when the Sabbatical [*shemitah*] laws were fully in effect. Thus Rabbi Moses Isserles stated: "We do not have the custom of *shemitah* at all in this era."[13] In the era contemporary with Rabbi Rosenberg, Rabbi Yeḥiel Mikhl ha-Levi Epstein, author of the influential halakhic work *'Arukh ha-Shulḥan,* expressed the opinion that there is no need at all for the custom of *prozbul.*[14]

In his pamphlet Rabbi Rosenberg argued, to the contrary, that *prozbul* continued to be valid outside the Land of Israel and in the present time, basing himself on the opinions of Rabbis Isaiah Horowitz (Shelah, c. 1555–1630) and Joel Sirkis (Baḥ, 1561–1640).[15] In parallel columns in Hebrew and Yiddish, Rosenberg explained in detail to his readers how exactly to enact a *prozbul.* As the year in which the guide was published, 5671 (1910/11), was considered to be a sabbatical year, Rosenberg's brief "public service" pamphlet discussed just the sort of topical issue that he hoped would gain the attention of the public. It is evident as well that Rabbi Rosenberg hoped that the pamphlet would generate some income for him. Indeed on the back page the reader is instructed to obtain the pamphlets at the *Prozbul* Organization [*Histadrut ha-Prozbul*], obviously led by Rabbi Rosenberg, who perhaps hoped many Jews would engage

12 Justin Jaron Lewis, "Verbal Exuberance and Social Engineering: Gossip in Hafetz Hayim," *Studies in Religion* 44, no. 2 (2015): 208. Cf. Binyamin Brown, "From Principles to Rules and From Musar to Halakha: The Hafetz Hayim's Rulings on Libel and Gossip," *Dine Yisrael: An Annual of Jewish Law and Israeli Family Law* 25 (2008): 171–256; Ira Robinson, "Introduction," in Simcha Fishbane, *The Boldness of an Halakhist: an Analysis of the Writings of Rabbi Yechiel Mechel Halevi Epstein* (Boston: Academic Studies Press, 2008), xiii–xxii.

13 *Shulḥan Arukh, Ḥoshen Mishpat* 67:1.

14 Alfred S. Cohen, "Pruzbul," *Journal of Halacha and Contemporary Society* 28 (1994): 22–23.

15 *Prozbul,* 1.

his help in this matter.[16] While it is possible that other publications specifically devoted to *prozbul* existed, it is to be noted that Yudel Rosenberg's 1910 publication on *prozbul* is the first printed publication entirely devoted to this custom extant in the collection of the National Library of Israel.

The second of Rabbi Yudel Rosenberg's publications dealing with halakhic matters published during his sojourn in Łódź was far more ambitious in scope and was designed to give him a reputation as a halakhic authority with respect to the impact of new technology on the major industry of Łódź—the manufacture of cloth. Like the *Prozbul* pamphlet, this publication advocated the renewed observance on a commandment of the Torah that had often been neglected by Jews—in this case, the prohibition of *sha'atnez,* cloth made from a mixture of wool and linen.

Łódź, often called the "Polish Manchester," was a major center for cloth manufacture in the Russian Empire. Many of its cloth factories were owned by Jews, and many of the workers in these factories were Jewish.[17] In the period just prior to World War I, when Rabbi Rosenberg was living in Łódź, the city was in economic recession resulting from the Revolutionary events of 1905–1907 as well as the worldwide aftereffects of the Panic of 1907. Yudel Rosenberg was convinced that he knew the reason for this recession, and hence its cure.[18] It all had to do with the introduction of new technology for cloth manufacturing which enabled manufacturers to recycle old garments into new thread. This new technology may have fostered more efficient manufacture of cloth, but at the same time it caused Jews to fall into the sin of manufacturing *sha'atnez*—the mingling of wool and linen. The recession was God's punishment.

Rabbi Rosenberg issued two pamphlets on this subject, one in Hebrew and the other in Yiddish. The Hebrew pamphlet, entitled *Darsha Tsemer u-Fishtim* was largely a halakhic discourse on the technicalities of the *sha'atnez* issue. Like his previous halakhic pamphlet that dealt with *prozbul,* it may be the first Hebrew publication devoted specifically to the halakha of *sha'atnez.*[19] Far more interesting

16 *Prozbul,* back page. It is to be noted that Yudel Rosenberg's publication on *prozbul* is the first such publication entirely devoted to this custom extant in the collection of the National Library of Israel.

17 *Jewish Encyclopedia,* s.v. "Łódź."

18 Leib Fox adds that the booklet was published during a strike. Fox, *100 Years of Hebrew and Yiddish Literature in Canada,* 274.

19 *Sefer Darsha Tsemer u-Fishtim* [hereafter *Darsha*] (Łódź: Yitsḥaq Shlomovits, 1912), especially 12–13. The National Library of Israel catalogue records no publication on *sha'atnez* published earlier than Rabbi Rosenberg's pamphlet. The Hebrew responsum was republished in *Omer,* part 2, 88–97.

is Rabbi Rosenberg's parallel Yiddish pamphlet, *Der Krizis fun Łódź Varshe.*[20] In this publication, Rabbi Rosenberg allowed himself go far beyond the technical halakhic analysis of *sha'atnez*. He rather sought to present his findings to a wider, Yiddish-speaking audience, one presumably less impressed with the fluency and dexterity of his halakhic argument. In *Krizis*, Rosenberg sought to expose the cause of the crisis that had hit the Jewish weavers of Łódź, which he lamented with rhetoric recalling the biblical book of Lamentations,[21] and possibly solve it.[22] He was at pains to present himself to his readers as having a firm grasp of much more than rabbinic literature, even though he realized that this work was not going to be acceptable to those who had already thrown off the yoke of Judaism.[23] It is important to understand that in presenting himself as a man familiar with secular subjects, Rabbi Rosenberg was not merely presenting a public image. It is likely that this was his self-image as well. As he stated in the introduction, "He who is speaking to you is no small-town rabbinic scholar (lit. "idler," *batlan*) who has no knowledge of economics, but ... rather a man who is knowledgeable in economics and in all worldly matters."[24]

Despite this bold assertion as well as some small attempts to back it up with an historical reference,[25] Rosenberg's approach to the problem faced by the Łódź textile industry was basically theological in nature. He attributed the recession which had struck Łódź, and which had resulted in unemployment, closed factories, starvation among the poor, and an increase in crime, to the new process of recycling old textiles to create new thread which resulted in the mingling of wool and linen and hence the transgression of the Biblical prohibition of *sha'atnez*.[26] As he stated, "It is only stupidity to say that the times are to blame for this [crisis]. ... We Jews must believe that the Creator of the world is [at work] here ... that this is a punishment from heaven for the sin of *sha'atnez*."[27]

Rabbi Rosenberg, of course, was hardly original in his theological analysis of economic cycles. Thus, the Orthodox weekly *Ha-Levanon* had similarly

---

20 See especially *Krizis*.

21 *Krizis*, 1.

22 *Darsha*, title page, 3

23 *Darsha*, 1, 3.

24 *Darsha*, 1.

25 *Darsha*, 7.

26 *Darsha*, 3. Cf. *Krizis*, 2–3.

27 *Krizis*, 5.

attributed the recession of 1874, which had a devastating effect on the city of Odessa, to the sins of its Jewish community.[28]

Rosenberg's purpose in publishing his pamphlets on the *sha'atnez* crisis in Łódź seems to have been twofold. He likely expected to gain more public recognition as well as a strengthened position within rabbinic circles in Łódź. There is also a distinct possibility that here as well he was looking to augment his income, because he ended his analysis with a plea to establish a rabbinic authority to certify the non-*sha'atnez* nature of recycled cloth. In other words, he wanted to make observant Jews as sensitive to the prohibition of *sha'atnez* as they were to halakhot concerning Shabbat and kashrut.[29] This was an endeavour that he, having been the first to bring public attention to the problem, was surely qualified to lead.[30]

If Yudel Rosenberg's halakhic works had not promoted his rabbinic career in Poland to the extent that he would have wished, he nonetheless had not given up on the idea that he could gain public recognition and advance his career through restoring or reviving halakhic issues that were being widely neglected in the Jewish community. It is thus telling that Rabbi Rosenberg persisted in his halakhic publications after his move to Canada despite the limited printing facilities available to him. It testifies to their importance in his plans.

The first of the halakhic works Rabbi Rosenberg published after he arrived in Canada in 1913 was *Miqveh Yehuda*, which was probably published circa 1917–1918[31] though it had likely been originally conceived earlier in Łódź. It dealt with the problematic situation in both Europe and North America of the Judaic laws of menstrual purification for married women. Judaic law and custom specified that married women who menstruated could not have sexual relations with their husbands until they had undergone ritual purification in a ritual pool [*miqveh*]. The major assault on the premodern Judaic tradition that was characteristic of modernity in nineteenth-century Europe included the issue of *miqveh*. By the turn of the twentieth century, it had become patently obvious to all observers—partisans as well as opponents of *miqveh*—that, along with many other Judaic rituals, the observance of female ritual purification in the *miqveh* had fallen upon hard times. That this was true also in Poland is evident in a letter written to Rabbi Rosenberg on March 29, 1913 by Rabbi Petaḥia

28 *ha-Levanon*, July 25, 1874, cited in Steven Zipperstein, *The Jews of Odessa*, 132.

29 *Krizis*, 10–11.

30 *Krizis*, 10.

31 At the earliest, this book may have been published sometime in 1917. See chapter 4 in this book, note 33.

Hornblass, one of the leading rabbis of Warsaw, which Rosenberg published in facsimile as a sort of "approbation" to his work.[32] Rabbi Hornblass stated that Yudel Rosenberg's book would be "useful in these times when the 'enlightenment' has spread greatly."[33] The situation for *miqveh* observance may have been bleak in Europe, but it was much more severe in North America, where some witnesses at the turn of the twentieth century felt that *miqveh* observance had all but disappeared from the American Jewish community.[34] As Rosenberg described the situation in the pamphlet's preface:

> There are some [women] who because of a foolish embarrassment refuse to travel [to a *miqveh*], and not merely to travel [long distances] but also to go [for a short distance] to the place of immersion. The enlightened ones among them say that according to the science of "hygiene," there is danger lurking in immersing in a communal *miqveh*. The prohibition [punished by] "cutting off" [*karet*, the exclusion from the community, here due to sexual relations while being] a menstruant has almost been [considered as] permitted for them for they have transgressed again and again. Woe to the ears that have heard this.[35]

The attitude Rabbi Rosenberg referred to seems to have been reasonably widespread among Jewish women in this era, one of whom recalls: "I told my mother ... you will not take me to the *mikve*. I have a nice clean *mikve* right in the house ... A nice, clean bath."[36] The woman in question may have been reacting to a report by the New York Board of Health at the beginning of the twentieth century that as many as 300 women immersed themselves in a *miqveh* before the water was changed.[37] Zionist leader Golda Meir shared this

32 This approbation is dated Saturday night, weekly Torah portion *Shmini*, 5673 (March 29, 1913).

33 *Miqveh*, 2. Cf. Yitzhak Alfasi, *Jewish Glimpses of Warsaw* (New York: CIS Communications, 1992), 37.

34 Weinberg, *The World of Our Mothers*, 94.

35 *Miqveh*, 3. Cf. *Omer*, part 2, 65. In a later sermon Yudel Rosenberg blamed a number of diseases like diphtheria and scarlet fever on the neglect of cleansing menstrual blood. *Omer*, part 1, 22.

36 Neil M. and Ruth S. Cowan, *Our Parents' Lives: The Americanization of Eastern European Jews* (New York: Basic Books, 1989), 277.

37 Michael A. Meyer, "New Waters in an Old Vessel: A History of Mikveh in Modern Judaism," in *Between Jewish Tradition and Modernity: Rethinking an Old Opposition, Essays in Honor of David Ellenson*, ed. Michael A. Meyer and David N. Myers (Detroit: Wayne State University

attitude and referred to immersion in the *miqveh* as "primitive,"[38] and her view was very clearly shared by many, including prominent American Reform rabbi David Phillipson, who referred to the practice as "barbarism."[39] While attempts were made to establish *miqvehs,* particularly in New York City,[40] and to promote their use through the publication of pamphlets and manuals, it was difficult in the extreme to overcome the public image of these ritual pools as uninviting, unsanitary and an invasion of one's privacy.[41]

Rabbi Rosenberg had come to understand that mere persuasion was unlikely to convince large numbers of North American Jewish women to immerse themselves in the communal *miqvehs* that actually existed. He also clearly knew that in many smaller Jewish communities there were no *miqveh* facilities whatsoever and that in general unmotivated women would be reluctant to visit *miqvehs,* however convenient the location.

Given the situation, Rabbi Rosenberg decided on a bold halakhic plan. He was going to render it possible for every Jewish home to contain its own *miqveh.* As he stated in the title page of his pamphlet: "it is possible to make a small kosher *miqveh* for ritual immersion in every home ... to save many souls from the punishment of 'cutting off.'"[42]

The major halakhic problem Rabbi Rosenberg faced in creating a viable home *miqveh* was that the water filling it needed to come from a source of flowing water, such as a lake or stream.[43] His basic halakhic argument was that, in modern cities, most dwellings had running water piped in from such natural sources. If, as he argued, the metal pipes that brought the water to the home did not invalidate the water for the purpose of *miqveh,* then he had solved the most important problem—the water source for the *miqveh.* All the rest was mere detail—how best to alter one's bathroom in order to construct a kosher immersion bath. This was the essential content of his pamphlet in both Hebrew and Yiddish. As in the *sha'atnez* pamphlet written in Łódź, Yudel Rosenberg

Press, 2014), 145. Cf. Celia J. Bergoffen, "The Lower East Side's Synagogues, Tenement, and Russian Bathhouse Mikva'ot and the Excavation of a Mikvah at 5 Allen Street," *American Jewish History* 101, no. 2 (April 2017): 163–196.

38 Cited in Guy Ben-Porat, *Between State and Synagogue: The Secularization of Contemporary Israel* (Cambridge: Cambridge University Press, 2013), 66.

39 Meyer, "New Waters in an Old Vessel," 145.

40 Andrew R. Heinze, *Adapting to Abundance: Jewish Immigrants, Mass Consumption, and the Search for American Identity* (New York: Columbia University Press, 1990), 57–58.

41 Joselit, *New York's Jewish Jews,* 117–121.

42 *Miqveh,* title page.

43 *Shulḥan Arukh, Yoreh De'ah,* chapter 201.

recognized the important impact that modern technology had made on the observance of halakha and the great potential beneficial results resulting from this recognition. As he stated, because of his publication: "there is no doubt that many Jewish souls will be spared the punishment of 'cutting off' for transgressing the prohibition of *niddah* [menstrual impurity]."[44]

Levi Cooper points out that Rabbi Rosenberg's idea to create individual home *miqvehs* as a response to the neglect of *miqveh* observance was shared by another Eastern European immigrant Orthodox rabbi, David Miller of Oakland California. Rabbi Miller, who was apparently unaware of Yudel Rosenberg's pamphlet, published in Oakland, California circa 1920 his own pamphlet, *Sefer Miqveh Yisra'el: Vegn 'Idishe Hofnung, 'Idishe Miqveh un di Dritte Ge'ula,* in which he expressed his hope that increased utilization of the *miqveh* would bring about the conditions that would result in the arrival of the messianic era.[45] There is evidence that Rabbi Miller's do-it-yourself *miqveh* plans were actually utilised.[46] However, though Rabbi Rosenberg later published several responsa on building a *miqveh,* indicating that he received more than one query on this subject,[47] no evidence exists that his *miqveh* plans were ever followed.

Rabbi Rosenberg's second foray into halakhic publication in North America took place in 1919, though it is likely that the manuscript of the book was completed well before then, since the book was listed as one of his works in his earlier *Miqveh Yehuda.*[48] At 128 pages, this publication was much longer and more ambitious than any of his previous halakhic guides, though it had in common with them the fact that it addressed a single halakhic subject. It was entitled *Ha-Qeri'ah ha-Qedosha* [The Holy Reading], and it concerned itself with one of the central ceremonies of the synagogue: the public reading of the Torah.[49]

---

44 *Miqveh,* 3.

45 Rabbi Miller's pamphlet is available online at http://www.hebrewbooks.org/41215, accessed March 23, 2016. On Rabbi Miller and his initiative, see Levi Cooper, "D.I.Y. Mikveh: The Challenge of Encouraging Commitment," *Jewish Educational Leadership* 9, no. 2 (Winter 2011): 58–63.

46 Barry L. Stiefel, "Beyond Synagogues and Cemeteries: The Built Environment as an Aspect of Vernacular Jewish Material Culture in Charleston, South Carolina," *American Jewish History* 101, no. 2 (April 2017): 225–227.

47 *Omer,* part 2, 63, 65, 71–72.

48 *Miqveh,* title page.

49 *Qeri'ah* was published in New York in 1919 thanks to a donation of $200.00 from a childless couple. The page numbers in the footnote correspond to the 1919 edition. On first publication, see *Qeri'ah,* 128.

Because Torah reading in the synagogue was one of the main foci of Jewish services on Sabbaths and holidays, many laws and customs had come to surround it. However, these laws were often only imperfectly understood by the vast majority of synagogue participants, including most of the lay leadership of the congregation.[50] This situation was especially true, as Rabbi Rosenberg stated in his introduction:

> In these last years ... in all large cities numerous ... small congregations have multiplied that have no halakhic decisor who can discern how to show them the clear path in these questions. ... If they were to run in the middle of the [Torah] reading to the chief rabbi or the [religious] judge to ask the question, who knows if they will find him at home? Meanwhile the Torah scroll remains on the reading desk idle, which is not to [its] honor.[51]

With Rabbi Rosenberg's book as a handy reference in every synagogue, however, this prevalent problem would be completely solved.[52]

Yudel Rosenberg divided the book into three sections. The first section included all the prayers, meditations and laws surrounding the Torah scroll while the Torah was removed from the Ark. This includes everything related to the etiquette of calling men to the Torah reading. It also includes several Hasidic and kabbalistic features, such as a *segulah* [protective charm] to prevent difficulties in childbirth taken from one of Rosenberg's other works,[53] and, importantly, Lurianic kabbalistic meditations [*kavvanot*] for the high holidays that first appeared in print in 1911.[54]

The second section, which included all the laws relevant to the reading of the Torah, was translated into Yiddish so all to be understood by "all classes of Jews."[55] This section constituted a greatly expanded restatement of the laws of Torah reading in comparison with other halakhic sources. For example, *Hilkhot Qeri'at Sefer Torah,* the section on Torah reading in the standard

50 Rosenberg remarks that these basically non-observant Jews need observant people as guides, see *Omer*, part 1, 18.

51 *Qeri'ah*, 4.

52 *Qeri'ah*, 4.

53 *Qeri'ah*, 8. Cf. *Refa'el*, passim. See Ira Robinson, "The Tarler rebbe of Łódź and His Medical Practice: Towards a History of Hasidic Life in Pre-First World War Poland," *Polin* 11 (1998): 53–61.

54 *Qeri'ah*, 9. On the printing of Lurianic *kavvanot*, see Jonatan Meir, *Kabbalistic Circles in Jerusalem (1896–1948)* (Leiden and Boston: Brill, 2016), 140ff.

55 *Qeri'ah*, title page.

sixteenth-century halakhic code, *Shulḥan 'Arukh*, encompasses fifteen chapters with a total of 72 paragraphs.[56] Rabbi Rosenberg's parallel section is much larger: it is organized in 27 chapters with 247 paragraphs. Major sources for this section include the halakhic works of Jacob Emden (1697–1776),[57] Jacob Lorberbaum of Lissa (1760–1832),[58] Shneur Zalman of Liadi (1745–1813),[59] and Ephraim ha-Kohen of Vilna (1616–1678),[60] as well as a few of Rabbi Rosenberg's own ideas [*ḥiddushim*].[61]

The third section of the book deals with the derivation of men's names and their Hebrew equivalents, so that Jews could be correctly called to the Torah reading.[62] This was important because the names by which men are called to the Torah determine their name for legal purposes, including divorce. Getting a man's name wrong on a divorce document, as Jacob Emden emphasized, meant invalidation of the divorce and potentially the creation of bastards [*mamzerim*].[63]

Yudel Rosenberg had grasped the reality: in literally thousands of small North American immigrant Orthodox synagogues there was no one with sufficient knowledge of rabbinic literature and halakha to give authoritative guidance in these matters. Thus Rosenberg clearly hoped he had a best-seller on his hands, dealing with a topic of immediate relevance to large numbers of Orthodox Jews in North America. However, this publication does not seem to have made much of a splash, and was not republished for fully eighty-five years, until Rabbi Rosenberg's great-grandson republished the first section only (Jerusalem, 2004).[64]

When Rabbi Yudel Rosenberg moved from Toronto to Montreal in 1919, he brought with him the conviction that a key way to address the important

---

56 *Shulḥan Arukh, Oraḥ Ḥayyim*, chapters 135–149.

57 Jacob Joseph Shacter, "The 'Siddur' of Rabbi Jacob Emden: From Commentary to Code," in *Torah and Wisdom; Studies in Jewish Philosophy, Kabbalah and Halacha. Essays in Honor of Arthur Hyman*, ed. Ruth Link-Salinger (New York: Shengold, 1992), 175–192.

58 "Jacob Ben Jacob Moses of Lissa," *Jewish Encyclopedia*, http://www.jewishencyclopedia.com/articles/8417-jacob-ben-jacob-moses-of-lissa, accessed December 6, 2016.

59 Immanuel Etkes, *Rabbi Shneur Zalman of Liady: The Origins of Chabad Hasidism* (Waltham: MA, Brandeis University Press, 2014).

60 Ephraim ben Yakov ha-Cohen, *Sha'ar Ephraim* (Lemberg, 1887).

61 *Qeri'ah*, 5.

62 In 1928 the Warsaw kehilla published a list of Jewish names eliminating many corruptions and nicknames which had led to confusion. Shapiro, "Jewish Self-Government in Łódź," 311.

63 *Qeri'ah*, 107. Cf. ibid., section 2, chapter 5, paragraph 7, 52.

64 Cf., however, Fox, *100 Years of Hebrew and Yiddish Literature in Canada*, 274 who claims to have seen a second edition of *Keriah* published in 1939.

issues facing Orthodox Judaism in its new North American setting was to come up with innovative ways to facilitate halakhic observance. In his first Montreal publications in the 1920s, Rabbi Rosenberg set his sights on facilitating wider Jewish observance of the Sabbath, which constitutes the central feature of rabbinic halakha and serves as an identity marker for Orthodox Jews. Sabbath observance formed a major topic for his sermons and moral discourses, like his 1924 *A Brivele Fun di Zisse Mame Shabbes Malkesa zu Ihre Zin und Tehter fun 'Idishn Folk,* which will be discussed in detail in chapter 7 below.

It is Rabbi Rosenberg's concern with the technological implications of contemporary Sabbath observance with which we are concerned in this chapter. This concern is present in several of his responsa. In one of them, he permitted the use by Torah-observant Jews of hot water from the tap on the Sabbath. Once again, as in previous cases we have seen, Rabbi Rosenberg began by commenting on his perception of contemporary Jewish practice: "Already in all the households they are accustomed to using this [hot] water on the Sabbath. It is not an easy thing to make thousands upon thousands of Jewish souls into Sabbath desecrators."[65]

Yet another halakhic decision he made concerning the Sabbath related to baby carriages. In a place with no symbolic enclosure [*'eruv*], the prohibition of "carrying" in public on the Sabbath would prevent parents from utilizing baby carriages outside their homes. Should the halakha concerning carrying on the Sabbath be strictly observed, mothers with children unable to walk by themselves would have to remain in the house for the duration of the Sabbath. The prevalence of baby carriages utilized on Saturdays made Rabbi Rosenberg determined to find a halakhic solution to this problem. His decision was originally published in 1924 in Yiddish as an appendix to his *Brivele* pamphlet. Only later would it be rendered into Hebrew in classic responsa form.

Rabbi Rosenberg began the Yiddish version by defining the women to whom he spoke: "I refer here not to the women who go on the Sabbath to buy bargains in the markets and carry the packages home ... but rather ... the women who are entitled to the name 'Jewish Daughters' [*'idishe tekhter*]." It is noteworthy that these "Jewish Daughters," as Rosenberg defines them, refrained from purchasing "bargains" on the Sabbath, which means that they adhered to the major Sabbath prohibition of commercial transactions. On the other hand, they did push their baby carriages in the streets on the Sabbath day.

65 *Omer,* part 2, 19.

How could one deal with this situation? Rosenberg's halakhic answer to the problem was to modify the carriages so that they would be at least forty-two inches high. Thus modified, they could be taken out on the Sabbath. In his Yiddish pamphlet, Rosenberg does not go into the halakhic reasoning which influenced his decision. It was sufficient for the women whom he addressed, presumably untutored in the fine points of halakhic discourse, that Rabbi Rosenberg said it was all right. In the Hebrew version, however, Rosenberg makes a halakhic case which is very weak. As Rosenberg himself admits, his altered baby carriage could only be considered permitted on the Sabbath if one combined three halakhic categories, each of which was only permitted in in a theoretical sense [*pattur aval assur*], with an opinion of Maimonides, meaning that, strictly speaking, those people who actually followed Rosenberg's instructions would actually be found in technical violation of the Sabbath laws, though only of a rabbinic ordinance and not Biblical law. Under ordinary circumstances, no Orthodox rabbi would be likely to give his permission for this and publicize his position in print on that basis alone. What, then, are the special circumstances according to which Rabbi Rosenberg's essentially extra-halakhic permission was granted?

It is apparent that he was concerned both with the comfort of the child and the attitude of the parents. As he wrote:

> One should not say because of [the fact that the baby cannot walk] that the father and mother should be imprisoned in the house all the Sabbath day. This is painful for them. Without doubt, their going to stroll with the child is part of their enjoyment of the Sabbath [*'oneg Shabbat*].[66]

From this evidence, it is clear that Rosenberg had arrived at a halakhic methodology that emphasized the possible leniencies within the halakhic process, going in this regard far beyond the efforts of most other contemporary Orthodox rabbis.[67] It is apparent that here, too, Rabbi Rosenberg was interested in the halakhic behavior of the masses of "traditional" Jews, and concerned with keeping them somehow within the folds of the Judaic tradition. He was certainly determined not to define them as Sabbath desecrators. Rabbi Rosenberg, in brief, could not conceive of a situation in which all but the most strictly

66 *Omer*, part 2, 26–27.

67 *'Ateret*, title page, 4. As Rabbi Rosenberg stated in one responsum, it is incumbent upon those who forbid to bring proof. *Omer*, part 2, 39.

observant would be in effect written off as Orthodox Jews. In establishing his halakhic positions, Rabbi Rosenberg adumbrated an attitude toward halakha in North America strongly advocated by another immigrant Orthodox rabbi, Ḥayyim Hirschenson (1857–1935). Rabbi Hirschenson's halakhic philosophy has been defined as:

> ... the imperative of trying to find *heterim* [permissions] for things which are a necessity of life in the U.S. By doing so, Jews will be able to remain loyal to tradition, and this will also strengthen the hand of the Orthodox rabbinate, as the people will feel that the rabbis are interested in their plight.[68]

Rabbi Rosenberg's attitude toward halakha is present as well in his 1920s responsum on the use of electricity. It is often taken as a given that Orthodox Jews have readily adopted modern technologies, and that, indeed, Orthodox Jews have flourished in contemporary urban settings.[69] It is, however, less clear how the process of adaptation to these technologies on the part of Orthodox Jews evolved in the nineteenth and twentieth centuries. Some light may be shed on this phenomenon by examining a moment in the rabbinic debate over the halakhic status of electricity[70] in the early twentieth century. In this episode, Rabbi Rosenberg played a notable part, though his halakhic arguments did not prevail against one of the most distinguished halakhic scholars of the twentieth century, Rabbi Shlomo Zalman Auerbach (1910–1995)[71] of Jerusalem.

---

68 Marc Shapiro, review of David Zohar, *Jewish Commitment in a Modern World: Rabbi Hayyim Hirschenson and His Attitude to Modernity* [Hebrew], *The Edah Journal* 5, no. 1 (Tammuz 5765): 2, http://www.edah.org/backend/journalarticle/5_1_shapiro.pdf, accessed March 25, 2016. Cf. Ari Ackerman, "'Judging the Sinner Favorably': R. Hayyim Hirschensohn on the Need for Leniency in Halakhic Decision-Making," *Modern Judaism* 22 (2002): 261–280; David Zohar, *Jewish Commitment in a Modern World*, 197–198.

69 On contemporary Orthodox Jews in urban settings, see Menachem Friedman, "Haredim Confront the Modern City," *Studies in Contemporary Jewry* 2 (1986): 74–96.

70 For a convenient summary of halakhic views on electricity, see Rabbi Michael Broyde and Rabbi Howard Jachter, "Electricity on Shabbat and Yom Tov," *Journal of Halacha and Contemporary Society* 21 (Spring 1991): 4–47, http://daat.co.il/daat/english/journal/broyde_1.htm. Cf. also Ze'ev Lev, "Electricity and Shabbat," *Crossroads (Alon Shvut)* 2 (1988): 7–28; H. J. Adler, "Some Halakhic Aspects of Electricity," *The Blessing of Eliyahu* (London: Bet ha-Midrash Golders Green, 1982), 197–210.

71 On Rabbi Auerbach's biography, see Rabbi Aaron Benzion Shurin, "Ha-Rav R. Shlomo-Zalman Auerbach N"e: Tsu Zayn 10-n Yartsayt," *Forward*, February 25, 2005, 8–9; D. Sofer, "Rav Shlomo Zalman Auerbach Zts"l," http://www.tzemachdovid.org/gedolim/

Rabbi Rosenberg first published his responsum as a pamphlet in 1924, entitled *Me'or ha-Hashmal.*[72] For his part, Rabbi Auerbach published his views in a book entitled *Me'orei Esh,* published in 1934.[73] An examination of these two treatises will yield much information concerning their respective halakhic, rhetorical, and communal strategies regarding halakha and its application to new technologies. The unpublished correspondence between Rabbi Auerbach and Rabbi Rosenberg will allow us further insight into both rabbis and their respective positions.

The issue that both rabbis addressed in common was the halakhic implications of the use of electric power by Jews on a Jewish holiday [*Yom Tov*]. By the early twentieth century, a consensus within the Orthodox Jewish community had emerged whereby nearly all halakha-observant Jews refrained from turning electric lights on and off on the Sabbath.[74] By contrast, in the first third of the twentieth century, the jury was definitely still out in these circles regarding the possibility of turning electric lights on and off on Jewish holidays. Eminent halakhic decisors, such as Rabbi Yeḥiel Mikhl ha-Levi Epstein, author of the widely known halakhic code *'Arukh ha-Shulḥan,* had pronounced in favor of

---

ravauerbach.html. Scholarship on R. Auerbach is concentrated on his decisions on halakha applied to medical problems. Cf. Mordecai Halperin, "The Laws of Saving Lives: The Teachings of Rabbi S. Z. Auerbach," *Medicine, Ethics, and Jewish Law* 2 (1996): 15–24; Avraham Steinberg, "Medical-Halachic Decisions of Rabbi Shlomo Zalman Auerbach (1910–1995)," *Assia* 3, no. 1 (1997): 30–43; idem, "Rabbi Shlomo Zalman Auerbach (1910–1995)," in *Pioneers in Jewish Medical Ethics,* ed. Fred Rosner (Northvale, NJ: Jason Aronson, 1997), 99–126.

72 Yehuda Yudel Rosenberg's *Me'or* was first published in Montreal in 1924. A second edition (Jerusalem, 1929) was presented as a supplement to the monthly *Sha'arei Tsion.* Page numbers follow the 1924 edition unless otherwise specified.

73 Shlomo Zalman Auerbach, *Sefer Me'orei Esh: Kollel Ḥiqrei Halakhot Ḥiddushim u-Bi'urim be-'Inyanim Shonim ha-Nog'im le-'Inyan Me'or ha-'Elektria be-Shabbat ve-Yom Tov* (Jerusalem: Defus Salomon, 1934; reprinted Jerusalem: Moriyah, 1980). The year of publication of the first edition is the Hebrew calendar year [5]695, which commenced in September 1934. As we will see, Rabbi Auerbach sent a copy to Rabbi Rosenberg in a letter dated January 8, 1935. From this we may assume that the book was printed sometime between September and December 1934.

74 Nonetheless, even that consensus was not completely uniform. One rabbi who held the opposite was Rabbi Yosef Zvi Dushinsky of Jerusalem. Menachem Keren-Kratz, "Mishmeret le-Moshmeret: R. Yosef Zvi (Maharitz) Dushinsky," in *The Gedoilim: Leaders Who Shaped the Israeli Haredi Society,* ed. Binyamin Brown and Nissim Leon (Jerusalem: Magnes Press, 2017), 365. Thus Rabbi Rosenberg polemicizes against some Jews, whom he characterized as "light of intellect" [*kalei ha-da'at*] who sought grounds to utilize electricity in this manner also on the Sabbath. *Me'or,* 7.

the utilization of electric lights on holidays,[75] while other well-known halakhic authorities, such as Rabbi Ḥayyim Ozer Grodzinsky (1863–1940),[76] opposed it. Rabbi Yudel Rosenberg stepped into this controversial area in 1924 with a responsum published in Montreal as a pamphlet.

It is instructive to note the way in which Rabbi Rosenberg posed the question he was to discuss and which thus framed his discussion: "I indeed see that the common people [*he-hamon*] act leniently in this matter ... whereas stringency [*ḥumra*] in this [matter] constitutes a decree that most of the public is not able to abide."[77] With respect to turning on lights on Jewish holidays, he concludes that: "Pressing a button to light the electricity on holidays is permissible *de jure* [*le-khatḥila*]. If [the people of] Israel are not prophets, they are the children of prophets,[78] but to do so on the Sabbath is prohibited."

In his 1929 edition, published as a supplement to the rabbinic journal *Sha'arei Tsion*, he also stated the prohibition of utilizing telephones and electric doorbells on Shabbat.[79] As for turning lights off on holidays, Rabbi Rosenberg stated:

> Now that we have come to this [conclusion] that pressing the button to extinguish [electricity] is only indirect [*garam*] extinguishing, and [if it is not extinguished] there is also a waste of money in that one will have to pay for electric light without need, and there is also bodily discomfort if the electric light will shine for the two days and nights of the holiday with no interruption, therefore ... it is permissible on the holiday to press the extinguishing button which is distant from the illuminated glass [bulb], but on the Sabbath it is certainly forbidden.[80]

Yudel Rosenberg further claimed in concluding that:

> Any person who possesses common sense [*sekhel ha-yashar*] will understand that the ... three reasons [for permitting use of electricity] are poured forth [smoothly] like a mirror. I have made the effort and found

75 Cf. Broyde and Jachter, "Electricity on Shabbat and Yom Tov," footnote 49.

76 Ḥayyim Ozer Grodzinsky, *Sh'elot u-Teshuvot Ahi'ezer* (Jerusalem, 1960), part 3, responsum 60.

77 *Me'or*, 2. Cf. Babylonian Talmud, Horayot 3b.

78 Cf. Babylonian Talmud, Pesaḥim 66a–b.

79 *Me'or*, 8.

80 Ibid., 7, 12.

> [a solution] with the help of the blessed God. ... Go and see what the people are doing, if they are not prophets, they are the children of prophets. ... May the blessed God enlighten my eyes in His Torah to advocate for the community of Israel. May my formulation justifying their [actions] be accepted in Heaven so that I may be among the enlightened who will shine like the splendor of the firmament and those who justify the multitude shall be like stars forever and ever.[81]

It is quite evident from Rabbi Rosenberg's presentation that he saw himself as an advocate for the people of Israel, finding sound halakhic reasons for their practice that had been questioned by some halakhic authorities. He had come to an unambiguous conclusion.

Rabbi Auerbach's *Me'orei Esh* was written, as we shall see, without knowledge of Rabbi Rosenberg's responsum, though *Me'or* had been republished in Jerusalem. It was prompted in general by the fact that the electrification of Palestine in the 1920s had made an abstract halakhic issue of pressing importance to halakha-observant Jews in that country.[82] Specifically, it was the result of a permissive halakhic ruling on electricity by prominent Jerusalem rabbi R. Tsvi Pesaḥ Frank (1873–1960) in 1934, published in the rabbinic journal, *Kol Torah*.[83] Rabbi Auerbach received letters of approbation from an impressive list of rabbis, including Rabbis Ḥayyim Ozer Grodzinsky of Vilna, Abraham Isaac ha-Kohen Kook, his teacher, Isser Zalman Meltzer (1870–1953), and Abba Yaakov ha-Kohen Borukhov (1840–1936), all of Jerusalem. All of these rabbis agreed that *Me'orei Esh* was reacting to the public discussion for, as Rabbi Kook stated, "many significant people [*rabbim ve-ken shelemim*] have begun to occupy themselves in this question."[84]

Whereas Rabbi Rosenberg had written his responsum with the object of coming to a definite conclusion, Rabbi Auerbach emphatically was not prepared to issue his own halakhic conclusion in a straightforward way. In fact, he constructed his book as if wished at all cost to avoid any definitive statement that might appear to be a halakhic ruling. As he wrote:

---

81 Cf. Daniel 12, 3.

82 Cf. David Zohar, *Jewish Commitment in a Modern World*, 251.

83 Auerbach, *Me'orei Esh*, 93. Cf. Broyde and Jachter, "Electricity on Shabbat and Yom Tov" footnote 49. The impact this rabbinic journal is clear in any reading of *Me'orei Esh*, especially 94, 96, 122, 144, 177. The issue of the proliferation of rabbinic journals and their readership in the late nineteenth and early twentieth centuries requires considerable clarification.

84 Auerbach, *Me'orei Esh*, unpaginated section.

> Indeed this is to announce that I have written all this only as a theoretical discussion [*pilpul*] in halakha and not for practical application [*le-ma'aseh*]. For even if it were true that [turning electric lights on and off on Jewish holidays] is permissible, it nonetheless looks entirely like weekday actions and it is possible to be concerned about an adverse reaction in that the common people [*he-hamon*] will think that [it is permitted] because it is not real fire and they will come to light and extinguish [electricity] on the Sabbath as well. Even though we should not add decrees to those of our sages, may their memory be a blessing, nonetheless leave Israel be, who have treated it at forbidden.[85]

Rabbi Auerbach further stated: "I have written all this only to illuminate the aspects of the doubtful issue. ... There is no joy like that of solving doubtful issues."[86] Perhaps this strategy of close analysis without coming to an unambiguous conclusion was influenced by the atmosphere of the yeshiva from which he emerged and its emphasis on the abstract and the academic.

Though he was loathe to come to a definitive conclusion, which was probably a wise course of action for a relatively young Jerusalem scholar, however brilliant his reputation, it is clear that Rabbi Auerbach's preference was to forbid electricity on holidays if only so as not to confuse "the people." It is interesting to note in this connection that Rabbi Auerbach, like Rabbi Rosenberg, had expressed concern for the welfare of the people, and he had used the same Talmudic citation as Rabbi Rosenberg to indicate that he wished to let them continue doing what they were doing. Clearly, Rabbi Rosenberg's "people," who were portrayed in his responsum as though they believed turning electric lights on and off on Jewish holidays were permitted, and Rabbi Auerbach's "people," who were portrayed in his book as treating this action as forbidden, were situated on opposite sides of the issue.

In Rabbi Rosenberg's papers there are two unpublished letters from Rabbi Auerbach as well as a draft of a letter from Yudel Rosenberg to Rabbi Auerbach,[87] which will be examined now. Rabbi Auerbach initiated the correspondence with a letter dated 4 Shevat 5695 (January 8, 1935), accompanied by a copy of his book. The letter was designed to make a number of points. First of

85 Ibid., 78, cf. also 155.

86 Ibid., 194.

87 From Rabbi Auerbach's letters, it is evident that he received at least two from Rabbi Rosenberg. Thus, even if the extant draft of Rabbi Rosenberg's letter reflects a letter actually sent to Rabbi Auerbach, there is still a missing part of the correspondence.

all, he wished Rabbi Rosenberg to know that he had not known of his responsum when he wrote the book.[88] He had been directed to Rabbi Rosenberg's responsum by a Jerusalem rabbi. He informed him that he desired his response to the book because "I saw that his [Rosenberg's] way of elucidating this halakha was honest [or straightforward, *yeshara*]." He told Rabbi Rosenberg that he was currently engaged in further research on the subject, and he assured him that his response would be published in a further projected volume. He also wished Rabbi Rosenberg to understand that "here in Jerusalem, the holy city, [Jews] had up to now been accustomed to forbidding [turning electric lights on and off on holidays]". He proffered the information that his rejection of Rabbi Epstein's arguments in favor of using electricity on holidays was because "it is evident that he [Epstein] did not understand at all the nature [*darkhei hithavut*] of electric light."[89] He hoped that Rabbi Rosenberg would promote his book, and he concluded with eight pages of a closely reasoned critique of Rabbi Rosenberg's responsum, asking for his reaction.

In his critique, while clearly maintaining a respectful tone, Rabbi Auerbach nonetheless tore into Rabbi Rosenberg's halakhic arguments, one by one. With respect to Rosenberg's interpretation of Maimonides's opinion of the concept of work on Jewish holidays for instance,[90] Rabbi Auerbach stated: "I do not know how it is so clear to him [Rosenberg]." Others of Rabbi Rosenberg's halakhic arguments were commented upon with expressions like "I am greatly astonished [*temehna tuba*] in this that [you] sir did not realize in this case that it is also to be considered work for the sake of food preparation [*okhel nefesh*]." Rabbi Auerbach also argued that Rabbi Rosenberg's halakhic analogy between electric current and oil in a lamp meant that turning off the light transgressed the negative commandment of extinguishing fire [*mekhabe*], but he stated: "It is ... astonishing to me since his excellency the rabbi [*ha-Rav ha-Ga'on*] himself came to this reasoning [but not to the same conclusion]." Another major pillar of Rabbi Rosenberg's halakhic argumentation, the analogy of a magnifying glass concentrating the rays of the sun to create fire, received somewhat milder treatment. For, as Rabbi Auerbach explained:

---

88 It is curious that Rabbi Auerbach did not come across the second edition of Rabbi Rosenberg's responsum, which was ostensibly published in Jerusalem in 1929. It is even more curious to realise, from the citations of *Me'or* in his letter to Rabbi Rosenberg, that he had the Montreal and not the Jerusalem edition in front of his eyes.

89 Rabbi Auerbach, like Rabbi Rosenberg, consulted books on popular science and electricity as well as having spoken with an expert in the subject. Auerbach, *Me'orei Esh*, 61, 153.

90 Maimonides, *Hilkhot Yom Tov* 1, 5–8; *Me'or*, 4.

> Truth be told, I also thought, at the beginning of this [line of] reasoning, that since the location of the glass [bulb] is distant from the [light] switch we have [an instance of] secondary force [*koaḥ sheni*]. However, I refuted this reasoning and remained with the concept of primary force.

In the end, Rabbi Auerbach confronted Yudel Rosenberg with a request that was, in essence, an ultimatum:

> Please let this great man [Rosenberg] examine [my arguments] and inform me with words of truth, for if I have erred, I will admit [it] and not be ashamed, God forbid. For about similar [matters], I believe that of him who admits and leaves [his transgression] [Proverbs 28, 13], his inadvertent errors become merits, and he receives a reward both for the explanation and the abstaining from explanation,[91] whereas one who does not admit [his error] is transformed, God forbid, from one who inadvertently errs to one who wilfully errs, far be it from me.

Though out of politeness, Rabbi Auerbach made his words refer to himself, it seems reasonably clear that he expected Rabbi Rosenberg to concede his position.

If Rabbi Rosenberg's draft response to Rabbi Auerbach's letter had actually been sent to him as it was set down, then Rabbi Auerbach was in for an unpleasant shock. Yudel Rosenberg considered the letter he had received to be a polemic [*ta'romet*] against his responsum. He showed no patience with Rabbi Auerbach's *pilpul*. He stated:

> Your Torahship knows that I also realize that here [in the case of electricity] there are factors [tending toward] prohibition and toward permission. However, there is a great obligation on the part of the rabbis of the generation to be on the side of permission as much as possible ... for just as it is an obligation [*mitzvah*] to say something that will be obeyed [*nishma'*], so it is an obligation not to say something that will not be obeyed.[92] For this [prohibiting turning electric lights on and off on Jewish holidays] is

91 Babylonian Talmud, Pesaḥim, 22b.

92 Babylonian Talmud, Yevamot 65b.

> a decree that the majority of the community is unable to uphold, and the masses will certainly not listen to the voice of the rabbis who prohibit.[93]

In this draft response, Rabbi Rosenberg did not attempt to deal in any serious way with Rabbi Auerbach's meticulously reasoned critique of his responsum. He merely repeated his assertion that:

> [T]he arguments for permission for which I laboured, and which I found ... are poured forth [smoothly] like a mirror, and they can be refuted neither by logical arguments [*sevarot*] nor by difficulties [*kushiyot*] from the latter halakhic authorities [*aḥaronim*]. It is understood that the gates of rejoinders [*terutsim*] have not been locked.

Yudel Rosenberg concluded his strong response with a rhetorical flourish:

> If they decree upon me the punishment of Hell [*Gehinom*] for this [responsum], it would be better for me to be in Hell along with the myriads of Israel who light and extinguish electricity on holidays, rather than to be in Paradise [*Gan Eden*] with the elite [*yeḥidei segulah*], who instead of loving righteousness have chosen love of wickedness.

Rabbi Auerbach's second letter to Yudel Rosenberg, dated 23 Adar I 5695 [February 26, 1935] expresses his shock and surprise at the response he had received. He tried to appease his older colleague by remarking how much his father, Rabbi Chaim Yehuda Leib Auerbach (1883–1954), had appreciated reading Rabbi Rosenberg's book on the *Zohar*. He claimed that he had no intention of either insulting or criticising him, and had taken no offence himself. His only thought had been to engage Rabbi Rosenberg in halakhic debate on the issue, which, in his mind, was the only way to truly solve the issue. He continued defending his position by pointing out that Rabbi Rosenberg's argument that his halakhic permission was plain and simple was disingenuous.

Rabbi Auerbach had shown his book manuscript to his teacher, Rabbi Isser Zalman Meltzer, who, he added, had actually read the text, unlike the case in most rabbinic approbations. Rabbis Abraham Isaac Kook and Ḥayyim Ozer Grodzinski had also agreed with his conclusions. Continuing in his attempt to appease Rosenberg, he tried to position himself as a young bystander

93 Cf. *Me'or*, 3.

attempting to deal with the strong opinions of his senior colleagues. Thus, Auerbach continued, just as Rabbi Rosenberg's response astonished him, so was he astonished upon reading a letter that Rabbi Grodzinski had written to his teacher, Rabbi Meltzer, in which:

> He [Grodzinski] complains greatly concerning those who are on the permissive side of this issue ... because it appears to him that it is plain and simple that it is prohibited. And I, in my poor, young opinion, for who am I to question [*leharher 'al*] the great [halakhic authorities]. ... With all of this I do not know why all this anger?

Rabbi Auerbach also sought to demonstrate to Rabbi Rosenberg that he did appreciate his situation: "For I know that the rabbis in the United States who fear God are very hurt by the degenerate situation there and therefore for them the power of permission is much preferable."[94]

At this moment in the history of halakha, two rabbis had clashed because, despite the important things they held in common, they came to the issue with different trajectories as representatives of two different rabbinic communities. Rabbi Rosenberg was a halakhic authority immersed in the problems of the communal rabbinate in North America. He saw it as his responsibility to give the sort of guidance to his community that would enable and empower them to remain faithful to the Judaic legal tradition under conditions that were often far from ideal.[95] Rabbi Auerbach in 1935 was a young scholar who had not yet emerged as the well-known and widely respected halakhic decisor that he was to become. He came from the world of the yeshiva, in which a scholarly elite pursued its vision of Torah scholarship without the necessity of taking into consideration the factors with which community rabbis had to deal. He also approached the issue from the perspective of the so-called "Old Yishuv," a Jewish community in Palestine with a strong orientation towards the perfection of "eternal life" [*ḥayyei 'olam*] as opposed to dealing with the mundane, in which

---

94 Yudel Rosenberg's great grandson, Yehoshua Ben Meir, was a student of Rabbi Auerbach. When the latter found out his connection with Yudel Rosenberg, he stated that in his youth he had indeed not given Rosenberg sufficient respect. Email from Yehoshua Ben Meir to the author, June 27, 2018.

95 On the issue of the ideal versus the attainable in twentieth-century halakhic discourse, see Ira Robinson, "Because of Our Many Sins: The Contemporary Jewish World as Reflected in the Responsa of Moses Feinstein," *Judaism* 35 (1986): 35–46.

standards of halakhic observance tended to be higher than among even those Jews in North America who identified with Orthodoxy.[96]

The subsequent development of halakhic opinion on the issue of turning electric lights on and off on Jewish holidays did not generally look kindly on Yudel Rosenberg's responsum. Rabbi Rosenberg, apparently, sent copies of *Me'or* to other rabbis in Palestine, including the Chief Rabbi, Rabbi Abraham Isaac Kook,[97] and Benzion Uziel, then Chief Rabbi of Jaffa and Tel-Aviv.[98] Rabbi Rosenberg's position was accepted and adopted by Rabbi Uziel, who had met him personally on a visit to Montreal in December 1927. Rabbi Uziel called Yudel Rosenberg "he who my soul loves,"[99] and acknowledged Rosenberg's work in his own responsum on the subject.[100] Other halakhic authorities, such as Rabbis Eliezer Valdenburg[101] and Ovadia Yosef,[102] were decidedly unimpressed by Rabbi Rosenberg's arguments. Rabbi Auerbach, on the other hand, emerged as one of the most important halakhic decisors of the twentieth century, whose responsa and halakhic arguments, particularly in the area of medical treatment and Sabbath observance, were respected by wide circles of halakha-observant Jews. Rabbi Auerbach became well known particularly for his opinions on the applications of electricity on the Sabbath.[103]

In 1934, near the end of his life, Rabbi Rosenberg decided to publish a book collecting his responsa, which he named *Yeḥeve Da'at*. He had been responding to halakhic questions since he had become a rabbi in Tarlow, and published occasional responsa in books dealing with other subjects.[104] As far back as 1919

---

96 On the society out of which Rabbi Auerbach emerged, see Menachem Friedman, *Ḥevrah va-Dat: ha-Ortodoqsia ha-lo' Tsionit be-Erets Yisra'el, 1918–1936* (Jerusalem: Yad Yitsḥak Ben Tsvi, 1977). For a portrait of the North American Orthodox society of this era, see Haym Soloveitchik, "Rapture and Reconstruction: The Transformation of Contemporary Orthodoxy," *Tradition* 28, no. 4 (1994): 64–130.

97 Yudel Rosenberg to Abraham Isaac Kook, 27 Shvat 5695 (January 31, 1935), BMA, Jerusalem.

98 Benzion Uziel to Yudel Rosenberg, 30 Adar I 5695 (March 5, 1935).

99 Benzion Uziel, *Mishpatei Uziel*, vol. 1, *'Oraḥ Ḥayyim* (Tel-Aviv, 1935), responsum 19.

100 Benzion Uziel to Yudel Rosenberg, 8 Tishrei 5691 (September 30, 1930), Arkhion Histori, Iriyat Tel-Aviv-Yaffo, 8/1018.

101 Eliezer Yehuda Valdenburg, *Tsits Eliezer*, vol. 1, number 20, chapter 7.

102 Ovadia Yosef, *Yabi'a Omer*, part 2, *Oraḥ Ḥayyim*, responsum 26.

103 Shlomo Zalman Auerbach, *Minḥat Shlomo*, chapters 9–13; Broyde and Jachter, "Electricity on Shabbat and Yom Tov," footnotes 2, 6, 9, 14, 23, 27, 33, 43, 46, 58, 61, 62, 64, 70, 71, 74, 78, 98, 105, 107.

104 Yudel Rosenberg's responsum on tefilin may be found in *'Ateret*, in an appendix to the book with separate pagination, 3–12.

he announced his intention to collect his responsa in a book that he at the time gave the name *Allufei Yehuda.*[105] Yudel Rosenberg proclaimed that his collection of some thirty responsa was being published not so that others will rely upon his judgement so much as to keep a record of how he ruled in these instances.[106] In his collection he republished most of the responsa he had already published starting with those he presented in his periodical *Kol Torah* (1908). Some of them he reedited for the collection. Thus in *Kol Torah* he had been asked three questions concerning cemeteries, two from Tsvi Ze'ev, the rabbi of Ladysmith, South Africa,[107] and the other from Rabbi Moshe Hinshparg of Kishinev, who, in the aftermath of the Kishinev pogroms asked concerning the placing of a privy on cemetery property for the use of the cemetery watchman.[108] In *Yeḥeve Da'at* Rabbi Rosenberg combined all three questions into one and presented the third as if it too had emanated from South Africa.[109]

Yudel Rosenberg's responsa collection presents other evidence of his abiding interest in the implications of technology for halakha. It includes a responsum in which he declares photographs permissible for Orthodox Jews.[110] With respect to the halakhic issue of photographs, Rosenberg had this to say:

> There is no permission for [even] the greatest [rabbi] of the generation to oppose a law that has been agreed upon in the *Shulḥan Arukh* ... because he has a question he does not know how to solve, for if so there would be no end to the matter. Anyone who is called in a letter *ga'on* and "great" may in error think that he should be thought of as among the *Ge'onim,* that he will receive a greater spirit ... in order to bring down the honor of the *Shulḥan Arukh,* saying that he is wiser. ... All this I write because I see some rabbis in the last while who have written in their books to prohibit images of people like photographs, a stringency that was never mentioned in the Talmud or the former halakhic authorities [*rishonim*] or the *Shulḥan Arukh.*[111]

105 *Qeri'ah*, 45.
106 *Omer*, part 2, 4.
107 KT, number 45, 44.
108 Ibid., number 46, 44–45.
109 *Omer*, part 2, 47–50.
110 Ibid., 78–82.
111 Ibid., 82.

In another responsum, Rabbi Rosenberg ruled that a small community could not fulfill its obligation to hear the shofar on the New Year by listening to a radio broadcast of the shofar blasts.[112]

The collection on responsa was not published in Yudel Rosenberg's lifetime. It was set in type and the page proofs reached Rabbi Rosenberg, but he was unable to afford to pay the printer and the edition was never printed. Examination of the page proofs shows Rabbi Rosenberg immersed in the communal problems of North American Jewry. He saw it as his responsibility to give the sort of guidance to his community that would enable them to remain faithful to the Judaic tradition under conditions that were often far from ideal.[113] He was particularly concerned with justifying the halakhic behavior of "traditional" Jews and not defining them as sinners. Rosenberg therefore pushed to the limit the lenient possibilities within the halakhic process, going in this regard far beyond most contemporary Orthodox rabbis.[114] Otherwise, he felt, all but the most strictly observant would be in effect written off as Orthodox Jews.

112 Ibid., 45–47.

113 See Robinson, "Because of Our Many Sins," 35–46.

114 See footnote 67 above.

CHAPTER 7

A "Folk Author": Yudel Rosenberg as Storyteller

As we have seen, starting in his Warsaw years, Rabbi Yudel Rosenberg was assiduously engaged in making a name for himself as a Talmudist, a halakhist, and a kabbalist. At the same time he was also busily writing a number of books for a popular Jewish book market that was growing and expanding.[1] These popular books would bring him his greatest fame, but would as well embroil him in controversy, for he published these works not as his own creations but rather as editions of centuries-old manuscripts taken from a non-existent archive—the Royal Library of Metz, which had been plundered "over one hundred years ago" with many of the old books and manuscripts finding their way into private hands.[2]

The tensions engendered by the challenges made to rabbinic Judaism in the modern era were expressed in many ways. Certainly one of the most interesting of these concerned the attention paid to texts and their authenticity. Those who challenged the pretensions of Orthodoxy to represent the continuation of the rabbinic Jewish tradition in modern times did so in large part through the application of modern standards of critical scholarship to the texts of the Jewish past. Thus the *Wissenschaft des Judentums* movement asserted its mastery of the Jewish past in large part through the publication of critical editions of ancient and medieval Jewish texts.[3]

---

1 Shmuel Feiner, *Haskalah and History: The Emergence of a Modern Jewish Historical Consciousness* (Oxford: Littman Library of Jewish Civilization, 2002), 205.

2 *Nifla'ot Maharal mi-Prag 'im ha-Golem* [hereafter *Nifla'ot*] (Warsaw: Aaron Cylingold, 1909), title page. Interestingly, this is contradicted in Yudel Rosenberg's introduction where he states that the manuscript had been stored away in the library "for about three hundred years until now." *Nifla'ot*, 3.

3 On *Wissenschaft des Judentums*, see Michael A. Meyer, *The Origins of the Modern Jew* (Detroit: 1967), 144ff.

The Orthodox more or less responded in kind.[4] Though they did not cease to polemicize against the perceived "treason" of the *maskilim* against the mythic structure of rabbinic Judaism, they proceeded to imitate them in many respects, not the least of which was a desire to publish ancient and medieval Judaic texts and thus, in Nahum Karlinsky's words, to "hitch the achievements of modern scholarship to [their] wagon."[5] As Norman Solomon comments, "the barrier which the traditionalists would have liked to exist and even imagined to exist between them and the *maskilim* was unreal."[6]

On both sides of the *Kulturkampf*, the legitimacy of Judaism was felt to be at stake. Thus, a polemical thrust can be detected in much of the publication of Judaic texts in the nineteenth century, both in Western and Eastern Europe. At the hand of both *maskil* and traditionalist, publication of all sorts of Hebraic material, to satisfy a growing demand, went on apace.[7] The highly charged ideological atmosphere as well as an ever-growing demand for Jewish books engendered a situation in which there was great temptation to forge documents.[8]

It is clear that a number of Westernized Judaic scholars could not resist this temptation. Some of the forgeries, such as Lazarus Goldschmidt's (1871–1950) *Baraita de-Ma'aseh Bere'shit*, or Solomon Friedlaender's (1860–1923) *Yerushalmi* may have been intended either as pranks or for the purposes of scholarly or pecuniary advancement.[9] Others, however, such as Saul Berlin's (1740–1794) publication of *Besamim Ro'sh*, ascribed to R. Asher of Toledo (1250–1327), and Joseph Perl's (1773–1839) *Megalleh Temirin* were specifically written with polemical purposes in mind—the advancement of maskilic views to the detriment of anti-*Haskala* forces such as Hasidism.[10] The

4 Ada Rapoport-Albert, "Hagiography with Footnotes: Edifying Tales and the Writing of History in Hasidism," *History and Theory* 27 (1988): 156.

5 Nahum Karlinsky, "The Dawn of Hasidic-Haredi Historiography," *Modern Judaism* 27, no. 1 (February 2007): 41. Cf. Uriel Gellman, "Stories," in *Studying Hasidism: Sources, Methods, Perspectives*, ed. Marcin Wodzinski (New Brunswick: Rutgers University Press, 2019), 65.

6 Solomon, "The Analytic Movement," 43–44.

7 Cf. David Roskies, "The Medium and Message of the Maskilic Chapbook," *Jewish Social Studies* 41, nos. 3–4 (Summer–Autumn 1979): 286.

8 On the issue of forgery in Jewish documents, see Jonathan Klawans, "Deceptive Intentions: Forgeries, Falsehoods, and the Study of Ancient Judaism," *Jewish Quarterly Review* 108, no. 4 (Fall 2018): 489–501.

9 Cf. Cecil Roth, "Forgeries," *Encyclopedia Judaica*, vol. 6, col. 1431–1432. Cf. Harry M. Rabinowicz, *Hasidism: The Movement and Its Masters* (Northvale, NJ: Jason Aronson, 1988), 268.

10 On Perl, see Raphael Mahler, *Hasidism and the Jewish Enlightenment: Their Confrontation in Galicia and Poland in the First Half of the Nineteenth Century* (Philadelphia: Jewish Publication Society of America, 1985), 7 Cf. Jonatan Meir, *Literary Hasidism: The Life and Works*

nineteenth-century Russian Karaite, Abraham Firkowicz (1786–1874), also published a series of forged tombstone inscriptions in order to establish a myth of Karaite origins.[11]

Within the Orthodox camp in Eastern Europe, the issue of the accuracy of "canonized" texts like the Talmud was indeed a recognized virtue practised in particular by such luminaries as the Vilna Gaon (1720–1797).[12] In the nineteenth century, there also was an increasing interest among Orthodox Jews in publishing manuscripts.[13] It is important to note that for the Orthodox, the temptation to forge documents, either for personal gain and advancement or for polemical purposes, was not less than in the camp of the *Wissenschaft*. This temptation was aided in particular by a growing realization that the vast amount of Hebrew manuscripts available in European libraries contained some very important unpublished material. As Solomon Schechter, a product of Hasidic Eastern Europe, put it:

> [Knowledge of the Hebrew collection of the British Museum] has penetrated into the remotest countries, and even the Bachurim [alumni] of some obscure place in Poland, who otherwise neither care nor know anything about British civilization, have a dim notion of the nature of these mines of Jewish learning.
>
> All sorts of legends circulate amongst them about the "millions" of books which belong to the "Queen of England." They speak mysteriously of an autograph copy of the Book of Proverbs, presented to the Queen

of Michael Levi Rodkinson (Syracuse: Syracuse University Press, 2016), 97–98, for the anti-maskilic factor in the production of Hasidic hagiography in the nineteenth century. Rabbi Abraham Mordecai Alter, the Gerrer Rebbe, encouraged the printing of the works of earlier rabbinical authorities as well as the writings of Ḥayyim Vital, primary exponent of Lurianic Kabbala, whose works remained largely in manuscript until the late nineteenth century. He was also one of the first to recognize that Friedlaender's publication of the *Talmud Yerushalmi* was a forgery. Harry M. Rabinowicz, *The World of Hasidism* (Hartford: Hartmore House, 1970), 164.

11 Dan Shapira, "On Firkowicz, Forgeries, and Forging Jewish Identities," in *Manufacturing a Past for the Present: Forgery and Authenticity in Medievalist Texts and Objects in Nineteenth-Century Europe*, ed. János M. Bak, Patrick J. Geary, and Gábor Klaniczay (Leiden: Brill, 2015, 156–169.

12 On the Vilna Gaon, see Immanuel Etkes, *The Gaon of Vilna: The Man and His Image* (Berkeley: University of California Press, 2002).

13 Gertner, *The Rabbi and the City*, 85, 378–379.

of Sheba on the occasion of her visit to Jerusalem[,][14] ... of a copy of the Talmud of Jerusalem which once belonged to Titus. ... of a manuscript of the book *Light is Sown* which is so large that no shelf can hold it.[15]

The Orthodox were tantalized by the stories of such legendary material known to exist in libraries and museums,[16] to which the vast majority of Eastern European Jews never dreamed of gaining access. In addition, the representatives of the "enlightened" were busily at work publishing texts from these libraries which were often used in polemics directed against the Orthodox. Due to these reasons, the temptation within Orthodox circles to forge texts was an ever-present factor.[17] Moreover, in the absence of an acknowledged genre of narrative fiction in classical Hebrew literature,[18] Moshe Rosman observes, Hasidic editors had been engaged in the practice of pseudepigraphy from the very beginnings of Hasidic publication.[19]

For some traditional Polish Jews, these unknown Hebrew manuscripts spelled opportunity. In the mid-nineteenth century, a Polish Jew named Judah b. Alexander Rosenberg (Yudel Rosenberg's great-grandfather) engaged in the publication of numerous Hebrew manuscripts, including the responsa of R. Judah Asheri (1846), a collection of Geonic works (1856) and the responsa of R. Hayyim, *Or Zaru'a* (1860).[20] It is apparent from the introductions to these works that this Judah Rosenberg made his somewhat precarious living from

14 Yudel Rosenberg himself claimed that some of Solomon's books are "hidden and guarded in the archives and treasures of the kings." *Sefer Divrei ha Yamim le-Shlomo ha-Melekh Yalkut ha-Ma'asiyot veha-Me'oraot she-yesh la-Hem Shayakhut el ha-Melekh Shlomo* [hereafter *Shlomo*] (Piótrkow, A. Y. Kleiman, 1913), 3.

15 Solomon Schechter, *Studies in Judaism*, first series (Philadelphia: Jewish Publication Society, 1896), 252. Cf. Yosef Dan, *Ha-Sippur ha-Ḥasidi* (Jerusalem: Keter, 1975), 241.

16 Yudel Rosenberg, in *Derekh Erets*, 20, tells the story of a king who goes to a library and takes out a Hebrew book. Rabinowicz, *Hasidism: The Movement and Its Masters*, 195, reports a story that the Hasidic leader Rabbi Gershon Henokh Leiner visited the Vatican Museum where he allegedly examined the garments belonging to the High Priest.

17 Levi Cooper, "'Neged Zarmei ha-Mayim ha-Zedonim': ha-Admor mi-Munkatsh R. Ḥayyim Elazar Shapira," in *The Gedoilim: Leaders Who Shaped the Israeli Haredi Society* (Jerusalem: Magnes Press, 2017), ed. Binyamin Brown and Nissim Leon, 268.

18 David Stern and Mark J. Mirsky, *Rabbinic Fantasies: Imaginative Narratives from Classical Rabbinic Literature* (New Haven: Yale University Press, 1990), introduction, 4.

19 Moshe Rosman, *Founder of Hasidism: A Quest for the Historical Ba'al Shem Tov* (Berkeley: University of California Press, 1996), 139. Cf. Uriel Gellman, "An Author's Guide: Authorship of Hasidic Compendia," *Zutot* 9 (2012): 85–96.

20 Judah b. Alexander Rosenberg, ed. *Zikhron Yehuda* (Berlin, 1846); *Kovetz Ma'asei Yedei Ge'onim Qadmonim* (Berlin, 1856); *She'elot u-Teshuvot Maharah Or Zaru'a* (Leipzig, 1860). For the relationship between the two Rosenbergs see Yehoshua Ben-Meir, "*ha-Rav Yehuda Yudel Rosenberg zts"l veha-Haggada she Pesaḥ shel ha-Maharal*" *ha-Me'ayen* 61, 2, no. 236 Tevet, 5781 [2021], 105–111.

these publishing ventures. We further learn that the dean of nineteenth-century Hebrew bibliographers, Moritz Steinschneider (1816–1907), accused this Judah Rosenberg of playing fast and loose with the generally accepted rules of publication by attributing an anonymous manuscript to the great Saadia Gaon, obviously with increased sales in mind![21]

In 1885, a man named Jacob Marshak of Polotsk published an anthology of short medieval texts, which he claimed to be publishing for the first time, entitled *Sefer Divrei Moshe*. In his introduction, Marshak squarely faced the fact that the authenticity of his documents, which included several Maimonidean letters, would be questioned. He stated that his book was published from a manuscript sold to him by Warsaw rabbi R. Tsvi Yeḥezkel Michelson (1863–1942), who assured him that the contents had never been published. He himself, however, was unable to guaranty that none of them had ever been published by "the researchers of antiquities and the revealer[s] of hidden things." He then proceeded to denounce the "modern critics" who came with evil intent to cast doubt on the authenticity of the documents he was publishing as they had done with the authenticity of the *Zohar* and other books. As he stated, "who can come to investigate matters written seven hundred years ago and more in the utmost limits of criticism?"[22] Significantly, Rabbi Samuel Mohilever (1824–1898), in his approbation of Marshak's book, leaves open the question of the documents' authenticity but nonetheless stated that they ought to be published.[23]

When Moses Cordovero's (1522–1570) book *Elimah Rabbati* was published from a manuscript in 1881 in Brody, the editor similarly faced up to anticipated scepticism concerning the authenticity of the document:

> Is [this book's] editor a prophet or a son of a prophet? Who has told him … that this is the holy book *Elimah*, a hidden treasure? Perhaps there is an error or perhaps malice in order to increase its monetary value. For thus some book peddlers[24] and booksellers cry out in the streets: Buy this

21 Moritz Steinschneider, *Der Siddur des Saadia Gaon (als Manuscript gedruckt)* (Berlin: Friedländer, March 28, 1856).

22 Jacob Marshak, *Sefer Divrei Moshe* (Warsaw, 1885), introduction, unpaginated.

23 Ibid.

24 Roskies notes that in the late nineteenth century the number of Jewish book peddlers increased. Roskies, "The Medium and the Message of the Maskilic Chapbook," 286.

> ancient book ... that we have found in a library. Perhaps this book you have called *Elimah* was written by someone other [than Cordovero]?[25]

Even a book of traditional folk-remedies, hardly the province of the Jewish intellectual elite, was getting into the act by announcing that it was being published from a manuscript found in an unspecified *bibliotek*.[26]

The late nineteenth-century Hasidic leader, R. Tsadok ha-Kohen (1823–1900) of Lublin, put it this way:

> Even with regard to works bearing the names of the early sages ... if the publisher is not known to be a God-fearing man who believes in all the words of the Torah, an investigation is required whether or not he has interpolated foreign matter into the books with the purpose of misleading the children of Israel, since it has become clear to me that they have done precisely this to a number of books.[27]

In such an atmosphere both of the miraculous recovery and publishing of important Judaic texts and suspicion lest these texts be found false, began the popular literary career of Yudel Rosenberg. Rosenberg, like other Orthodox observers of the current scene, believed that the younger generation was falling prey to the wiles of the secularists because they, as Abraham Mordecai Alter (1866–1948), the Gerrer Rebbe, stated, "read wicked books and newspapers which poison the body and soul."[28] What was needed, obviously, was to fight fire with fire. Thus the Gerrer Rebbe, having spoken of the poison of "wicked" books and newspapers at work on the younger generation, accompanied it with a proposal for the establishment of an Orthodox press. Yudel Rosenberg was certainly in full agreement with this assessment of the situation. He felt that Jewish youth were "like sheep without a shepherd who drink the bitter waters of the foreign schools and have not even the ability to pray with a siddur."[29] As he further stated in the introduction to his *Zohar* translation:

---

25 Moses Cordovero, *Elimah Rabbati*, ed. David ha-Kohen (Jerusalem, 1984, photo-offset of Brody, 1881 edition) editor's introduction, unpaginated.

26 *Sefer Refu'ot* (Vienna, 1927). Reprinted in *'Otsar ha-Segullot* (Jerusalem, 1987), title page.

27 Cited in Louis Jacobs, *Hasidic Thought* (New York: Behrman House, 1976), 232.

28 Cited in Rabinowicz, *The World of Hasidism*, 163. Cf. idem, *Chassidic Rebbes: From the Baal Shem Tov to Modern Times* (Southfield, MI: Targum/Feldheim, 1989), 195, 238.

29 *Omer*, part 1, 18.

> We see, because of our many sins, that books of heresy are greatly multiplying in this era and they have many buyers. It is as if they [the heretical authors] are hunting for souls by the fact that they beautify their books with all sorts of beauty. Moreover these books are written in a pure and simple language, while the holy books are left in a corner.[30]

What Rabbi Rosenberg realized was that the old style of pious literature was not "working" any more. In the introduction to a collection of moralistic excepts from various rabbinic and medieval sources that he originally wrote in the late nineteenth century but remained unpublished by him, Rosenberg stated: "Hasidic books speak only to the Hasidim while moralistic books which speak of hellfire ... have none to seek them."[31] Scoffers were making light of traditional tales and legends because they were not written down in modern-style histories.[32] To Yudel Rosenberg, it was obvious that the situation could be changed for the better by offering the public new-fangled stories purveying the traditional message, thus creating an opposition to modern Yiddish and Hebrew literatures, whose general idea was the diminished relevance of the Jewish tradition in the present day.[33]

Since the object was to attract the younger generation to Orthodoxy through the literary medium, Rabbi Rosenberg determined to imitate contemporary works of Yiddish fiction and, at least in retrospect, he presented himself as a "folk" author (*folk* or *'ammamit*).[34] In that sense, Yudel Rosenberg's "folk narratives" could be characterized, as Shaul Magid observes, as "a rich interaction of materials from the lived reality and experience, with elements of creative

30 *Sha'arei*, 7. On the necessity for Orthodox Jews to publish and counter the publications of the "freethinkers" Cf. Solomon, "The Analytic Movement," 283. On the dangers of these publications, see Sholom DovBer Schneerson "The Foundation of Education" [Ḥanokh la-na'ar], tr. Eliezer Danziger, www.chabad.org/library/article_cdo/aid/150276/jewish/The-Foundation-of-Education.htm.

31 *Derekh Erets*, 3.

32 *Nifla'ot*, 3.

33 In *Derekh Erets*, one of Yudel Rosenberg's earliest works, he included stories dealing with the acquisition of secular knowledge (6–10). In that book he also expressed his opposition to the spoken Hebrew of the Zionists in Palestine with its "Sefardic" pronunciation (27–28). Cf. Gellman, "Stories," 65.

34 On the concept of "folk author" see *Yassif, The Golem of Prague*, 8ff. In the 1956 edition of *Yadot*, the preface makes the claim that Rosenberg was one of the first creators of "traditional Jewish folk literature" because he saw the need to spread the light of Torah and Hasidism to the masses who were not able to explore the original sources (5).

imagination and fantasy."[35] His work may also constitute an example of David Roskies's categorization of a "Warsaw school" of Yiddish fiction in the latter part of the nineteenth century that concentrated on folklore, local events and the Hasidic milieu.[36] Yudel Rosenberg would thus use new means in conveying his Orthodox message. He would serve in the role of a sort of Orthodox narrator-transmitter embodying the Judaic heritage and illuminating the Jewish collective memory from his perspective.[37] His literary work would thus constitute an alternative to modern fiction aimed at a traditional audience.[38] Like later purveyors of Orthodox-oriented stories of great rabbis of the past, Rosenberg undoubtedly felt empowered to make changes and additions to existing stories and even to invent stories for the sake of inspiring his readers.[39]

In 1904, two years after the publication of his Talmudic work, *Yadot Nedarim*, Yudel Rosenberg together with his eldest son, Meir Joshua, then eighteen years old,[40] published a popular book entitled *Sefer Goral ha-'Assiriyot* [Book of the Lots of Ten].[41] The book describes a system in which, by following the instructions in the book, people would be able to receive oracular answers to their queries. Meir Rosenberg was credited in the title page with editing the text[42] and Rabbi Yudel Rosenberg in his own name was credited with contributing a "halakhic word" on the propriety of consulting oracles [*goralot*].[43]

---

35 Shaul Magid, "Folk Narratives," in *Studying Hasidism: Sources, Methods, Perspectives*, ed. Marcin Wodzinski (New Brunswick, NJ: Rutgers University Press, 2019), 128.

36 Cf. Roskies, "Medium and Message," 285; Dan Miron, "Folklore and Antifolklore in the Yiddish Fiction of the Haskala," in *Studies in Jewish Folklore*, ed. Frank Talmage (Cambridge, MA: Association for Jewish Studies, 1980), 249.

37 Haya Bar-Itzhak, *Jewish Poland: Legends of Origin* (Detroit: Wayne State University Press, 2001), 14.

38 Biale et al., *Hasidism: A New History* (Princeton: Princeton University Press, 2018), 465, 467.

39 Marc Shapiro, *Changing the Immutable: How Judaism Rewrites Its History* (Oxford: Oxford University Press, 2015), 282–283.

40 On Meir Joshua Rosenberg, see the introduction to the Jerusalem, 1968 edition of his work, *Kur ha-Mivḥan*. It is interesting to note that Michael Rodkinson, at a similar age of eighteen, published a book dealing with oracular responses to questions: *Sefer Urim ve-Tumim ha-Ḥadash*. See Jonatan Meir, "Michael Levi Rodkinson: Beyn Ḥasidut le-Haskala," *Kabbalah* 18 (2008): 240–241.

41 *Goral* passed the Russian censorship on November 26, 1903.

42 Interestingly, the manuscript was supposed to have included an introduction by Ḥasdai, son of Tsemaḥ Gaon. Perhaps this is a parallel to the collaboration of the father and son Rosenbergs on this book. Meir Joshua Rosenberg, ed., *Sefer Goral ha-'Assiriyot* [hereafter *Goral*] (Warsaw: Ephraim Baumritter, 5664), 13.

43 Rosenberg reedited and republished this responsum in his *Omer*, part 1, 84–88.

How did Yudel Rosenberg come to be associated with a popular book on oracles? There is no clear answer other than there was a demand in the Jewish book market for works enabling its readers to get a glimpse into the murky future. Why did Rabbi Rosenberg choose to play second fiddle in this publication to his young son? There are two likely reasons why he let his son take the main credit. First, it would allow Yudel Rosenberg to distance himself somewhat from the work should its authenticity come into question. Secondly, young Meir Joshua was then on the marriage market and the family might have felt that having this publication to his credit could help him get a good match.[44]

The work published by the Rosenbergs was ascribed to "Rav Tsemaḥ bar Mar Rav Aḥai Gaon," and it presented itself as being published from a manuscript originating in the "Imperial Library of Metz." Neither the Gaon Tsemaḥ b. Aḥai,[45] nor the Imperial Library of Metz existed.[46] The assertion of an archival origin was obviously considered important for the acceptance of the text, and, as we have seen, Yudel Rosenberg shared this need with an impressive array of authors—non-Jewish as well as Jewish—through the centuries. His work required what Anthony Grafton called an "archival pedigree" which offered "an apparent guarantee that what might seem an individual's free invention had in fact been preserved for uninterrupted centuries in an inviolable archive."[47] It is noteworthy, in light of the Rosenbergs' collaboration in publishing the text of the forged manuscript, that the fake "introduction" was written by the son of the alleged author, R. Tsemaḥ Gaon, Ḥasdai.[48]

Rabbi Rosenberg claimed in the introduction to have obtained the manuscript from a Ḥayyim Sharfstein and published a letter, purportedly from Sharfstein, in his introductory material.[49] The Sharfstein letter, which was dated

44 For a similar instance of an author "assigning" a book to a relative (in this instance, a brother) see Yosef M. Boimel, "In Memoriam," in Yehoshua M. Boimel, *A Blaze in the Darkening Gloom: The Life of Rav Meir Shapiro* (Jerusalem: Feldheim, 1994), xxi.

45 Meir Bar-Ilan, "The Miracles of R. Yehuda Yudel Rozenberg" [Hebrew], *Alei Sefer* 19 (2001): 177. Bar-Ilan also notes that the language of the book uses medieval terms not known to the Geonic era.

46 Leiman, "The Adventure of the Maharal of Prague in London," 26–58. Yudel Rosenberg had royal libraries on his mind as early as 1896. Cf. *Derekh Erets*, 20.

47 Anthony Grafton, *Forgers and Critics: Creativity and Duplicity in Western Scholarship* (Princeton: Princeton University Press, 1990).

48 *Goral*, 13.

49 Rosenberg claims Sharfstein as a relative in his letter to Joseph Levy, April 18, 1906, BMA. Similarly Yehuda Ashlag published a volume of Hasidic hagiography in 1914 that he claimed to have purchased from a Shlomo Zalman Breitstein. Yonatan Meir, "Giluyyim ḥadashim 'al R. Yehuda Leib Ashlag," *Kabbalah* 20 (2009): 351, note 26.

Cracow, Tuesday, weekly Torah portion *Shemot* 5656 (December 31, 1895), told of the difficulties of copying the manuscripts, which "have nearly faded away because of [their] age." The letter also states that together with the manuscript of *Goral ha-'Assiriyot* he was enclosing other manuscripts: an anonymous manuscript, written in Arabic, entitled *Quntres 'Ikkarei ha-Emunah leha-Karaim* [Treatise on the Fundamentals of Karaite Belief], obviously having to do with the Karaites, and a manuscript, by the seventeenth-century Lurianic kabbalist Meir Poppers (c. 1624–1662), entitled *Quntres Tsiyyurei 'Amidat ha-'Eser Sefirot min ha-Heh Partsufim* [The Drawing of the Stance of the Ten Sefirot from the Five Configurations].[50] The listing of these other manuscripts was obviously intended to give the cover story verisimilitude. It also indicates the fact that Rabbi Rosenberg was aware, at least in a general way, that manuscripts extant in libraries included a considerable amount of Karaitica, that Karaite writings were often in Arabic, and that unpublished manuscripts of renowned kabbalists were also to be found in library collections.[51]

Despite anachronisms like mention of "masters of Kabbala" in a work purportedly written in the Geonic era, before the appearance of Kabbala in the twelfth century,[52] there is no evidence that the authenticity of *Goral ha-'Assiriyot* was ever questioned by the popular audience for which it was intended.[53] This is indicated by the fact that Rabbi Rosenberg was able to publish a year later, in 1905, yet another manuscript purportedly from the Imperial Library of Metz, though not any of those mentioned in the Sharfstein letter. This one was also a work designed for a popular audience, though it, too, had some scholarly pretensions. Again, Rabbi Rosenberg contributed something in his own name. The publication in question was an edition of the Passover Haggada with a

50 Meir Poppers did have a number of unpublished works, the majority of which have the word *or* [light] in the title, making it more certain that we are dealing with a spurious title.

51 In the preliminary material to his *ZT*, Yudel Rosenberg includes a letter from Professor Alexander Harkavy of St. Petersburg. The letter, in which Harkavy acknowledges, among other things, a request for help in translating foreign words in the *Zohar*, indicates that Rabbi Rosenberg may have had more intellectual contact with the world of "modern" scholarship, perhaps through articles in the Hebrew press, than he was prepared to admit. *ZT* volume 1, 8.

52 *Goral*, 13.

53 On popular reading audiences in Russia at the turn of the twentieth century, see Jeffrey Brooks, *When Russia Learned to Read: Literacy and Popular Literature, 1861–1917* (Princeton, Princeton University Press, 1985).

commentary ascribed to the famed sixteenth-century Rabbi Judah Loewe of Prague, the Maharal (1520–1609).[54]

The book was supposed to be based on a manuscript from Metz obligingly sent by Ḥayyim Sharfstein, the source of the 1904 publication. In the covering letter Sharfstein, writing now from Metz itself, explained to Yudel Rosenberg, whom he now claimed as a relative, that the manuscript had come into the possession of his uncle along with a number of other valuable manuscripts. Rabbi Rosenberg published the Maharal Haggada, unlike *Goral ha-'Assiriyot,* with the approbations of two prominent Warsaw rabbis, Petaḥia Hornblass and Isaac ha-Kohen Feigenbaum (1830–1911), an indication that this book aimed to engage a more mainstream audience than the previous one and thus required approbations.[55]

The manuscript of the Maharal's Haggada commentary, according to Yudel Rosenberg's narrative, was ostensibly copied in the year 1599 by Rabbi Loewe's son-in-law Isaac Katz, and was described as containing a long introduction by the latter (which Rabbi Rosenberg said he chose not to publish). There were parts of the Maharal Haggada that Rabbi Rosenberg specifically claimed as his own. These included a preface with a compendium of laws and customs related to the month of Nissan and the holiday of Passover that Rabbi Rosenberg entitled *Mateh Yehuda* [The Staff of Judah]. As he noted, this work was similar to Rabbi Ephraim Zalman Margaliot's (1762–1828) *Mateh Ephraim* [The Staff of Ephraim] on the laws and *minhagim* of Ellul and the High Holidays.[56] Yudel Rosenberg also wrote in his own name a commentary on the concluding hymn of the Passover Seder, *Ḥad Gadya,* in which he interpreted the poem as speaking of the Jewish destiny from the time of the giving of the Torah until the coming of the messiah,[57] as well as occasional "editor's notes."[58]

---

54 *Haggada shel Pessaḥ* (Warsaw, 1905). On Hasidic affinity for the Maharal, see Hillel Kieval, *Languages of Community: The Jewish Experience in the Czech Lands* (Berkeley: University of California Press, 2000), 102; David Sorotzkin, "'Geula shel Ḥoshekh va-Afela': R. Yoel Teitelbaum ha-Rabi mi-Satmar," in *The Gedoilim: Leaders Who Shaped the Israeli Haredi Society,* ed. Binyamin Brown and Nissim Leon (Jerusalem: Magnes Press, 2017), 379.

55 Both rabbis had provided Yudel Rosenberg with approbations for previous works. Feigenbaum's approbation mentions the "fact" (obviously conveyed to him by Rosenberg) that he had to pay for the manuscript.

56 *Haggada,* 1. The first edition.of *Mateh Ephraim* was published in Zolkwa, 1834.

57 *Haggada,* 1–9, 71–72.

58 Some of these editorial notes involve halakhic matters, such as the recitation of Hallel with a blessing (47, note). Others make points that would have involved obvious anachronisms had they been inserted into the commentary, such as Rabbi Rosenberg's denunciation of Darwinism and Spinozism (59, note).

The "Maharal commentary" was in fact largely composed of material excerpted from Maharal's genuine works, particularly *Gevurot ha-Shem.*[59] However, much of the material in the commentary attributed to the Maharal can be shown not to have emanated from Yudel Rosenberg's pen, particularly in those sections that relate to Kabbala.[60]

For a second time Rabbi Rosenberg had succeeded in passing his creation as a genuine work. The Maharal Haggada was published in numerous editions, both by Rosenberg and others, and was accepted by a number of rabbis as halakhic authority with respect to the laws and customs of the Passover Seder.[61] Only in the year 1985 did a challenge to the authenticity of this document appear in print and cause something of a controversy.[62]

Obviously fortified by the success of his first two editions of manuscripts from the Metz library, Yudel Rosenberg proceeded in 1909 to publish another document from the treasure-trove of the non-existing Royal Library of Metz. Once again, his relative Ḥayyim Sharfstein provided Rabbi Rosenberg with a Maharal manuscript[63] and spoke of yet another Maharal manuscript of over 100 pages, which he was prepared to sell for the sum of 800 *kronen.* Prospective buyers were urged to contact Rabbi Rosenberg.[64]

The manuscript that Yudel Rosenberg published in 1909 was entitled *Nifla'ot Maharal mi-Prag 'im ha-Golem* [The Wonders of the Maharal of Prague with the Golem].[65] It has been described by Yosef Dan as the most important

---

59 Yudel Rosenberg may have gotten the idea of using Katz as the recorder of his Maharal manuscripts through a publication in the Hebrew periodical *ha-Maggid* in 1872 containing an eyewitness account of Katz who had accompanied his father-in-law to a meeting with the Holy Roman Emperor. Arnold Goldsmith, *The Golem Remembered, 1909–1980* (Detroit: Wayne State University Press, 1981), 40. On the makeup of "Maharal's" commentary, see the criticism of Abraham Benedict, "Haggadat Maharal o Aggadat Maharal?," *Moriah* 14, nos. 3–4 (1985): 102–113.

60 Benedict, "Haggadat Maharal," 105, 113; Yosef Dan, *Ha-Sippur ha-Ḥasidi* (Jerusalem: Keter, 1975), 221.

61 Benedict, "Haggadat Maharal," 102.

62 Ibid.

63 *Nifla'ot,* 3. Cf. the *haskama* of Yisrael Goldblum, ed., *Sefer Yere'im,* cited in Ira Robinson and Simcha Fishbane, "Ketavim Ḥadashim shel ha-Rav Yitsḥak Nissenbaum mi-Geniza Russit," in *Turim: Studies in Jewish History and Literature Presented to Dr. Bernard Lander,* ed. Michael Shmidman, vol. 2 (New York, Touro College Press, 2008), Hebrew pagination, 97–129.

64 *Nifla'ot,* 4.

65 This was translated into English by Joachim Neugroschel and published in *Yenne Velt: The Great Works of Jewish Fantasy and Occult* (New York: Pocket Books, 1976), vol. 1, 162–225. See the translator's note (351). A later translation is *The Golem and the Wondrous Deeds of*

twentieth-century contribution of Hebrew literature to world literature.[66] As with the 1905 Maharal Haggada commentary, the manuscript was presented as written by Isaac Katz, Maharal's son-in-law. It is an account of the creation, by the Maharal, of a humanoid golem and the role of the Maharal and his golem in protecting the Jews of Prague against Christian persecution specifically in the context of the blood libel.[67] In doing so, Rosenberg would leave his mark on what has been called "one of the most enduring and imaginative tales in modern Jewish folklore."[68]

The notion that by means of esoteric knowledge it was possible to create a humanoid has a long history in the Jewish tradition.[69] However, the name of Rabbi Judah Loewe of Prague was not connected with the concept of the Golem until the early nineteenth century,[70] though Moshe Idel does show that the Maharal related to the Talmudic passage on the creation of artificial life in his work, *Ḥiddushei Aggadot* [New Interpretations of Rabbinic Legends].[71] In the 1830s and 1840s the tale of the Golem became located in Prague, and was published in a story some 350 words long.[72] It is possible that Yudel Rosenberg

---

the Maharal of Prague, trans., ed., and with an introduction and notes by Curt Leviant (New Haven: Yale University Press, 2007).

66 Dan, "The Beginnings of Hebrew Hagiographic Literature," 85.

67 On the Golem legend, see Hillel Kieval, "Pursuing the Golem of Prague: Jewish Culture and the Invention of a Tradition," *Modern Judaism* 17, no. 1 (1997): 1–23; Maya Barzilai, *Golem: Modern Wars and Their Monsters* (New York: New York University Press, 2016), 17.

68 Edan Dekel and David Gantt Gurley, "How the Golem Came to Prague," *Jewish Quarterly Review* 103, no. 2 (2013): 241.

69 See Gershom Scholem, "The Idea of the Golem," in his *On the Kabbalah and Its Symbolism* (New York: Schocken Books, 1965), 158–204; Moshe Idel, *Golem: Jewish Magical and Mystical Traditions on the Artificial Anthropoid* (Albany: SUNY Press, 1990); Maya Barzilai, *Golem: Modern Wars and Their Monsters* (New York: New York University Press, 2016), 15–16. Cf. the vast literature on this subject cited by Edan Dekel and Gurley, "How the Golem Came to Prague," 241, note 1.

70 Bar-Ilan, "The Miracles of R. Yehuda Yudel Rozenberg," 174; Isaac Yudlov, "Maharal of Prague and His Writings," in *Maharal: Overtures, Biography, Doctrine, Influence* [Hebrew], ed. Elchanan Reiner (Jerusalem: Zalman Shazar Center for Jewish History, 2015), 70–71.

71 Moshe Idel, "The Golem in Jewish Magic and Mysticism," in Emily D. Bilski, *Golem! Danger, Deliverance, and Art* (New York: Jewish Museum, 1988), 28.

72 Goldsmith, *The Golem Remembered*, 28, 35; Vladimir Sadek, "Stories of the Golem and Their Relation to the Work of Rabbi Löw of Prague," *Judaica Bohemiae* 23, no. 2 (1987): 86; Hillel Kieval, *Languages of Community: The Jewish Experience in the Czech Lands* (Berkeley: University of California Press, 2000), 95–113; Maya Barzilai, *Golem: Modern Wars and Their Monsters* (New York: New York University Press, 2016), 16–17; Cathy S. Gelbin, *The Golem Returns: From German Romantic Literature to Global Jewish Culture, 1808–2008* (Ann Arbor: University of Michigan Press, 2011), 90.

got wind of the story through its inclusion as an appendix to a chronicle published in Warsaw in 1869.[73] Alternatively, he may have read Yiddish writer Isaac Leyb Perets's (1852–1915) version of the legend, published in 1893, or that of Sholom Aleykhem (Sholom Rabinovitch, 1859–1916), published in 1901,[74] or else hear it transmitted orally, and decided to present it in a book-length form.[75]

In creating his tale of the Maharal of Prague and the Golem, Rabbi Yudel Rosenberg was presumably looking to supplement his rabbinic income, which seems always to have been insufficient for the support of his large family. A special consideration was that his daughters were fast approaching marriageable age and needed to be provided with dowries.[76] The situation on the Jewish book market was difficult: as Yudel Rosenberg himself once observed in an introduction to another publication, "It is a known fact that all authors of books in our times rather than inheriting honor suffer contempt; in place of profit there is baldness."[77] Doubtless, it was to his advantage to present this book, like his previous two popular works, as the writing of a major luminary of the Jewish past. This would likely increase sales.

However, merely ascribing the book to the Maharal was only half the battle. It remained for Rabbi Rosenberg to create a work worthy of the illustrious name it bore. By all accounts, he succeeded. He filled out the nineteenth-century short story about the Maharal and the Golem, among other things, with motifs found in the tales of Rabbi Naḥman of Bratslav (1772–1810).[78] More importantly, Yudel Rosenberg took the skeleton of the story that he found and

73 Frederic Thieburger, *The Great Rabbi Loew of Prague* (London: East & West Library, 1954), 80; Idel, *Golem: Jewish Magical and Mystical Traditions on the Artificial Anthropoid*, 252.

74 Gelbin, *The Golem Returns*, 71–72.

75 Rosenberg may have come to his knowledge of the Maharal's family through the *Megillat Yuhasin mi-Rabbenu Maharal mi-Prag* (Warsaw, 1864 and 1889). Cf. Gabriele Von Glasenapp, "'Wie eine schaurige Sage der Vorzeit': Die Ritualmordbeschuldigung in der Jüdischen literatur des frühen 20. Jahrhunderts," in *Integration und Ausgrenzung*, ed. Mark H. Gelber, Jacob Hessing and Robert Jütte (Tübingen: Niemeyer, 2009), 200, note 22.

76 On the financial difficulties of the Rosenberg family, particularly with regard to providing dowries for the daughters, see Leah Rosenberg, *Errand Runner*, 24.

77 *Derekh Erets*, 3.

78 *Sefer Tiferet Mahar'el mi-Shpole* [hereafter *Shpoler*] (Piotrkow: Hanokh Henikh Folman, 1912), 53. Moshe Idel comments on the absence of the Golem legend in Hasidic literature prior to Rosenberg. Moshe Idel, "The Golem in Jewish Magic and Mysticism," in Bilski, *Golem! Danger, Deliverance, and Art*, 35. Cf. Yehuda Moraly, "Representations of the Maharal in Theater and Film," in *Maharal: Overtures, Biography, Doctrine, Influence* [Hebrew], ed. Elchanan Reiner (Jerusalem: Zalman Shazar Center for Jewish History, 2015), 570; Yassif, *The Golem of Prague*, 19.

attached it to a theme of great dramatic appeal and unceasing Jewish communal concern—the blood libel.

The notion that Jews used the blood of Christian children in their rites developed in medieval Europe and was especially prevalent in fifteenth- and sixteenth-century Germany. The actual persecution of Jews on this charge petered out in the seventeenth century due to structural changes in the legal and judicial system of the Holy Roman Empire, developments in Reformation theology, and the efforts of the Jews themselves to refute it.[79] Nonetheless, the legend remained intact, particularly in rural areas. In the late nineteenth century, the anti-Semitic movement, as part of its campaign against the Jews becoming an integral part of modern society, caused a revival of the myth and, starting in the late nineteenth century, a number of well-publicized trials of related to the charge of ritual murder were held in Central Europe, the Russian Empire, and North America.[80]

In the Russian Empire, after the dissolution of the second Duma in 1907 and the concurrent victory of reactionaries in the Russian government, there was a concerted effort on the part of the Russian government, as part of its anti-revolutionary campaign, to use the Blood Libel against the Jews.[81] Doubtless, this situation led Rabbi Rosenberg to tie the Maharal of Prague and his Golem to this very theme. As the title page of the book proclaimed, "The Maharal created the Golem through kabbalistic wisdom to fight the Blood libel, which was common in his time and to show to all the truth that Israel is innocent [of that libel]."[82]

Rosenberg tried to go even farther in an attempt to exonerate the Jews from gentile accusations. At one point in the book, he attempted to demonstrate that the Jews were not in fact responsible for the trial and condemnation of Jesus. He did this by asserting that those who participated in the trial of Jesus were the sectarian Saducees alone, "whereas the true Jews, that is the Pharisees and the Essenes, who did not desire to recognize Herod's government, did not at all wish to take part in this trial."[83]

---

79 On the history of the Blood Libel, see *R. Po-Chia Hsia, The Myth of Ritual Murder: Jews and Magic in Reformation Germany* (New Haven: Yale University Press, 1988).

80 David Fraser, "The Blood Libel in North America: Jews, Law, and Citizenship in the Early 20th Century," *Law & Literature* 28, no. 1 (2016): 1–53.

81 *Encyclopedia Judaica*, vol. 4, col. 1130, s.v. "Blood Libel".

82 *Nifla'ot*, title page.

83 *Nifla'ot*, 7.

In point of historical fact, as has been shown by several critics, the Blood Libel appears not to have been a factor in Jewish-Christian relations in Prague during the era of the historical Rabbi Loewe.[84] However this and other historical and geographical errors committed by Rosenberg[85] do not diminish the dramatic power of the confrontation of the kabbalist rabbi, aided by his Golem with the priest-sorcerer, Thaddeus, with victory going to the rabbi and vindication to the Jews.[86]

Rosenberg's *Nifla'ot Maharal* story was immensely popular and influential.[87] It and the other Rosenberg stories earned this praise from Yiddish journalist A. Litwin:

> [Rosenberg has] a full, colourful, popular [*folkstimlikhen*] style of narration. The purity, spirituality, and great love of the author for his heroes raises his style to a higher more artistic level without thereby abandoning the charm of the unartistic, popular work. [He is] a man with a poetic soul and a strong attraction to mysticism.[88]

Maya Barzilay calls him "a sophisticated modern writer even when his text uses traditional storytelling tropes."[89] Arnold Goldsmith criticises Yudel Rosenberg for presenting a work that is "too journalistic with [a] preference for stock character types" but nonetheless concludes, "he resurrected for twentieth-century readers a new folk hero."[90] Cathy Gelbin sees Rosenberg as emulating "the supposedly authentic style of legend writing generated by the Grimms" and understands that "the literary quality of Rosenberg's text emerges in the

---

84 Goldsmith, *The Golem Remembered*, 35.

85 An example of one of the errors made by Rosenberg is that he gave the cardinal in Prague the name Jan Sylvester. This is the name of a sixteenth-century Christian Hebraist. No cardinal of that name existed in the Maharal's era. See Leiman, "The Adventure of the Maharal of Prague in London: R. Yudl Rosenberg and the Golem of Prague," *Tradition* 36, no. 1 (2002): 26–58; Goldsmith, *The Golem Remembered*, 40.

86 Rosenberg returns to the theme of a priest-sorcerer in *Greiditser*, part 4, 19–20. The theme of the "evil priest" is common in Hasidic tales. See Biale et al., *Hasidism: A New History*, 454.

87 Edan Dekel and David Gantt Gurley, "Kafka's Golem," *Jewish Quarterly Review* 107, no. 4 (Fall 2017): 535.

88 A. Litwin, cited in Zalman Reizin, *Leksikon fun der Yiddisher Literatur, Presse un Filologie*, vol. 4, col. 117.

89 Maya Barzilai, *Golem: Modern Wars and Their Monsters* (New York: New York University Press, 2016), 229, note 7.

90 Goldsmith, *The Golem Remembered*, 50; Gelbin, *The Golem Returns*, 91.

aesthetic choice of style and its implicit references to a host of high and low culture literary models."[91]

A sure sign that Yudel Rosenberg's experiment in presenting his Maharal work was a success was that it spawned numerous other literary works. One of them, entitled *Ḥokhmat Maharal,* purports to be an account of a religious disputation held between Maharal and Cardinal Jan Sylvester. This work is clearly dependent on Rabbi Rosenberg's publication, for the "fact" of this disputation was widely known only through it.[92] However, Rosenberg's own work merely summarizes the debate and, in *Ḥokhmat Maharal,* four of the five topics listed by Rosenberg are not treated.[93] On the basis of internal evidence, Sid Leiman assumes that its author is Dovberish Tursh (ca. 1863–1935), two of whose works are mentioned in the course of the disputation.[94] Yudel Rosenberg's *Nifla'ot Maharal* was further anthologized by the Hebrew author and folklorist Micha Ben Gurion in his *Meqor Yehuda* [Fountain of Judah],[95] by David Ignatof in *Ma'asiyot fun Altn Prag,* and by Y. Y. Trunk in his *Letste Ḥasidishe Folks Mayses,*[96] The book was translated into both German[97] and Judeo-Bukharan,[98] and adapted by the Yiddish poet H. Leivick for a drama entitled *Der Goylem.*[99]

Apparently, nearly all early twentieth-century readers of *Nifla'ot Maharal* accepted Yudel Rosenberg's presentation of the work as genuine and treated the book as the publication of a sixteenth-century manuscript. Thus Zalman Reizin, in his lexicon of Yiddish literature, reported that "[Rosenberg's] relative, a bookseller, found it in the City Library of Metz."[100] Not all readers were

---

91 Cathy S. Gelbin, *The Golem Returns,* 91–92, 146–147.

92 On anti-Christian polemical themes in the Maharal's commentary on the aggadot, *Be'er ha-Gola,* see Mordecai Breuer, "Vikkuḥo shel Maharal mi-Prag 'im ha-Notsrim: Mabat Ḥadash 'al sefer Be'er ha-Gola," *Tarbiz* (1986): 253–260. On manuscript evidence for the Maharal's involvment in a disputation with a Christian cleric, see Avraham David, "The Involvement of the Maharal of Prague in a Jewish-Christian Debate" [Hebrew], *Kiryat Sefer* 64 (1992/1993): 1433–1434.

93 Leiman, "The Adventure of the Maharal of Prague in London," 26–58.

94 Ibid. On Tursh, see Uriel Gellman, "An Author's Guide: Authorship Of Hasidic Compendia," *Zutot* 9 (2012): 87.

95 Cf. Goldsmith, *The Golem Remembered,* 41. Eli Yassif discerns similarities between Rosenberg and Berdichevsky. Yassif, *The Golem of Prague,* 41–42.

96 Fox, *100 Years,* 275.

97 Chaim Bloch adapted Yudel Rosenberg's work (attributing it to a Polish Jew from Chelm he met in a prisoner-of-war camp). It was serialized in 1917 and published in 1920 as *Der Prager Golem.* Barzilai, *Golem: Modern Wars and Their Monsters,* 4, 12.

98 Ibid., 53.

99 Ibid., 41, 76, 79; Fox, *100 Years,* 275.

100 Reizin, *Leksikon fun der Yiddisher Literatur, Presse un Filologie,* vol. 4, col. 116.

taken in, however. In the far-off town of Marmoroszighet, Rabbi Emmanuel Eckstein noted that the work contradicted previous rabbinic statements on the creation of a golem and possessed other internal contradictions. Having sent to Prague for accurate information, Rabbi Eckstein declared the work a lie and a sham in a pamphlet he published in Marmoroszighet in 1910.[101] Eckstein's criticism was picked up by the young Gershom Scholem, who, in a review of a work edited by Chaim Bloch that contained another purported Maharal letter dependent on Yudel Rosenberg's work, condemned the publication as a late forgery.[102] Forgery or not, a study of the issue of the *Golem* by Moshe Idel holds out the possibility that Rosenberg's account may nonetheless preserve some important ancient traditions.[103] In a later essay on the *Golem*, Scholem would give the author of *Nifla'ot Maharal* the following grudging compliment:

> Toward the end of this Hebrew novel there are nineteen apocryphal utterances of Rabbi Loew on the nature of the Golem, which, in reality, do no less honor to the kabbalistic frame of mind than to the imagination of the author.[104]

However, the animadversions of Eckstein and Scholem do not appear to have influenced the broad audience in Eastern Europe that accepted the book at face value.[105] The publication of *Nifla'ot Maharal* seems thus to have consolidated Rosenberg's reputation as an "editor."

---

101 Emmanuel Eckstein, *Sefer Yetsira* (Marmorosszighet, 1910).

102 Gershom Scholem, review of Chaim Bloch, *Qovets Mikhtavim Meqoriim meha-Besh"t ve-Talmidav*, *Kiryat Sefer* 1 (1924/5): 104–106. Arnold Goldsmith in *The Golem Remembered* demonstrates that Bloch is dependent on Rosenberg's publication though Bloch did not acknowledge this. Cf. Leiman, "The Adventure of the Maharal of Prague in London," 26–58; Nicola Morris, *The Golem in Jewish American Literature* (New York: Peter Lang, 2007), 15; Jonatan Meir, *Literary Hasidism: The Life and Works of Michael Levi Rodkinson* (Syracuse: Syracuse University Press, 2016), 105.

103 Idel, *Golem: Jewish Magical and Mystical*, 85.

104 Scholem, "Idea of the Golem," 189, note 1; idem, *Elements in the Kabbalah and Its Symbolism* [Hebrew] (Jerusalem: Mossad Bialik, 1980), 410.

105 The eight editions of the book I have thus far discovered indicate that it was almost continuously in print at least until the late 1960s. This would seem to indicate its continuing acceptance. Cf. A. Brosh, "Mikhtav 'Maqor' shel ha-Maharal mi-Prag," *Ha-Modi'a*, 20 Nisan 5750 (1990). For evidence of the influence of these tales, see Joseph I. Schneersohn, *Lubavicher Rebbe's Memoirs*, vol. 1 (Brooklyn: Otzar Hachassidim, 1956), 167ff, and volume 2 (Brooklyn: Otzar Hachassidim 1960), 218–219; *Haqqafot* (Montreal, 1919), title page. There were and are a number of manuscripts within the Hassidic community ascribed to Pinḥas of Korets. See Rabinowicz, *Chassidic Rebbes*, 44.

This reputation enabled Yudel Rosenberg to publish other purported manuscripts. In 1909 Rosenberg published a new document from another "manuscript," which he did not claim to have come from the Metz archive. The publication consisted of a service for the processions of the Torah [*haqqafot*] on the holiday of Simḥat Torah according to the custom of the early Hasidic master Pinḥas of Korets (1726–1791), along with some pious customs and Torah thoughts ascribed to Rabbi Pinḥas. Rabbi Rosenberg claimed to have obtained this document from a man named Yitsḥak Lerner, the grandson of R. Pinḥas's student and colleague, R. Bertsche Katz of Siedlkov.[106] Yudel Rosenberg's claim is based upon some accurate traditions concerning the relationship between these two figures and also reflects knowledge of the existence of unpublished manuscripts of Rabbi Pinḥas.[107] On the other hand, bibliographer Abraham Schischa brings evidence that Rabbi Pinḥas did not in fact create his own *haqqafot* service.[108] Given what we know about Yudel Rosenberg's Maharal publications, Schischa's evidence should be taken seriously. In any event, this publication is the first in a series of Hasidic "documents" and stories which Rabbi Rosenberg would publish in the ensuing years.

In Łódź as in Warsaw, Rabbi Yudel Rosenberg was forced by his penurious circumstances to use his literary talents both to make ends meet as well as to try and consolidate his position as spiritual leader. As a creative writer, the years between 1910 and 1913 were the most prolific of Yudel Rosenberg's life. Of the works he published in this period, no less than five were based upon "editions" of texts which, it was claimed, were either unpublished old manuscripts or at least not readily available to the average reader.

The first of these, *Sefer Eliyahu ha-Navi'*, was a collection of tales concerning the prophet Elijah. Most of them were culled from various midrashic collections, but some of them bear traces of Yudel Rosenberg's editorial hand.[109] Rosenberg's idea for the publication of this book may well have stemmed from the widespread custom among Hungarian and Galician Hassidim to read designated portions of a midrashic collection entitled *Tanna de-Be Eliyahu*, popularly

106 *Haqqafot*, title page.

107 On this relationship, see Yehezkel Frankel, ed. *Sefer Imrei Pinḥas ha-Shalem* (Bnei Brak, 1988), 169, 239. On the existence of Rabbi Pinḥas's manuscripts in the twentieth century see Michael Marmur, *Abraham Joshua Heschel and the Sources of Wonder* (Toronto: University of Toronto Press, 2016), 112.

108 Abraham Schischa, letter to the author, June 29, 1988.

109 Eli Yassif comments that Rosenberg was a careful anthologizer who, nonetheless, allowed himself a great deal of freedom in his treatment of his sources. Yassif, *The Golem of Prague*, 14.

ascribed to the prophet Elijah,[110] at the end of every Sabbath and thereby merit success in the study of Torah, bodily health, and economic prosperity.[111] Rabbi Rosenberg presented his book to the public as fulfilling the same purpose, since he recommended reading from it at the same time period—after the end of the Sabbath—and with the same goal in mind, "to ensure a good living [*parnasa*], success, and blessing."[112]

Along with placing his new collection in direct competition with *Tanna de-Be Eliyahu*, Yudel Rosenberg moved to put into question the very authenticity of that midrash. In his introduction, he stated that he would not cite passages in his book in the name of the midrash *Tanna de-Be Eliyahu*: "because of the doubt which the critics [*mevaqrim*] have expressed that the author of *Tanna de-Be Eliyahu* is not the prophet Elijah but rather the Tanna Elijah who lived in the times of the *Tannaim* [mishnaic rabbis]."[113]

He also stated that his version of the "Prayer of Elijah the Prophet for the Community of Israel [*Knesset Yisrael*]" was parallel to that printed in chapter 19 of *Tanna de-Be Eliyahu*, but was more complete than in the ordinary version of *Tanna de-Be Eliyahu* and had less scribal errors [*shigegat ha-ma'atiqim*].[114] At the same time, he asserted the authenticity of his own publication by demanding that the reader "be in no hurry to suspect that—God forbid—I forged this [document] by myself [*mi-libi*]."[115]

Rabbi Rosenberg announced that in his Elijah book he was relying on other *midrashim*, such as *Midrash Tadshe* and *Midrash va-Yosha'*. The texts of these *midrashim* that he used, he claimed, were superior to those contained in the standard printed editions: "In our *Midrash va-Yosha'* we find only the second half of this wonderful tale. This transcription is from the manuscript *Midrash va-Yosha'*, which includes many wonderful tales not published in our country."[116]

---

110 The source of this attribution is Babylonian Talmud, Ketubot 106a: "Elijah used to come to R. Anan, upon which occasions the prophet recited the Seder Eliyahu to him."

111 William G. Braude and Israel J. Kapstein, *Tanna Debe Eliyyahu: The Lore of the School of Elijah* (Philadelphia: Jewish Publication Society, 1981), 12. Cf. also Rabinowicz, *Chassidic Rebbes*, 108.

112 *Sefer Eliyahu ha-Navi': Hitgaluto, Nifle'otav, 'Inyene Eliyahu ha-Navi' 'al Devar ha-Ge'ulah, Nilketu min Talmud Bavli ve-Yerushalmi veha-Zohar* ... [hereafter *Eliyahu*] (Piotrków: Mordecai Tsederboym, 1910), 3. Cf. also *Refa'el*, 85–6, where Rabbi Rosenberg prescribes reading this book in order to prevent sexual thoughts during prayer.

113 *Eliyahu*, 4. Cf. Braude and Kapstein, *Tanna Debe Eliyyahu*, 9, note 27.

114 *Eliyahu*, 67.

115 *Eliyahu*, 3.

116 *Eliyahu*, 34, note.

The source of his superior texts, Rabbi Rosenberg asserted, was the Land of Israel. He stated that he received a superior copy of *Midrash va-Yosha'* from the Land of Israel through his friend, Joshua Teitelbaum of Warsaw.[117] The superior text of Elijah's prayer, mentioned above, was sent to him, so Rabbi Rosenberg claimed, directly from the city of Safed along with other copies of old books from which he copied many items.[118] Yudel Rosenberg's claim was no doubt given some verisimilitude from the publications of his contemporary, Rabbi Solomon Aaron Wertheimer (1866–1935) who claimed to have derived many of the manuscripts for his collections of *midrashim*, which he began publishing in 1893, from manuscripts found in the Land of Israel.[119] Rabbi Rosenberg also included in this book the Zoharic passage Pataḥ Eliyahu (pages 71–89), which will be examined in chapter 7.

In publishing his Elijah book, Rosenberg once more demonstrated that he was capable of adapting some techniques of critical scholarship in order to enhance the chances of success for his work on the Hasidic book market. It also shows that he had a keen eye for a niche in the book market. The many editions of this work, both in its original Hebrew and in Yiddish translation, testify to both the intrinsic appeal of the stories he presented as well as to the correctness of his strategy.[120]

From the realm of *midrash*, Yudel Rosenberg next turned his hand to Hasidic hagiography.[121] In 1910, a collection of stories on Rabbi Levi Isaac of Berdichev was published anonymously and has been ascribed to Rabbi Rosenberg.[122] While the style of the stories in this book, entitled *Nifla'ot Qedushat Levi* [The Wonders of The Holiness of Levi], may indicate Yudel Rosenberg's hand, there is, at this point, no way of proving his authorship. Given his previous track record, it would seem most uncharacteristic of him to publish anonymously.

117 *Eliyahu*, 4. Cf. the long story extracted from this manuscript on 34–40.

118 *Eliyahu*, 67.

119 Cf. "Wertheimer, Solomon Aaron," *Encyclopedia Judaica*, vol. 16, col. 459. Wertheimer, it seems, also played fast and loose with the manuscripts he possessed. For evidence of his censorship of *midrashim*, see Deborah F. Sawyer, "Heterodoxy and Censorship: Some Critical Remarks on Wertheimer's Edition of Midrash Aleph-Beth," *Journal of Jewish Studies* 42 (1991): 115–121.

120 Of all Yudel Rosenberg's works, *Eliyahu* has been republished the most times. I have counted twenty-three editions, the latest published in 1986.

121 On the state of hasidic hagiography in the late nineteenth century, see Yosef Dan, "A Bow to Frumkinian Hasidism," *Modern Judaism* 11 (1991): 175–193; Jonatan Meir, *Literary Hasidism: The Life and Works of Michael Levi Rodkinson* (Syracuse: Syracuse University Press, 2016); Biale et al., *Hasidism: A New History*, 469–470.

122 *Nifla'ot Qedushat Levi* (Bilgoray, 1910/1). Cf. Fox, *100 Years*, 275.

In 1912, however, he published a series of tales of the early Hasidic leader, Rabbi Arye Leib, the "Grandfather" of Shpole, in a conscious celebration of the one hundredth anniversary of his death in 1812.[123] In the *Shpoler Rebbe*, Rosenberg had an ideal subject. Rabbi Aryeh Leib was famous in Hasidic lore for his conflict with and persecution of one of the most original minds to emerge from the Hasidic movement in the early nineteenth century—Rabbi Naḥman of Bratslav.[124] Despite his fame, however, precious little was actually known concerning this important figure. Moreover, Hasidic legend saw Rabbi Aryeh Leib as a descendant of the Maharal.[125] This situation was tailor made for Yudel Rosenberg to unleash his literary talent; his work would itself become a source for "Hasidic history."[126]

As Rabbi Rosenberg stated, the tales in the collection, entitled *Tif'eret Mahar'el mi-Shpole* [The Glory of Rabbi Aryeh Leib of Shpole], were gathered, "from printed books, from sources who are learned sages [*talmidei ḥakhamim*]," and also, as we have come to expect, from a faded manuscript which was allegedly written by R. Arye Leib's servant, Isaac Skvirer, whose descendents, Isaac Orshatov and Ḥazkele Kalmanovitz of Warsaw, sold it to Rosenberg.[127] Yudel Rosenberg stated that he copied and edited this manuscript. He also stated that he had received information from Rabbi Aaron Mordecai Kromer, the current rabbi of

123 R. Aryeh Leib died in 1812. The centenary is specifically mentioned in *Shpoler*, 22. The book also came out in Yiddish as *Der Shpoler Zeyde* (Piotrkow, n.d.). There are a number of differences between the Hebrew and the Yiddish versions. On page 4 of the Yiddish version, the translator remarks: "Up to now we have translated the forward which has been written in the holy language by the famous *ga'on* and rabbi, R. Yudel Rosenberg ... living today in Łódź, who is the author of many books, as well as the writer of the book in the holy language *Tif'eret Mahar'el*. Unfortunately, we have to confess the truth: many things remained which the author did not allow us to translate into *zhargon* [Yiddish] for the sake of his own reasons and hidden motives." Cf. Susanne Galley, "Holy Men in Their Infancy: The Childhood of *Tsakidim* in Hasidic Legends," *Polin* 15 (2002): 173, note 24.

124 On Naḥman, see Arthur Green, *Tormented Master* (Alabama: PUBLISHER, 1978).

125 *Shpoler*, 3, 7, 10; Rabinowicz, *The World of Hasidism*, 81; Mintz, *Legends of the Hasidim*, 183. For other Hasidic connections with the Maharal, see ibid., 95, 108; Klepfisz, *Culture of Compassion*, 90; Sorotzkin, *Orthodoxy and Modern Disciplination*, 143, 349; Bezalel Safran, "Maharal and Early Hasidism," in *Hasidism: Continuity or Innovation*, ed. Bezalel Safran (Cambridge: Harvard University Press, 1988), 47–144.

126 On the dependence of Hasidic history on such hagiographical works, see Yosef Salmon, "R. Naftali Zvi Horovits mi-Ropshitz—Qavvim biografiim," in *Hasidism in Poland*, ed. Rahel Elior, Yisrael Bartal and Chone Shmeruk (Jerusalem: Bialik Institute, 1994), 91; Assaf, "Ḥasidut Polin be Me'ah ha-19," 363.

127 *Shpoler*, 3. This suggests comparison with Yudel Rosenberg's other claims that manuscripts had been sold to him. Cf. Rabinowicz, *World of Hasidism*, 81. Rabbi Rosenberg also mentioned a tradition concerning the interest of Israel of Rizhin, *Shpoler*, 67.

Shpole, as well as Rabbi Tsvi Yeḥezkel Mikhelson of Plonsk who was serving as a member of the Warsaw rabbinate (1863–1942), a man with a wide reputation as an expert in Hasidic tales,[128] and Rabbi Abraham Segal Etinga of Dukla.[129]

Reviewing this work, Gedaliahu Nigal, a student of Hasidic literature, has stated that "there is no doubt that before us is a modern literary creation. The question is who wrote it: the relative or Rosenberg?" Nigal was satisfied that Rosenberg authored a large part of the book, though he also noted that a considerable portion indeed consisted of reworkings of stories published in earlier hagiographical collections.[130]

An examination of the content of the stories bears Nigal out. The fact that Rabbi Aryeh Leib in one of the stories prevents a blood libel against Jews brings to mind the major theme of Rosenberg's Maharal book.[131] Indeed, Rabbi Aryeh Leib is said in the book to have been a soul-descendent [*gilgul*] of the Maharal, which perhaps explains at least part of Rabbi Rosenberg's particular interest in his character.[132] Another detail which links the Shpoler tales and those of the Maharal consists of a literary parallel. In the Maharal book, a story is told of two men from Romania, both named Berel.[133] In the tales of R. Aryeh Leib, a story is told of two men from Romania, both named Mendel.[134] Eli Yasif readily discerns motifs borrowed from Daniel Defoe's *Robinson Crusoe* and Alexander Dumas's *The Count of Monte Cristo*, as well as *Shivḥei ha-Besht* and the Tales of Rabbi Naḥman of Bratslav.[135]

Finally, Yudel Rosenberg's continuing fascination with modern technology, so evident in his non-literary works,[136] is betrayed at one point in the tales where the Shpoler Grandfather is made to say:

---

128 On Mikhelson, see Justin Jaron Lewis, *Imagining Holiness: Classic Hasidic Tales in Modern Times* (Montreal and Kingston: McGill-Queen's University Press, 2009), 48–49. Cf. Gellman, "Stories," 66.

129 *Shpoler*, 4.

130 Gedalyahu Nigal, *The Hasidic Tale: Its History and Topics* (Jerusalem: ha-Makhon le-Ḥeqer ha-Sifrut ha-Ḥasidit, 1981), 50.

131 *Shpoler*, 3, 7, 10.

132 *Shpoler*, 3. Dan suggests that Rosenberg considered himself a descendant of the Maharal but Rabbi Rosenberg never stated that fact clearly even though he did not hesitate to claim descent from Judah the Pietist. Leiman, "The Adventure of the Maharal of Prague in London," 26–58.

133 *Nifla'ot*, 41.

134 *Shpoler*, 38.

135 Yassif, *The Golem of Prague*, 25, 54.

136 See Ira Robinson, "Reviving the Study of the Zohar in First Half of the 20th Century: A Consideration of the Roles of Gershom Scholem, Yudel Rosenberg, and Yehuda Ashlag,"

> What we do on earth is "photographed" and preserved in heaven with live action [*ḥayyut u-tenu'ah*]. Know that in the future on earth men will be able to make such a miracle to make photographs which have motion and sound and to record what happens at that time even after hundreds of years [have passed].[137]

In his Shpoler book, Rabbi Rosenberg demonstrated yet again his ability to make use of aspects of the "outside" scholarly world in order to enhance the credibility and, presumably, the saleability of his book. Beyond claiming to base his work on the discovery of a manuscript, he also published letters he received from informants, including the current rabbi of Shpole, who gave him details of the sparse local traditions concerning the Grandfather.[138] The publication of the Shpoler book in 1912 may indicate that Rosenberg was aware of and in a certain sense inspired by Solomon An-ski's (1863–1920) ethnographic expedition. This expedition was launched in 1911, the time Rosenberg must have been compiling his book. An-sky aimed to collect and preserve ethnographic data from an Eastern European Jewry, which he perceived as undergoing a radical cultural transformation.[139]

In 1913, Yudel Rosenberg published a sequel to his tale of the Maharal and the Golem, entitled *Sefer Ḥoshen ha-Mishpat shel ha-Kohen ha-Gadol* [Book of the High Priest's Breastplate]. Once again, he claimed to have derived the manuscript he was publishing from the Imperial Library of Metz, now identified by him as located in the land of Lotharingia.[140] In this work, there is no mention of the mediation of Ḥayyim Sharfstein. The manuscript, entitled *Klei ha-Miqdash,* was supposedly authored by a Rabbi Manoaḥ Hendel of France.

---

in *From Something to Nothing: Jewish Mysticism in Contemporary Canadian Jewish Studies,* ed. Harry Fox, Daniel Maoz and Tirzah Meacham (Newcastle upon Tyne: Cambridge Scholars Publishing, 2019), 41–50.

137 *Shpoler*, 61. Cf. PY, 55: "All the speeches of men are found in the air. And through the power of the radio we are able to hear ... peoples' voices ... from a distance of thousands of parasangs."

138 *Shpoler*, 106. On the paucity of pre-Rosenberg tales of the Shpoler, see Yassif, *The Golem of Prague*, 61.

139 On the An-ski expedition, see Nathaniel Deutsch, *The Jewish Dark Continent: Life and Death in the Russian Pale of Settlement* (Cambridge: Harvard University Press, 2011).

140 *Sefer Ḥoshen ha-Mishpat shel ha-Kohen ha-Gadol* [hereafter *Ḥoshen*] (Piótrkow: Ḥanokh Henikh Folman, 1913), 3. It is likely that the geographical term "Lothar" was taken from references in the Tosafistic commentaries on the Talmud.

The story begins in the year 1590, the very year in which the narrative of Yudel Rosenberg's 1909 Maharal book comes to an end.[141] The book makes the assumption that the vessels of the Temple of Jerusalem, which had been seized by the Romans in 70 C.E., were now in the hands of the French and the English, "as is well known among the investigators of antiquity and the scholars of archaeology." The 1913 book further asserts that the breastplate of the high priest was on display at London's "Belmore Street Museum."[142] This assertion would have been plausible to many Rosenberg's audience, who already heard the stories stating that some of the booty from the Jerusalem Temple had been preserved at the Vatican.[143]

The plot of this book revolves around the theft of the breastplate from the Museum. When the breastplate was stolen, the Maharal journeyed from Prague to London. He solved the crime, committed by a Captain Wilson, and converted the thief to Judaism. Rosenberg concluded his tale by asserting that a latter-day descendent of this Captain Wilson was none other than President Woodrow Wilson of the United States, just elected to the presidency in 1912, who was rumored to be a philo-Semite.[144]

It is easily established that the story of the theft of the High Priest's breastplate was in fact taken by Yudel Rosenberg from a story of Arthur Conan Doyle, "The Jew's Breastplate," which had been published in 1908.[145] Rosenberg cites Conan Doyle by name in the work as a "great English author and researcher," and he states clearly that he translated part of Conan Doyle's work from Russian.[146] What Rosenberg did with Conan Doyle's story was to "Judaize" it both by making the Maharal the dectective-hero of the story[147] and by constructing

141 This was noticed by Leiman, "The Adventure of the Maharal of Prague in London," 26–58.

142 *Ḥoshen*, 4.

143 Rabinowicz, *Hasidism: The Movement and Its Masters*, 195. Cf. Steven Fine, *The Menorah: from the Bible to Modern Israel* (Cambridge: Harvard University Press, 2017), chapter 6.

144 *Ḥoshen*, 40.

145 Arthur Conan Doyle, "The Jews' Breastplate," in his *Round the Fire Stories* (London: Smith, Elder and Company, 1908), https://www.arthur-conan-doyle.com/index.php?title=The_Story_of_the_Jew%27s_Breast-Plate, accessed December 18, 2019. Cf. Salomon Alter Halpern, *The Prisoner and Other Tales of Faith* (Jerusalem and New York: Feldheim, 1981), 12.

146 *Ḥoshen*, 5, 40. In Russian popular literature of the turn of the twentieth century there was much republication as well as local adaptation of the character and plots of Doyle's Sherlock Holmes stories. Brooks, *When Russia Learned to Read*, 115–117, 141–144, 208.

147 Most likely, Arnold Goldsmith did not know of this particular work of Rosenberg's but only commented on the Maharal's portrayal in *Nifla'ot*. But interestingly, he stated that

an independent subplot concerning two Jewish museum guards (at a time prior to the readmission of Jews into England in the seventeenth century) who were accused of having engineered the theft.[148]

Rabbi Rosenberg concluded this work on the same scholarly note in which he had begun by publishing a letter he claimed to have been written to him from London by a Mr. I. Werner, "a great sage and investigator of antiquity [and] a Jew devoted to the religion and belief of Israel from the city ... of London." In his letter dated April 1, 1913, Mr. Werner gave Rosenberg information on the Conan Doyle story, the likely whereabouts of remnants of the Temple vessels and implements in Italian museums, on the likelihood of Woodrow Wilson's descent from Captain Wilson, and on translations of the *Zohar* into European languages.[149] In the book, Rosenberg gives evidence of some knowledge of Roman history.[150] Anachronisms include the Maharal placing advertisements in newspapers and the use of calling cards, cameras, and spectroscopes.[151] In the 1950s Rabbi Shim'on Aharon Hershkovitz of Bnei Brak published a Yiddish version of this story, without attribution to Rosenberg, as *Di Gneive in Britishen Muzeum fun Maharal mi-Prag*.[152]

Later in 1913, the year Rosenberg moved to Canada, he wrote a series of tales concerning Rabbi Elijah Guttmacher (1795–1874), the Greiditser Rabbi.[153] The Greiditser book was the only one of Rosenberg's known hagiographical works that was published solely in Yiddish, though it claims on the title page to be a translation of a Hebrew work entitled *Hadrat Eliyahu*. The five tales in the collection, for which Rosenberg claimed literary as well as eyewitness sources,[154] did not center on the figure of the rabbi as in normative Hasidic hagiography. They rather concerned Jews caught in the bewildering maze of modernity. Having rejected the life of tradition, they got into various sorts of

---

Rosenberg's Maharal took on the character of a Sherlock Holmes. Goldsmith, *The Golem Remembered*, 56. Cf. Yassif, *The Golem of Prague*, 26–27.

148 *Ḥoshen*, 33.

149 Ibid., 40.

150 *Ḥoshen*, 3–4.

151 *Ḥoshen*, 6, 11, 31. The *Shpoler* book also exhibits the anachronism of newspapers (32, 36).

152 This tale is bound together with another obvious adaptation of Rosenberg, also published without attribution: *Dem Maharals Droshe: A Mayse* (Bnei Brak: Der Heyliger Kval, 1950).

153 On this work, see Ira Robinson, "The Uses of the Hasidic Story: Rabbi Yudel Rosenberg and His Tales of the Greiditzer Rabbi," *Journal of the Society of Rabbis in Academia* 1, nos. 1–2 (1991): 17–24. On Guttmacher, see Glenn Dynner, *Yankel's Tavern: Jews, Liquor, and Life in the Kingdom of Poland* (Oxford: Oxford University Press, 2014), 131ff.

154 *Greiditser*, part 5, 3, 17.

trouble only to be saved by repentance and by the supernatural power of the rabbi. The tales have to do only marginally with the historical Greiditser Rabbi, who achieved a widespread reputation as a master of Kabbala.[155] Perhaps because this work was published only in Yiddish, it is the least concerned with the facade of scholarly research and manuscript publication.

All five Greiditser stories attempted to provide the Jews who constituted Rosenberg's audience with ways for understanding the situation of the traditional Jew in the modern world. One thread which connects all five stories is the threatening omnipresence of the secularized gentile world. It treats traditional Judaism with disdain and causes the ruin of several characters through a pursuit of "aristocratic" luxury, theatrical performances, secular education, and illicit sex.

To counter the threatening forces of the non-Jewish world, the remedies of that world were of no avail. Thus, in the case of two Jewish girls held in a Catholic convent against their will,[156] lawyers and court orders were powerless. Physicians were unable to cure boys possessed by *dybbuks*. Only the rabbi and the Judaism he represented could save the day. The stories make eminently clear that the protagonists' abandonment of Judaism and its principles caused their downfall while their repentance and resolve henceforth to live strictly as Orthodox Jews lead to their salvation. Those who live an Orthodox life prosper.

The Greiditser Rabbi himself never leaves his small town. Nonetheless, he is in full control of events in places as far afield as Africa and Brazil.[157] In an era of unprecedented emigration of Eastern European Jews to far-flung lands, Yudel Rosenberg felt it important to underline the notion that the rabbi's power was not confined to "the old country" but rather extended worldwide.[158] The fact that the Greiditser Rabbi lived a mere generation before Rabbi Rosenberg

155 Nigal, *The Hasidic Tale*, 203, note 74.

156 For a contemporary report of a Jewish girl in danger of conversion, see Edward J. Bristow, *Prostitution and Prejudice: The Jewish Fight against White Slavery, 1870–1939* (New York: Schocken Books, 1983), 218. Cf. Robert P. Lockwood, "Convent Horror Stories," *Catholic Answers Magazine* 19, no. 3 (March 2008), http://www.catholic.com/magazine/articles/convent-horror-stories, accessed March 28, 2016.

157 On exotic locations in the nineteenth-century Yiddish fiction of Isaac Mayer Dik, see Iris Parush, *Reading Jewish Women: Marginality and Modernization in Nineteenth-Century Eastern European Jewish Society* (Waltham: Brandeis University Press, 2004), 149.

158 The historical Rabbi Elijah Guttmacher received *kvitlakh* (petitions) from throughout Eastern Europe and from places as far afield as Western Europe and America. Dynner, *Yankel's Tavern*, 134.

took pen in hand was a powerful sign that, even in modern times, Judaism's rabbi-defenders had not lost any portion of their spiritual power.[159]

Utilizing many of the sensationalist themes of popular Yiddish fiction [*shund*], Yudel Rosenberg had produced a work of fiction disguised as hagiography. Thus, one of the tales centers on a murder committed in São Paulo, Brazil, while yet another turns on whether Moishele, the ex-yeshiva student, will succeed in escaping from a penal colony in French Equatorial Africa. Moreover, in further contrast to more normative Hasidic hagiographies, the Greiditser rabbi is not the center of attention, either as subject or narrator. He rather becomes the symbol of the spiritual power of Judaism in the modern world.[160]

The last work Rabbi Rosenberg wrote and published in Łódź, though it was only published after his emigration to Canada in 1914, was his *Sefer Divrei ha-Yamim le-Shlomo ha-Melekh* [Book of the Chronicles of King Solomon]. Perhaps because he was about to leave for Canada and knew that he would not have easy access to his publishers in Poland, he sold his rights to the book to the publisher, something he had not done hitherto.[161]

This collection of tales concerning King Solomon is largely created by reworking various *midrashim*, including some that "were not so well known like *Midrash Mishlei Rabbati*."[162] Mordecai Ben Yehezkel has tried to trace the stories presented in this book in various editions of *Midrash Mishlei* and could not find them. He concludes that the stories Yudel Rosenberg attributed to *Midrash Mishlei Rabbati* were the fruit of his own imagination, a pattern we have seen in Rosenberg's other works.[163] Eli Yassif concludes that Rosenberg in this book took relatively brief midrashic tales and expanded them into complete stories.[164]

What is of great interest in Rabbi Rosenberg's presentation of King Solomon is his claimed use of non-Jewish material in order to present the voyage of the Queen of Sheba to King Solomon as portrayed in the "Chronicles of the Kings of Sheba in the Land of Abyssinia." For this task, Rosenberg claimed that

---

159 On the continuing power of the righteous "in our time" see *Tif'eret ha-Yehudi* (Piotrkow, 1912), unpaginated introduction.

160 Robinson, "The Uses of the Hasidic Story," 17–24.

161 *Shlomo*, 2.

162 *Shlomo*, 5. Yassif believes that these midrashic sources were invented by Rosenberg. Yassif, *The Golem of Prague*, 16.

163 Mordecai Ben Yehezkel, "*Sefer 'Va-Yehe ha-Yom*,'" in *Byalik: Yetsirato le-Sugeha bi-Rei ha-Biqoret: Antologyah*, ed. Gershon Shaked (Jerusalem: Mossad Bialik, 1974), 360.

164 Yassif, *The Golem of Prague*, 17.

he relied upon a number of books written by "researchers into antiquity" that were sent to him from the "library of the city of London which is next to the great university."[165] From this library, Rosenberg claims to have received copies or extracts from the following:

1) *Voyage historique d'Abissinie* by the Portuguese Jesuit, Jeronimo Lobo (Paris, 1728);[166]
2) *History of Kush and the Land of Abyssinia* by Berossus the Chaldean;[167]
3) *Sefer ha-Yalkut* of Yohanan Alemanno,[168] in which he copied extracts from a work on alchemy; and
4) *Sefer ha-Matspun*, which was ascribed to King Suleiman I of Abyssinia. Rosenberg felt that it might well be a translation of the writings of King Solomon himself, possibly identical to the "Book of Remedies" hidden by King Hezekiah which was extant "in the library of the Kingdom of Armenia and the Kingdom of Sheba which is called Abyssinia."[169]

In all this carefully contrived display of learning, much of which he might have come across in articles on the Falashas of Abyssinia published in the Hebrew or Yiddish press,[170] Yudel Rosenberg was able to maintain the illusion of scholarship, though he did make certain errors, like attributing the conversion of the Ethiopians to Christianity to the activities of English missionaries![171] In any event, his generally scholarly tone tended to give his message more authority

165 What gives some verisimilitude to this account is that Yudel Rosenberg's book speaks of the conversion of Falashas to Christianity by an English missionary, which could only refer to the exploits of Reverend Henry Aaron Stern (1820–1885), published in his *Wanderings among the Falashas in Abyssinia: Together With a Description of the Country and its Various Inhabitants* (1862). See William George Dimock Fletcher, "Stern, Henry Aaron," in *Dictionary of National Biography, 1885–1900*, vol. 54, https://en.wikisource.org/wiki/Stern,_Henry_Aaron_(DNB00), accessed March 30, 2016.

166 *Shlomo*, 29. The bibliographical reference is valid. Cf. *Encyclopedia Brittanica* (Chicago, 1961), vol. 14, 261.

167 On Berossus, see *Encyclopedia Brittanica*, vol. 3, 461.

168 Presumably, these were excerpts from Alemanno`s book, *Ḥesheq Shlomo* to which Yudel Rosenberg refers in *Shlomo*, 63.

169 *Shlomo*, 29. Cf. *Encyclopedia Judaica*, vol. 2, col. 646.

170 There would have presumably been some Jewish press reaction to the expedition of Professor Jacques Faitlovich to the Falashas in the early 1900s. On Yudel Rosenberg's reasonably accurate etymology of the word "Falasha," see *Shlomo*, 34.

171 *Shlomo*, 34.

to his presumably traditional audience as well as holding out the prospect of better sales.

Another interesting aspect of the Solomon book was his meticulous description of Solomon's miraculous throne, which, Rabbi Rosenberg opined, was operated by electricity.[172] Inspired by seeing a model of the Tabernacle [*mishkan*] which was being exhibited in large cities and which was supposedly making its owners rich, Yudel Rosenberg invited craftsmen to build a model of Solomon's throne according to his specifications which could be exhibited "in order to earn much money."[173] Once again we see him as an opportunist and promoter, though there is no evidence that this scheme ever came to fruition.

The case of Yudel Rosenberg as manufacturer of Judaic texts has its own intrinsic interest. However, it must also be seen as well as part of a wider Orthodox response to modernity. In the aftermath of the First World War, a number of documents related to the origins of the Hasidic movement were supposedly found in the Russian city of Kherson.[174] These documents, which were ultimately dismissed by most scholars as forgeries, are still claimed as genuine by many Hasidim. They reflect the same atmosphere and the same motivations which seem to have driven Rabbi Rosenberg.

Ada Rapoport-Albert, in her analysis of the Kherson texts, sees their manufacture as going beyond mere greed, though that motivation is certainly not discounted by her.[175] She rather sees them as responding to: "A keen awareness of extrinsic historiographical sensibilities and a novel, extraneously inspired sense of the inadequacy of hagiographical traditions as historical source material."[176] For her, the Kherson material was both symptom of the breakdown of Orthodox morale due to the onslaught of modern ideologies and modern secular historiography and a creative response to this breakdown. As she stated, "The Kherson Geniza offers verification of hagiography whose traditional modes of authentication had lost their validity through the assimilation, however unconscious, of modern historical criteria."[177]

Like the creators of the Kherson documents, but much more openly and consciously, Yudel Rosenberg attempted through his publication of

---

172 *Shlomo*, 18, 22–23.

173 *Shlomo*, 24.

174 Cf. Ada Rapoport-Albert, "Hagiography with Footnotes: Edifying Tales and the Writing of History in Hasidism," *History and Theory* 27 (1988).

175 Ibid., 130.

176 Ibid., 129.

177 Ibid., 130, 132.

"manuscript" material to offer an "antidote" to secular literature by providing the public with "Orthodox" scholarship. The many editions of his creative works testify to the fact that they fulfilled a perceived need within the Hasidic community.

That community, by and large, was and is still mostly unaware of the liberties Rosenberg took in his publications. Even those who are aware of their controversial nature, however, would not necessarily see them as aberrant. Hasidim are quite aware that "printed stories are usually amended in some way, according to the editor's personal whim."[178] Thus, as Jiri Langer wrote in his evocation of Hasidic life in the era immediately prior to 1914—the very time of the flowering of Rosenberg's literary talents:

> The Chassidim are aware that by no means everything they relate about their saints actually happened; but that does not matter. If a saint never really worked the miracle they describe, it must still have been one such as only he was capable of performing. Rabbi Nachman of Bratzlav goes out of his way to point out that not everything related about the holy Baal Shem (for instance) is true, but even the things which are untrue are holy if told by devout people.[179]

178 Mintz, *Legends of the Hasidim*, 6.
179 Langer, *Nine Gates to the Hasidic Mysteries*, 23.

CHAPTER 8

"Almost Alone": Yudel Rosenberg as Preacher

In examining Rabbi Yudel Rosenberg's writing from his Canadian period, one thing is immediately noticeable: he seems to have given up his work as a "folk author" that featured so prominently in his Polish period. The major exception to this, a volume of stories he adapted from the *Zohar* as part of his translation project, will be dealt with in chapter ten. One major reason for this change might be that he had lost the possibility of immediate contact with his publishers in Poland. What is clear is that he seems to have utilized the energy he expended on his tales with sermons addressed to his community.

One of the finest examples of his activity in Canada is a sermon from 1924, which actually incorporated much of the creativity he had developed in Poland, for it addressed Montreal Jewry in the voice of the "Sabbath Queen." It is entitled *A Brivele fun di Zisse Mame Shabbes Malkese zu Ihre Zin un Tekhter fun 'Idishn Folk* [A Letter of the Sweet Mother Sabbath Queen to Her Sons and Daughters of the Jewish People]. As one can gather from the title, Rosenberg chose to speak through a fictional interlocutor, the Sabbath Queen, mother of the Jewish people. He maintained the fiction throughout, asserting on the title page that the letter appeared "through [the auspices] of the Montreal rabbi, Yudel Rosenberg."

What did the Sabbath Queen, through Rabbi Rosenberg, wish to impart to her children, the Jews? The central theme of her discourse was the lack of observance of the Sabbath within the Jewish community.[1] Rabbi Rosenberg was certainly not the first Jew to reprove his community for its neglect of the Sabbath. In the Middle Ages, Abraham ibn Ezra (c. 1092–1167) composed a tractate entitled *Iggeret ha-Shabbat* [Sabbath Epistle], which begins with an angel delivering to the author a letter from the Sabbath that decries lapses in Jewish Sabbath observance. He may have also been influenced by a Hasidic

1 On this issue, see PY, 16.

classic in which the Sabbath is compared to a love letter from God to the Jewish people.[2]

In Rabbi Rosenberg's letter, the Sabbath Queen tells her "dear beloved children" that she has heard their prayers and their questions as to why the exile of the Jewish people has lasted so long and why Jews suffer so much. Her answer is that very many Jews have desecrated the Sabbath and thus they have abandoned the peace and protection afforded by the Sabbath Queen, who in Kabbala was identified with the Divine Presence [*Shekhina*].[3]

Most of what the Sabbath Queen says consists of arguments for Sabbath observance. From these arguments we can readily discern the position of Sabbath observance and Orthodox Judaism in the Montreal Jewish community of the 1920s. The first thing to note is that the Sabbath Queen is not addressing the entire Jewish community, for there are Jews who cannot be reached. The Sabbath Queen can only effectively address those in whom the holy spark has not yet been entirely extinguished.[4]

To those willing to listen, the Sabbath Queen spoke of the notion prevalent among many Jews that Sabbath observance was not compatible with modern civilization. This refers to the contemporary positivistic view of science which was quite widespread within North American society and which contended that contemporary science "completely repudiates the theological and cosmological outlook of Holy Scripture."[5] On the contrary, the Sabbath Queen exhorted, Maimonides and other Jewish Sabbath observers who were great scientists, astronomers, doctors, and philosophers proved that Torah and civilization are compatible:

> Possibly you believe that civilization is connected to the profanation of the Sabbath. However you must know that among the Jewish people there have always been found great sages, researchers, philosophers, doctors, astronomers who were quite Orthodox and strictly observed

---

2 Abraham Ibn Ezra's *Iggeret ha-Shabbat* was published by S. D. Luzzatto in *Kerem Ḥemed* 4 (1839): 158–160. Cf. Joseph Jacobs, *The Jews of Angevin England* (London: D. Nutt, 1893), 35–38. On the Sabbath as a love letter, see Jacob Joseph of Polnoye cited in Joseph Dan, *The Teachings of Hasidism* (New York: Behrman, 1983), 135.

3 Denunciations of Jewish desecration of the Shabbat are often found in Yudel Rosenberg's sermons. See, for example, *Omer*, part 1, 22; PY, 16.

4 *Brivele*, 8.

5 Rachel S. A. Pear, "Differences over Darwinism: American Orthodox Jewish Responses to Evolution in the 1920s," *Aleph: Historical Studies in Science and Judaism* 15, no. 2 (2015): 370.

> the Sabbath. ... Now you understand very well [from the example of] Maimonides that the holy Jewish Torah does not relate to civilization as fire [to] water.[6]

The Sabbath Queen was also greatly annoyed by the fact that many Jews who showed no respect at all to her, nonetheless, showed great respect for the memory of their deceased parents and honored them through the recitation of the memorial prayers of *Qaddish* and *Yizkor*:

> When they have an anniversary of [a loved one's] death [*yortseit*] or on the High Holidays they come to the synagogue and purchase a "fat" *'aliyah* [Torah reading]. The ritual director [*gabbai*] and the president delight in such a fine guest and beckon to the caretaker [*shames*] to seat him in a good place. Is this not a desecration of God's name and a disgrace for the Torah?[7]

Such people, in the opinion of the Sabbath Queen, do not understand what they are doing. They are aware that their deceased loved ones have souls, which live on after their death. How, then, will it appear to these souls when their loved ones publicly desecrate the Sabbath and yet ask God to give their parents a "proper rest under the wings of the *Shekhina*"? Having insulted the *Shekhina,* represented by the Sabbath Queen, they now ask for a favor?[8]

The Sabbath Queen also offers a nationalist argument for Sabbath observance. Christians and Muslims both observe their day of rest. There is even a Christian sect that observes Saturday as the Sabbath "because it is against the Ten Commandments of the Bible" [*vayl dos is against* (sic) *di 'aseres ha-dibros funm Baybl*]. But the Jews have abandoned their national day of rest and hence their national pride.[9]

Many Jews excused their non-observance by blaming economic conditions, which made it difficult, if not impossible, to obtain jobs that allowed for Sabbath observance. The Sabbath Queen acknowledged this argument and stated that the solution to this problem was to be found in the five-day,

---

6 *Brivele*, 4.

7 Ibid., 14. For a further condemnation of such synagogue leaders, see *Omer*, part 1, 69.

8 *Brivele*, 5.

9 Ibid., 6.

forty-hour week, then advocated by Labor.[10] Owners of stores and factories that employed Jews on the Sabbath and festivals were warned of divine punishment awaiting them in the next world.[11]

With respect to non-Orthodox Judaism, the Sabbath Queen comments on the phenomenon, well-attested in North America, of Jewish immigrants attending services in Reform Temples in order to hear the polished English sermons of their rabbis. The Sabbath Queen warns:

> Hear not the poisoned speeches of the Reform "rabbis," [as they] possess the selfsame sinful souls of the prophets of Baal who caused ... the destruction of the First Temple, or else the selfsame sinful souls of the Hellenistic leaders who brought upon the Jewish people the destruction of the Second Temple.[12]

While he had preached sermons as far back as Tarlow, and published occasional sermons as part of his other books, it was only in 1931 that Rabbi Yudel Rosenberg published his first sermon collection. Perhaps, in part his sermon collections are the result of the efforts made by his son, Aaron Elimelech, who was entrusted with the task of writing down his father's remarks after each Sabbath.[13] In the last few years of his life, Rabbi Rosenberg published two volumes of sermons and prepared another collection for publication (it was in page proof form at his death).

Anyone who investigates Jewish sermonic literature, as Marc Saperstein points out, faces the well-nigh insoluble problem of reconstructing sermons as they were originally delivered. In its published form, the date and place of a sermon are often missing. Many incidental details, of much interest to historians, are edited out. The very language of the sermon is often changed in the course of its finding its way into print. One has no way at all of reconstructing the voice of the preacher, the attentiveness (or lack thereof) of the audience, or any one

---

10 Ibid., 7. Other contemporary Jewish leaders such as Cyrus Adler, President of the Jewish Theological Seminary of America, likewise looked to the forty-hour week as the solution to the problem of Sabbath observance. Cf. Ira Robinson, ed., Cyrus *Adler: Selected Letters* (Philadelphia: Jewish Publication Society, 1985), vol. 1, 183–185.

11 *Brivele*, 6.

12 Ibid., 11. Despite this, Yudel Rosenberg seems to have maintained amicable enough relations with the local Reform rabbi, Harry Stern, as evidenced by Stern's letter included in the souvenir program for Rosenberg's seventieth birthday. Cf. *Omer*, part 1, 69, 109–110: ZT, vol. 5, 176; ZT, vol. 4, 114.

13 Aaron Rosenberg, *Liqqutei Beit Aharon*, 6.

of the myriad details we would like to know but cannot.[14] That is certainly the case with the sermons collected by Rabbi Rosenberg. What we can say is that Rabbi Rosenberg, in at least one place, reflected on the art of preaching to a Jewish congregation. In that passage, he advocated not to speak deceptively to the congregation and to stick to the verses of the Bible and the sayings of the Rabbis. He urged his readers who might have the chance to preach not to tell the congregation that they can do what they please, "and all of this should be done with pleasantness and not with an angry, loud voice."[15]

Rabbi Rosenberg's first published collection of sermons, *'Ateret Tif'eret,* is a tribute to that all-important life-cycle event in North American Judaism—the bar mitzvah[16]—and its effect on a North American Orthodox rabbinate in the throes of Americanization and professionalization.[17]

The ancient rabbinic concept of bar mitzvah refers to Jewish boys starting from their thirteenth birthday, when they are considered to have reached their religious majority. The boy, and not his parents, is now fully responsible for the legal and moral consequences of his deeds. This milestone, however, did not become a publicly celebrated *rite de passage* until medieval times, at which time the following points began to emerge as major elements in the synagogue celebration (though it was and is not necessary that all these elements be combined in any one ceremony): being called to the reading of the Torah; publicly reading the *haftarah*;[18] putting on *tefillin* (on weekdays); and delivering a public address on a relevant topic. This celebration was also called bar mitzvah.

In North America, where much of the traditional ritual of Orthodox Judaism had been abandoned by many of the immigrants, the bar mitzvah ceremony

---

14 Marc Saperstein, *Jewish Preaching, 1200–1800* (New Haven: Yale University Press, 1980); idem, *Your Voice Like a Ram's Horn: Themes and Texts in Traditional Jewish Preaching* (Cincinnati: Hebrew Union College Press, 1996).

15 *Omer*, part 1, 4.

16 Isaac Rivkind, *Bar Mitzvah: a Study in Jewish Cultural History* [Hebrew] (New York: Bloch, 1942); Norma Joseph "Ritual, Law, and Praxis: An American Response/a to Bat Mitsva Celebrations" *Modern Judaism* 22, no. 3 (2002): 234–260; Jenna Weissman Joselit, "Red-Letter Days," in her *The Wonders of America: Reinventing Jewish Culture 1880–1950* (New York: Hill and Wang, 1994), 89–133; Byron Sherwin, "Bar Mitzvah, Bat Mitzvah," in his In Partnership With God: Contemporary Jewish Law and Ethics (Syracuse: Syracuse University Press, 1990), 150–168.

17 Kimmy Caplan, *Orthodoxy in the New World: Immigrant Rabbis and Preaching in America* [Hebrew] (Jerusalem: Zalman Shazar Center for Jewish History, 2002).

18 Selection from the prophetic literature of the Hebrew Bible, recited in the synagogue after the Torah reading.

was, if anything, strengthened. It became (and remains) a focus for family ties, Jewish education, and rabbinic involvement.[19]

In Eastern Europe, rabbis were but little interested in bar mitzvah other than as a halakhic concept. Not so in America. As Rabbi Samuel Fine of Detroit, Michigan states in the introduction to his 1935 book of sermons, *Yalkut Shmuel*:

> The rabbi's way of life has changed [in America], and with it has come also a change in the rabbi's work. The rabbi is forced to speak and preach at all opportunities, and especially at the joyous occasions of weddings and bar mitzvahs. A hard task is placed upon the rabbi with this work which wastes all his energies and does not give him rest to investigate and search in various books, and to find that which he requires. Therefore I think that my book will with God's help bring benefit and blessing to the rabbis. ... Here they will find much material for their homilies and speeches on these matters.[20]

The bar mitzvah, and the speeches which often marked its celebration, encouraged the publication of a number of books designed to offer those bar mitzvah boys, who did not have the time, talent, or inclination to write their own addresses, appropriate words in English, Yiddish, and/or Hebrew to present to their family and guests.[21] That was all well and good for the boys themselves, but what of the long-suffering and time-challenged rabbis described by Rabbi Fine? There were literally hundreds of books of sermons circulating among the Eastern European immigrant Orthodox rabbinate in North America in the early twentieth century, but there were apparently none solely addressed to this specific niche in the market, until the appearance of Rabbi Yudel Rosenberg's *'Ateret Tif'eret* in 1931. It advertises itself as containing fifty sermons appropriate for rabbis addressing the bar mitzvah boy. In each of these sermons, the weekly

19 Joselit, *Wonders of America*, 89–133.

20 Samuel Fine, *Yalkut Shmuel* (St. Louis: Salz and Gellman Publishing, 1935), 3, http://www.hebrewbooks.org/pdf/yalkutshmuel.pdf, accessed April 13, 2008.

21 Examples of such books are G. Zelikovitz, *Bar Mitsva Redes* (New York: Hebrew Publishing Company, 1925), and R. M. Zalmanovitz, *Derashot le-Bar Mitsva*, ed. M. Stern (New York: Hebrew Publishing Company, 1935). A generation later, other books were designed to be appropriate as gifts for the bar mitzvah. An example of this is Azriel Eisenberg, *The Bar Mitzvah Treasury* (New York: Behrman, 1952). The phenomenon of publications directed toward bar mitzvah boys requires more research.

haftarah is connected to the Torah portion of the week, and further connected to the theme of *tefillin* and the general obligations of a bar mitzvah.

The first thing that is apparent in Rabbi Rosenberg's book of bar mitzvah sermons is its artificiality, not least because of the fact that it was written in Hebrew, whereas in this milieu, sermons were generally delivered in Yiddish. The book was clearly designed to offer a complete array of bar mitzvah sermons for use by rabbis, and was probably published as a means of generating income. In his preface, which is addressed to "rabbinic preachers" [*rabbanim darshanim*], Yudel Rosenberg frankly addresses its origins and the use to which it will be put:

> Indeed I also know that books of sermons are not lacking in the last generation. They increase and multiply greatly until they are found sixty to each shelf[22] at the booksellers. ... However ... a book like this has not yet appeared in our literature. It is simply like a useful and workmanlike tool so that the rabbinic preacher, who is mostly busy with other matters, will not have to search and to sharpen his brain every Sabbath when he sits to compose something of the material relevant for the day of the bar mitzvah. Here you have bread and here a knife. Each rabbi has permission to eat all the bread or a portion thereof.[23]

On the other hand, it would be foolish indeed to assume that the sermons in their entirety were all mechanically written and never delivered. That is because the reader gains a sense that these sermons are the expression of an underlying reality. In his introduction, Rabbi Rosenberg addresses the probable audience that would be listening to these bar mitzvah sermons in a way that indicates his feel for some realities of the bar mitzvah sermon as it was delivered in the synagogues of Eastern European immigrants in North America.

In discussing the genre of the bar mitzvah sermon in general, Yudel Rosenberg began by questioning whether anyone—from the bar mitzvah himself to the audience—is listening? He agreed that most people are not listening to the rabbi's admonitions. On the other hand, Rosenberg averred, we cannot be certain that no one is listening. Some boys may be attentive and even retain a bit of

---

22 There is a play of words between *qeresh* ("board," here translated "shelf") and *keres* ("belly"), reminding us of the *midrash* in which the Israelite women in Egypt gave birth to sixty babies in one womb. Cf. *Midrash Tanḥuma*, ed. Shlomo Buber (reprint edition, Jerusalem: Ortsel, 1964), vol. 2, 4.

23 *'Ateret*, 6.

what the rabbi is saying. Moreover, the rabbi is also addressing the adults in the synagogue, who may well need a timely reminder that they, too, are *bnei* (plural of bar) mitzvah and thus obligated to observe the commandments.[24]

The fifty sermons that make up the volume are, then, the product of a rabbi who knew his audience and was a master of the rabbinic raw material out of which the sermons emerged. What did he want to convey to young boys and their guests? By far the strongest impression given by a reading of the sermons as a whole is that Judaism is under siege. It is attacked mainly from within the Jewish people, because the sermons pay relatively little attention to overt anti-Semitism on the part of the non-Jews.[25] As far as Rosenberg was concerned, the enemies of Judaism within the Jewish people were legion. They included Jewish communists, especially those in Russia, whom he called "Haman's Jews."[26] They also included Reform Jews, and particularly Reform rabbis.[27] Most prominent, however, was Rabbi Rosenberg's sustained polemic against the promoters of secular education,[28] which he considered to be a major cause of the destruction of the Temple.[29] For Jews influenced by this education, the Torah, which is the greatest body of knowledge in existence,[30] becomes a mere collection of old stories and out-of-date laws.[31] Secular education is compared by Rosenberg to the Egyptian civilization, with Pharaoh as a philosopher and advocate of

---

24 Ibid., 5–6. On refusal to specifically put on tefilin, see *'Ateret*, 122.

25 For an oblique reference to antisemitism on the part of university students, see *'Ateret*, 144.

26 Ibid., 187. Cf. also ibid., 131, 199, 213. Yudel Rosenberg's own son and daughter-in-law were fervent communists. See Suzanne Rosenberg, *A Soviet Odyssey* (Toronto: Oxford University Press, 1988), 10, 21. He was somewhat tolerant of other Jewish leftists, and considered them part of the Jewish people [*kelal Yisra'el*] provided that they did not deny their origin or God [*kofer be-'iqqar*]. *'Ateret*, 213; *Omer*, part 1, 6–67.

27 *'Ateret*, 33, 35, 165, 176; PY, 34; Ira Robinson, "Kabbalist and Communal Leader," 46.

28 *'Ateret*, 129—130, 144; *Omer*, part 1, 80–81.

29 *Sha'arei*, 20.

30 *'Ateret*, 21, 120, 143.

31 *'Ateret*, 18, 165. Rabbi Rosenberg's reference to Egypt as representing philosophy and the sciences may be taken from the polemics of the mediaeval Maimonidean controversy. See Caterina Rigo, "*Dux Neutrorum* and the Jewish Tradition," in *Maimonides' Guide of the Perplexed in Translation: A History from the Thirteenth Century to the Twentieth*, ed. Josef Stern, James T. Robinson, and Yonatan Shemesh (Chicago: University of Chicago Press, 2019), 103–104. For an oblique reference to contemporary Biblical critics, see *'Ateret*, 51; PY, 34. Yudel Rosenberg's concern with education likely stemmed from a contemporary controversy in Montreal concerning whether Jewish children should obtain their education in schools of the Protestant School Board, or in specifically Jewish schools. On this issue, see Arlette Corcos, *Montréal, les Juifs et l'École* (Sillery, QC: Septentrion, 1997), 75–112.

assimilation.[32] Spinoza, too, with his identification of God and nature comes in for considerable criticism.[33] Jewish students engaged in "Egyptian" or "Greek" schools turn their backs on the older generation, are steeped in foreign cultures, desire only to be doctors and lawyers, and are ashamed to speak in Yiddish, even at home.[34]

The "four sons" of the Passover Haggada symbolize for Rabbi Rosenberg, as for other commentators throughout the ages, differing attitudes toward Judaism to be found among the Jewish people. It is instructive to hear what he has to say about them. In contrast to numerous interpretations, the wise son, for Rabbi Rosenberg, is not one learned in the Torah who follows the correct path. If it were so, asked Rabbi Rosenberg, why is his question so similar to that of the wicked son? Evidently, there is not really much difference between the wise and the wicked sons. For the wise son is wise only in the natural sciences and philosophy. His real question is:

> What importance is there in my eyes for those commandments which God commanded you. ... Only of you, the older generation, simple men with little wisdom, could it be said that He commanded you to observe these commandments. But he [the wise son] is wise and has no relationship with these lowly and simple matters. For does he not occupy himself with higher intellectual matters? However the wise one does not grudge that the older generation continues to observe the 613 commandments and does not prevent them from observing the commandments.[35]

32 *'Ateret*, 55, 159. Cf. *Omer*, part 1, 4, 48; PY, 45. Rabbi Rosenberg may have absorbed this trope from Hirsch Wolofsky's book *Oyf Eybiken Kvall: Gedanken un Batrachtungen fun dem Hayntigen Idishen Leben un Shtreben, in likht fun Unzer Alter un Eybig-Nayer Tora, Eingeteylt loyt di Parshiyos fun der Vokh* [From the Eternal Source: Thoughts and Observations from Contemporary Jewish Life and Aspirations in the Light of Our Old and Eternally New Torah, Organized According to the Weekly (Torah) Portions] (Montreal: Eagle Publishing Company, 1930). On Wolofsky and his book, Cf. Ira Robinson, *Rabbis and Their Community*, 119–126

33 *'Ateret*, 126, 129, 158–159, 218, 220, 222. Cf. *Haggada*, 59, note; PY, 151–152; *Omer* part 1, 48.

34 *'Ateret*, 55, 130; Cf. *Omer*, part 1, 38.

35 *'Ateret*, 65. Cf. also *'Ateret*, 174 for a condemnation of this attitude toward the commandments on the part of skeptics. On contemporary unbelieving scientists, see *Omer*, part 1, 48.

On the contrary, the wicked son, like contemporary Jewish communists[36] and other radical secularist ideologues, does not wish others to perform the commandments and works unceasingly to prevent them from doing so.

The son "who does not know how to ask" is not a fool for Rosenberg. Rather, he is one "whose belief in the Torah and the commandments is so great that it does not occur to him to ... ask questions about them." The "innocent" [*tam*] son does ask a question, but, like the "son who does not know how to ask," he does not mock or belittle. Rather, he genuinely wants to know the reasons for things.[37]

In an atmosphere where the Torah is beleaguered and "secular wisdom" seems set against the Torah, saying it was no longer relevant in the present day,[38] Rabbi Rosenberg needed to assert the supremacy of the wisdom of the Torah. He does that particularly in a sermon I have chosen to deal with at length. The sermon belongs to the Torah portion *be-Ha'alotekha*,[39] and deals with the symbolism of the candelabrum [*menorah*] which appears in both the Torah portion and the corresponding *haftara* from the Book of Zechariah.[40] In this sermon Rosenberg utilizes the metaphor of oil as source of light to indicate that all of the secular sciences derive their power and validity from the Torah. It was an attempt to completely reverse the way in which so many in Rosenberg's community seemed to see things. As he stated, basing on the verse from Proverbs 9, 1, "The wise woman built her house and hewed out its seven pillars":

> The Torah built her house with all the sciences in the world. She hewed its seven pillars which hints at the seven sciences in which all the sciences in the world are included. All of them are rooted and find their foundation in the oral Torah and the Written Torah. Thus the Gaon, Rabbi Elijah stated that all the sciences are necessary for our holy Torah and are included in it. Therefore it is possible to say that this is the matter hinted at in the symbol of the candelabrum with its seven lamps. The body of the candelabrum hints at the essence of the holy Torah. Its seven lamps hint at the source and root of the seven sciences of the world which are fundamental [*avot*] to all the other sciences in the world. Therefore we may understand that

36 Yudel Rosenberg condemns Jewish communists in *Omer*, part 1, 67.

37 Ibid., 65–66.

38 Cf. PY, 95.

39 Numbers 8, 1–12, 16.

40 Zechariah 2, 14–4, 7.

> the sources of the seven sciences which are rooted in the holy Torah are properly called "the faces of the candelabrum."[41]

Another attempt to effect a reversal of perspective stems from Rosenberg's interpretation of Zechariah's message to Zerubavel. "Not by might," for Rosenberg, was a reference to bringing about the redemption of the Land of Israel through human endeavor and military force. Though Rosenberg does not use the name "Zionist," it is clear that Zerubavel constitutes a symbol for the movement. Thus, he states:

> For then, in the Babylonian exile, just as now in the final exile, there were many who strayed to exalt and magnify the other sciences over the science of Torah saying "why is [Torah] important?" Because their faith in the words of Torah was weakened, their faith in divine providence was automatically weakened, saying "God has abandoned the earth." Therefore they gathered assemblies to take counsel on the use of force and natural power to throw off from themselves the yoke of the Babylonian exile and to return to the Land of Israel, and not to wait until the arousal of redemption from heaven. At their head stood the noble Zerubavel. Because of this the angel showed the prophet Zechariah this wondrous vision: that the seven lamps of the candelabrum, which symbolize the seven sciences that are fundamental to the rest of the sciences in the world, derive [their light from] the overflow of their oil from the bowl which is on its head, in order to give light to the world. Oil drips into the bowl from two olive trees, which symbolize the two Torahs—the written Torah and the oral Torah. From that bowl flows the oil which symbolizes the overflow of wisdom to be apportioned to the seven lamps of the candelabrum, which symbolize the seven sciences. ... The entire issue of this vision is to know and understand that the science of the holy Torah is supreme above all the other sciences since it is from heaven. Therefore it is impossible for any force or wisdom on earth to nullify anything from the words of Torah, which teaches that everything transpires according to divine providence, according to the will of the Creator, may his name be blessed.
>
> That is why the angel concludes: "This is the word of God to Zerubavel saying, 'Not by force and not by might but by my spirit says the Lord of Hosts.'" ... The meaning is that only through the will of the Holy One,

41 *'Ateret*, 142–143. Cf. *Omer*, part 1, 21.

> blessed be He, can there be the awakening of redemption, and not through the will of Zerubavel and his associates to go out in force and natural strength. Thus it is written,[42] "There is no wisdom, or understanding, or counsel against God."[43]

Finally, it is interesting how, in this sermon, Rabbi Rosenberg reflects on the task confronting the Jewish preachers. On the Torah portion on which he comments, Rosenberg finds the following allusion to preachers:

> ... the rabbis and preachers who toil in Torah in order to bring the children of Israel to the highest level through their sermons of moral reproof [*tokhaḥat musar*]. Of them it is written, "when you raise the lamps." That is to say when you preach your words in a sermon in order to raise the two lamps of the bar mitzvah—the lamp of his good inclination and the lamp of his supernal soul. Make sure to teach him knowledge and to make him understand that "opposite the face of the lamp the seven lamps will shine." The body of the candelabrum symbolizes the essence of the holy Torah. The faces of the candelabrum are the sources in the Torah from which flow all the seven sciences in the world, fundamental categories for all the sciences which are hinted at in the seven branches of the candelabrum.

Ideally, through the efforts of these preachers:

> ... the bar mitzvah will know that he should not listen to the words of the evil inclination which seeks to belittle the wisdom of the Torah in his eyes and to elevate the other sciences.[44] You should make him understand him that it is not so. It is only that all seven sciences give light opposite the face of the candelabrum, which is the holy Torah—written and oral. All the seven sciences receive their enlightenment from our holy Torah. Therefore the bar mitzvah should know that the science of the Torah is supreme above all the sciences in the world.

Thus, the preacher concludes, addressing the bar mitzvah directly:

---

42 Proverbs 21, 30.

43 *'Ateret*, 144. Cf. ZT, vol. 5, 195–6.

44 For a condemnation of those who felt that the Torah might have been valid in previous times but has lost its validity in the present, see *'Ateret*, 165.

> ... do not cease and distance [yourself from] the study of Torah, both written Torah and oral Torah. More than anything else, the study of Torah adds light to the two lamps of the bar mitzvah which are the good inclination and the supernal soul which will be found inside him and will not flee from him, because study of Torah purifies the soul and plants in the heart of man all good qualities.[45]

In 1934 Yudel Rosenberg continued his fight for the Torah with the publication of another book, *Sefer Omer va-Da'at*. This book contained a section with fifty sermons, entitled *Yabia Omer* after Psalm 19, 2, "pouring forth speech"; and another section with thirty-three responsa, entitled *Yeḥeve Da'at*, after the second part of this verse, "revealing knowledge." The book came to the page proof stage but was apparently not published at that time, most likely because there was not enough money to finance the printing.[46] The sermons were eventually published by Rosenberg's descendants in Israel in 1996.

In this collection as well, Rosenberg fights the good fight against those who consider the Torah irrelevant in the present day and rely only on enlightened opinions and scientific books. He speaks against the congregations that, instead of truly pious men [*yar'ei ve-ḥared*], choose "enlightened" rabbis, who can insert references to Greek philosophers in their sermons and are ashamed to cite the Bible and the Talmudic sages.[47]

Rabbi Yudel Rosenberg's last book published during his lifetime was entitled *Peri Yehuda*. It was written in 1932 and published in 1935. It consists of a collection of sermons arranged according to the Torah portion of the week. It is possible to discern in this book many reflections of the problems and struggles faced by Orthodox rabbis in North America.

The following passage is typical:

> We see with our own eyes ... that pious scholars are despised by the people. Their life [is one of] penury and shame. Similarly the religious schools are in a lowly state, for the rich men among the people do not wish to support and strengthen them. On the contrary, they ... give for the support of those schools where they make Jewish children into gentiles

45 Ibid., 143–144.

46 The page proofs, RFA, Savannah, frequently contain "reminders" by the printer that money is owed.

47 *Omer*, 3–4.

> through the teachers … who educate the holy flock in an alien education opposed to the Torah and [Jewish] faith as well as through their directors who are called by the name of "rabbi"—that is to say, "there is evil in him" [*ra' bei*]. … For these leaders and shepherds there is no financial want.[48]

Rosenberg refers here not to the Protestant school system, which educated the vast majority of Jewish children in Montreal, but rather to non-Orthodox Jewish schools which he felt were detrimental to the preservation of Judaism. The teachers in these schools were characterized by Rosenberg in the following way:

> Evil men [*anshe belia'al*] who mock the words of our holy Torah, cast off [its yoke] and deny God [*kofrim be-'iqar*] … they are enlightened and masters of [Hebrew] grammar. … They are clean-shaven, dressed like the gentiles without … ritual fringes [*tsitsit*] and … do not put on tefillin. Everyone who sees them will think they are gentiles. However despite all that they pride themselves that they are enlightened sages with great knowledge of the Bible, experts in grammar and able to teach the children "Hebrew in Hebrew."[49] … In their blindness they think that our holy Torah is just a "legend" [*legenda*] and no more.[50]

On the other hand, Jewish education was hardly being served by itinerant melamdim who come to homes for a half hour to teach some blessings or to prepare boys for their bar mitzvah.[51] As a result the younger generation in Rosenberg's estimation was the sort "that they will be ashamed and refuse even to stand to the left side of their parents in one row. … They will mock every holy thing and despise the Torah and the [Judaic] faith."[52] Rabbi Rosenberg further stated in his *Zohar* commentary:

---

48 PY, 34. Cf. *'Ateret*, 176.For a similar remark by a European Hasidic leader, Moshe of Kozienice, see the citation in Mahler, *Hasidism and the Jewish Enlightenment*, 246.

49 This was a "modern" method of teaching Hebrew to Jewish children. See Jonathan B. Krasner, *The Benderly Boys and American Jewish Education* (Waltham: Brandeis University Press, 2011), 23–26.

50 *Omer*, part 1, 66. Cf. *'Ateret*, 176; ZT, vol. 5, 27.

51 *Omer*, 80–81.

52 PY, 139.

> There does not exist a person who will say to his friend take an amount of money to engage in Torah. Rather to the despair of our heart we find the exact opposite that a man will say to his friend take a sum of money for you not to engage in Torah. May the blessed God have mercy on us and act for the sake of his Torah to quickly bring us from darkness to light.[53]

Despite all this, however, Rosenberg recognized that the support of the non-observant was essential for the continuation of Orthodox institutions. To discuss this somewhat ambivalent relationship, Rosenberg recalled the birds that Noah sent out of the ark:

> The raven which fled from Noah symbolizes those merchants who do not observe the Sabbath properly and flee from it in order to earn money. ... Yet they obtain some merit if they support the Torah and bring bread and livelihood to those who occupy themselves in the Torah. The dove which did not flee ... designates those who observe the Torah ... [who] say it is better [to obtain] a bitter livelihood from the hand of the Holy One, blessed be He, ... and to avoid desecration of the Sabbath than [to obtain] a sweet, bountiful [livelihood] from flesh and blood [in which] he is forced to desecrate the Sabbath.[54]

Kashrut, of course, was Rosenberg's primary concern in his sermons. He expressed this concern in one of his homilies in this fashion:

> Our sages, their memory be a blessing, stated, "The most proper among butchers is a partner of Amalek." ... For the war of Amalek in every generation is [against] the impure power which seeks to defile the mouths of Israel with forbidden foods. This is a very grave sin. For a sin [committed] outside the body can be erased through repentance and disappear. However, if the body has been fattened with forbidden foods ... even if he does repent, the body remains with the sickness of impurity. ... Thus ... the butcher who boasts that he is kosher and yet does not wish to place

53 ZT, vol. 2, 135.

54 PY, 16. On the phenomenon of the non-observant "Orthodox" Jew, see Jeffrey Gurock, "The Winnowing of American Orthodoxy," in *Approaches to Modern Judaism*, ed. Marc L. Raphael (Chico, CA: Scholars' Press, 1984), 41–53, 106–110. Yudel Rosenberg also discusses Jewish students forced to attend school on the Sabbath. *'Ateret*, 116.

> himself under the supervision of the local rabbi ... signifies that he feeds [the public] non-kosher food.[55]

Moreover, according to Rabbi Rosenberg, other Jews felt that *kashrut* in general was not worth the trouble, since, as they asked: "what did it matter whatever was eaten. Does not everything become dung in the intestines? What holiness is attached to the intenstines?"[56]

In general, the impression given by a perusal of Rabbi Yudel Rosenberg's sermonic writings is that the life of the Orthodox rabbi in Canada was a ceaseless struggle: "Pious sages are despised by the people. They live in want and shame. Also the [religious] schools are in a lowly state because the rich among the people do not wish to support them."[57] Even worse: as Rosenberg put it, somewhat apocalytically, faithful Jews were engaged in a fight:

> ... between the pious remnants of Israel and the helpers of Satan ... in the end of days. At that time, Jacob, the spirit of Ancient Israel [*Yisra'el sabba*] will remain almost alone with no help or support. For the people will go in darkness and will not wish to go in the spirit of Ancient Israel. Only a tiny minority will be the remnant which God calls. Then Jacob will remain limping on his hip because of the coldness of those who support the Torah "until the dawn breaks"—that is, until the light of messiah glimmers.[58]

For these reasons, Yudel Rosenberg felt that he was engaged in a war against secularism. His weapon was the pen. He perhaps best expressed his motivations in preaching and publishing his sermons addressing the Jewish masses in the following passage:

> Why must you bring into your houses impure books and stories full of poison, whether the poison of heresy or the poison of immodesty, and read them. They sully the mind and deaden the heart. ... Would it not be better for you to bring into your homes books of ethics and wisdom which are not against the Torah for your sons and daughters to read especially in

---

55 *PY*, 56. Cf. *Omer*, 65.

56 Ibid.

57 *PY*, 34.

58 Ibid., 34–35. Cf. *Omer*, part 1, 67. The reference is to the Biblical story recounted in Genesis 32, 25–29. For a similar evaluation by a contemporary European rabbinic figure, see Elḥonon Wasserman, *Ma'amar Ikvete de-Meshiḥa* (New York, 1937).

these times of the "footsteps of the messiah." For heresy is strengthened every day as our sages, their memory be a blessing, foresaw in the period prior to the revelation of king messiah.[59] Therefore there is a holy obligation upon everyone who possesses the fear of God to fight with all his strength against heresy. ... The strongest weapon to fight against it is the pen, to distribute to the people books like these from which the heart will be able to understand without going into the "counsel of the wicked."[60]

59 For contemporary use of messianic themes in sermons, see Motti Inbari, "Messianic Expectations in Hungarian Orthodox Theology before and during the Second World War: A Comparative Study," *Jewish Quarterly Review* 107, no. 4 (2017): 517–519.

60 NZ, 6.

CHAPTER 9

Magic, Science, and Healing

From his earliest writings, we know that Rabbi Yudel Rosenberg was keenly aware of the necessity according to the way of Torah and of nature [*teva'*] of a healthy soul in a healthy body."[1] This necessarily made him think about the interconnected issues of magic, science, and healing. In particular, there is considerable evidence that, while living in Łódź between 1909 and 1913, Rabbi Rosenberg actively practiced as a healer, relying heavily on the knowledge he gained of homeopathic medicine.

The connection between magic, religion, and healing is an ancient one, for Jews no less than others.[2] Within the Hassidic movement, to which Rabbi Yudel Rosenberg belonged, there were numerous leaders, including Israel ben Eliezer (*Ba'al Shem Tov*),[3] and Pinḥas of Korets who had combined spiritual leadership and healing.[4] There were also medical professionals associated with Hasidism. For instance, Dr. Ḥayyim David Bernhard, a disciple of the Seer of Lublin was a qualified physician.[5] The Hasidic leader, Rabbi Simḥa Bunem of Przysucha (1765–1827), was widely known to have received a diploma as a certified druggist and to have taught this profession to his students.[6] In a later generation, Rabbi Gershon Henokh Leiner of Radzyn (1839–1890) was well

---

1 *Derekh Erets*, 3, 82.

2 On this nexus, see W. H. R. Rivers, *Medicine, Magic, and Religion: The Fitzpatrick Lectures Delivered before the Royal College of Physicians of London in 1915 and 1916* (London and New York: Routledge, 2001). On Jewish aspects of this nexus, see H. J. Zimmels, *Magicians, Theologians and Doctors: Studies in Folk-Medicine and Folk-Lore as Reflected in the Rabbinical Responsa (12th–19th Centuries)* (London: Goldston, 1952); David Ruderman, *Jewish Thought and Scientific Discovery in Early Modern Europe* (New Haven: Yale University Press, 1995).

3 On the Ba'al Shem Tov as a healer, see M. Rosman, "Miedzyboz and Rabbi Israel Baal Shem-Tov," in *Essential Papers on Hasidism*, ed. Gershon Hundert (New York: New York University Press, 1991), 218.

4 Raphael Mahler, *A History of Modern Jewry, 1780–1815* (London: Vallentine, Mitchell, 1971), 450.

5 Glenn Dynner, *Men of Silk: The Hasidic Conquest of Polish Jewish Society* (Oxford: Oxford University Press, 2006), 161.

6 The same was claimed for Rabbi Simḥa Bunim of Przysucha, who was, among other things, a registered pharmacist. Cf. Rabinowicz, *Chassidic Rebbes*, 94.

known for his knowledge of medicine and was said to have written prescriptions in Latin, which were accepted by the local pharmacies.[7] The same was said of Rabbi Yitsḥak Zelig Morgenstern of Sokolow (1866–1939).[8] Yet another man who combined Hasidic spiritual leadership and healing was Rabbi Ḥayyim Dov of Piotrków, a disciple of Shlomo Hakohen Rabinowicz, the first Rebbe of Radomsk.[9] A younger contemporary of Yudel Rosenberg, Rabbi Kalonymous Kalman Shapiro (1889–1943), the Rebbe of Piaseczno:

> took a special interest in medical problems ... and learned as much as he could about the science of medicine. ... His fame as a counsellor on medical problems spread until it became a regular practice in the Jewish community of Warsaw ... to ask his advice in particularly dangerous or complex situations.[10]

According to Y. Y. Trunk, Rabbi Yeraḥmiel Yisroel Yitsḥak (the Aleksander Rebbe, 1854–1910), regularly patronized the Łódź physician Dr. Jonscher (a Polish patriot of German origins); and he advised all of his followers in Łódź to go to Dr. Jonscher as well. Aleksander sources themselves indicate that Rebbe Yeraḥmiel Yisroel Yitsḥak was fairly well acquainted with a variety of Łódź physicians and other medical personnel, due to his many efforts on behalf of those seeking both medical advice and spiritual intercession.[11]

Thus, when Rabbi Yudel Rosenberg set himself up as the Tarler Rebbe in Łódź, he could expect to be approached, practically as a matter of course, to give medical advice.[12] Nor would Rabbi Rosenberg's advice necessarily be inferior to that of the physicians available to his followers. In this period of transition from ancient to modern medicine, from traditional to scientific theories,

7 Rabinowicz, *Hasidism: The Movement and Its Masters*, 196.

8 Biale et al., *Hasidism: A New History*, 618.

9 David Margalit, "Gedolei ha-Ḥasidut ke-Rof'im," *Qor'ot* 7 (1976): 81–88. Cf. Assaf, "Ḥasidut Polin be-Me'ah ha-19," 365–366.

10 Aharon Sorasky, "Kalonymous Kalman Shapiro: Rebbe of the Warsaw Ghetto," in Kalonymus Kalman Shapiro, *A Student's Obligation*, trans. Micha Odenheimer (Northvale, NJ: Jason Aaronson, 1991), xxix. On the practice of consulting tsaddiqim as healers, see Zimmels, *Magicians, Theologians and Doctors*, 36–37.

11 Yedida Sharona Kanfer, "Lodz: Industry, Religion, and Nationalism in Russian Poland, 1880–1914" (PhD diss., Yale University, May 2011), 154; Efraim Shmueli, *With the Last Generation of Jews in Poland* [Hebrew] (Tel-Aviv: Aleph, 1986), 94, 96.

12 Shmueli, *With the Last Generation of Jews in Poland*, 9.

even trained physicians were often helpless, unable to cure most diseases or to convince their patients that prayer was useless.[13]

In such a context, Rabbi Rosenberg was able to serve a useful purpose, particularly to the poor Jews who tended to be his followers. These people might not have been able to afford a physician's fees, and even if they could, they would not have been well served by existing medical facilities that were never sufficient to provide adequately for a rapidly growing population.[14] In attempting to help the sick who called upon him, Yudel Rosenberg had at his disposal the full range of traditional remedies of Eastern European Jewry.[15] However, he could also offer them access to Western medicine contained in Russian medical books. In a letter he wrote near the end of his life, he recalled this period:

> When I lived for five years in the city of Łódź as a rebbe of Hassidim, and I needed to dispense cures and remedies, I wrote the book *Raphael ha-Malakh* ... for I did not wish to take fees [*pidyonim*] for nothing. Thus I was obliged to seek cures and remedies which were good and effective. I especially employed homeopathic remedies which were effective. The medical books which I had were from great professors, all in the Russian language.[16]

This letter tells us several things. First of all, it indicates that Rabbi Rosenberg practiced medicine in Łódź (and there is no indication that his acquisition of medical knowledge began with his move to that city). Secondly, it indicates that his medical publications from his Łódź period emerged out of an actual medical practice. Thirdly, it tells us that his practice of medicine was influenced not merely by traditional folk remedies, but also by modern, Western medicine,[17] albeit by its somewhat controversial offshoot—homeopathy.

Homeopathic medicine was a therapeutic doctrine first propounded by the German physician, Samuel Hahnemann (1755–1843) in the late eighteenth century. As a homeopathic practitioner, Rabbi Rosenberg believed in

---

13 Neil M. and Ruth Schwartz Cowan, *Our Parents' Lives: The Americanization of Eastern European Jews* (New York: Basic Books, 1989), 109.

14 Martin Kaufman, *Homeopathy in America: The Rise and Fall of a Medical Heresy* (Baltimore: Johns Hopkins University Press, 1974), 63.

15 Cf. Mahler, *History of Modern Jewry*, 450.

16 Yudel Rosenberg to Moshe Blistreich, Ḥanukkah, 5695 (1934). RFA, Savannah.

17 Cf. Gideon Bohak, "How Jewish Magic Survived the Disenchantment of the World," *Aries—Journal for the Study of Western Esotericism* 19 (2009): 22.

Hahnemann's cardinal principle that the cure of disease is effected through the action of minute doses of drugs, which produce in healthy individuals symptoms similar to those of the disease being treated.[18] He further would have likely understood that homeopathy was denigrated by contemporary orthodox physicians as superstition. As such, homeopathy was connected by these physicians with Hasidic healing pretensions.[19] As a rabbinic practitioner of homeopathy, Rabbi Rosenberg was part of a larger pattern. A student of Russian homeopathy, Alexander Kotok, notes that in pre-revolutionary Russia, there was a great deal of support for, and practice of, homeopathic medicine on the part of the Russian Orthodox clergy.[20]

Rabbi Yudel Rosenberg composed no less than three books on healing during his Łódź period, a sign that this issue took up a great deal of his attention. The first book, published in Piotrków in 1912, is entitled *Homeopatia* and deals with the principles of homeopathic medicine.[21] Yudel Rosenberg did not write it, but rather translated it, presumably from Russian, and possibly with the collaboration of his son, Aaron Elimelech. It was published at the behest and with the support of the owner of a homeopathic pharmacy in Łódź.[22] The owner of this pharmacy, J. Pogonowski, evidently wished to help Jews understand the principles of homeopathic medicine and, thereby, to drum up more business for himself. In doing so, Rabbi Rosenberg was following a centuries-old tradition of collaboration between kabbalists and pharmacists in Poland.[23]

---

18 In *Refu'at*, Rabbi Rosenberg often referred to obtaining medicines in a "homeopathic pharmacy." Cf. *Refu'at*, 24–26, 36–37. For another reference to homeopathy in his works, see *'Ateret*, 157.

19 Lisa Epstein, "Caring for the Soul's House: The Jews of Russia and Health Care, 1860–1914" (PhD diss., Yale University, 1995), chapter 4, 16, note 32.

20 Alexander Kotok, "Homeopathy and the Russian Orthodox Clergy: Russian Homeopathy in Search of Allies in the Second Part of the 19th and Beginning of the 20th Centuries," *Medizin, Gesellschaft und Geschichte* 16 (1997): 171–193.

21 For the attribution of *Homeopatia* to Rosenberg, see Fox, *100 Years*, 276; Cohen, *Sefer ha-Zikkaron*, 6. In the copy of *Homeopatia* preserved in the library of Mr. Baruch Rosenberg of Toronto, a handwritten note refers to Yudel Rosenberg's translation and the collaboration of his son, Aaron Elimelech.

22 The homeopathic pharmacy in Łódź was one of approximately thirty existing in the Russian Empire at that time. Alexander Kotok, "The history of Homeopathy in the Russian Empire until World War I, as Compared with other European Countries and the USA: Similarities and Discrepancies," http://homeoint.org/books4/kotok/2400.htm#2410, accessed July 31, 2017.

23 Yohanan Petrovsky-Shtern, "'You Will Find It in the Pharmacy': Practical Kabbalah and Natural Medicine in the Polish-Lithuanian Commonwealth, 1690–1750," in *Holy Dissent: Jewish*

The introduction to the book, written by Pogonowski, stated that: "The Jewish nation is certainly known, much more than other peoples, to cure themselves with medicine."[24] The introduction further noted that "the greatly learned Jewish rabbis" strongly support homeopathy.[25] An incident in Góra Kalwaria was cited in which the Gerrer rebbe refused to allow an operation according to the principles of mainstream Western medicine and instead referred the patient to a homeopathic physician. The introduction further claimed that the Alexander Rebbe had sent prescriptions for homeopathic medicines to Pogonowski's pharmacy. Finally, the introduction noted: "Today, moreover, the well-known Rabbi Rosenberg, who lives here in Łódź, also very often sends me homeopathic prescriptions."[26]

Homeopatia is divided into three sections. The first section consists of a short introduction to homeopathy written by a Dr. Z. Graf.[27] The second section is an alphabetical list, in Latin characters, of the entire homeopathic pharmacopeia, from *Abelmoschus* to *Zizia aurea*.[28] The following section, entitled "*Pharmakologia*," consists of a short description in Yiddish of the healing properties of ninety-eight drugs.[29] A typical example of the way these *materia medica* are presented is the entry on cannabis:

> This medium [*mitel*] would also only be recommended for urinary diseases. For example, in the beginning stages of gonorrhoea; burning in the kidneys or in the bladder; sand or stones in the kidney or bladder; retention of urine by a stoppage or through typhus; bloody urine; nipple pain in women.[30]

---

and Christian Mystics in Eastern Europe, ed. Glen Dynner (Detroit: Wayne State University Press, 2011), 33, 35, 40.

24 Yudel Rosenberg, *Homeopatia* (Piotrków, 1912), introduction, 3. Cf. Epstein, "Caring for the Soul's House," chapter 4, 3, note 6.

25 Cf. Shmueli, *With the Last Generation of Jews in Poland*, 97.

26 *Homeopatia*, 4. A draft of a business agreement from Yudel Rosenberg's Toronto period is written on the other side of a Homeopathic prescription form from Łódź, RFA, Savannah.

27 Graf's name appears only on the title page. *Homeopatia*, 5–48.

28 Ibid., 49–64.

29 Ibid., 65–98.

30 Ibid., 73.

The book concludes with a price list of all the medicinal ingredients available at Pogonowski's pharmacy along with instructions for ordering these materials by post.[31]

One actual prescription written by Rabbi Rosenberg is preserved in a letter he wrote from Łódź to his son, Meir Joshua, dated August 9, 1910. Meir Joshua's infant son's circumcision had apparently not healed properly, and his wife's nipples were also irritated. The following is Yudel Rosenberg's letter with directions to his son, followed by a prescription:

> Today I received your letter and I am distressed that the circumcision has not healed and also the nipples. [?] Water well on the circumcision for in this way the swelling will lessen. Now you have to wash the circumcision with camomile water with kvass [mixed with] borax[?] every day. After cleaning the circumcision put this powder on. Also in the day you need to clean the circumcision with hot camomile water and vinegar [mixed with borax?] after urination and put on this powder and it will soon heal. For those nipples I send to you another ointment. It is strange to me that the first ointment did not succeed, for many women were healed with that ointment. However the most important thing is cleaning the nipples as I wrote to you in the first letter. Instead of the first ointment put on this ointment and conduct yourself with cleanliness as I have written.

The prescription, written in Latin letters, includes the following:

> Zinci oxydat, albi [white zinc oxide]
> Talci [Talc] 15,0 [grams]
> Arg. nitrici [silver oxide] 0,1 [gram]
> Cocaini nitrici [cocaine nitrate] 0,05 [gram][32]

The second, and by far the most significant of Rabbi Rosenberg's publications in this field, is *Refa'el ha-Mal'aḥ* [The Angel Raphael]. This book combines two elements in Rabbi Rosenberg's medical practice: traditional remedies, including amulets [*kame'ot*] and incantations [*leḥashim*], and modern cures. It thus represents the continuation of a centuries-old tradition among Eastern European Jews.[33] As noted above, it was customary among Hasidic spiritual leaders

31 Ibid., 99–112.

32 BMA. It is to be noted that camomile water, kvass, borax, and vinegar all have antiseptic qualities, as does silver nitrate. Zinc oxide is a skin protectant. Cocaine was widely utilized medically and was not at that time a controlled substance.

33 Epstein, "Caring for the Soul's House," chapter 4, 3, note 5.

to possess traditional cures for maladies, which were generally not for publication.[34] *Refa'el ha-Mal'aḥ* also follows a broader European tradition, stemming at least from the eighteenth century, of manuals of home remedies designed to help the poor, who did not have ready access to qualified physicians, to cope with sickness and improve their health. A prominent example of this genre is the eighteenth-century publication *Primitive Physick, or, an Easy and Natural Method of Curing Most Diseases,* written by the English religious leader, John Wesley. *Primitive Physick* was said to have been "far and away the most popular" of Wesley's writings.[35] Among Eastern European Jews, this genre was well represented by publications of such eighteenth-century figures as Mendel Lefin (1749–1826), Barukh of Shklov (c. 1740–c.1812), and Dr. Moses Markuse (b. 1740s).[36] Closer to Rosenberg's time, Dr. Meir Gotlib (b. 1866) published a series of booklets on public health issues in Yiddish entitled *Zayt Gezunt* (Warsaw, 1899–1903) and Dr. Y. Frekel published a similar work *Der Hoyz Doctor* [The Home Doctor] (Warsaw, 1895).[37]

In his introduction to *Refa'el ha-Mal'aḥ,* Rabbi Rosenberg gives an indication that there were certain tensions between the traditional and modern remedies contained in his work.[38] To his readers he announced that he would be presenting them with several sorts of remedies: home remedies, medicines obtainable from pharmacies without a doctor's prescription, amulets, and incantations.[39] For each of these categories, Yudel Rosenberg carefully outlined how his work was not only useful, especially to the poor who could not readily afford a physician's fees, but also an improvement over its predecessors.

34 Aharon Wertheim, *Halakhot ve-Halikhot ba-Ḥassidut* (Jerusalem: Mossad ha-Rav Kook, 5720 [1960]), 236. Cf. Yoram Bilu, "Refu'a Mesoratit be-Kerev Yotsei Maroko," in *Jews of the Middle East: Anthropological Perspectives on Past and Present,* ed. Shlomo Deshen and Moshe Shokeid (Tel-Aviv: Schocken, 1984), 170, 172.

35 Richard L. and Claudia L. Bushman, "The Early History of Cleanliness in America," *Journal of American History* 74 (1988): 1218. Cf. Epstein, "Caring for the Soul's House," chapter 4, 6, note 10.

36 Mahler, *History of Modern Jewry,* 593.

37 Nathan Cohen, "Distributing Knowledge: Warsaw as a Center of Jewish Publishing, 1850–1914," in *Warsaw. The Jewish Metropolis: Essays in Honor of the 75th Birthday of Professor Antony Polonsky,* ed. Glenn Dynner and Francois Guesnet (Leiden: Brill, 2015), 201.

38 See Epstein, "Caring for the Soul's House," chapter 4, 39.

39 *Refa'el,* title page. On amulets and other remedies in the practice of early twentieth-century kabbalists in Jerusalem, see Jonatan Meir, *Kabbalistic Circles in Jerusalem (1896–1948)* (Leiden and Boston: Brill, 2016), 47, 50, 61. It is worthy of note that Yudel Rosenberg in his tale of the Maharal of Prague has the Maharal prescribe an amulet and gives its text. *Nifla'ot,* 53.

With regard to the remedies and medicines he prescribed, Rabbi Rosenberg stated that previous books in this area, even those that were not to be found "in our country," some of which he also consulted, were hopelessly outdated. These books stemmed from an era when knowledge of medicine was relatively primitive, and when the large, well-stocked pharmacies of today simply did not exist. For him, the best of this lot was Tobias Cohen's (1652–1729) *Ma'aseh Toviya.*[40] Regarding the amulets and incantations found in those older books, Yudel Rosenberg warned his readers that they are mostly forbidden, since ordinary people do not have the holiness or power to control the power of the great angels invoked by them.[41]

Rabbi Rosenberg reassured his readers that he had taken care to collect remedies "from many books of the wise physicians who lived in this era" and included their Latin names, which would enable his readers to obtain the medicines from pharmacies all over the world.[42] With regard to the other remedies he presented in his book, he stated that his aim was to avoid "stupidities and vain [remedies]." The criteria he used were, first of all, that the remedies should be available to all and, secondly, that "they not be very foreign to the science of medicine as it is practiced in this era."[43]

The amulets Rabbi Rosenberg included in his work had to fulfil two criteria. Their texts had to be accurate and not garbled. They also had to be free of theologically problematic injunctions to angels but rather simply contain holy names and prayers. In this respect Yudel Rosenberg recommended especially the amulets he claimed to have received from the Rebbe of Trisk, Abraham Twersky (1806–1889), who was well-known for his use of medicinal amulets.[44] Indeed, for Rabbi Rosenberg the book *Refa'el ha-Mal'aḥ* itself constituted a form of protective amulet for women in childbirth, like *Sefer Razi'el,* of which Rabbi Rosenberg was critical.[45]

---

40 On this book, see David Ruderman, "Medicine and Scientific Thought: The World of Tobias Cohen," in Robert C. Davis and Benjamin Ravid, eds., *The Jews of Early Modern Venice* (Baltimore: Johns Hopkins University Press, 2001), 191–210.

41 *Refa'el,* 3. There is some evidence of reticence among at least some Hasidic leaders with respect to the use of amulets and *segulot.* See Wertheim, *Halakhot ve-Halikhot ba-Ḥassidut,* 236. On the ambivalence with respect to publishing books devoted to these esoteric areas among Jews, see J. H. Chajes, "'Too Holy to Print: Taboo Anxiety and the Printing of Practical Hebrew Esoterica," *Jewish History* 26 (2012): 247–262.

42 *Refa'el,* 4–5.

43 Ibid., 4.

44 Biale et al., *Hasidism: A New History,* 316.

45 *Refa'el,* 4. Cf. ibid., 115, for Yudel Rosenberg's criticism of the "rival" *Sefer Razi'el.*

Yudel Rosenberg was careful not to advocate indiscriminate use of the incantations he included in the book. He pointedly stated that they were effective only in the hands of holy men and were not for ordinary people, who would be better served by relying on natural remedies.[46] Indeed, ordinary people who attempted these incantations on their own were "destroying the faith and mocking the sages."[47]

Rabbi Rosenberg, of course was far from the sole Hasidic healer practicing in Łódź, and his career as a healer evidently evoked opposition. Thus, in his introduction to *Refa'el ha-Mal'aḥ*, he stated that there would be no lack of opposition to his book, implying clearly that this opposition would be a result of intra-Hasidic rivalry, which Satan has devised in order to "delay the Redemption."[48] In *Refa'el ha-Mal'aḥ*, Rosenberg surely gave his critics as good as he got. For example, he strongly opposed a remedy for a childless woman who was to eat the foreskin of a circumcised child in order for her to have children. The rabbi who prescribed this remedy had engaged in a lengthy discussion in order to prove the halakhic permissibility of this remedy.[49] Against this practice Rabbi Rosenberg declared:

> Enough of such stupidities and foolishness! They merely make a jest and a mockery that such things can be found in the literature of Israel. Those minor rebbes [*rebbelekh*] who dispense such a remedy are of inferior intellect and without sense. ... They think that all things printed in books have substance.[50]

Yudel Rosenberg's *Refa'el ha-Mal'aḥ* was, therefore, a curious mixture of the old and the new, of modern medicine, folk remedies, charms, and incantations. On the one hand, he agreed with Rabbi Menaḥem Mendel Schneersohn (1789–1866) of Lubavitch that at present, as opposed to earlier generations, dreams are not portentious. He thus stated that anyone familiar with "anatomy"

46 *Refa'el*, 4; cf. also 64, 70–71.

47 Ibid., 4; cf. also 110ff.

48 Ibid., 4; cf. also 58.

49 This is mentioned as a Moroccan custom where women ate the foreskin in order to have male children. Hayyim Yosef David Azulai, *Mahazik Berakha, Yoreh De'ah* (Salonika, 5572), responsum 79, 98a, section 2. It is also mentioned in the *Responsa of Rabbi Shim'on ben Tsemaḥ Duran* (Livorno, 1742), responsum 518, 103b.

50 *Refa'el*, 6.

will understand that dreams have a physical cause.[51] On the other hand, in presenting an amulet designed to benefit a woman in a difficult childbirth, Rabbi Rosenberg stated: "This amulet was revealed to me from Heaven. I earnestly give a very great warning that no man should utilize this amulet unless he know and understand the secret of the combination of these three [divine] names."[52]

On the one hand, he is aware that, in case of being bitten by a mad dog: "in this era experienced doctors in this [disease] are found in the large towns who are appointed by the government for the good of the country." On the other hand, the intervention of physicians is by no means the only possible treatment. As he wrote immediately afterward:

> Before you are able to get to the physician, you should make this home remedy. Take an onion and crush it or grate it with a grater and mix with salt and liquid honey until it becomes like a salve. Rub it on the place of the bite several times a day.[53]

In this book, amulets against cholera are juxtaposed with hygienic advice "according to the science of medicine."[54] While these differing ways of curing diseases are normally found in separate paragraphs, where possible Rosenberg commented on the areas of agreement between traditional healing and modern medicine such as that between the theory of disease of the kabbalist Rabbi Ḥayyim Vital (1543–1620) and "the science of medicine."[55] Gideon Bohak, in an interesting article, asserts that "in Europe, even in Eastern Europe[,] ... mixture of ancient magic and modern men and pharmacology was quite rare by the late 19th century."[56] The case of Rabbi Yudel Rosenberg demonstrates that this combination of magic and science did have a continuation.

---

51 *Refa'el*, 34. Yudel Rosenberg occasionally shows off his knowledge of human anatomy elsewhere in his works. Cf. *'Ateret*, 106.

52 *Refa'el*, 64. Belief in amulets was not at all universal among contemporary Hasidim. Rabbi Yizhak Meir Alter of Ger is reported to have stated, "Woe to us if we had to resort to sorcery and amulet writing." Cited in Max Lipschitz, *The Faith of a Hassid* (New York: n.p., 1967), 160.

53 *Refa'el*, 47.

54 Ibid., 50.

55 Ibid., 52–53. On Vital's medical knowledge, see Yael Buchman and Zohar Amar, *Practical Medicine of Rabbi Hayyim Vital (1543–1620): Healer in the Land of Israel and Vicinity* (Ramat-Gan: Bar-Ilan University, 2006).

56 Bohak, "How Jewish Magic Survived the Disenchantment of the World," 22–23.

In a manuscript preserved at the Montreal Jewish Public Library, we can see some of the raw material Rabbi Rosenberg prepared for the writing of this book. The manuscript is untitled and unattributed, but the handwriting appears to be Yudel Rosenberg's. The manuscript is a small booklet that contains a numbered series of eighty-seven incantations and remedies (there appears to be a leaf lost because the numbers 2 and 12–22 are missing). This is not simply a copy of a portion of Rabbi Rosenberg's *Refa'el ha-Mal'aḥ*. It rather appears to be a sort of notebook in which he listed the remedies and spells as he heard them, in no particular order, and then edited them for publication. One comparative example is the remedy for a mad dog bite contained in both the book and the manuscript:

Jewish Public Library manuscript, number 31:	*Refa'el ha-Mal'aḥ*, 47:
Immediately put on the place of the bite onion mixed with honey.	Take an onion and crush it or grate it with a grater and mix with salt and liquid honey until it becomes like a salve. Rub it on the place of the bite several times a day.

It is immediately noticeable that the formulation in *Rafael ha-Mal'aḥ* is much more elaborate whereas the manuscript is much briefer, which makes considerable sense if we understand it to be a notebook. The range of ailments included in the Jewish Public Library manuscript includes remedies for sore throat, stomach worms, bloody urine and much more. There are also spells against the evil eye, to engender love between husband and wife (number 48), to deal with mice infestation in a house ("take meat from a wolf and burn it and scatter the ashes in the four corners of the house," number 30), and for getting the answer to questions in one's dreams (*she'elat ḥalom*, numbers 49 and 51).[57]

Refa'el ha- Mal'aḥ became one of Rabbi Rosenberg's most influential books, constituting a handbook of Hassidic healing that was, apparently, widely utilized within the Hassidic community as well as by traditional Jewish healers from North Africa.[58] Within months, it was translated into Yiddish, though not, apparently, with Rabbi Rosenberg's initial approval, for he hesitated to make things which contained, among other things, "secret" holy names available on the popular Yiddish market. Only after some persuasion did he agree to an

57 Jewish Public Library, Montreal, Jewish Canadiana Collection: Yehuda Rosenberg.

58 Cf. Reizin, *Lexicon fun der Yiddisher Literatur, Presse un Filologie*, vol. 4, col. 117; Baumeil, "Rosenberg," 276.

abridged Yiddish edition in which he controlled which items to translate and which not.[59]

Rosenberg's last medically oriented work from this period (1913) is essentially a Yiddish translation of Maimonides's *Hilkhot De'ot* [laws of personality development] of his *Mishneh Torah*. In this section, Maimonides gives a number of precepts concerning the health of the body and the mind. Rosenberg, accordingly, entitled the work *Refu'at ha-Nefesh u-Refu'at ha-Guf* [Cure of the Soul and the Body]. Appended to it was a short biography of Maimonides which the author claimed to have translated from an original text by Israel Ḥayyim Zagorodsky (1864–1931).[60] This biography was designed to give the Yiddish reader an idea of Maimonides's philosophical and scientific greatness.[61]

In accordance with the book's title, its purpose was to offer to all Jews the way to achieve a healthy body and soul as well as a synthesis between Judaism [*yiddishkeit*] and humane living [*menshlikhkeit*][62] The contents of the book go somewhat beyond a mere translation of Maimonides's words, for, just as in *Refa'el ha-Mal'aḥ*, Rabbi Rosenberg was acutely aware that the science of medicine had greatly progressed since Maimonides's lifetime. Thus, interspersed in the Yiddish translation, Rabbi Rosenberg added numerous comments of his own. He remarks, for instance, that the advice Maimonides gives against eating too much fish is contradicted by "the newest research" which demonstrates that fish is digested in the stomach as well as flesh.[63] Similarly, Rabbi Rosenberg comments that the advice Maimonides gives to not wash the head in cold water is contradicted by almost all contemporary medical books.[64] Another example is found in chapter 4, paragraph 13, which presents Maimonides's cure for constipation. After the translation of Maimonides's words, Rabbi Rosenberg comments: "According to today's science of medicine, there are [remedies] much better than that, such as 'Karlsbader Salt.'"[65] Recalling his collaboration with pharmacist Pogonowski, Rabbi Rosenberg also managed to introduce a plug for homeopathic pharmacies.[66]

---

59 *Segulot*, 3.

60 Jacob I. Dienstag, "Maimonides in Yiddish Literature," *Yiddish* 7 (1987): 92, 99–100.

61 *Refu'at*, 3.

62 Ibid., title page, 4.

63 Ibid., 29.

64 Ibid., 36.

65 Ibid., 33. Yudel Rosenberg also recommended mineral water from spas such as Karsbad, Marienbad, Kissingen, and Yessentuki in the Caucasus. *Refu'at*, 51.

66 Ibid., 26, 36–37.

Despite these comments, Rabbi Rosenberg continued to emphasize that "all contemporary professors [of medicine] agree with Maimonides's statements."[67] In *Refu'at*, as in *Refa'el*, Rabbi Rosenberg repeated his dual theme: the acceptance of the methods and cures of modern Western medicine[68] coupled with reassurances as to the essential validity of the Jewish way in maintaining health.[69] A major element in Rabbi Rosenberg's comments is also the criticism of small-town Jewish society noted above in chapter 2 concerning *shtetl* hygiene and mores.[70]

Rabbi Yudel Rosenberg did not publish any more works dealing directly with medicine, and as noted in chapter 4, apparently gave up his public healing practice. However, throughout his publications, he maintained an intellectual interest in the connections between Torah, science, and medicine. Rabbi Yudel Rosenberg was, of course, not unique in this. As Kimmy Caplan comments, many of Yudel Rosenberg's Orthodox rabbinical contemporaries were likewise prone to discussing scientific and technological concepts in their writings.[71]

Rabbi Rosenberg sporadically referred in his writings to issues related to pharmacology and chemistry,[72] as well as homeopathic medicine,[73] geography,[74] and electricity.[75] In a responsum, he commented that earlier halakhic authorities were in error because they were not sufficiently aware of the science of bacteriology.[76] Similarly, in one of his sermons, he referred to the power of incense to drive out *mazikin* [demons], which he identified with microbes:

> Scientists have shown that there exist in the air very small worms [*tola'im*] that are called "bacilli" which are not visible to the eye without the instrument of the microscope which magnifies things very greatly. From the air they go into the water and they bring forth a terrible poison and all diseases come from these small creatures as is known to medical scientists. One may ask from what are these demons created? The answer is that we see now that all the words of men are found in the air. Through the power

67 Ibid., 33.
68 Ibid., 23.
69 Ibid., 34.
70 Ibid., 38, 52–54, 63.
71 Caplan, "The Concerns of an Immigrant Rabbi," 208.
72 *Omer*, part 1, 47; part 2, 38–39.
73 *'Ateret*, 157.
74 PY, 85.
75 PY, 123.
76 *Omer*, part 2, 77.

> of the radio we are able to hear with an instrument called a radiophone the voices, cries, and conversations of men that are found in the air from thousands of miles away. Thus all the curses and outcries and evil speech are found in the air. From all of this the air is defiled and in it are created these tiny poisonous destroyers. If the Holy One Blessed be He did not purify the air and water it would not be possible to live in the world.[77]

As Yudel Rosenberg put it, doctors who do not recite the biblical passages concerning the incense [*qetoret*] have only the use of carbolic acid to oppose these creatures.[78]

Rabbi Rosenberg included among the sciences he was interested in hypnotism[79] and spiritualism, which claimed to scientifically prove the existence of the soul after physical death.[80] Such new discoveries had implications for him with respect to giving reasons for the commandments of the Torah.[81] With respect to Kabbala, he would compare the emanation of the *sefirot* (kabbalistic term for stages of emanation of God's power) to the radioactivity of radium and to cosmic rays.[82]

Many similar analogies are to be found in Yudel Rosenberg's work on the *Zohar*, to be discussed in chapter 10. In accordance with his program of presenting Kabbala as the key to the salvation of Judaism, Rabbi Rosenberg took pains to describe Kabbala as "the source of all spiritual sciences and also the source of the highest and noblest morality."[83] His goal was to present his material in such a way that there was agreement between Kabbala and science, "so that all the nations of the world and their sages should see that everything is implicit in the holy Torah."[84]

Thus, woven in among his commentaries and homilies are a number of instances in which Rabbi Rosenberg combined Kabbala and science. In dealing with the creation account in Genesis, Yudel Rosenberg connected the Sun and

77 PY, 55, 120–121. Cf. also *Sha'arei*, 20–21; ZT, vol. 3, 51, 73; ZT, vol. 4, 46; ZT, vol. 5, 148. See especially ZT, vol. 1, 43 where Rabbi Rosenberg asserts that all this was known to R. Shim'on bar Yoḥai.

78 ZT, vol. 4, 46; PY, 55, 120–121.

79 ZT, vol. 5, 108.

80 ZT, vol. 5, 35. Cf. ZT, vol. 4, 95 where he identifies contemporary spiritualism as something anticipated by the Zohar.

81 ZT, vol. 5, 35–36.

82 *Omer*, part 1, 47, cf. also pages 61, 76, 100; *Yadot*, 37–38.

83 *Haqqafot*, 15

84 PY, 5. Cf. ZK, 7.

the six planets (Mercury, Venus, Earth, Mars, Jupiter, and Saturn) to the seven lower *sefirot*. He continued:

> And if recently the astronomers have discovered other planets greater and farther away whose orbit is connected with the sun, it must be said that they are symbolized by the three first *sefirot* of the *'olam ha-'assiya* [World of Formation, the third, in descending order, of the four supernal worlds in Lurianic Kabbala]. Thus Kabbala and science do not contradict each other.[85]

The fact that scientists believed the world was considerably older than the few thousand years provided for by the Jewish calendar was not a matter of concern for Yudel Rosenberg. He did not consider this a contradiction because the kabbalistic book, *Sefer ha-Temuna* [Book of the Image], had stated that the world had passed through a number of aeons [*shemitot*] prior to the commencement of the present one.[86]

Indeed, Rabbi Rosenberg was not content to claim that Kabbala did not contradict the scientists. He believed in principle that seeming discrepancies between science and the tradition of Kabbala can be satisfactorily explained,[87] though he admitted he could be mistaken and if so, God would forgive him for his purpose was to deflect objections to Kabbala.[88] He also declared that the *Zohar* had anticipated the scientists in a number of discoveries. Thus, he claimed to be able to derive the fact that the Earth and the Moon revolve around the Sun from the *Zohar*:[89]

> The holy *Zohar* is not merely a book for the pious. ... It also contains many matters of natural science. ... It is known that the *Zohar* appeared in the world a hundred [sic] years before the discovery of the portion of the Earth [which includes] America.[90] ... Yet there is found in it the science of geography,[91] just as it was later discovered by the two scientists, [Christopher] Columbus (1451–1506) and Nicholas Copernicus (1473–1543). That is,

85 ZK, 7.
86 PY, 6.
87 ZK Tehilim, 221; PY, 132.
88 *Eliyahu*, 80–81.
89 ZK Tehilim, 221.
90 Cf. ZT, vol. 4, 95.
91 For other references to geography see *Sha'arei*, 10.

> that the earth is round like a ball, that it is inhabited on all sides and that it possesses two types of motion, one motion spherical ... like a wheel on its axle and the other motion elliptical around the Sun. ...
>
> Everyone who understands will be able to see that almost the same things were hinted at [in the *Zohar*] as were discovered by the scientist Copernicus about three hundred years after the *Zohar* appeared in the world.[92]

Another example: Rosenberg considered that the "tower floating in the air," which Jewish legend ascribed to King Solomon, was a machine, similar to the modern airplane, which worked in accordance with natural properties such as electricity and magnetism.[93]

Rabbi Rosenberg knew from his reading of geography that the Land of Israel was not the center of the world,[94] but some discrepancies between science and the *Zohar* needed quite a bit of massaging on his part. Thus, in a sermon he attempted to reconcile the *Zohar*, which states that the distance from the earth to the moon is 36,000 cubits (slightly more than 10 miles), and the astronomers, who hold that it is a distance of 240,000 miles. Yudel Rosenberg attempted to reconcile this vast discrepancy by asserting that the shorter distance holds only with respect to the Land of Israel but elsewhere on earth there is a greater distance.[95] Even evolution, that most threatening of nineteenth-century scientific theories for traditional religious belief, and one which Yudel Rosenberg condemned in no uncertain terms,[96] had its connection with Kabbala:

> It must be seen that the science called ... "evolution," which was established by the mad scientist Darwin, has something stolen from the words of the *Zohar*, which speaks here of the creatures and types of men found in the other portions of the earth. Darwin, however, wrote that all men are descended from the apes. And it certainly seems that he was like an ape

92 NZ, 145–146,149; ZT, vol. 1, 23–24. Adolphe Frank commented that the *Zohar*'s text on the roundness of the world could have been written by a disciple of Copernicus. Cited in André Neher, *Jewish Thought and the Scientific Revolution of the Sixteenth Century* (Oxford: Oxford University Press, 1986), 104.

93 NZ, 126–127.

94 *Sha'arei*, 35. Cf. ibid., 10.

95 PY, 7, ZK, 7.

96 ZT, vol. 1, 62.

> which is accustomed to imitate men in their movements. Thus he desired to imitate and say [things] similar to the words of the *Zohar* only in a spirit of madness. ... On the contrary, in several places in the *Zohar* the opposite is stated that the apes are the descendants of sinful men. Something similar is agreed upon by the honest scientists of the nations of the world.[97]

Nonetheless, he was not willing to relativize everything. He affirmed, for instance, that the sun did stand still for Joshua at Gibeon.[98] In general, Rosenberg wished to leave the impression that the *Zohar* was respected by the scholars of the gentiles, who seek in it knowledge of divine philosophy and who had even translated it into their own languages. After all, the great Maimonides was also a kabbalist.[99] How much more so, then, should the Jews honor and study this book "which is ours and which [contains] our soul and the length of our lives."[100]

---

97 NZ, 147. Cf. also NZ, 22–23, 146; ZT, vol. 1, 40, where Yudel Rosenberg speaks of gorillas as descendants of Cain; ZT, vol. 1, 62; ZK Tehillim, 23; *Haggada*, 59, note. For a more positive attitude toward evolution by a contemporary kabbalist, Yehuda Ashlag, cf. Boaz Huss, "Komunizm Altruisti: Ha-Kabala ha-Modernistit shel ha-Rav Ashlag," in *'Iyunim bi-Tekumat Yisrael: Me'asef li-Ve'ayot ha-Tsionut, ha-Yishuv u-Medinat Yisrael* 16 (2006): 118.

98 PY, 93.

99 PY, 161. Cf. Moshe Idel, "Maimonides and Kabbalah," in *Studies in Maimonides*, ed. Isadore Twersky (Cambridge, MA: Harvard University Press, 1990), 31–81.

100 PY, 159.

CHAPTER 10

"Those Who Understand Kabbala Are Extremely Rare in Our Generation":[1] Yudel Rosenberg as Kabbalist

At the beginning of the twenty-first century, the Judaic mystical tradition of Kabbala is experiencing a veritable renaissance. It has achieved the sustained attention of academic scholars and ordinary people alike. It attracts Jews of all degrees of commitment, from Ḥaredi to secular, as well as many non-Jews. Publications of its major and minor texts in their original languages fill multiple bookshelves; translations and interpretations in multiple languages and formats compete for the reader's attention. Celebrities like Madonna[2] and rabbis of all denominations endorse its wisdom and prescribe its teachings as the solution for most of life's problems.[3]

This was hardly the case at the beginning of the twentieth century, however. In that era, academic scholars of Judaism often tended to dismiss Kabbala as irrelevant at best, and as positively harmful to Judaism at worst. Liberal Jews thought of it, if at all, as a dark stain on the Judaic tradition that went directly counter to the true, rationalistic basis of Judaism. For them, Kabbala was a sort of estranged relative, best left unmentioned in polite company. Orthodox Jews, for whom Kabbala and its texts constituted an integral part of their revered Judaic tradition, were certainly not willing or able to repudiate the Kabbalistic tradition outright. They tended, nonetheless, to handle its contents gingerly, asserting that Kabbala was not something meant for the attention of ordinary Jews.

---

1 Cited in Jonathan Garb, *The Chosen Will Become Herds: Studies in Twentieth-Century Kabbalah* [Hebrew] (Jerusalem: Karmel, 2005), 26.

2 Boaz Huss, "All You Need Is LAV: Madonna and Postmodern Kabbalah," *Jewish Quarterly Review* 95, no. 4 (2005): 611–624.

3 Jody Myers, "Kabbalah at the Turn of the 21st Century," in *Jewish Mysticism and Kabbalah: New Insights and Scholarship*, ed. Frederick E. Greenspahn (New York: New York University Press, 2011), 175–190.

The Orthodox often asserted that only scholars who had achieved full mastery of the Talmudic literature (a requirement that practically eliminated all but a very few) should be allowed to study Kabbala.

Against this background of non-interest at best and outright dismissal at worst, which spread across nearly the entire spectrum of Judaic belief (and non-belief), we come to examine the efforts of Rabbi Yudel Rosenberg and a few of his contemporaries, who directed their considerable scholarly talents, efforts, and publications toward restoring Kabbala to what they considered to be its true, central place in Judaism's present and future. This chapter will especially examine Yudel Rosenberg's decades-long quest to spread public knowledge of the greatest Kabbalistic classic, the *Zohar,* through the publication of its translation from Aramaic to Hebrew, accompanied by his commentary.[4] In studying Rabbi Rosenberg's effort, the place of the *Zohar* and of Kabbala in general in the first half of the twentieth century, will come into sharper focus.

From nearly the beginning of Rabbi Rosenberg's writing career to practically its end, he wrote and published works related to Kabbala. His major writing project of translating and reediting the *Zohar* occupied a full quarter-century of his life. He certainly considered his work on the *Zohar* to be his magnum opus.[5] This makes it abundantly clear that Kabbala in general, and his *Zohar* project in particular, were of immense importance to him. As we shall see, Kabbala and the truth, which, he felt, was contained there, are keys to understanding much of Rabbi Rosenberg's thought, including his attitudes toward science and its discoveries as well as his ideas concerning the imminent coming of the messiah and the messianic age, which, for Rosenberg, would bring about the solution to all the difficulties faced by the Jews.[6] Rabbi Rosenberg was morally certain that the solution to all of these problems lay in the *Zohar*. What needed to

---

4 On the history of the Zohar as a literary document, see Boaz Huss, *Like the Radiance of the Sky: Chapters in the Reception History of the Zohar and the Construction of its Symbolic Value* [Hebrew] (Jerusalem: Bialik Institute, 2008)

5 The title pages of nearly all of Yudel Rosenberg's books identify him first and foremost as the author of the *Zohar* translation.

6 Yudel Rosenberg's conviction was shared by Rabbi Yehuda Ashlag. See Jonatan Meir, "Gilui ve-Gilui be-Hester: 'Al Mamshikhei ha-R. Y. L. Ashlag, ha-Hitnagdut la-Hem ve-Hafatsat Sifrut ha-Sod," *Kabbalah* 16 (2007): 154. On messianic expectations in that era among Orthodox rabbis, see Binyamin Brown, "Ha-Ba'al Bayit: R. Yisrael Meir ha-Kohen, 'ha-Ḥafets Ḥayyim,'" in *The Gedoilim: Leaders Who Shaped the Israeli Haredi Society*, ed. Binyamin Brown and Nissim Leon (Jerusalem: Magnes Press, 2017), 145–146; Gershon C. Bacon, "Birthpangs of the Messiah: The Reflections of Two Polish Rabbis on Their Era," in *Jews and Messianism in the Modern Era: Metaphor and Meaning. Studies in Contemporary Judaism, an Annual* 7 (1991): 86–99; Biale et al., *Hasidism: A New History*, 301. Cf. Zeev Gries,

happen, as far as he was concerned, was for multitudes of Jews to access its wisdom and bring it into their lives. If this could happen, all would be well because Rosenberg was certain that the *Zohar* contained "all the wisdoms of the world" as well as the ultimate secret of the coming of the Messiah.[7]

Rabbi Yudel Rosenberg obviously immersed himself in the study of Kabbala, as we will see. However, in his time and place it was hardly a given that even a Hasidic rabbi would necessarily become expert in Kabbala. Even though the Hasidic tradition, in which Yudel Rosenberg was raised and educated, contained many ideas based on Kabbala, for many Hasidic leaders in the second half of the nineteenth century, with the notable exception of Rabbi Tsvi Hirsh Eichenstein of Zhidachov (1763–1831),[8] study of Kabbala in general, and of Lurianic Kabbala in particular were deemphasized.[9] On the other hand, as Jonatan Meir states, the world of late nineteenth- and early twentieth-century Kabbala "still awaits a full accounting" and we have much to learn on this issue using Yudel Rosenberg as a guide.[10]

Rabbi Rosenberg was well aware that in his milieu many contemporary rabbis had no interest in Kabbala. Writing toward the end of his life, he condemned:

> Rabbis ... and Rosh Yeshivas who study Torah but occupy themselves [only] in keen observations [*pshetlekh*] and do not occupy themselves with the knowledge of God. ... They suffice themselves with casuistry [*pilpul*] in the oral Torah. There is a well-known saying of our sages: "Those who only have Torah do not even have Torah."[11]

The Book in the Jewish World 1700–1900 (Oxford and Portland: Littman Library of Jewish Civilization, 2007), 126, note 32.

7 Rosenberg, in *Sha'arei*, 56, specifically states that he is revealing a secret and asks God to forgive him, because his intention was to strengthen the weak with the knowledge that the redemption is near. Cf. ZT, vol. 4, section "Sod Zman Kets ha-Aḥaron" unpaginated [last page]; ZK, vol. 7, 3; Jonatan Meir, *Kabbalistic Circles in Jerusalem (1896–1948)* (Leiden and Boston: Brill, 2016), 117.

8 Biale et al., *Hasidism: A New History*, 383–384, 770. Cf. Raya Haran, "Ḥerut be-Tokh Emuna: Ha-Hatafa le-Limud ha-Nigleh veha-Nistar be-Hagut ha-Tsaddiqim le-Veyt Ziditschov-Komarna," in *Sefer Zikkaron le-Gershom Sholem: bi-Me'lot 'Esrim ve-Ḥamesh Shanim li-Fetirato*, ed. Yosef Dan (Jerusalem: Makhon le-Mada'ei ha-Yahadut, 2007), 305–352.

9 Shaul Magid, *Hasidism on the Margin: Reconciliation, Antinomianism, and Messianism in Izbica/Radzin Hasidism* (Madison: University of Wisconsin Press, 2003), 12.

10 Meir, *Kabbalistic Circles in Jerusalem*, ix. Cf. idem, "Giluyyim Ḥadashim 'al R. Yehuda Leib Ashlag," *Kabbalah* 20 (2009): 350.

11 *'Ateret*, 176.

With whom did Rabbi Rosenberg study Kabbala? One hint is contained in an undated amulet in his handwriting against plague [*magefa*] which he claimed to have derived from Rabbi Ḥayyim Vital's *Sha'ar ha-Yiḥudim* [Gate of Unifications], chapter 12. At the end of his description of the utilization of this amulet, Rabbi Rosenberg wrote: "I have a tradition [*qabbala*] from our Rabbi Yehuda Leib Eger ... of Lublin to hang the amulet on the man."[12] We know that Rabbi Rosenberg visited Rabbi Eger in 1886, shortly before his death in 1889.[13] We further learn that he elsewhere explicitly states that Rabbi Eger gave him guidance in the reading of the *Zohar.*[14] It is thus likely that Rabbi Eger was at least one of his primary teachers in Kabbala, as he was to Rabbi Tsadok ha-Kohen, and that factor may partially explain why Rabbi Rosenberg originally considered moving to Lublin in the first place.

In Yudel Rosenberg's very first published work of Talmudic commentary, *Yadot Nedarim,* we see his interest in Kabbala manifested. At the end of part one of that book, Rosenberg included a sermon which had been originally delivered at a ceremony formally marking the end of the study of the Talmudic tractate *Nedarim.* It was entitled "The Power of Speech and Thought."[15] The sermon speaks of the theme of the relation of Judaism to the natural sciences through the medium of Kabbala.

It was the thesis of Rabbi Rosenberg's sermon that a fruitful analogy may be made between the kabbalistic concept of a cause-and-effect relationship between humans and *Eyn Sof* [God in His absolute transcendence] and similar relationships in natural sciences. In the sermon, Yudel Rosenberg referred to human prayer metaphorically "ascending" on wings of thought and compared it to the movement of electricity and the ascension of balloons. He also compared other spiritual matters with recent scientific discoveries and technological innovations such as the speed of light, magnetism, electricity, the telephone, the phonograph, and the radio.[16] For Rosenberg, all these new discoveries demonstrate the truth of Torah and the falsity of the claims of the unbelievers:

---

12 The text of an amulet, presumably utilized by Yudel Rosenberg, is found in the BMA, Jerusalem. On Rabbi Eger as Rosenberg's guide in the reading of the *Zohar,* see *Sha'arei,* 111.

13 Meir Joshua Rosenberg, *Kur ha-Mivḥan,* introduction; Stein, *Radom,* 116. Rosenberg mentions his 1886 visit in *Sha'arei,* 111. Cf. PY, 92.

14 *Sha'arei,* 111

15 *Yadot,* 37–38.

16 ZK Tehilim, 76, 224; ZT, vol. 2, 163, 180; ZT, vol. 2, 106; ZT, vol. 5, 100; PY, 123.

> The unbelievers [*apikorsim*] mocked and did not believe that human prayer can rise to heaven and be heard there, or that human [expression of] Torah can be heard in the Garden of Eden. However in recent times natural scientists continually find hidden powers in the world such as the power of electricity by which it is possible to hear news from thousands of parasangs away even without metal wires. Some years ago they discovered the power of "radio" and have constructed an instrument called a radiophone through which it is possible to hear in America the music of a musician in Berlin. And it would be possible to hear in a synagogue in New York the sermon of the preacher in the Great Synagogue in Vilna as it is preached. With no exaggeration, when the Temple is rebuilt, speedily in our days, and the High Priest performs his service ... it will be possible to hear his voice in every synagogue in the world.[17]

Soon after he finished the publishing of *Yadot Nedarim*, Rabbi Rosenberg commenced a project that would become his major life work—a Hebrew translation and reedition of the classic work of Kabbala, the *Zohar*.[18] This was a bold and ambitious project indeed. Its publication would not be completed until 1930.

In order to comprehend the magnitude and originality of Rabbi Rosenberg's project, it is necessary to understand the position of the *Zohar* within the Judaism of his time. It is widely understood that Kabbala received its classic representation in the *Zohar*.[19] Though modern scholarship has concluded that the *Zohar* was largely created in the medieval period, particularly but not exclusively by the thirteenth-century Spanish kabbalist, Moses de Leon (1240–1305),[20] Orthodox Jews for the most part accepted the composition as it presents itself: the work of the renowned second-century rabbi, Shim'on bar Yoḥai. From the sixteenth through the eighteenth centuries, the *Zohar* constituted a major source of authority in Judaism, approaching at times that of the Bible and Talmud. In that era, no Jew thought himself well-educated unless he

17 ZT, vol. 5, 100. Cf. ZK Tehilim, 224.

18 On publication history of Rosenberg's translation and commentary, see chapter 3, note XXX.

19 On the *Zohar* and its historical reception, see Boaz Huss, *Like the Radiance of the Sky: Chapters in the Reception History of the Zohar and the Construction of its Symbolic Value* [Hebrew] (Jerusalem: Bialik Institute and Ben-Zvi Institute, 2008).

20 On the development of the Zohar, see Boaz Huss, *Like the Radiance of the Sky: Chapters in the Reception History of the Zohar and the Construction of its Symbolic Value* [Hebrew] (Jerusalem: Bialik Institute and Ben-Zvi Institute, 2008).

possessed some knowledge of Kabbala, including the *Zohar*. Kabbala, with the *Zohar* taking pride of place, provided an intellectual basis for many significant ideological developments within Judaism, not the least among which was the Hasidic movement.[21]

From the end of the seventeenth century, however, the position of the *Zohar* began to decline. On the one hand, the broad popularization of Kabbala and kabbalistic practice that began to intensify in the last decades of the seventeenth century[22] was in a large part due to the rise of Lurianic Kabbala. This meant that, as much as the *Zohar* continued to be revered, it also tended to be supplanted in prominence by the study of the Lurianic writings.[23] The seventeenth-century messianic movement of Sabbatai Tsvi also impacted on the *Zohar* and its study. The Sabbatian movement was largely inspired by kabbalistic ideology, and its notorious and noxious aftermath necessarily caused further hesitancy concerning Kabbala among those many Jews who decried the movement's perceived excesses.[24]

On top of this, the rationalistic spirit that marked the *Haskala* eventually caused a marked devaluation of Kabbala study among "enlightened" Jews. By the mid-nineteenth century, therefore, Kabbala and the *Zohar* with it had been thoroughly discredited among nearly all non-Orthodox Jews, who saw them as a divergence from the essentially rationalistic "essence" of Judaism.[25] Traditionalists themselves showed a marked ambivalence concerning this issue. Among non-Hasidic Jews [*mitnagdim*], the *Zohar* was formally revered but was largely removed from the curriculum of even the scholarly class.[26] Even the Hasidim, whose ideology was ultimately dependent upon Kabbala and its teachings,

---

21 Gershom Scholem, *Major Trends in Jewish Mysticism* (New York: Schocken Books, 1941), 244–350.

22 Gershon David Hundert, "Jewish Popular Spirituality in the Eighteenth Century," *Polin* 15 (2002): 95.

23 Jonathan Garb, *Kabbalist in the Heart of the Storm: R. Moshe Hayyim Luzzatto* [Hebrew] (Tel-Aviv: Haim Rubin Tel Aviv University Press, 2014), 51.

24 Gershom Scholem, *Sabbatai Sevi: The Mystical Messiah* (Princeton: Princeton University Press, 1973), 1–76.

25 A prime example of this attitude is Heinrich Graetz's treatment of the *Zohar* in his *Geschichte der Juden* (Leipzig, 1863), vol. 7, 235–249.

26 Scholem, *Kabbalah* (New York: Schocken Books, 1974), 85; Jonathan Garb, *Yearnings of the Soul: Psychological Thought in Modern Kabbala* (Chicago: University of Chicago Press, 2015), 67. On Lithuanian Kabbala and its characteristics, see Raphael Shuchat, "Kabbalat Lita ke-Zerem Atsma'i be-Sifrut ha-Qabbala," *Kabbalah* 10 (2004): 181–206. Cf. Benjamin Brown, "Substitutes for Mysticism: a General Model for the Theological Development of Hasidism in the Nineteenth Century," *History of Religions* 56, no. 3 (2017): 249–250, 260.

often tended to shy away from direct contact with such texts.[27] For example, nineteenth-century Hasidic Rabbi Ḥayyim Halberstam (1797–1876) of Sanz could state, "We concentrate on Talmud and the Codes. We study Kabbala when others are asleep."[28] Hardly anyone seemed to advocate the bringing of Kabbala as such to the masses.[29] While some Hasidic leaders, like Rabbi Israel Hopstein (1737–1814), the Maggid of Koznits,[30] and Rabbi Yeḥezkel Shraga Halberstam (1818–1898) of Sieniawa encouraged the publication of kabbalistic books,[31] others, such as Rabbi Abraham Joshua Heschel (1748–1825) of Apt, refused to give his approbation for Kabbala books. [32] When venturing beyond standard rabbinic literature, many nineteenth-century Hasidic leaders tended to emphasize and encourage the study of the literature of the classical period of Hasidism, which maintained an indirect link with the *Zohar* and its ethos, over the direct study of the *Zohar* itself.[33] For other Jewish scholars, such as Rabbi Samuel Landau of Prague (1752–1834), the *Zohar* was to be addressed only insofar as it was cited by later Kabbalistic writings.[34] As late as 1925 in Jerusalem, the leadership of the Kabbalistic Yeshiva Sha'ar ha-Shamayim emphasized the danger of Kabbala becoming "incomprehensible and removed" for Jews[35] Rabbi Rosenberg himself took note of the contemporary non-attractiveness of the study of *Zohar* in a letter he wrote in 1904 to Rabbi Moses Naḥum Yerusalimsky, where he stated that Jews "almost detested it."[36]

Thus, devoting his major literary effort to encouragement of the popular study of *Zohar*, Yudel Rosenberg was seemingly bucking a major trend within

27 Tsvi Hirsh Shapira, *Tif'eret Banim* (Jerusalem: Emet, 2000), 20 (citation of Biala Rebbe); David Sorotzkin, "'Geula shel Ḥoshekh va-Afela': R. Yoel Teitelbaum ha-Rabi mi-Satmar," in *The Gedoilim: Leaders Who Shaped the Israeli Haredi Society*, ed. Binyamin Brown and Nissim Leon (Jerusalem: Magnes Press, 2017), 381.

28 Rabinowicz, *The World of Hasidism*, 137. Cf. Langer, *Nine Gates to the Hasidic Mysteries*, 37; Isaac Bashevis Singer, *Love and Exile: a Memoir* (Garden City, NY: Doubleday, 1984), 9.

29 Yohanan Petrovsky-Shtern, "Hasidei De'ar'a and Hasidei Dekokhvaya': Two Trends in Modern Jewish Historiography," *AJS Review* 32, no. 1 (2008): 153–154.

30 Rabinowicz, *Chassidic Rebbes*, 78.

31 Ibid., 187.

32 Ibid., 102.

33 Mahler, *Hasidism and the Jewish Enlightenment*, 269–270; Shaul Magid, *Hasidism on the Margin: Reconciliation, Antinomianism, and Messianism in Izbica/Radzin Hasidism* (Madison: University of Wisconsin Press, 2003), 12–13; Shim'on Fogel, "Pe'ilato ha-Safrutit shel R. Gershon Ḥanokh Henikh Leiner mi-Radzin," *Da'at* 68–69 (2010): 178–179.

34 Garb, *Yearnings of the Soul*, 170.

35 Ibid., 120.

36 Yerusalimsky Papers, Schocken Library, Jerusalem.

the Jewish world in which he lived.[37] But in his desire to promote the study and comprehension of Kabbala, Rabbi Rosenberg was far from alone. Indeed, at the very time Yudel Rosenberg was in the process of inaugurating his *Zohar* project, circa 1900, Jonathan Garb claims that a new period in the history of Kabbala begins.[38] Other men of Rabbi Rosenberg's time and place, like Hillel Zeitlin (1872–1942), Rabbi Samuel Alexandrov (1865–1941), and Rabbi Abraham Isaac ha-Kohen Kook (1865–1935), were also becoming active in their advocacy of Kabbala and *Zohar* study.[39] A younger contemporary, Rabbi Yehuda Leib Ashlag (1885–1954), was equally engaged in promoting the study of the *Zohar*,[40] and has been called by Jonathan Garb "instrumental in developing the twentieth-century ideology of the centrality of the *Zohar*."[41] It is perhaps significant that Rabbi Ashlag, like Rabbi Rosenberg, was a product of Hasidic Warsaw, and a rabbinical decisor [*moreh tsedeq*].[42] Significantly, also like Rabbi Rosenberg, Yehuda Ashlag had significant connections with Rabbi Meir Yeḥiel ha-Levi (1854–1928), the Ostrovtser Rebbe.[43]

Why did Rabbi Rosenberg and these others see fit to engage in attempts to revive Kabbala study? Yudel Rosenberg clearly and at length sets out his reasons in his first book devoted to the *Zohar*, published in 1905, entitled *Sha'arei Zohar Torah* [The Gates of the Splendor of Torah], the title of which perhaps signalled a compliment to Rosenberg's acquaintance Rabbi Isaac ha-Levi Feigenbaum

---

37 Among Mizrahi Jews the *Zohar* retained somewhat more of its influence.

38 Jonathan Garb, "Contemporary Kabbalah and Classical Kabbalah: Breaks and Continuities" in *After Spirituality: Studies in Mystical Traditions*, ed. P. H. Wexler and J. Garb (New York: Peter Lang Publishing, 2012), 23.

39 Meir, "Gilui ve-Gilui," 151; idem, "The Imagined Decline of Kabbalah: The Kabbalistic Yeshiva Shaar ha-Shamayim and Kabbalah in Jerusalem in the Beginning of the Twentieth Century," in *Kabbalah and Modernity: Interpretations, Transformations, Adaptations*, ed. Boaz Huss, Marco Pasi, and Kocku von Stuckrad (Leiden: Brill, 2010), 213; Boaz Huss, "Komunizm Altruisti: ha-Kabala ha-Modernistit shel ha-Rav Ashlag," in *'Iyunim bi-Tekumat Yisra'el: Me'asef li-Ve'ayot ha-Tsiyonut, ha-Yishuv u-Medinat Yisrael* 16 (2006): 111.

40 On Rabbi Ashlag, see David Hansel, "Une nouvelle école cabaliste au XXe siècle: Rabbi Yehuda Halevi Ashlag," in *Réceptions de la cabale*, ed. Pierre Gisel and Lucie Kaennel (Paris and Tel-Aviv: Éditions de l'Éclat, 2007), 227–240; Huss, "Komunizm alternativi," 109–130. See Jonathan Garb, *The Chosen Will Become Herds: Studies in Twentieth-Century Kabbalah* (New Haven: Yale University Press, 2009).

41 See Garb, *Yearnings of the Soul*, 110. Cf. idem, *The Chosen Will Become Herds: Studies in Twentieth-Century Kabbalah* (New Haven, Yale University Press, 2009).

42 Yaakov Elman, "Rav Isaac Hutner's *Paḥad Yitzḥak*: a Torah Map of the Human Mind and Psyche in Changing Times," in *Books of the People: Revisiting Classic Works of Jewish Thought*, ed. Stuart W. Halpern (New York: Maggid Books, 2017), 307.

43 Jonatan Meir, "Gilui ve-Gilui," 152–153.

(1830–1911), a senior member of the Warsaw rabbinate and editor of a rabbinic journal entitled *Sha'arei Torah,* in which Rosenberg had published some pieces. In his introduction to *Sha'arei Zohar Torah,* Rosenberg boldly stated that nothing less than the ultimate salvation of the Jewish people[44] was at stake in the publication of his book.[45] In this conviction, Rabbi Rosenberg was following in a long line of kabbalists who had often expressed the thought that the messianic redemption was to be preceded by widespread study of Kabbala among the Jewish people.[46] All of them based themselves on the following *Zoharic* statement: "Israel will come to taste of the tree of life which is this book of *Zohar.* With it they will go out of the exile with [divine] mercy."[47]

Rabbi Rosenberg and other contemporary Orthodox rabbis, including Rabbis Ashlag and Elḥanan Wasserman (1874–1941)[48] were utterly convinced that they were living at the threshold of the messianic era.[49] He certainly agreed that bringing about the conditions for the coming of the messiah required, as Rabbi Ashlag put it, the breaking of the "iron curtain" [*meḥizat ha-barzel*] that separated Jews from the study of Kabbala.[50] Many rabbis also believed that after the Jewish calendrical year 5600 (1840) heavenly "permission" had been given to study more widely esoteric subjects like Kabbala whose study had

---

44 Huss notes that Yudel Rosenberg, in paraphrasing Abraham Azulai in his introduction to ZT, vol. 1, 9, uses the word *le'umi* [national] to modify the word *shekhina.* Boaz Huss, "Translations of the Zohar: Historical Contexts and Ideological Frameworks," *Correspondences* 4 (2016): 110.

45 *Sha'arei,* introduction.

46 *Sha'arei,* title page; ZT, vol. 1, 9, 20; ZK, vol. 2, 3. Rabinowicz, *Hasidism: The Movement and Its Masters,* 248, speaks of Rabbi Tsvi Elimelech of Dynow making this connection. Cf. Shim'on Zvi Horowitz, *Or ha-Me'ir,* cited in Meir, "The Imagined Decline of Kabbalah," 203, 207.

47 *Ra'aya Mehemna, Zohar* III, 124b. On messianism as expressed in the *Zohar,* see Yehuda Liebes, "*Ha-Mashiaḥ shel ha-Zohar,*" in Yehuda Liebes and Yair Zakovits, eds., *The Messianic Idea in Jewish Thought* (Jerusalem: ha-Akademia ha-Le'umit ha-Yisra'elit la-Mada'im, 1982), 87–236. Cf. also the statement attributed to Israel b. Eliezer, the Ba'al Shem Tov, that the messiah would come when his teachings "have been revealed in the world and become famous." Cited in Joseph Dan, *The Teachings of Hasidism* (New York: Behrman House, 1983), 97. On the problematic relationship of messianism to Hasidism, see Gershom Scholem, *The Messianic Idea in Judaism* (New York: Allen & Unwin, 1971), 176–202. Cf. also Morris Faierstein, "Gershom Scholem and Hasidism," *Journal of Jewish Studies* 38 (1987): 230–232.

48 Gershon Greenberg, "'Da'at Torah' neged 'Amalek': R. Elhanan Wasserman," in *The Gedoilim: Leaders Who Shaped the Israeli Haredi Society,* Binyamin Brown and Nissim Leon (Jerusalem: Magnes Press, 2017), 228–231.

49 Huss, "Translations of the Zohar," 111.

50 Yehuda Leib Ashlag, *Sefer ha-Haqdamot* (Jerusalem, 1978), 1. Cf. Meir, *Kabbalistic Circles in Jerusalem,* 177.

previously been restricted. Thus, an older contemporary of Rabbi Rosenberg, the Lithuanian kabbalist Rabbi Shlomo Eliashiv (1841–1926) stated:

> Permission has been granted to all those who engage this wisdom [Kabbala] to understand these ideas, each according to their level. And specifically from the year 5600 and onwards as it is written in the *Zohar* (2:117), "and in the six-hundredth year of the sixth millennium, the gates of the higher-wisdom [*ḥokhma li-'elah*] were opened." ... This means that permission has been granted to all those who yearn to cleave to the living God, to engage with true wisdom [*ḥokhmat ha-emet*] ... and to utilize the [divine] Name properly. Anyone who delves into this matter will be enlightened. ... This was not the case before the year 5600 because then it was still hidden and enclosed, except for a few exceptional individuals as I heard in the name of ... Rabbi Israel Salanter (1810–1883). All of this is rooted in the revelation of supernal light ... as it draws additional light into this world and secrets of Torah are revealed in order to rectify the world for the eventual rectification [*tiqqun*].[51]

Similarly, Rabbi Shalom Ullman stated:

> In the darkness of the fourth exile at the end of the reign of Edom, the inner light of the Torah and its secrets will be revealed ... in order to help [God's] children to withstand the brazen lies and materialism that will reign in the world at that time.[52]

It was obvious to all these men that for the sake of the world's salvation the spread of Kabbala study had to proceed apace. However, the problem was how exactly to spread the knowledge of Kabbala? Rabbi Rosenberg stated in his introduction to *Sha'arei Zohar Torah* that the problem of bringing the Jews to the *Zohar* needed to be considered "scientifically." As he stated:

---

51 Shlomo Elyashiv, *Leshem Shevo ve-Aḥlama: Drushei 'Olam ha-Tohu, Ḥelek Alef, Drush Hei* (no. 4), 76, cited in Joey Rosenfeld, "A Tribute to Rav Shlomo Elyashiv, Author of Leshem Shevo v-Achloma: On his Ninetieth Yahrzeit," The Seforim Blog, March 19, 2016, http://seforim.blogspot.ca, accessed March 15, 2016.

52 Shalom b. Yisrael Ullman, *Sefer Maftehot Ḥokhma* (Jerusalem: Ha-Messora, 1987), 3. Cf. Meir, *Kabbalistic Circles in Jerusalem*, 72.

> But let us judge and see with scientific eyes [*be-'eynei ha-mada'*]. How can this revelation [of Kabbalistic knowledge] come about if the language of the *Zohar* is in Aramaic which is not well understood except by the elite? Will a man buy a book that is not understandable? We see, because of our many sins, that books of heresy are greatly multiplying in this era and they have many purchasers. It is as if they [the heretical authors] are hunting for souls by the fact that they beautify their books with all sorts of beauty. These [heretical] books are especially written in a pure and simple language while holy books ... are left in a corner, especially the holy *Zohar* which is looked upon as something esoteric and not understood, like an amulet. ... In this situation, how can the *Zohar* arrive at a new revelation and spread further among the masses of Jews?[53]

Rabbi Rosenberg thought that the key problem to surmount was the language barrier. Zoharic Aramaic was incomprehensible to nearly all contemporary Jews, many of whom, however, could read Hebrew. If the *Zohar* could only be rendered into a clear and simple Hebrew,[54] fully two-thirds of the book would become immediately accessible to great masses of Jews.[55] Such a translation would appeal to a Jewish audience far wider than that of the habitués of rabbinic houses of study, thereby beating the "heretical" authors Yudel Rosenberg referred to at their own game.[56] Rabbi Rosenberg's other consideration was to make the *Zohar* as accessible as possible to beginners and simple students of Torah.[57] His solution was to reedit the Zoharic text such that it would become a kind of running commentary on the verses of the Pentateuch, Psalms, Song of

---

53 ZT, vol. 1, title page, 9. On books of Hasidic tales as antidotes to "modern" literature, see Jonatan Meir, "Michael Levi Rodkinson: beyn Ḥasidut le-Haskala," *Kabbalah* 18 (2008): 246–247. For other contemporary projects to translate the Zohar, see Meir, *Kabbalistic Circles in Jerusalem*, 177–178.

54 This involved the creation of some new Hebrew terminology. See J. Fox in Cohen, *Sefer ha-Zikkaron*, 10.

55 ZT, vol. 1, 9. Rabbi Ashlag, for his part, was motivated to take on his own monumental task of Zoharic exposition for reasons entirely similar to those of Yudel Rosenberg. His goal as well was to make it possible for all Jews to study Kabbala and the Zohar. He was convinced that the divine plan for his generation was to bring kabbalistic texts and ideas, hitherto confined to limited circles and specially gifted scholars, to the attention of the widest possible public. Ashlag, *Sefer ha-Haqdamot*, 88–89.

56 The threat of "outside" books as a spur to the publication of kabbalistic texts is a continuing theme in ultra-Orthodox publications to the present. See, for example, Raphael Blum, "Mikhtav," introduction to Immanuel Hai Ricchi, *Mishnat Ḥasidim* (Brooklyn, 1975).

57 ZT, vol. 3, introduction, 3.

Songs, Proverbs, and Ecclesiastes.[58] This adaptation would further encourage its study among broad circles of Jews.

Accomplishing all of this was, of course, far from a simple task. Prior to attempting it, Rabbi Rosenberg needed to overcome his own serious doubts concerning the propriety of the entire enterprise. These doubts clearly existed among a great many Orthodox Jews of his time and place.[59] As Rabbi Rosenberg was keenly aware, many of them held that the very act of translating the *Zohar* from Aramaic to Hebrew constituted a sacrilege; that there was an esoteric reason why it was originally written in Aramaic and not Hebrew. Furthermore, many Jews feared that a Hebrew translation might lead to a general neglect of the original Aramaic text.[60] On top of that, Yudel Rosenberg, no less than any of his potential critics, believed that the *Zohar* contained great esoteric mysteries, not supposed to be revealed to the ordinary Jews who were the target audience of his translation. How, then, could he proceed?

Rabbi Rosenberg was greatly encouraged by his discovery of an earlier kabbalist, whom he considered a model. In the early seventeenth century, Rabbi Yissakhar Baer of Kremnits published a partial Hebrew translation of the *Zohar*, accompanied by approbations by some of the leading rabbinical authorities of that generation. This provided a valuable precedent for Yudel Rosenberg to deal with an Orthodox Jewish society that revered precedent. As he stated:

> When I began to occupy myself with [the translation of the *Zohar*] I saw that I was not the first with this idea. There arose a great man [*gadol*] in the days of the *Shla* [Rabbi Isaiah Horowitz (1555–1630)] and the *Levush* [Rabbi Mordecai Jaffe (1530–1612)], ... our teacher Rabbi Yissakhar Baer, author of the commentary *Imrei Bina* [Sayings of Understanding] on the *Zohar*. He translated the passages of the *Zohar* that are easily understood into the Holy Language [Hebrew], arranged them according to the order of the sections [*parshiyyot*] of the Torah, and called the

---

58 Ibid., 3. Rosenberg comments on this reordering of the Zohar text in his "Third Introduction," ZT, vol. 4, unpaginated. A similar answer was given by Moses Gelernter, *Sefer Tehillim 'im Perush ha-Zohar ha-Shalem* (Brooklyn: Samet, 1980), 5–6.

59 On the issue of translating the Zohar in the early twentieth century, see Boaz Huss, "Admiration and Disgust: The Ambivalent Re-Canonization of the Zohar in the Modern Period," in *Study and Knowledge in Jewish Thought*, ed. Howard Kreisel (Beersheva: Ben-Gurion University, 2006), 222–223; Jonatan Meir, "Naftulei Sod: Hillel Tseitlin, ha-Rav Y. Ashlag, veha-Kabbala be-Erets Yisra'el," in *Yahadut: Sugyot, Qeta'im, Panim, Zehuyot: Sefer Rivqah*, ed. Haviva Pedaya and Ephraim Meir (Beersheva: Ben-Gurion University, 2007), 623–624.

60 ZT, vol. 1, 3.

> book *Meqor Ḥokhma* [Source of Wisdom]. The holy rabbi, author of the *Shlah* [Rabbi Isaiah Horowitz], and the sage [*ga'on*] Rabbi Mordecai Jaffe, author of *Levush*, as well as other great ones of the generation approved the printing of the book. In his introduction [Yissakhar Baer] wrote that his work would be useful in that all the words of the *Zohar* will be open and explained in the eyes of all those that read it.[61]

Rabbi Rosenberg was evidently unaware of the nineteenth-century attempt to translate the Zohar into Hebrew by the Hungarian rabbi Elyakim Getzel Halmilzahagi.[62]

A preliminary step that Yudel Rosenberg took before he commenced his labors was to consult with one of the most eminent rabbis of his generation, Rabbi Ḥayyim Hezekiah Medini (1834–1905), well known for his encyclopedic work on rabbinic literature, *Sdei Ḥemed* [Fields of Pleasantness], and then resident in Hebron. [63] Shortly before his death in 1905, Rabbi Medini wrote Rosenberg a reply to his queries, which was prominently featured in the introductory section of *Sha'arei Zohar Torah.*[64] In his response, Rabbi Medini gave Yudel Rosenberg's project his conditional approval as long as some specific guidelines were followed.

The letter of Rabbi Medini as published by Yudel Rosenberg has been challenged as a forgery by Rabbis Yaakov Ḥayyim Sofer, David Zvi Hillman, and Marc B. Shapiro on the grounds that some linguistic elements of the letter are foreign to Rabbi Medini's style and may well have come from the pen of Rabbi Rosenberg.[65] This challenge has a serious basis, given that Yudel Rosenberg

---

61 ZT, vol. 1, 9. Yissakhar Baer's precedent was also cited in the approbation letter of Rabbi Yerusalimsky (ibid., 2) and in the letter of Rabbi Medini (ibid., 5). On Yissakhar Baer of Kremnits, a pioneer popularizer of Kabbala, see Andrea Gondos, "Kabbalah in Print: Literary Strategies of Popular Mysiticsm in Early Modernity" (PhD diss., Concordia University, 2013), http://spectrum.library.concordia.ca/977951/1/Gondos_PhD_F2013.pdf. Cf. Meir Benayahu, *Sefer Toledot ha-Ari* (Jerusalem, 1967), 42–45.

62 Jonatan Meir, "Haskala and Esotericism: The Strange Case of Elyakim Getzel Hamilzahagi (1780–1854)," *Aries—Journal for the Study of Western Esotericism* 18 (2018): 153–187; Huss, "Translations of the Zohar," 97.

63 *Sha'arei*, introduction, 7–8. On Rabbi Medini, see David Ben-Naeh, "R. Ḥayyim Ḥizkia Medini: Posek u-Mehanekh Sefardi be-'Idan shel Temurot," in his *Mayim mi-Dalyo* (Jerusalem: Mikhlelet Lipshitz, 1996), 209–221.

64 *Sha'arei*, title page, 5–6.

65 Marc B. Shapiro, "Concerning the Zohar and Other Matters," The Seforim Blog, August 29, 2012, http://seforim2.rssing.com/chan-9044709/all_p1.html, accessed September 2, 2019. Cf. *Ets Ḥayyim* 10, 379. On one of his points Shapiro is mistaken. He wrote in his blog:

presented several of his publications, discussed in earlier chapters, as editions of manuscripts obtained from untraceable libraries and people, but these works have later been cogently attributed to the pen of Yudel Rosenberg himself. I agree that Yudel Rosenberg's hand was very likely present in this letter for the following reason. When he first published the Medini letter in *Sha'arei Zohar Torah*, Rabbi Rosenberg noted that he presented Rabbi Medini's letter against the rabbi's explicit instructions, since he considered that Rabbi Medini's death had rendered the condition, under which he had forbidden its publication, null and void. This sentence was deleted in later editions of *Zohar Torah*. If Yudel Rosenberg thus clearly advertised that he did not follow Rabbi Medini's explicit instructions, it is no great stretch to assume that he may have edited or embellished the letter in other ways. However, if the letter were a complete forgery, the question remains why, if Rabbi Rosenberg wrote the entire letter himself, he would have included the detail indicating that he was going against Rabbi Medini's wishes in publishing it, rather than simply presenting the letter, as in all later editions, as a provisional "go ahead" for his *Zohar* project.

Whether or not Rabbi Medini authored the letter Yudel Rosenberg published, in whole or in part, the guidelines contained in it were certainly ones that Rabbi Rosenberg followed throughout his *Zohar* project. They included the following points: first, to be careful to print the original Aramaic text of the *Zohar* side by side with its translation, emphasizing the fact that the translation was meant to be a sort of bridge, allowing novices access to the original text in the hope that for at least some readers the translation might eventually be dispensed with.[66] The second condition was to refrain from translating those portions of the *Zohar* that were considered esoteric in nature and required knowledge of Lurianic Kabbala for their proper comprehension.[67] Rabbi

---

"In the authentic letters, before his name Medini always adds ... *ha-tsa'ir*, which he does not do in the forged haskamah." In Yudel Rosenberg's work, the Medini letter does close with *yedido ha-tsa'ir*.

66 This was an issue with the Artscroll translation of the Babylonian Talmud in the late twentieth century: "It is not the purpose of this edition of the Talmud to provide a substitute for the original text or a detour around the classic manner of study." "Publisher's Preface," in *Tractate Makkos*, ed. Hersh Goldwurm and Nossen Scherman (Brooklyn: Mesorah Publications, 1990), xv.

67 For example, ZT, vol. 2, 40. Thus, in a sermon on the blowing of the shofar, Rosenberg referred to the "secrets and intentions [*kavvanot*] of the shofar blasts" but continued immediately and without explanation to deal with the plain meaning of the shofar. *Omer*, part 1, 41. Cf. PY, 163 where Yudel Rosenberg censors *Qabbala ma'asit*. Similarly, Rabbi Rosenberg asserted that the formula *le-shem yiḥud* could be said by anyone, not only the experts in Kabbala. *Omer*, part 1, 46. Cf. PY, 71. Concerning restrictions on the dissemination of

Rosenberg, accordingly, placed such passages in the original Aramaic, untranslated, at the end of his *Zohar* volumes.[68] This step served to ensure that the esoteric ideas not designed for exposure to the masses would not get into the wrong hands.[69]

Rabbi Rosenberg strongly felt that knowledge of Lurianic Kabbala should be restricted.[70] Practical Kabbala, though it was certainly practiced in the twentieth century,[71] was also a subject that Rabbi Rosenberg was reticent to address publicly.[72] He felt, on the other hand, that the Kabbala taught by Moses Cordovero's (1522–1570) *Pardes Rimmonim* and Joseph Gikatilla's (1248–c. 1305) *Sha'arei Orah* poses no danger to any Jew.[73] As a rule, Yudel Rosenberg remained true to this limitation of the amount of kabbalistic information. For example, when he commented on a passage in the *Zohar* that spoke of the Ark of the Covenant, he stated, "This is a very deep matter … therefore we will only interpret the meaning of the words."[74] His attitude to the secrets of Kabbala is again apparent in his commentary on the sin of Adam and Eve:

> Many men bereft of knowledge [*mada'*] think that the matter is as [the Torah] plainly states [*ke-peshuto*] that because of the eating of the apple the Creator got angry and decreed death for the entire world. For this reason Rashbi [Rabbi Shim'on bar Yoḥai] here reveals the hidden secret in

Lurianic Kabbala, see Meir, "The Imagined Decline of Kabbalah," 211–212. Cf. idem, *Kabbalistic Circles in Jerusalem*, 159, note 70.

68 These sections, always entitled "Hashlamat ha-Zohar, mah she-lo Ne'etaq el Leshon qodesh," consisted of twenty-four pages after ZT, vol. 1, thirty-six pages after ZT, vol. 2, twenty-six pages after ZT, vol. 3, and forty-one pages after ZT, vol. 4.

69 ZT, vol. 1, 4. Cf. *Haggada*, in which Yudel Rosenberg asserts that the Maharal agrees with the Zohar and disagrees with Lurianic Kabbala (12, note, 16, note, 30, note). This is where Rabbi Ashlag differed from Rabbi Rosenberg. Ashlag's project contained an exposition of the entire Zoharic text, whereas Rosenberg refrained from translating those parts of the *Zohar* that, in his opinion, required knowledge of the Lurianic interpretation of Kabbala. Concerning restrictions on the dissemination of Lurianic Kabbala, see Meir, "The Imagined Decline of Kabbalah," 211–212. Cf. idem, *Kabbalistic Circles in Jerusalem*, 159, note 70.

70 *Sha'arei*, 4. In his tendency to limit exposure of Lurianic Kabbala, Rabbi Rosenberg was anticipated by Rabbi Isaiah Horowitz. Cf. Haran, "Ḥerut be-Tokh Emuna," 328; Ronit Meroz, "The Archaeology of the Zohar: Sifra Ditseni'uta as a Sample Text," *Da'at* 82 (2016): xiii.

71 Yuval Harari, "Three Charms for Killing Adolf Hitler: Practical Kabbala in WW2," *Aries—Journal for the Study of Western Esotericism* 17 (2017): 171–214.

72 PY, 163.

73 ZK, vol. 7, 138.

74 ZT, vol. 2, 174.

> this parable [*mashal*] concerning the essence of the sin, even though we hold that scripture does not depart from its plain meaning. Since I do not have the power to explain the matter in a way that all will understand, I will therefore put a block [*maḥsom*] to my pen and I rely on everyone who understands the science of Kabbala so that each one will understand ... according to the knowledge in his head.[75]

Similarly, in 1935 Yudel Rosenberg received a kabbalistic query from Rabbi Aaron Simḥa Blumenthal of New York related to the creation of the universe in its relation to the godhead and whether one can truly believe in creation ex nihilo. In his draft response, written on the back of Blumenthal's letter, Yudel Rosenberg refers him to a passage in Moses Cordovero's *Pardes Rimmonim* but pointedly does not mention any Lurianic writings. Rabbi Rosenberg goes on to say that true knowledge of the godhead is not possible and that the true task of humanity is to understand that the universe was created by God and given to humans in order to draw down God's good abundance [*shefa tov*] through the observance of the commandments of the Torah.[76]

As most kabbalists, Rabbi Rosenberg believed that Lurianic Kabbala was superior to the kabbalistic systems that proceeded it. He even had something of a reputation as a kabbalist who understood Lurianic matters. Thus, in 1923 Rabbi Rosenberg received a letter from Rabbi Benjamin Barashi of Kotsk with a question on an aspect of Lurianic Kabbala that Barashi had asked of other experts on Lurianic Kabbala but found no one able to explain it.[77] Furthermore, in his book of sermons, *Peri Yehuda*, Yudel Rosenberg spoke of the superiority of Lurianic understandings of Kabbala over those taught by Moses Cordovero in understanding the universe, and of the superiority of both over philosophy, "which establishes laws to limit the Creator."[78] He consistently opposed the study of philosophy because it "deceives a person away from the way of pure faith ... and brings him to heresy."[79]

---

75 Ibid., vol. 1, 37.

76 Rabbi Aharon Simḥa Blumenthal to Yudel Rosenberg, 1935, RFA, Savannah.

77 Benjamin Barashi of Kotsk to Rosenberg, 5683, RFA, Savannah. Barashi is acknowledged as a purveyor of a manuscript source in the book of Hasidic tales, *Siaḥ Sarfei Kodesh*, ed. Yo'ets Kim Qadish of Przytyk, part 5, 8, http://www.daat.ac.il/daat/vl/sarfeikodesh/sarfeikodesh23.pdf, accessed September 2, 2019.

78 PY, 164.

79 ZT, vol. 1, 62, 132–133, 139, 159.

Rabbi Rosenberg's understanding of Lurianic Kabbala is eloquently expressed in some of his sermons where he deals with the permutation of letters.[80] Similarly, he adds a table of the seventy-two letter name of God to his *Zohar* commentary.[81] Perhaps most importantly, Rabbi Rosenberg possessed for himself, and possibly for the instruction of others, an *ilan* [tree]: a depiction on a rotulus, in words and diagrams, of the entirety of supernal reality as understood from a kabbalistic, sefirotic perspective. Rabbi Rosenberg's *ilan* is based on that of the seventeenth-century Polish kabbalist, Meir Poppers.[82] J. H. Chajes describes the *ilan* as "a genre of kabbalistic creativity" that "had a variety of functions, from meditative to mnemonic ... they are performative, ritually-used artefacts. The Ilan is thus a tool of kabbalistic practice."[83]

Yudel Rosenberg's reedition of the *Zohar* was no less bold a step than its translation, for it involved a complete change in the way the work presented itself to the reader. As originally edited, the *Zohar* presents itself as a sort of *midrash*. Like other midrashic collections, it was organized in sections corresponding to the weekly portions of the Pentateuch read in synagogues. However, the Zoharic material, like midrashic material generally, did not strictly conform to the subject matter of the individual Torah portion. A Zoharic statement pertinent to a discussion of Genesis, for instance, might be found in the *Zohar* on the Book of Numbers.

Rabbi Rosenberg proposed to change the original Zoharic format entirely by rearranging the passages of the *Zohar* to form a sequential commentary on the Biblical verses. In his initial 1905 volume, *Sha'arei Zohar Torah,* he implemented this format change for the book of Genesis. In that volume's introduction he claimed that he had material already prepared for the rest of the

---

80 PY, 13–15, 71.

81 ZT, vol. 2, 48.

82 J. H. Chajes and Eliezer Baumgarten, "About Faces: Kabbalistic Visualizations of the Divine Visage in the Gross Family Collection," in *Windows on Jewish Worlds: Essays in Honor of William Gross, Collector of Judaica,* ed. Emile Schrijver (Uitgeverig: Walburg Pers B.V., 2019), 77.

83 Rabbi Rosenberg's *ilan* is in the archives of the Jewish Public Library of Montreal, Fonds 1399. On the genre of *ilanot,* see J. H. Chajes, "Kabbalah Practices / Practical Kabbalah: The Magic of Kabbalistic Trees," *Aries—Journal for the Study of Western Esotericism* 19 (2019): 112–145. Cf. idem, "Duchgelässige Grenzen: Die Visualierung Gottes zwischen jüdischer und christlicher Kabbala bei Knorr von Rosenroth und van Helmont," *Morgen-Glanz: Zeitschrift der Christian Knorr von Rosenroth-Gesellschaft* 27 (2017): 99–147; Eliezer Baumgarten, Uri Safrai, and J. S. Chajes, "'He Saw the Entire World Resembling a Ladder:' Rabbi Yehoshua ben Rabbi David of Kurdistan's Kabbalistic Tree" [Hebrew], in *Meir Benayahu Memorial Volume,* ed. Moshe Bar-Asher, Yehuda Liebes, Moshe Assis, and Yosef Kaplan, vol. 2, 843–871.

Pentateuch as well as for Psalms and Song of Songs. He stated that he eventually hoped to accomplish this task for the entire Hebrew Bible, and thus to have all the *Zohar* translated except that which constituted "deep Kabbala" [*qabbala 'amukah*].[84] It would take him twenty-five years before he more or less completed the program that he started in 1905.[85]

In choosing to reedit the *Zohar*, Yudel Rosenberg had assumed the role of redactor as well as translator, with all the creative possibilities implied by editorship. His aspiration was to open the *Zohar* to contemporary Jews in the same manner that Rabbi Solomon ben Isaac (Rashi, 1040–1105) had opened rabbinic literature to a wider audience through his biblical and Talmudic commentaries.

Yudel Rosenberg's confidence in his powers as editor was fortified because he did not view his reedition of the *Zohar* as the first the *Zohar* had undergone. On the contrary, he believed that the *Zohar* was originally written by Rabbi Shim'on bar Yoḥai (fl. second century C.E.), and that it had evidently been edited in the thirteenth century by Spanish Rabbi Moses de Leon (1240–1305), a major figure in the diffusion of the Zoharic writings. He was thus far from simply accepting the *Zohar* as it presents itself. He did not for a moment think that that the text of the *Zohar* in the printed editions was in any way identical to the work that had supposedly left the hands of Rabbi Shim'on bar Yoḥai, who is credited by nearly all traditional Jews as the Zohar's "author." On the contrary, Rabbi Rosenberg asserted that that what had come into the hands of Rabbi Moses de Leon was not one manuscript, but rather a series of documents [*quntresim*] that were garbled [*metushtashim*] and out of order.[86] In this, he agreed with academic students of Kabbala, who assert Moses de Leon is the "author" of the *Zohar* in one or another sense. As to the manner of their transmission, Yudel Rosenberg reasoned that the writings of the *Zohar* had been concealed in a cave for hundreds of years, so that the parchment likely rotted or was erased. Even after the Zoharic writings were revealed, the printing press did not exist and these writings were copied one manuscript from another. All this necessarily introduced errors in the text, since not every copyist had adequate knowledge of Kabbala or Aramaic grammar.[87] For Yudel Rosenberg,

---

84 *Sha'arei*, 4. Cf. ZT, vol. 5, 5.

85 In addition to the biblical books Yudel Rosenberg mentioned in 1905, he created a Zoharic commentary to Proverbs and Ecclesiastes.

86 ZT, vol. 3, 6. It is interesting in this context to note that Yudel Rosenberg's description of the manuscripts of the *Zohar* resemble his description of the "manuscripts" he "edited" in many of this other works.

87 Ibid., 4.

Rabbi Moses de Leon had in effect reedited the "original" *Zohar*. And if Rabbi Moses could do it, for good and sufficient reasons, so could he![88] Furthermore, because he understood that the Zohar's text had been garbled in places, the result of manuscript deterioration and transmission, it required emendation.[89] Emending the text of the *Zohar* was thus not an issue Rabbi Rosenberg feared at all. On the contrary, as he stated:

> First of all the reader should know that the reason for almost all difficulties encountered by the commentators on the *Zohar* is that they have not investigated the errors [*shibbushim*] that occurred in the copying of old manuscripts. … Many letters were mixed up and erased. … With printed [editions], most of the typesetters are not Torah scholars and the proofreaders are more or less lazy. … The interpreters of the *Zohar* have feared to edit properly. … Any understanding person who admits to the truth will see that my words are correct.[90]

Moreover, however holy the *Zohar* was to Rabbi Rosenberg, it was no holier than the text of the Talmud. If great Talmudic scholars of the past, like Rabbi Joel Sirkes (Baḥ, 1561–1640) and Rabbi Elijah (Vilna Gaon, 1720–1797) could emend the Talmudic text, he could do the same for the *Zohar*. Thus Rabbi Rosenberg was certainly a fervent believer in the holiness and the religious potential of the *Zohar*, but he was far from an uncritical one.[91] In a similar way, Rabbi Ashlag, like Yudel Rosenberg, was not unaware that academic students of Kabbala had concluded that R. Moses de Leon and not R. Simeon bar Yoḥai had composed the *Zohar*. With respect to this issue, Rabbi Ashlag asserted that the *Zohar* itself was more important than its authorship. Though he was unshaken in his belief that R. Shim'on was the *Zohar*'s author, he nonetheless stated that if, hypothetically, there appeared conclusive proof that R. Moses de Leon was in fact the author, it would only increase his conception of R. Moses's eminence [*ma'alah*].[92]

Yudel Rosenberg's goal in his work was make the *Zohar* a genuinely popular work. In specifically aiming at a wide, popular audience, Rabbi Rosenberg stated:

---

88 Ibid., vol. 4, 1. Cf. ibid., vol. 5, 6.

89 *Sha'arei*, 77, 107; ZK Tehillim, 78, 134; ZT, vol. 1, 53, 133; ibid., vol. 2, 174; ibid., vol. 3, 4, 137; ibid., vol. 4, 23, 128–129.

90 ZT, vol. 4, 23.

91 Ibid., 3.

92 Yehuda Ashlag, *Sefer ha-Haqdamot*, 88–89.

> I know that my book ... is not needed by the great men who are comparable to divine angels. ... However they, too, will rejoice ... when they see the awakening of ordinary men to study and understand the statements of the holy *Zohar*. For that is a sign that salvation will soon be revealed. ... The good of the community of Israel will arise through the study of the *Zohar*. We cannot say that [salvation] depends upon [the study of the *Zohar*] by the great ones of the generation alone ... For there will yet come a new revelation [of the *Zohar*] to the masses of Israel ... who will taste of the Tree of Life.[93]

As we have seen, to do this, Yudel Rosenberg programmatically abandoned the esoteric parts of the Zohar that required deeper kabbalistic knowledge. In essence, he did the same as the Italian Rabbi Elijah Benmozegh (1822–1900) in his mid-nineteenth-century work on the *Zohar*, even though Rabbi Rosenberg was probably unaware of this earlier effort. Indeed, he shared Rabbi Benmozegh's conviction that "progress consisted of gradually disseminating Kabbalistic knowledge and abandoning the esoteric aspect that made it the strict preserve of the initiated."[94] Yudel Rosenberg thus thought that his *Zohar* edition could be studied by schoolchildren as young as age nine as well as by synagogue study groups in the same way that rabbinic texts like the *Mishna* and *Eyn Ya'aqov* were studied.[95] He did not think that the work would be any danger to any reader, even the youngest.[96] In this spirit Rabbi Rosenberg advocated that ordinary Jews take on kabbalistic customs such as the recitation of the formula *le-shem yiḥud* [for the sake of the (supernal) unity], which, as many Jews assumed, were only appropriate for righteous people who were also kabbalists.[97] He let his readers understand that while kabbalists indeed had their own specialized understanding of the Torah, there was, nonetheless, value in ordinary people studying the "plain intention" [*kavvana peshuta*] of the Torah.[98]

This was, of course, a far cry from the attitude of those of his contemporaries who felt that the reading of the *Zohar* by the masses should either be

---

93 *Sha'arei*, 7. In ZT, vol. 4, 2, Yudel Rosenberg refutes the idea that there is no permission to reveal the secrets of the Zohar until after the coming of the messiah. Cf. Jonatan Meir, *Literary Hasidism: The Life and Works of Michael Levi Rodkinson* (Syracuse, Syracuse University Press, 2016), 99.

94 Alessandro Guetta, *Philosophy and Kabbalah: Elijah Benmozegh and the Reconciliation of Western Thought and Jewish Esoterism* (Albany, SUNY Press, 2009), 102.

95 ZT, vol. 5, 5.

96 ZT, vol. 3, 5.

97 PY, 151.

98 PY, 154.

forbidden entirely or else undertaken as a simple pious recitation without any attempt at comprehension of the text.[99] Very much to the contrary, Rosenberg strongly believed that it was a great error to assert that mere exposure to the words of the *Zohar* without comprehension is at all efficacious. As he put it: "It is a stupid mistake [*ta'ut shel shtut*] to think that all is the same in the study of the *Zohar*."[100] Because Rabbi Rosenberg was interested in his readers' comprehension, he added to his translation a short, succinct commentary, entitled *Ziv ha-Zohar* [Splendor of the Zohar], that enabled the reader, at least on a superficial level, to follow the Zoharic text's sefirotic symbolism.[101] Frequently, however, his commentary also dealt with the nature of the relationship between Jewish tradition and the world of modern science, with the clear implication that Torah was ultimately superior to science.[102]

In their evaluation of the necessity for the actual comprehension of the Zoharic text, Rabbis Rosenberg and Ashlag decisively parted company. While Yudel Rosenberg asserted that undertaking to study the *Zohar* without comprehension was a huge mistake, Rabbi Ashlag felt that those who study Kabbala, even without comprehension, have acquired a great "treasure" [*segulah*].[103] Rabbi Ashlag's attitude, not by happenstance, is echoed in the ethos of the contemporary Kabbala Center movement, for which scanning kabbalistic texts, even without comprehension, may be mystically effective.[104]

Moreover, Rabbi Rosenberg thought that his *Zohar* constituted an answer to the great challenge faced by Orthodox Jews in his time. Supplemented by the study of other kabbalistic books, like Joseph ben Abraham Gikatilla's *Sha'arei Orah*,[105] the study of *Zohar* by Jews would suffice to overcome heretical ideas [*epikorsut*] among them.[106] Another important issue *Zohar* study might remedy was the perception on the part of many Orthodox Jews that they were under

99 ZK Tehilim, 3.

100 Ibid., 3.

101 ZT, vol. 1, 15.

102 *'Ateret*, 142–143. Another writer of the time to make the connection between Kabbala and science was Zev Wolf Tannenbaum. Cf. Boaz Huss, "Komunizm Altruisti," 112. Cf. also Meir, "Naftulei Sod," 635–636.

103 Ashlag, *Sefer ha-Haqdamot*, 35.

104 On the Kabbala Center movement and its relation to the teachings of Rabbi Ashlag, see Jody Myers, *Kabbalah and the Spiritual Quest: The Kabbalah Centre in America* (Westport, CT: Praeger, 2007), 33–108.

105 On Gikatilla, see Hartley Lachter, "Kabbalah, Philosophy, and the Jewish-Christian Debate: Reconsidering the Early Works of Joseph Gikatilla," *Journal of Jewish Thought and Philosophy* 16, no. 1 (2008): 1–58.

106 ZT, vol. 5, 5.

siege by the forces of modernity in its various guises.[107] Yudel Rosenberg did not accept the widespread feeling by "modern" Jews that science and religion had little to say to each other, and that adaptation to modernity implied a rejection of the Orthodox Jewish tradition.[108] If the study of the *Zohar* was, indeed, to be the salvation of Judaism, it had to deal with science in such a way as to demonstrate its relevance to the modern world. Rabbi Rosenberg clearly stated that one of his primary goals was: "to explain creation so that it will be comprehended according to Kabbala and science [*ḥokhmat ha-meḥqar*] so that all the peoples of the world and their sages will see that everything is alluded to in the Holy Torah."[109] Indeed, in several places Yudel Rosenberg announced a project to write a book entitled *Mequbal ve-Ḥoqer* [Kabbalist and Researcher] that would be devoted to just this issue, but this project apparently never came to fruition.[110] On the other hand, Rabbi Rosenberg's *Zohar* commentary frequently mentioned scientific concepts on the assumption that the text of the *Zohar* referred to them.[111] The clear implication was that the *Zohar* was indeed not merely a book for the pious; it retained its cogency in the modern world.[112]

Since Yudel Rosenberg saw the renewal of *Zohar* study as a key element in helping to bring about the messianic salvation of the Jewish people, it is not entirely surprising that he made a detailed messianic prediction in his *Zohar* commentary.[113] Knowing full well that other Jews had in the past mistakenly predicted the date of messianic advent, Rabbi Rosenberg posited that his predecessors' error stemmed from their lack of comprehension that the exile of the Jewish people would last so very long. At this moment in history, however, it seemed to Rabbi Rosenberg that the meaning of the *Zohar* regarding the messiah was now clear [*pashut*].[114] Even so, he expressed the caveat that even if his own predicted date for the coming of the messiah would not turn out to be valid, Jews must still "wait for him."[115]

---

107 ZK, vol. 7, 3.

108 *Sha'arei*, 9; ZT, vol. 1, 21; *Brivele*, 3–4.

109 PY, 5.

110 PY, 9; In his Zohar book, Yudel Rosenberg called the planned work *Hoqer u-Mequbal*. ZK Tehilim, 221.

111 For example, ZT, vol. 1, 21; PY, 5.

112 *Brivele*, 3–4.

113 On other early twentieth-century messianic predictions, see Meir, "Naftulei Sod," 614–615.

114 ZK, vol. 7, 205. For a refutation of mistaken interpretations of these messianic dates, see PY, 160.

115 *Eliyahu*, 63.

Based on a Zoharic text speculating on the messianic advent, Yudel Rosenberg posited that salvation for the Jewish people would come about in stages.[116] In his opinion, the first stage had already occurred. Thus, Rabbi Rosenberg wrote that the year 5660 (1899/1900) had seen a divine "visitation," heralding the onset of the troubles and persecutions of the Jews which would precede the messiah's coming.[117] In *Sha'arei Zohar Torah*, published in 1905, he announced that in Nissan of 5666 (Spring 1906), about a year away, the messiah would appear in the Galilee.[118] He would not say, however, whether this messianic appearance would be "public" or not. Further stages of messianic redemption would occur in 5673 (1912/3) and in 5700 (1939/40).[119] The latter date would see the final ingathering of the Jews to the Land of Israel.[120] When 1906 came and went with no apparent messianic "sign," Yudel Rosenberg pinned his hopes on 1913. After that date, too, came and went with no messianic appearance, he speculated that the absolutely final date for the messianic advent would be either 5726 (1965/6)[121] or 5728 (1967/8),[122] with the resurrection of the dead scheduled for 5800 (2039/40).[123]

Sha'arei Zohar Torah, the initial volume of the *Zohar* translation project, passed the Russian censorship in April 1905.[124] The book was published with the approbations [*haskamot*] of four rabbis, though one of them, Rabbi Ḥayyim

116 *Sha'arei*, 55–56; PY, 160. This Zoharic text had inspired previous generations of messianic speculators. See Ira Robinson, "Abraham ben Eliezer Halevi: Kabbalist and Messianic Visionary of the Early Sixteenth Century" (PhD diss., Harvard University, 1980), 87–122. Cf. also A. Morgenstern, *Messianism and the Settlement of the Land of Israel* [Hebrew] (Jerusalem: Yad Ben-Zvi, 1985), 39ff; Haran, "Ḥerut be-Tokh Emuna," 325.

117 *Sha'arei*, 55–56; ZT, vol. 1, 98. Cf. ibid., vol. 3, 142; ibid., vol. 5, 52.

118 For a contemporary prediction of 1906 as a messianic year, see Meir, *Kabbalistic Circles in Jerusalem*, 112, 123. For a messianic prediction for 1905, see ibid., 100, note 12.

119 ZT, vol. 1, 97–98; ibid., vol. 3, 143 Cf. Gedalia ibn Yahya, *Shalshelet ha-Qabbala* (Warsaw, 1899), 64, who spoke of "signs" of the Messiah in 5700. Cited in Shimon Huberband, *Kiddush Hashem: Jewish Religious and Cultural Life in Poland During the Holocaust*, trans. David Fishman (Hoboken, NJ: Ktav, 1987), 121–125. Rabbi Hayyim Shapira of Munkacz predicted the coming of the messiah in Fall 1941. Allan Nadler, "The War on Modernity of R. Hayyim Elazar Shapira of Munkacz, *Modern Judaism* 14 (1994): 237.

120 *Sha'arei*, 55–56. For evidence of Jewish belief in the coming of the messiah in the year 5666 see Singer, *Of a World That Is No More*, 226–234. Though Singer does not specify the source of the belief, it may well have been Yudel Rosenberg's book.

121 ZK Tehilim, 177; ZK, vol. 7, 80–81.

122 ZK Tehilim, 179; ZK, vol. 7, 80, 206; PY, 138. Yudel Rosenberg apparently received a number of inquiries concerning this prediction, as it required that the *shemita* [Sabbatical] and *yovel* [Jubilee] years be the same, impossible in the present Hebrew calendar. His undated draft response is extant in RFA, Savannah.

123 ZK, vol. 7, 81.

124 *Sha'arei*, [2].

Hezekiah Medini, as we have seen, had specifically forbade Rosenberg to print his letter as an approbation, though Rabbi Rosenberg defended publishing the letter by arguing that since its author had already passed away, there was no longer a need to suppress it.[125] The other rabbis were Moses Naḥum Yerusalimsky of Kielce, Shalom Mordecai ha-Kohen Schwadron (1835–1911) of Berezhany, and Isaac ha-Kohen Feigenbaum (1830–1911) of Warsaw who, alone of the three, had also written an approbation of Rabbi Rosenberg's *Yadot Nedarim*. None of the three rabbis was known especially for expertise in Kabbala.

Obtaining letters of approbation for a work such as *Sha'arei Zohar Torah*, which attempted to deal with a sacred, esoteric text in a strikingly new manner, was evidently fraught with difficulty for Rabbi Rosenberg. His problems are amply illustrated by three letters he wrote Rabbi Yerusalimsky in the year 1904 seeking his approbation. The first letter was accompanied by eight pages of the manuscript, a copy of his book, *Yadot Nedarim*, as well as three stamps for return postage. It briefly described the aim of the book. Alluding to the difficulty of obtaining letters of approbation in the Hasidic world, Rosenberg stated:

> Your Torahship knows well that seeking approbations from the *admorim* [Hasidic spiritual leaders] is a difficult task for various reasons. The most important is that he who is not a Hasid of [the *admor*] is [considered] a stranger in his eyes. Only [from] two *admorim* who know me, that is, the holy, righteous Rabbi etc., etc., the *admor* Rabbi A[braham] Eger of Lublin … and the holy, righteous rabbi, etc., etc., Rabbi Y[eḥiel] M[eir] … of Ostroviec have I received two approbations.[126]

It is likely that Rabbi Rosenberg did not in fact have approbations from these *admorim* in hand, though he may have been hopeful as he wrote to Rabbi Yerusalimsky that his personal connection with these men would finally get him what he wanted. In any event, approbations from the two *admorim* he mentioned were not printed in the first edition.

Another example of the difficulties Yudel Rosenberg had with the Hasidic authorities to whom he turned is the outright refusal of the Radziner Rebbe, Rabbi Mordecai Joseph El'azar Leiner (1877–1929), who had settled in

125 *Sha'arei*, 6. In later editions of ZT, Rabbi Rosenberg omitted that portion of Rabbi Medini's letter forbidding him to publish it.

126 Yerusalimsky Papers, Schocken Library, Jerusalem. It should be noted that even if the approbations he mentioned were received, they were not printed in the first edition.

Warsaw, to give his approbation on the grounds that the difficulties of translating the *Zohar* would result in Rabbi Rosenberg's work becoming a failure. As he stated: "will the expressions in the book have any reason [*ta'am*]?"[127]

Rabbi Rosenberg's second letter to Rabbi Yerusalimsky, which also enclosed a stamp for reply, included a copy of the approbation by Rabbi Schwadron that was published. By the third letter, Rabbi Yerusalimsky's lack of response had Rosenberg thoroughly worried.[128] Once the book was already published Yudel Rosenberg received a number of laudatory letters from prominent rabbis to whom he sent the book. In later editions of the work these were also published as letters of approbation. Included in this group were the following rabbis: Meir Yeḥiel ha-Levi, the Ostrovtser Rebbe, Abraham Eger of Lublin, Ḥayyim Berlin of Elizavetgrad (1832–1912), Elijah Ḥayyim Miesel (1821–1912) of Łódź, and Jacob Mazeh (1859–1924) of Moscow.[129] Interestingly, Rabbi Rosenberg also sent a copy to a non-rabbi, Professor Abraham Harkavy (1835–1919), head of the Department of Jewish literature and oriental manuscripts in the Russian Imperial Library of St. Petersburg, along with a request for aid in translating certain foreign terms into Hebrew, and published his reply.[130] Through this action, Rosenberg showed himself capable of reaching out to scholarly circles well beyond the confines of Orthodoxy.

Rosenberg's *Sha'arei Zohar Torah* covered the book of Genesis alone. However it was clear that even at the time of its 1905 publication, he had ambitions to complete this project. As he stated in his introduction to that work: "I have already arranged this commentary on the five books of the Torah and on the Book of Psalms and the Song of Songs. And God willing ... after all that is prepared is printed, I will begin to prepare this commentary on the rest of the Prophets and Hagiographa so that all the *Zohar* will be translated except for places of deep Kabbala that may are not be translated."[131] This project, however, was destined to remain dormant until 1919, as we will see.

In 1910, as part of his anthology of material on Elijah the Prophet, discussed in chapter seven, Rabbi Rosenberg included the well-known passage from *Tiqqunei Zohar* 17a known as *Pataḥ Eliyahu* ["Elijah commenced"], which

127 N. Baumeil, "Rosenberg," 112.

128 Yerusalimsky Papers, Schocken Library, Jerusalem.

129 ZT, vol. 1, 5, 7–8.

130 Ibid., 8. Harkavy, apparently, followed the writings of Orthodox rabbis. Thus, he hailed the publication by Rabbi Jacob David Wilowsky, the Slutsker Rav, of his commentary on the Palestinian Talmud. See Karp, "The Ridwas," 222.

131 *Sha'arei*, 4.

deals with the sefirot. He presented a vowelized text to which he attached his own running commentary, entitled *Or Tsaḥ* [Clear Light].[132] In a short separate introduction to this commentary Yudel Rosenberg stated that the main sources for his commentary were Moses Cordovero's (1522–1570) *Pardes Rimmonim, Hadrat Melekh,* a Lurianic commentary on the Zohar written in the eighteenth century by Rabbi Shalom Buzaglo (1700–1780), *Shefa Tal,* written by Shabetai Sheftel ben Akiva ha-Levi of Prague (d. 1619), and the *Siddur* [Prayerbook] of Rabbi Shneur Zalman of Liadi (1745–1812). As he put it, "I have smoothed out [*hirḥavti*] their holy words" with an easy and clear commentary in which I added a small contribution [*nofekh*] ... so that it will be easier for the reader to understand these holy words that stand at the pinnacle of the universe and constitute the basis of faith. In the absence of such understanding Jews will spend their days in the aspect of limited minds [*qatnut ha-moḥin*]."[133] Unlike the *Ziv ha-Zohar* commentary, which is a series of disconnected notes on various issues in the text of the *Zohar,* Rabbi Rosenberg's commentary to *Pataḥ Eliyahu* is a lengthy, running commentary explaining the passage conceptually and giving definitions of its sefirotic terminology. As elsewhere, he understood that he was writing in an atmosphere in which the "enlightened" [*maskilim*] mocked kabbalists and accused them of not having room in their sefirotic system for scientific concepts of nature such as magnetism and electricity. Rabbi Rosenberg remarked that previous commentators on the Zohar had indeed not adequately explained the correspondence between Kabbala and science. However, he continued, "God opened my eyes" to understand and explain these matters, though he did hedge his bets and asked God's forgiveness in advance in case he interpreted wrongly, "for He knows the truth that I meant it for the good to enlighten blinded eyes and to remove all objections to the wisdom of Kabbala."[134] *Pataḥ Eliyahu* remains the only running commentary Yudel Rosenberg ever published for a kabbalistic text.

In 1912, Rabbi Rosenberg published a section of the *Zohar* dealing with *sha'atnez* [mingled threads] in his pamphlet on that subject, discussed in chapter six, in the same format as the one he utilized in *Sha'arei Zohar Torah.*[135] However, there is no evidence that he took any active steps to fulfil his ambition for a full Hebrew translation and reedition of the *Zohar* until he settled in Montreal.

132 *Eliyahu,* 69–89.

133 *Ibid.,* 71.

134 Ibid., 80. The commentary on *Pataḥ Eliyahu* was reprinted at the end of ZT, vol. 3.

135 *Darsha,* 23–25.

In the year 1919, his first in Montreal, Yudel Rosenberg reprinted his 1909 publication of Pinḥas of Korets's *Haqqafot,* discussed in chapter seven. In that publication, his first in Montreal, Rabbi Rosenberg inserted an announcement that he intended to complete the job he had commenced in 1905 and publish his full translation of the *Zohar* on the Torah. He asked for advanced subscribers to pay $20.00 for a five-volume set.[136] From hints contained in his *Zohar* commentaries, it is possible to follow Rabbi Rosenberg's progress on the work. He was likely working on his commentary on the *Zohar* to Leviticus in 1920 when he wrote the following remarkable passage commenting on the years that had passed since 1914. He spoke of:

> The terrible war in our days that commenced in 5674 [1914], in which all the kings of Europe and America shook the earth [contending] with each other. Six years have passed and an apparent peace has been made. But there is no peace as it should be [*ka-ra'ui*]. Israel's blood flows like a river in Russia, Ukraine, Poland, Galicia, Hungary, and Romania where Jews, including women and children, have been subjected to destruction with great cruelty that makes each hearer's hair stand up. ... There was never a time of trouble for Jacob like these years.[137]

Rabbi Rosenberg was, apparently, at work on *Zohar* to Deuteronomy in 1922, when he referred to an article of that year he had read in the New York Yiddish newspaper the *Tageblatt* on the subject of hypnotism.[138] He states that he completed his work on the entire five books of the Torah on the holiday of Purim 5683 (March 3, 1923), in the very midst of the bitter controversy regarding kosher meat supervision in Montreal discussed in chapter five.[139] Rabbi Rosenberg's five volumes of *Zohar Torah* were published in New York by the Trio Press on Fourth Street, with the first volume on Genesis appearing in 1924.[140]

His volume on the *Zohar* to *Mishlei* [Proverbs] was completed on 1 Ḥeshvan 5687 (9 October, 1926).[141] He finished *Zohar* to Kohelet on the *hilula*

---

136 *Haqqafot,* unpaginated (after page 14).

137 ZT, vol. 3, 142.

138 ZT, vol. 5, 35.

139 ZT, vol. 5, 256.

140 The volumes were evidently published in the years 1924–1926, if one follows the date of the copyright, registered in Washington, D.C. ZT on Genesis was published in 1924, ZT on Exodus, Numbers, and Leviticus were copyrighted 1925, and ZT on Deuteronomy in 1926.

141 ZK, vol. 7, 151.

[celebration of the passing] of Rabbi Shim'on bar Yoḥai 5627 (May 27, 1927).[142] His work on *Zohar* to the Song of Songs was finished in Nisan 5688 (March/April 1928).[143] His labor on *Zohar* to the book of Psalms was finished between Rosh ha-Shana and Yom Kippur of 5689 (14–24 September, 1928).[144] Whereas he published the five volumes of *Zohar Torah* in New York, Yudel Rosenberg published part 6 of his series, covering the Book of Psalms, in 1929, in Biłgoraj, Poland at the printing house of the Brothers Wajnberg, though the inner page indicates that the actual printing was done by Sz. Sikora and I. Milner of Nowolipki 6 in Warsaw. The same printer was utilized for volume 7, published in 1930. The change in printer was presumably because Hebrew typesetting was much cheaper in Poland.

This change in printer emphasizes the shoestring nature of the finances that made possible the publication of Rabbi Rosenberg's *Zohar* project. In a 1931 letter Rabbi Rosenberg wrote to Yitsḥak Gershtenkorn, he gives some interesting details on the financing of the sixth and seventh volumes of the series:

> Two years ago [1929], I gave to the printers another two volumes of the *Zohar ha-Qadosh* … and after a tremendous effort and great difficulty I succeeded in redeeming [paying for] the *Zohar Tehilim* [from the printers]. My thought was that I would redeem *Zohar Tehilim* and then I would finish and redeem the seventh volume. However at that time there arose a great crisis in the world of business and the rich were made poor … because of the purchase of stock that all Jews participated in thinking to become rich easily … and the opposite came about, and because of this the time was not right for selling books. … And when I realized there was no prospect of redeeming [the seventh volume] from the sale of *Zohar Tehilim* … I agreed to have a banquet [in honor of my seventieth birthday] because I imagined that … everyone will buy the book, and the calculation was to gather the $1500.00 needed to redeem the seventh volume from the printers and to pay the small debt remaining from [the printing of] *Zohar Tehilim*, but it did not happen as I imagined for now is not conducive to raise funds.[145]

142 ZK volume 7, 208.

143 ZK volume 7, 104.

144 ZK Tehilim, 280.

145 Letter of Yudel Rosenberg to Yitsḥak Gershenkorn, 5 Adar 5691 (February 22, 1931), Bidspirit Auction 4180, lot 114694, https://il.bidspirit.com/ui/lotPage/source/catalog/auction/4180/lot/114694/Letter-from-Rabbi-Yehuda-Yudel?lang=en, accessed March 29, 2020.

Yudel Rosenberg's *Zohar* project was still not quite finished with the publication of the seventh volume, however. In 1927, he published *Nifla'ot ha-Zohar* [wonders of the *Zohar*], a book of stories from the Zohar presented in both Hebrew and Yiddish. He intended this book to be an eighth and supplementary volume to his seven part *Zohar* translation.[146] Through his Yiddish stories of the *Zohar*, he hoped specifically to address women as well as men.[147] This book was therefore designed for a more popular audience, to whom Rabbi Rosenberg wished to give the understanding that beyond the physical world of bodies there is a great and profound spiritual knowledge expressed by the masters of the *Zohar*.[148] Beyond that publication, Rabbi Rosenberg continued writing other stories from the *Zohar*, preparing a manuscript of the *Zohar* story of the prophet Jonah in 1931, presumably for publication in a pamphlet.[149]

Rabbi Rosenberg's translation and reedition of the *Zohar* earned him considerable critical notice, much of it negative. The first substantive criticism came from Hillel Zeitlin, whose own attempt to translate the *Zohar* into Hebrew was mentioned in a 1922 letter Rabbi Rosenberg wrote to his son, Meir Joshua, in which he remarked that Zeitlin had published some excerpts from the *Zohar*.[150] Zeitlin critiqued Yudel Rosenberg's 1905 *Sha'arei Zohar Torah* as well as Azriel Natan Frenk's (1863–1924) *Aggadot ha-Zohar*[151] in a letter to Simon Rawidowicz, contrasting it with his own project for a complete scientific translation of the *Zohar* into Hebrew. In criticism of Yudel Rosenberg, he stated:

---

146 NZ, 159.

147 Rosenberg was following in a tradition of other collections of stories of Rabbi Shim'on bar Yoḥai and his companions. See, for example, *Sefer Nifla'ot ha-Qedoshim* (Warsaw: M. Knoster, 1911).

148 NZ, 5.

149 "Maftir de-Yona loyt dem Pshat fun Zohar ha-Qadosh," Erev Yom Kippur, 5692 (20 September, 1931), manuscript, Jewish Public Library. It was eventually published with an English translation by Baruch Rosenberg, *Qovets Ma'amar Yehuda: Collected Discourses of Rabbi Yehuda Yudel Rosenberg Zt"l*, part 2: *Commentary on the Book of Jonah according to the Zohar* (Toronto: Eitz Yehuda Publishing Society, 1989).

150 Postcard from Yudel Rosenberg to Meir Joshua Rosenberg, not dated but postmarked May 16, 1922, BMA, Jerusalem. On Zeitlin's translation project see Jonatan Meir, "Hithavuto ve-Gilgulav shel Mif'al Targum u-Be'ur Sefer ha-Zohar le-Hillel Zeitlin," *Kabbalah* 10 (2004): 119–157.

151 Azriel Natan Frenk, *Aggadot ha-Zohar*, 2 volumes (Warsaw, 1923–1924). On Frenk, see François Guesnet, "Frenk, Azriel Natan," in YIVO Encyclopedia of Jews in Eastern Europe, http://www.yivoencyclopedia.org/article.aspx/Frenk_Azriel_Natan, accessed August 10, 2016.

> [Rosenberg's] translation has neither religious nor scientific validity. The rabbi who translated it merely gathered a few homilies from each section and translated them into an inaccurate and inelegant Rabbinic Hebrew. For instance, from the entire section of Bere'shit, which [in the Zohar] contains over seventy pages, in [Rosenberg's translation] there are only twelve pages.[152]

Academic scholars of Kabbala, such as Gershom Scholem (1897–1982) and Isaiah Tishby (1909–1992), dismissed Yudel Rosenberg's work on the *Zohar* as largely unworthy of scholarly interest.[153] Scholem wrote echoing Zeitlin that the translation is "devoid of any literary qualities."[154] Tishby wrote of Rabbi Rosenberg's translation that "instead of clarifying the subject matter, the translator's system forced him to mix up the *parshiyot,* and chop up the passages into small pieces. The translation itself is unreliable."[155] Kabbala scholar Yosef Dan likewise stated that Yudel Rosenberg's translation was not precise according to currently accepted scientific criteria.[156]

When Rabbi Rosenberg's first volume of *Zohar Torah* was published in New York in 1924, Getsel Zelikovits (1863–1926),[157] the reviewer in the *Tageblatt,* the New York Yiddish newspaper catering to Orthodox Jews, praised it moderately, stating that it was the greatest Hebrew work to come out of Canada to date. However, Zelikovits, who was evidently well acquainted with the *Zohar* and with scholars of Kabbala like Hillel Zeitlin and Samuel Abba Horodetsky (1871–1957), however, did not think that Yudel Rosenberg's translation was necessarily as good as Zeitlin's projected translation was likely to be, and he had some specific criticisms of the translation of various passages. Nonetheless, he

---

152 Jonatan Meir, "Hithavuto ve-Gilgulav," 145–146.

153 Cf. Gershom Scholem, *Major Trends in Jewish Mysticism* (New York: Schocken, 1961), 373; Isaiah Tishby and Fishel Lachover, *Mishnat ha-Zohar* (Jerusalem: Mossad Bialik, 1957), vol. 1, 113, 116. This attitude may have had something to do with Scholem's generally negative attitude toward contemporary traditional kabbalists. Cf. Boaz Huss, "The Translations of the Zohar" [Hebrew], in *New Developments in Zohar Studies,* ed. Ronit Meroz (Tel Aviv: Tel Aviv University Press, 2007, 79; idem, "'Authorized Guardians': The Polemics of Academic Scholars of Jewish Mysticism against Kabbalah Practitioners," in *Polemical Encounters: Esoteric Discourse and its Others,* ed. Kocku von Stuckrad and Olav Hammer (Leiden, Brill, 2007), 81–103.

154 Scholem, *Kabbalah,* 240.

155 Cited in Huss, "Translations of the Zohar," 115. It is interesting to note that Tishby, in his *Mishnat ha-Zohar,* himself "chopped up" passages from the Zohar into smaller pieces.

156 Cited in Yassif, *The Golem of Prague,* 11.

157 On Zelikovits see G. Selikovitsch, *Collection of Writings: Prose and Poetry* [Yiddish] (New York: Zelikovitsh Yibileum Komite, 1913), iii–xiv.

concluded, these small quibbles do not take anything away from the importance of Rosenberg's "clear" translation.[158] In his further review of the second volume of *Zohar Torah* on Exodus, which appeared a few months later, Zelikovits deplored the fact that Rabbi Rosenberg had refrained from translating important sections of the *Zohar* such as *Idra Rabba* and *Idra Zuta*, but nonetheless recommended the book to those people who wished to receive an introduction to the philosophy of Kabbala.[159]

In 1931, Rabbi Rosenberg's now complete *Zohar* publication was reviewed twice in Montreal; neither review praised it unequivocally. On February 18, Tsvi ha-Kohen, editor of the souvenir volume for Rabbi Rosenberg's seventieth birthday celebration, published a tribute in which over half of the space was devoted to the theme of the utter impossibility of translating the *Zohar* into other languages, including Hebrew. Ha-Kohen then added the following faint praise: "Nothwithstanding [*yihyeh asher yihyeh*] the translation [of the *Zohar*] is a gigantic labor ... and in this he has done a great thing [*higdil la'asot*].[160] The next month, Montreal's Yiddish daily, the *Keneder Adler*, published a lengthy review by Montreal Yiddishist educator Shimshon Dunsky (1899–1982),[161] who attacked Rabbi Rosenberg's translation as incomplete, inconsistent, inaccurate, and not "scientific" [*vissnshaftlikh*].[162]

Rabbi Rosenberg's response to this critique was not long in coming. It is notable in being his longest sustained statement in defense of his *Zohar* project at its completion. He began by synthesizing the five questions brought up by Dunsky in his critique:

1) Why is the original order of the Zohar changed to follow the verses of the Torah?
2) Why were parts left out?

---

158 G. Zelikovits, "Zohar Iberzettst oyf Loshn Qoydesh," *Tageblatt*, December 7, 1924.

159 Idem, "Literatur un Lomdus," *Tageblatt*, March 27, 1925. Cf. idem, "Literatur un Lomdus," *Tageblatt*, November 5, 1926.

160 Cohen, *Sefer ha Zikkaron*, 7–8.

161 On Dunsky, see "Shimshon Dunsky, 1899–1982," Jewish Public Library, http://www.jewishpubliclibrary.org/modules/archives/heritagevex/heritagedunsky.html, accessed September 1, 2016.

162 Shimson Dunsky, "Iz Shoyn be-Emes Faran a Falshtendige Iberzetzung fun zohar?," *KA*, March 19, 1931, 4, 8. A modern critic, Meir Bar-Ilan, asserts that a comprehensive comparison of the original to Yudel Rosenberg's translation would reveal "portions of the Zohar written by Rosenberg." Meir Bar-Ilan, "The Miracles of R. Yehuda Yudel Rozenberg" [Hebrew], *Alei Sefer* 19 (2001): 183.

3) Why was it written for those who had a *ḥeder* [traditional elementary] education?
4) The translation has stylistic and linguistic problems.
5) The translation has grammatical faults.

Yudel Rosenberg took Dunsky's criticisms and discussed them at length in the order they were presented.

1) Rabbi Rosenberg defended the editorial changes in order as an aid to comprehension, benefitting those who only wish to know what the *Zohar* has to say about a particular verse. The work, however, is also useful for those who can study the *Zohar* in the original Aramaic. As for changing the *Zohar*'s order, just as Isaac Alfasi reordered the Babylonian Talmud for his own purposes, and the *Yalkut Shimoni* re-ordered the Midrash, just so he has reedited the *Zohar*. In this connection, Rabbi Rosenberg emphasized that Rabbi Moses de Leon did not receive the Zohar in its present order, and thus the Vilna Gaon wrote that the text Rabbi Moses de Leon received was perhaps only a thousandth part of what Rabbi Shim'on bar Yoḥai and his colleagues produced, and what he did receive was not received in any particular order.
2) Rabbi Rosenberg asserted that not all that much text was in fact left out, and the material not translated constitutes "deep [*tifer*] Kabbala." Why was this material not translated? First of all, Rabbi Rosenberg replied, such abstruse matters cannot be translated into understandable Hebrew. Any word-for-word Hebrew translation would be essentially meaningless and the Zoharic text had been purposefully concealed with not readily understandable Aramaic. Moreover, he said, in a reference to the 1905 letter of Rabbi Ḥayyim Ḥizkiah Medini, the great rabbis he consulted did not give him permission to translate these deep matters. Yudel Rosenberg further defended the educational value of the translation in that it would enable a person who had mastered the translation to transition to the study of the *Zohar* in the original.[163]
3) The translation was indeed meant for those with a traditional elementary [*ḥeder*] education. It was certainly not meant for children

163 Rosenberg utilized his Zohar translation in his other works. Cf. PY, 135–138.

studying in modern "schools" or for the "Einstein" academics. These people possess telescopes instead of *Zohar* and we have *Zohar* instead of their telescopes. It is also certainly not written for great and learned rabbis, who can easily read the *Zohar* in the original. It is rather aimed at ordinary Torah Jews whose goal in studying *Zohar* is its moral lessons [*mussar*].

4) Rabbi Rosenberg dismissed the argument that the translation was inadequate by asserting that it was fine for the ordinary Jews for whom it was intended and that Shimshon Dunsky had ulterior motives in his criticism that did not deserve a response.
5) As for the issue of grammatical errors in Hebrew, Rabbi Rosenberg conceded that, according to "enlightened" [*maskilic*] standards of Hebrew grammar, his translation may have come up occasionally short. However, he argued, he had translated the *Zohar* into a midrashic Hebrew which, like biblical Hebrew, did not always follow the "rules" of Hebrew grammar.[164]

If the critical response to *Zohar Torah* was far from unanimous praise, the book, apparently, did sell. The five volume set of *Zohar Torah* was produced in an initial print run of 5000 copies, costing $20.00 for a set of five volumes.[165] According to Rabbi Rosenberg's account, the first edition sold out within two years.[166] From his surviving correspondence, we are able to piece together some details about how the book was marketed and distributed.

In 1925, when Rabbi Rosenberg had published the first two volumes of his *Zohar Torah,* he sent copies to a number of prominent rabbis. Among them was Rabbi Abraham Isaac ha-Kohen Kook, Chief Ashkenazic rabbi of Palestine. In his generous response, Rabbi Kook praised Rabbi Rosenberg's work of translating the Zohar into a "pure and clear" Hebrew as a public benefit and approved of his arranging the columns of Hebrew and Aramaic so that the reader could easily follow the text.[167] Rabbi Rosenberg also developed a warm relationship with Rabbi Benzion Uziel (1880–1953), a future Chief Sephardic Rabbi of Israel, when he visited Montreal in 1927. In 1932, Rabbi Uziel wrote that he

---

164 "Entfer oyf der Zohar Kritik," *KA*, March 31, 1931.

165 *Haqqafot*, 15

166 ZK, vol. 7, 3.

167 Abraham Isaac Kook, *Igrot ha-Raiy'a* (Jerusalem: Zvi Yehuda Kook Foundation, 1984), vol. 4, 247. Rabbi Kook's letter was published by Rosenberg in ZT, vol. 4, unpaginated. Cf. Jonatan Meir, "Hithavuto ve-Gilgulav," 145, note 104.

had read the sixth volume of Rabbi Rosenberg's *Zohar* translation and spoke of its "exact Hebrew translation and its enlightening notes." He also wrote of the importance of distributing the book widely in synagogues and Houses of Study and furthermore offered to help distribute them.[168]

Indeed, Yudel Rosenberg carefully crafted what amounted to a worldwide distribution network for his work, and his surviving correspondence gives us interesting details of how it worked. His will, written on September 3, 1935, indicates that he stored copies for sale in three places, Montreal, Warsaw, and New York. In a 1930 letter to his son, Meir Joshua, Rabbi Rosenberg mentioned that he had given 1000 copies of his *Zohar* on Psalms, published in 1929, to the New York bookseller Reznick and Menschel,[169] presumably the New York depository mentioned in the will, on commission. He further wrote that he was planning to send a representative to the upcoming Agudat ha-Rabbanim convention where he expected that many Orthodox rabbis, potential buyers, would congregate. In that letter, Rabbi Rosenberg also asked his son for the address of Rabbi Leo Jung (1892–1987), an influential Orthodox rabbi in New York, whom he presumably wished to send a copy.[170]

Another prominent American Jew to whom Rosenberg sent a set of his *Zohar* work was Dr. Cyrus Adler (1863–1940), President of Dropsie College for Hebrew and Cognate Learning in Philadelphia. Along with the publication, Rabbi Rosenberg evidently made a request that Dropsie College grant him a PhD on the basis of his publication. Dr. Adler politely refused this request.[171]

Rabbi Rosenberg also corresponded with booksellers worldwide, including Moshe Bleitrakh in Metz, France, Mardoché Sitruk in Tunisia, Meir Gabbai in Egypt, and N. E. B. Ezra in Shanghai, China.

Another aspect of Rabbi Rosenberg's campaign to increase circulation of his work was the development of his connection with Kabbalists from the Land of Israel. In 5692 (1931/2) Rabbi Rosenberg met with Rabbi Hayyim Yehuda Leib Auerbach (1883–1954), head of Jerusalem kabbalistic yeshiva

168 Rabbi Benzion Uziel to Yudel Rosenberg, 10 Adar II 5692 (March 18, 1932), Arkhion Histori, Iriyat Tel-Aviv-Yaffo, Rabbi Benzion Uziel papers 92/975. These sentiments are reiterated in another letter from Uziel to Rosenberg of 15 Sivan 5692 (June 19, 1932), ibid., 92/1505. On Rabbi Uziel as a supporter of kabbalistic yeshivot, see Meir, *Kabbalistic Circles in Jerusalem*, 56.

169 This company was located on Canal Street. Shnayer Leiman, "From the Pages of Tradition: Montague Lawrence Marks in a Jewish Bookstore," *Tradition* 25, no. 1 (Fall 1989): 59–60.

170 Yudel Rosenberg to Meir Joshua Rosenberg 16 Iyyar 5690 (May 14, 1930), BMA, Jerusalem.

171 Cyrus Adler to Yudel Rosenberg, March 8, 1932, RFA, Savannah.

Sha'ar ha-Shamayim during Rabbi Auerbach's fundraising trip in North America.[172] He was also evidently helpful in Rabbi Auerbach's mission and as a token of appreciation, the Sha'ar ha-Shamayim yeshiva bestowed on him the title of *ḥaver* [fellow] and *gabbai qodesh* [honorary officer].[173]

Despite all these efforts, and apparently appreciable sales of his *Zohar* work, in 1934 Rabbi Rosenberg stated that he had essentially made no money on this publication and that he had not even recovered his expenses despite the fact that it had been published in a second edition.[174] As we will see in the next chapter, Rabbi Rosenberg's work on the Zohar has never been out of print and continues to beckon to readers from booksellers' shelves.

One must conclude that for Rabbi Yudel Rosenberg, there was something fundamentally important about Kabbala in general, and the *Zohar* in particular, for the future of Judaism. This attitude he certainly shared, despite all their differences, with scholars like Gershom Scholem and with rabbis like Yehuda Ashlag. He and they certainly understood that for Kabbala to take its rightful place among Jews there would have to be a revolution in Jewish thought. He and they undertook to create that revolution in Judaism against much perceived opposition.[175] He and they approached their redemptive and revolutionary task by means of "translations" of the *Zohar* from its original language, which had become all but incomprehensible to contemporary Jews, to one which was accessible to them.[176]

172 "Ha-Rav Hayyim Yehuda Leib Auerbach," in *Encyclopedia of the Founders and Builders of Israel*, ed. David Tidhar, http://www.tidhar.tourolib.org/files/tidhar/index/assoc/HASH01db.dir/images/V03_375.jpg.

173 Cohen, *Sefer ha-Zikkaron*, 29. In a letter of 13 Tishrei 5686 (October 1, 1925) to Rabbi Yosef Haim Sonnenfeld in Jerusalem, Rosenberg sent $10.00 as a contribution to the yeshiva. See il.bidspirit.com, auction 3455, lot 130363, accessed June 20, 2018. On the activities of the Sha'ar ha-Shamayim yeshiva, see Meir, *Kabbalistic Circles in Jerusalem*, 63–76.

174 *Omer*, part 2, 5.

175 Yudel Rosenberg acknowledged that there were deniers of the Zohar's validity. PY, 62.

176 For a detailed comparison between the three, see Ira Robinson, "Reviving the Study of the Zohar in First Half of the 20th Century: A Consideration of Roles of Gershom Scholem, Yudel Rosenberg, and Yehuda Ashlag," in *From Something to Nothing: Jewish Mysticism in Contemporary Canadian Jewish Studies*, ed. Harry Fox, Daniel Maoz, and Tirzah Meacham (Newcastle upon Tyne: Cambridge Scholars Publishing, 2019), 41–50.

CHAPTER 11

What Is Rabbi Yudel Rosenberg's Legacy?

Having surveyed the life and works of Rabbi Yehuda Yudel Rosenberg in the previous chapters of this volume, we end by asking what his legacy was. What did Rabbi Rosenberg write or do during his lifetime that makes us pay attention to him a century after he lived and wrote?

At his death in 1935, it was not at all clear that Yudel Rosenberg had much of a legacy to leave to anyone, with the exception of his own family. His death left his family almost literally penniless in the middle of the Great Depression. The family had to plead with a financially challenged Jewish Community Council of Montreal to provide a pension for his widow.[1] Rabbi Rosenberg left several manuscripts ready for the printer at his death, but there were no funds available to get them printed, or even to get a book that was already in the page-proof stage published. In 1934 Rabbi Rosenberg's printer in Biłgoraj, Poland, Szloma Wajnberg, inserted a note in the page-proofs of Yudel Rosenberg's book, *Omer*, stating that he would not do any more work for Rabbi Rosenberg until he was paid what he was owed, more than 300 złoty [*zehuvim*].[2] That book would only partially see the light of day after many decades,[3] even though, after Rabbi Rosenberg's death, his family started a fund with the express purpose of publishing *Omer*. In the fundraising circular the family issued, the publication was promised by the first anniversary of Rabbi Rosenberg's death, October 1936.[4] No publication resulted from this effort, and so there was evidently little or no public interest in supporting the publication of any posthumous book by Rabbi Rosenberg. At this point, only his immediate family seemed at all interested in Yudel Rosenberg's literary heritage.

1 Leah Rosenberg, *The Errand Runner*, 121.

2 At that time, this was worth approximately $US60.00. *Omer*, part 2, 114.

3 The publication began in 1996.

4 "A request to those who receive this book," undated, RFA, file 5.

The extended Rosenberg family certainly remembered him. His daughter Leah's reverence for her father comes out quite clearly in her memoir.[5] Leah's son, Mordecai Richler, mentioned his grandfather numerous times in his writings, though he was only five when his grandfather died. In one place, he recalled his grandfather's custom of testing his quill by writing the name "Amalek" in Hebrew, and then crossing it out.[6]

But the members of the Rosenberg family not merely remembered him; they also remained committed to Yudel Rosenberg's heritage for a considerable period of time. In the 1950s, family members supported a new edition of Rabbi Rosenberg's *Zohar Torah,* and the idea was expressed that any profit from the sales of the new edition should be used to publish Rabbi Rosenberg's unpublished manuscripts.[7] However, it would not be until the late 1980s that one of his grandchildren living in Toronto, Baruch Rosenberg, began to publish some of the unpublished works.[8] Starting in the 1990s, the Ben-Meir family in Israel, descendants of Rabbi Rosenberg's son Meir Joshua, would also reprint some of Rabbi Rosenberg's already published works and publish some hitherto unpublished material.[9]

But what of Rabbi Rosenberg's influence beyond his numerous descendants? It is clear from chapter ten of this book that Yudel Rosenberg spent a great deal of his time and creative effort on his *Zohar* project. Did that project have any effect? The answer has to begin by acknowledging that Rabbi Yudel Rosenberg did not acquire any acknowledged disciples in Kabbala. The one exception to this statement, which proves the rule, was Rabbi Rosenberg's son, Aaron Elimelech (1881–1960). Aaron Elimelech, who made his living as a poultry *shoḥet* in Montreal, was described by Chaim Leib Fox in his book on Canadian Yiddish and Hebrew authors as a "kabbalist" [*mekubal*].[10] Aaron Elimelech's sole published book, *Likkutei Beit Aharon* (1954) does contain some kabbalistic

5 Leah Rosenberg, *The Errand Runner.*

6 Mordecai Richler, *This Year in Jerusalem* (Toronto: Knopf, 1994), 204. For other examples of this custom, see Elliot Horowitz, *Reckless Rites: Purim and the Legacy of Jewish Violence* (Princeton and Oxford: Princeton University Press, 2006), 107, 109.

7 RFA, Savannah.

8 Baruch Rosenberg published *Kovets Ma'amar Yehudah* (Toronto, 1988), including a discourse on Tefillin by Rabbi Yudel Rosenberg from an unpublished manuscript, and *'Ets Yehudah: Ve-hu Kol Kitve Yehudah Yudel Rozenberg* (Toronto, 1988).

9 Meir Yehoshua Ben Meir edited and published with additional notes *Prozbul* in 2001 and *Qeri'ah* in 2004.

10 Fox, *100 Years of Hebrew and Yiddish Literature in Canada,* 273.

citations that he apparently learned from his father.[11] In the matter of disciples, Rabbi Rosenberg fared differently from other kabbalists of that era who lived in the Land of Israel, such as Rabbis Yehuda Ashlag, Yehuda Petaya (1859–1942), and Shlomo Eliashiv (1841–1926), all of whom sought to spread kabbalistic knowledge and all of whom possessed identifiable students. These students, especially those of Rabbi Ashlag, served to enhance their teacher's reputation by their intensive marketing of their mentor's teachings.[12] One result of this situation is that Rabbi Rosenberg's work on the *Zohar* has been largely ignored in the burgeoning contemporary literature on Kabbala, whether addressed to Orthodox, popular, or scholarly audiences, whereas Rabbi Ashlag's work on the *Zohar* has been widely published and is considered by an academic Kabbala scholar of the calibre of Arthur Green as "a most important aid."[13]

Notwithstanding this general lack of acknowledged disciples, many Jews, and occasionally non-Jewish scholars like Scottish Professor Oliver Shaw Rankin (1885–1954) consulted Rabbi Rosenberg's *Zohar* translation over the years.[14] There were certainly enough readers in the twenty years following Rabbi Rosenberg's death to exhaust the extant stock of Rabbi Rosenberg's *Zohar* works, and there was apparently some continuing demand for them, enough to encourage his family to finance a new edition in 1955. In that year, the seven volumes of Rabbi Rosenberg's *Zohar* work were republished in a reduced-format edition of 2000 sets.[15] The work was again reprinted in Israel in 1967 and in New York in 1970. It has remained available in print, on bookstore shelves, and on the internet into the twenty-first century.[16]

What is the legacy of Yudel Rosenberg's many published stories? Despite Yosef Dan's bold statement that Rabbi Rosenberg's story of the Maharal and the Golem constitutes the most important twentieth-century contribution of

---

11 Aaron Rosenberg, *Likkutei Bet Aharon*, 41–42.

12 Jonatan Meir, "Gilui ve-Gilui Behester: 'Al Mamshikhei ha-R.Y.L. Ashlag, ha-Hitnagdut la-Hem ve-Hafatsat Sifrut ha-Sod," *Kabbala* 16 (2007): 155.

13 Arthur Green, *A Guide to the Zohar* (Stanford: Stanford University Press, 2004), 177.

14 Oliver Shaw Rankin, *Jewish Religious Polemic* (New York: Ktav, 1970), 223. Cf. Harry Joshua Stern, "Commentaries," *Canadian Jewish Review*, November 1, 1935.

15 Harry Glass, letter to "Uncle and Aunt," April 26, 1955, RFA, Savannah. Dr. Jacob Goldstein, "Zohar mit ha-Rav Yudel Rosenbergs Barimter Hebraisher Iberzetsung Dersheynt Kumendiken Ḥodesh," *Tog-Morgen Zhurnal* (1955): undated clipping. Cf. Y. Y. Zahavi, "Zohar mit ha-Rav Yudel Rosenbergs Hebraisher Iberzetsung Desrshynt dem Hodesh," *Der 'Yid*, October 14, 1955, 6.

16 See, for example, the website of My Sefer bookstore, https://mysefer.com/Zohar—Zohar-Torah-Commentary-Rabbi-Yehuda-Yudel-Rosenberg__p-3721.aspx, accessed October 18, 2019.

Hebrew literature to world literature,[17] Yudel Rosenberg is not included in any history of Modern Hebrew literature.[18] It is likely that his work was passed over by scholars of Modern Hebrew Literature for two reasons. The first is that his work was written for, and circulated in the popular Orthodox book market, and thus would tend to be considered irrelevant by those interested in "modern," "secular" Hebrew literature. The other, perhaps more important factor, was that Yudel Rosenberg never quite presented himself as the "author" of his works. He rather painted a picture of himself as the "editor" of centuries-old manuscripts, and as such he was accepted for many years, essentially until the 1970s. Thus, Rabbi Rosenberg's tales of King Solomon were accepted as genuine folk material and provided Ḥayyim Naḥman Bialik source material for his work on Jewish legends.[19] Similarly, Rabbi Rosenberg's tales of Rabbi Yehuda Leib (1724–1811), the *Shpoler Zayde,* still informs accounts of his life.[20]

In 1975 a column in the Israeli newspaper *Davar* copied a number of spells [*leḥashim*] from Rosenberg's *Refa'el ha-Mal'akh,* correctly identifying him as the translator of the *Zohar* and the writer of the Maharal legend.[21] In the 1980s, and 1990s, scholars like Shnayer Leiman[22] in the United States and Eli Yassif[23] in Israel discovered him, pulled away his "editorial" façade and revealed him as an interesting and creative writer in his own right. Thus, when Rabbi Rosenberg's tale of the Maharal and the Golem was translated into English by Joachim Neugroschel in the 1970s, Rabbi Rosenberg's name was absent.[24] However, in

17 Yosef Dan, "The Beginnings of Hebrew Hagiographic Literature" [Hebrew], *Jerusalem Studies in Jewish Folklore* 1 [1981], 85.

18 Yassif, *The Golem of Prague,* 10, note 1.

19 Mordecai Ben Yehezkel, "Sefer 'va-Yehe ha-Yom,'" in *Byalik: Yetsirato le-Sugeha bi-Rei ha-Biqoret: Antologyah,* ed. Gershon Shaked (Jerusalem: Mossad Bialik, 1974), 360.

20 Elie Wiesel, *Sages and Dreamers: Biblical, Talmudic and Hasidic Portraits and Legends* (New York: Summit Books, 1991), 351–366; Zev Kitzis, "From the treasury of Chassidic Stories," *Shabbat B'Shabbato* 2369 (January 18, 2014): 5–6, http://www.zomet.org.il/eng/?CategoryID=160&SectionID=-1&ChapterID=-1&Archive=&ArchVolID=&AuthorID=89&searchMode=0&Search=1&SString=&Page=5, accessed January 27, 2016.

21 Shlomo Saba, "Kama Leḥashim Tovim le-Kavod he-Ḥagim mi-Sefer Yashan u-Baduq," *Davar,* September 19, 1975, 43.

22 Shnayer Z. Leiman, "The Adventure of the Maharal of Prague in London: R. Yudl Rosenberg and the Golem of Prague," *Tradition* 36, no. 1 (2002): 26–58.

23 Yassif, *The Golem of Prague.*

24 Joachim Neugroschel, *Yenne Velt.*

2007, Curt Leviant's English translation of Yudel Rosenberg's Maharal story clearly acknowledged his authorship.[25]

The growing recognition of Rabbi Rosenberg's literary talent by scholars does not mean, however, that this recognition has penetrated non-scholarly circles, which remain quite taken with the Golem of Prague, especially in the Golem's putative home city. Thus in 2009 a New York Times reporter in Prague found "Golem hotels, Golem door-making companies, Golem clay figurines[,] ... a recent musical starring a dancing Golem and a Czech strongman called the Golem."[26] This phenomenon is an illustration of a point made by Eli Yassif: "Any story ... becomes folk literature if it is taken up by society at large—that is, if it is told and retold in a society that comes to see the legend as a cultural asset, through which it expresses its wishes and fears."[27]

In the contemporary ultraorthodox [*Ḥaredi*] world, a world with strong connections to the tales of Jewish tradition Yudel Rosenberg told, his stories are still reprinted, though they are not always attributed to him. The ultraorthodox community, as opposed to the community of Jewish scholarship, still cares whether the Maharal of Prague actually created a Golem, and the evidence for and against Rabbi Rosenberg's authorship of this and other works is still debated.[28] Thus in a *Ḥaredi* publication, *Or Torah,* a reader asked for help finding a book mentioned by Rabbi Rosenberg in his *Zohar Torah* on Leviticus, ascribed to a student of Rabbi Jacob Emden.[29] This reader was answered in the next month's *Or Torah* by two other readers who asserted that the Emden work

25 Yudel Rosenberg, *The Golem and the Wondrous Deeds of the Maharal of Prague,* trans. and ed. with an introduction and notes by Curt Leviant (New Haven: Yale University Press, 2007).

26 Dan Bilefsky, "Hard Times Give New Life to Prague's Golem," *New York Times,* May 11, 2009.

27 Eli Yassif, *The Legend of Safed: Life and Fantasy in the City of Kabbalah* (Detroit: Wayne State University Press, 2019), 4.

28 Binyomin Y. Rabinowitz, "The Golem of Prague—Fact or Fiction?," *De'ah ve-Dibur,* March 1, 2006, http://www.chareidi.org/archives5766/terumoh/TRM66features.htm, accessed January 19, 2016. Cf. Shneur Z. Leiman, "Did a Disciple of the Maharal Create a Golem?," *Seforim Blog,* February 8, 2007, http://seforim.blogspot.ca/2007/02/shnayer-z-leiman-did-disciple-of.html, accessed January 19, 2016; idem., "The Letter of the Maharal on the Creation of the Golem: A Modern Forgery," *Seforim Blog,* January 3, 2010, http://seforim.blogspot.ca/2010/01/letter-of-maharal-on-creation-of-golem.html, accessed January 19, 2016; idem., "The Golem of Prague in Recent Rabbinic Literature," *Seforim Blog,* May 4, 2010, http://seforim.blogspot.ca/2010/05/golem-of-prague-in-recent-rabbinic.html, accessed January 19, 2016.

29 *Or Torah* (Tevet 5772): 362.

mentioned by Rabbi Rosenberg did not in fact exist and that Rabbi Rosenberg was a master of imagination [*ba'al dimayon*].[30]

The fictiveness of Yudel Rosenberg's tales of the adventures of the Maharal of Prague in England is not apparent to many *Ḥaredi* Jews, and the stories are still extant and republished in *Ḥaredi* media and databases.[31] British Orthodox Rabbi and author Salomon Alter Halpern has had visitors from Israel ask him "more than once" whether Rabbi Rosenberg's story was really true that the High Priest's Breastplate was in the British Museum. Rabbi Halpern, who fully realizes the fictiveness of Rabbi Rosenberg's Maharal narrations, tries to excuse him by writing:

> Though I should hesitate to write a complete fiction about a real person myself, I do not blame him for it, because he probably thought it was perfectly obvious to anyone that it was fiction.[32]

Jewish studies scholar Marc Shapiro tends to mitigate the issue of Rabbi Rosenberg's "forgery" on similar lines:

> With some of Rosenberg's "forgeries", it seems that what he was doing was creating a form of literature, and anyone who takes the story literally has only himself to blame (much like anyone who thinks that *Animal Farm* is really about animals has no one to complain to but himself). At times, Rosenberg would even hint to the reader what he was doing, as in *Ḥoshen ha-Mishpat shel ha-Kohen ha-Gadol*, where in the preface he mentions that part of the story also appeared in a work of Arthur Conan Doyle. If any reader would have taken the time to find out who this was, he would have realized that we are dealing with a fictional account. At other times, however, Rosenberg offers no such hint, at least none that I am aware of, and what we have appears to be a simple forgery.[33]

30 *Or Torah* (Adar 5772): 555–557.

31 Steven Fine, *The Menorah: From the Bible to Modern Israel* (Cambridge: Harvard University Press, 2017), 189.

32 Salomon Alter Halpern, *The Prisoner and Other Tales of Faith* (Jerusalem and New York: 1981), 11–12.

33 Marc B. Shapiro, "Concerning the Zohar and Other Matters," *Seforim Blog*, August 29, 2012, http://seforim2.rssing.com/chan-9044709/all_p1.html, accessed September 2, 2019.

In the end, we are left with the story of a man, Rabbi Yehuda Yudel Rosenberg, confronted in his generation with a seemingly relentless onslaught on the viability of Orthodox Judaism. It is apparent that Rabbi Rosenberg felt obliged to help save Orthodox Judaism through a variety of means that must have seemed quite quixotic to many of his contemporaries. In the face of those wishing to minimize or even eliminate the study of Kabbala among Jews, Rabbi Rosenberg advocated a broad popularization of the study of Kabbala among Jews, and devoted years of his life to creating a version of the *Zohar* that would be accessible to ordinary Jews. In the face of those who thought that the findings of science negated the traditional teachings of Orthodox Judaism, Rabbi Rosenberg worked assiduously to promote the idea that science and Judaism, properly understood, were not antagonistic but mutually supportive. In the face of those who asserted that the literary future of the Jews inhered in stories that told of the decline and fall of Jewish traditional life, Rabbi Rosenberg set out to create a body of literature that asserted the strength and persistence of that tradition. In the face of contemporary observers of the Jewish immigrant community in North America at the beginning of the twentieth century, who could see no future for Orthodox Judaism there, Rabbi Rosenberg set out to help create an institutional basis for Orthodoxy in Montreal that had staying power.

It is easy to say that Rabbi Rosenberg's ideas concerning the accommodation of science to Kabbala—and vice versa—are naive. It is possible to say that his considerable literary output was significantly tainted by his attribution of his works to prominent rabbis of past ages. Yet his work was part and parcel of the opening phase of a process which, perhaps in a more sophisticated way, marks the intellectual history of Judaism in the past century.

It is perhaps significant that Rabbi Rosenberg published his edition and translation of the *Zohar* in the 1920s—the same era in which Gershom Scholem began in earnest his masterful life-work of rescuing Kabbala from neglect in the academic world. In a certain way, both men had much the same mission. Each was to take Kabbala, which was neglected and misunderstood in the context of contemporary Judaism, and to make it the key element in the regeneration of Judaism in the modern era. The difference, of course, is in the audiences they addressed. Gershom Scholem and his works found popularity in the academy. Rabbi Rosenberg's translation found a considerable readership among Orthodox Jews, judging from the numerous reprints of the work. Moreover both men seem—in their respective spheres—to have anticipated that Kabbala was to become a prime factor in Judaic thought. Yudel Rosenberg must, then, be considered a predecessor of later popularizers of Kabbala among Orthodox Jews such as Adin Steinsaltz and Aryeh Kaplan.[34]

Yudel Rosenberg was certainly no scientist. He was rather a man who absorbed a good deal of scientific information available to him in Hebrew, Yiddish, and Russian. Yet here, too, he anticipated some of the major strategies of contemporary Orthodox Judaism in dealing with scientific theories and discoveries. These include the notion that all valid science is to be found in the Torah in some form, that there is no basic contradiction between Torah and true science, and that science is the handmaiden of Torah.[35]

In short, we have been dealing with a man whose life and works have been obscured by the passage of time, but which have amply rewarded our study. Through Rabbi Yehuda Yudel Rosenberg, we have come to a more nuanced understanding not merely of the pressures of the modern world upon Orthodox Judaism in the late nineteenth and early twentieth centuries, but also of the beginnings of the creative response to these pressures, which ultimately enabled Orthodoxy to emerge as a viable force within Judaism of the early twenty-first century.

As we stand at the beginning of the twenty-first century, we find ourselves in the midst of a Jewish community many of whose ideas are fed from Judaic sources in one sort of "translation" or another. Contemporary Jews often take for granted the availability and accessibility of these sources in translation. But their availability and relevance to the present must be seen as the culmination of a revolution in Judaic thought that began in earnest in the early twentieth century. It was a revolution that was made possible, at least in some small measure, by the life and work of the person examined in this book—Rabbi Yehuda Yudel Rosenberg.

34 Adin Steinsaltz, *The Thirteen-Petalled Rose* (New York: Basic Books, 1980); Aryeh Kaplan, *Mediation and Kabbala* (York Beach, ME: Samuel Weiser, 1982).

35 See Leo Levi, *Torah and Science: Their Interplay in the World Scheme* (New York: Association of Orthodox Jewish Scientists, 1983).

A Chronological Bibliography of the Writings of Rabbi Yehuda Yudel Rosenberg

1902

Yadot Nedarim: Ve-Hu Be'ur Maspiq 'al Kol ke-Lomar asher be-Ferush Rashi uva-Ran ... uvi-She'ar Meqomot ... shebe-Masekhet Nedarim. Warsaw: Ephraim Baumritter, 5663. Subsequent printings in 1925, 1956, 1986, 2008, and 2015.

1903

"Number 118." *Sha'arei Torah* 1, no. 11 (1903): 356.

1904

"Devar Halakha 'im Mutar le-She'ol ba-Goral," in *Sefer Goral ha-'Assiriyot*, edited by Meir Joshua Rosenberg, 19–23. Warsaw: Ephraim Baumritter, 5664. Subsequent printings in 1965 and 1995 without attribution to Yudel Rosenberg.

"Number 40." *Sha'arei Torah* 2, no. 4 (1904): 130–132.

"Number 79." *Sha'arei Torah* 2, no. 9 (1904): 280–285.

1905

Haggada shel Pḥesaḥ 'im Perush R. Yehuda Liva' ... 'im Hosafot ba-Quntres Mateh Yehuda Me'et ha-Mo'l. ... Warsaw: F. Baumritter, 5665. Subsequent printings in 1920, 1951, 1964, 1971, 1984, 1989.

Haggada shel Pesaḥ. Warsaw: H. Odelstein, 5665.

Sefer Sha'arei Zohar Torah. Hu Perush ha-Zohar ha-Qadosh 'al ha-Torah ... Ḥelek 'A Sefer Bere'shit. Warsaw: J. Edelstein, 5666.

1908

Sefer Kol Torah. Hu Qovets Ḥiddushei Torah. ... Warsaw: n.p., 1908. Subsequent printings in 1992 and 2015.

1909

Sefer Nifla'ot Maharal mi-Prag 'im ha-Golem. Warsaw: Aaron Cylingold, 1909. Other editions: Podgórze: Shaul Ḥanannia Daytsher, 1909; Piotrkow: Ḥanokh Henikh Folman, 1909. Subsequent printings and translations in 1910, 1913, 1914, 1920, 1980, 1987, 1991, 1996, 2007, and 2013.

Seder Haqqafot le-Shmini Atseret ule-Simḥat Torah. ... Kemo she-Ne'emru be-Veyt Midrasho shel ... Pinḥas mi-Korets. Piotrków: Ḥanokh Henikh Folman, 1909. Subsequent printings 1919, 1996, 2005.

1910

Sefer Eliyahu ha-Navi': Hitgaluto, Nifle'otav, 'Inyene Eliyahu ha-Navi' 'al Devar ha-Ge'ulah, Nilketu min Talmud Bavli ve-Yerushalmi veha-Zohar. ... Piotrków: Mordecai Tsederboym, 1910. Also published in Yiddish as *Ale Ma'asiyos fun Eliyohu ha-Novi.* Piotrków: Aaron Cajlingold and Mordecai Tsederboym, 1910. Subsequent Hebrew printings 1911, 1913, 1920, 1953, 1964, 1974, 1975, 1986.

Segules u-Refu'es. ... Warsaw: n.p., 1910. Yiddish translation of *Refa'el ha-Mal'aḥ.*

Sefer Segulot u-Refu'ot. Piotrków: Yitsḥaq Shlomovits, 1910. Subsequent printings 1911, 1920, 1930.

Seder ha-Prozbul. Piotrków: Mordecai Tsederboym, 1910. Subsequent printings 2008, 2014.

Ma'aseh fun'm Maharal mi-Prag. Lemberg: H. Steinmetz, 1910.

Sefer Nifla'ot Maharal. Lemberg: H. Steinmetz, 1910.

Di Geshikhte Nifla'os Maharal mit dem Goylem. Warsaw: Aaron Cylingold, 1910[?].

"Haskama" to Yisrael Isser Rosenberg, *Sefer Zemirot Yisra'el.* Warsaw: Benjamin Lipshitz, 1910.

1911

Sefer Refa'el ha-Mal'aḥ. Piotrków: Shlomo Belkhatovski, (1911). Subsequent printings 1920, 1929, 1930, 1944, 1960, 1963, 1965, 1967, 1976, 1984, 1986.

Segules u-Refu'es. Łódź: Yitsḥaq Shlomovits, 1911. Yiddish translation of *Refa'el ha-Mal'aḥ.*

Sefer Eliyahu ha-Navi'. Piotrków: Mordecai Tsederboym, 1911. Also published Warsaw: Aaron Cylingold, 1911; and Podgórze: Shaul Ḥanannia Daytsher, 1911. Also published as *Eliyahu ha-Navi'.* Kraków: n.p., 1911. Published in Yiddish as *Ale Ma'yses fun Eliyohu ha-Navi'.* Piotrków: Mordecai Tsederboym, 1911; Warsaw: Aaron Cylingold, 1911).

Ḥokhmas Maharal. Piotrków: Belkhatovsky, 5671 (1911).

"Haskama" to Yitsḥaq Me'ir Garnet, *Sefer Agra Deve Ḥillulei.* Piotrków: Belkhatovski, 1911.

1912

Sefer Tif'eret Mahar'el mi-Shpole. Piotrkow: Ḥanokh Henikh Folman, 1912. Subsequent printings and translations 1914, 1919, 1920, 1926, 1930, 1951, 1960, 1969, 1975, 1987, 1996.

Published in Yiddish as *Der Shpoler Zayde. ... Vunderkikhe Mofsim vos hot Bavayzn Leyb Shpoler.* Piótrkow: Belkhatovsky, 1912[?]. As indicated in this book, it is a translation of *Sefer Tif'eret Mahar'el*, compiled by the Tarler Rebbe, Yudel Rosenberg.

Sefer Darsha Tsemer u-Fishtim. Łódź: Yitsḥaq Shlomovits, 1912.

Der Krizis fun Lodz Varshe. Piotrków: Ḥanokh Henikh Folman 1912.

Ma'ase fun Maharal mi-Prag. Warsaw: Ephraim Baumritter, 1912.

Homeopatia: A Hekhst Interessants Vissenshaftlikhes Bukh, Velkhes Bashraybt ve azoy Men Ken Kurern ale Krankheiten mit Homeopatia. Piótrkow: Shlomo Belkhatovsky, 1912.

1913

Sefer Ḥoshen ha-Mishpat shel ha-Kohen ha-Gadol. Piótrkow: Ḥanokh Henikh Folman, 1913. Subsequent printings 1951, 1975, 1985, 1994.

Sefer Refu'at ha-Nefesh u-Refu'at ha-Guf, bilingual edition. Warsaw: Aaron Cajlingold, 1913. This edition also includes *Der Rambam Hilkhot De'ot.* Subsequent printings 1920, 1950, 1960, 1967, 1968, 1986, 1987.

Niflo'es Maharal: ... Vos er hot Bevizen dorkh der Hilf fun dem Goylem. ... Warsaw: Yudel Rozenberg, [1913].

Sefer Eliyahu ha-Navi'. Warsaw: Aaron Cylingold, 1913; Warsaw: Ephraim Baumritter, 1913.

Der Maharal mi-Prag mit dem Ḥoshen Mishpat fun Kohen Godol. Piotrkow: Yitsḥaq Shlomovits, 1913.

Sefer Divrei ha Yamim le-Shlomo ha-Melekh Yalkut ha-Ma'asiyot veha-Me'oraot she-yesh la-Hem Shayakhut el ha-Melekh Shlomo. Piótrkow: A. Y. Kleiman, 1913. Subsequent printings 1914, 1980, 1982, 1985.

Der Greiditser. Łódź: Yitsḥaq Shlomovits, 1913; Piótrkow: Shlomo Belkhatovsky, 1913. As indicated in the book, this is an Yiddish translation of *Sefer Hadrat Eliyahu.* Subsequent printings 1920, 1930, 1940, 1962, 1988.

Ma'aseh fun Maharal mi-Prag: ... Di Moftim vos er hot Bavayzen durkh der Hilf fun dem Golem, bilingual edition. Warsaw: Aaron Cylingold, 1913.

1914

Nifla'ot Maharal [Judeo-Bukharan/Judeo-Tadjik], translated by Maman Suleimanoff. Jerusalem: Bet 'Eked Sefarim, 1914.

Sefer Divrei ha Yamim asher le-Shlomo ha-Melekh Yalkut ha-Ma'asiyot veha-Me'oraot she-yesh la-Hem Shayakhut el ha-Melekh Shlomo he-Ḥakham mi-kol ha-Adam, composed by Yehudah Yudel b. R. Yisra'el Yitsḥaq of Rozenberg family. Pyótrkow: Mordekhai Tsederboim, 1914.

Ḥokhmes Shloyme ha-Meylekh [Yiddish], translated by Yosef Y'avets. Warsaw: Avraham Yosef Klaiman, 1914; Piotrków: Libeskind, 1914.

Segules u-Refu'es. Łódź: Yitsḥaq Shlomovits, 1914; Przemyśl: Amkraut et Fraynd, 1914. Yiddish translation of *Refa'el ha-Mal'aḥ.*

Sefer Tiferet Mahar'el mi Shpole. Piótrkow: Shlomo Belkhatovsky, 1914.

1915

"A Brif fun Poylishn Rov vegn di Basar Kosher Frage." *THJ*, January 3, 1915.
"Etlikhe Verter fun Rabi Rosenberg vegn Toronter Kashrus." *THJ*, January 23, 1915, 2.
"Fun ha-Rov Rosenberg Toronto." *KA*, April 1, 1915.

1916

"A Brif fun ha-Rav Y. Rosenberg." *THJ*, March 23, 1916, 3, 5.
"Der Maharal mi-Prag." *THJ*, April 17, 1916.
"Hodu'ah vegn Basar Kosher." *THJ*, August 17, 1916.
"Mikveh fir Kontri 'Iden." *THJ*, November 27, 1916.

1917

Miqveh Yehuda. Toronto: n.p., 1917–1919[?].
"A Ma'asele fun Midrash." *THJ*, April 6, 1917.

1918

"An Erklerung fun Rabi Rosenberg." *THJ*, February 3, 1918.

1919

Sefer ha-Qeri'ah ha-Qedosha Hu Shulḥan 'Arukh 'al Halakhot u-Minhagim shel Qeri'at ha-Torah. New York: Rosenberg Printing Company, 5679.
Seder Haqqafot le-Shmini Atseret ule-Simḥat Torah. Montreal: Keneder Adler Press, 1919.
Der Shpoler Zayde. Łódź: J. Przemiarover, 1919; Warsaw: B. Lewin-Epstein, 1919.
"A Brif mit an Antwort." *KA*, February 27, 1919, 5.

1920

Der Mal'aḥ Refa'el ... Segulot zu Alerlei Krankheiten. Przemyśl: S. Freund, 1920[?].
Di Geshikhte Nifla'os Maharal mit dem Golem: A Historishe Bashraybung. Warsaw: Aaron Cylingold, 1920.
Sefer Refa'el ha-Mal'aḥ. Łódź: Yitsḥaq Shlomovits, 1920[?].
Tif'eret Mahar'el mi-Shpole. Łódź: A. Przemiarover, 1920[?]; Warsaw: Sikora i Milner, 1920[?].
Der Shpoler Zayde. Warsaw: Abraham Cylingold, 1920[?].
Der Greiditser. Łódź: Yitsḥaq Shlomovits, 1920[?]; Piotrków: Shlomo Belkhatovsky, 1920[?].
Sefer Segulot u-Refu'ot. Łódź: Yitsḥaq Shlomovits, 1920[?].
Haggada shel Pesaḥ 'im Perush R. Yehuda Liva'. Warsaw: Y. Knoster, 1920[?].

Sefer Refu'at ha-Nefesh u-Refu'at ha-Guf. Warsaw: Abraham Cylingold, 1920[?].
Ale Ma'yses fun Eliyohu ha-Navi'. Warsaw: Abraham Cylingold, 1920[?].

1921

"Number 1", Sha'arei Torah 11, number 3 (1921).
"Azhara." *KA*, February 9, 1921.
"Matamim zum Talmud Torah Kampyn." *KA*, February 22, 1921.
"Pesaḥdike Hekhsherim." *KA*, April 17, 1921.
"Kosher Gebeks." *KA*, May 13, 1921.
"A Sharfer Protest gegn Ḥillul Shabbat in Montreal fun Rabbi Rosenberg." *KA*, November 6, 1921.

1922

"Statement vegn di Montrealer 'Oyfes Shoḥtim." *KA*, February 6, 1922.
"Le-Kavod Purim di Droshe le-Parshat Zakhor." *KA*, February 14, 1922.
"Vegn Sheḥitat 'Oyfes." *KA*, June 18, 1922.
"Kol Qore."" *KA*, July 4, 1922.
"Yom Kippur Qaton." *KA*, August 20, 1922.
"Mayn Erklerung vegn Basor Kosher." *KA*, September 10, 1922.

1924

Sefer Zohar Torah, 5 volumes. New York: Trio Pressin, 1924–1926. The volumes were evidently published in the years 1924–1926, if one follows the date of the copyright in Washington, D.C. Exodus, Numbers, and Leviticus were copyrighted 1925, Genesis and Deuteronomy in 1926. Subsequent printings in 1955, 1967, 1970, 1990, 2013.
Me'or ha-Ḥashmal She'ela u-Teshuva 'al Dvar Me'or ha-Elektrin be-Shabat ve-Yom Tov. Montreal: Rapid Printing Co., 1924. Reprinted 1929, 1990.
A Brivele Fun di Zisse Mame Shabbes Malkesa zu Ihre Zin und Tehter fun Idishn Folk. Montreal: City Printing Co., 1924.

1925

Yadot Nedarim: Ve-Hu Be'ur Maspiq 'al Kol ke-Lomar asher be-Ferush Rashi uva-Ran ... uvi-She'ar Meqomot ... shebe-Masekhet Nedarim. Warsaw: Y. Knoster, 1925.
"Shoḥatim u-Memartim, Memartim ve-Shoḥatim." *Apirion* 2 (5685/1925): 19–20.

1926

Der Shpoler Zayde. Łódź: n.p. 1926.
"Di Ekzamens in der Higer Yeshive." *KA*, March 26, 1926.
"Zakhrenu le-Ḥayyim!" *KA*, August 29, 1926.

1927

Nifla'ot ha-Zohar. Montreal: City Printing Company, 1927. Subsrquent printings 1967, 1968, 1969, 1986, 1989.
"Kaved Lev Par'o." *KA*, February 13, 1927.
"Oyfruf fun Rabi Rosenberg." *KA*, March 14, 1927, 6.
"Hakhasha." *KA*, April 15, 1927.

1928

"Meshulaḥ fun Yeshivas Ohel Moshe Yerushalyim a Gast in Montreal." *KA*, November 23, 1928.

1929

Sefer ha-Zohar ha-Qadosh, vol. 6 on Psalms. Bilgoraj: Braci Wajnberg, 1929. This volume is a continuation of *Zohar Torah* (1924). The inner page indicates that the actual printing was done by Sz. Sikora and I. Milner of Nowolipki 6 in Warsaw. For subsequent printings see *Zohar Torah* (1924).
Me'or ha-Ḥashmal She'ela u-Teshuva 'al Dvar Me'or ha-Elektrin be-Shabat ve-Yom Tov. Jerusalem: Sha'arei Tsion, 1929. Revised version of 1924 publication presented as a supplement to the monthly *Sha'arei Tsion.*
Der Mal'aḥ Refa'el. Przemyśl: S. Fraynd, 1929[?].
"Davar ha-Ne'esar be-Minyan." *Pardes* 3, no. 9 (December 1929): 12–13.

1930

Sefer ha-Zohar ha-Qadosh, vol. 7 on Song of Songs, Proverbs, and Ecclesiastes. Bilgoraj: Braci Wajnberg, 5690 (1930). The actual printing was done by Sz. Sikora and I. Milner of Nowolipki 6 in Warsaw. For subsequent printings see *Zohar Torah* (1924).
Segulot u-Refu'ot. Jerusalem: Shlomovits, 1930[?]; Łódź, Y. Shlomovits, 1930[?].
Refa'el ha-Mal'aḥ. Jerusalem and Tel-Aviv: Shlomovits, 1930[?].
Der Greiditser. Łódź: Y. Shlomovits, 1930[?].
Vunderlike Moftim vos hot Bavayzen R. Leyb Shpoler. Łódź: Y. Psemiarover, 1930[?].
"Teqi'at Shofar be-Kol Radio" *Pardes* 4, no. 7 (October 1930): 12–14.

1931

Sefer 'Ateret Tif'eret. New York: Reznick Menshil, 1931.
"Be-'Inyan Natan Se'a ve-Natal Se'a." *Pardes* 4, no, 12 (Adar 5691): 5
"Birkat 'Av," preface to Meir Joshua Rosenberg, *Kur ha-Mivḥan.* Siene: n.p., 1931.
"Vending zum Montrealer 'Identum fun Rabi Rosenberg." *KA*, February 24, 1931.
"Entfer oyf der Zohar Kritik." *KA*, March 31, 1931.

"Kol Qore' vegn dem Envelop Kampayn be-Yeme ha-Nora'im far di Fareynigte T"T." *KA*, September 7, 1931.

1932

"Ḥurban un Oyfbau." *Unzer Gajst* (Zamosc) 3, no. 8 (1932), 5–7.
"Azhara Gedola vegen Sheḥitas 'Oyfes." *KA*, February 17, 1932.
"Vegn dem Talmud Torah Kampayn." *KA*, March 14, 1932.
"A Refarat." *Der Shtern* (Montreal), April 8, 1932, 3.
"Bakantmakhung vegen Rokeaḥs Artiklen." *KA*, April 17, 1932.
"Der Va'ad ha-'Ir." *KA*, October 21, 1932, 1.

1933

"Has Kategor." *Unzer Gajst* (Zamosc) 4 (1933), no. 10, 17.
"Oyfruf fun Va'ad ha-Rabonim vegen di Farmakhte Talmud Toyres." *KA*, January 20, 1933.

1934

Sefer Omer va-Da'at. Piotrkow: Ḥanokh Henikh Folman, 5694. This book was not printed. Page-proofs found in RFA. It was published in part in 1996, and in full in 2007 and 2020.

1935

Peri Yehuda: Ḥidushim Perushim 'al Ḥamishah Ḥumshe Torah 'al pi Pardes Bilgoraj: Szloma Wajnberg, 1935. Subsequent printing, 1991.
"Hakḥasha fun ha-Rav Yudel Rosenberg." *KA*, March 17, 1935.
"Hodo'a meha-Rav Yudel Rosenberg." *KA*, May 26, 1935.
"Haskama" to Yehuda Leyb Mendelson, *Masekhet 'Eduyot Beḥirta.* Warsaw: Shlomo Shtainsaltz, 1935.

1940

Der Greiditser. Jerusalem: B. Motzen, 1940[?].

1944

Refa'el ha-Mal'aḥ. Jerusalem: Bet 'Eked Sefarim, 1944.

1950

Ale Ma'yses fun Eliyohu ha-Navi'. New York: Mifitzei Sefarim be-'Ivri Taytsh, 5710 (1950).
Refu'at ha-Nefesh u-Refu'at ha-Guf. Brooklyn: Shlomo Yosef Meisels, 1950.

1951

Sefer Ḥoshen ha-Mishpat. Jerusalem: Hershkovitz, 1951.
Tiferet Mahar'el mi-Shpole. Jerusalem: Hershkovitz, 1951.
Sefer Nifla'ot Maharal. Jerusalem: Hershkovitz, 1951.
Haggada shel Pesaḥ 'im Perush R. Yehuda Liva'. Brooklyn: Shraga, 1951.

1953

Sefer Eliyahu ha-Navi'. Jerusalem: Hershkovitz, 5713 (1953).

1954

"Derush le-Kol Nidrei." In Aaron Elimelech Rosenberg, *Liqqutei Beit Aharon*, 46–47. Montreal: Friedman, 1954.
"Derush le-Rosh ha-Shana." In Aaron Elimelech Rosenberg, *Likkutei Beit Aharon*, 44–45. Montreal: Friedman, 1954.

1955

Sefer Zohar Torah, 7 volumes. New York: Rosalg Corp., 1955.

1956

Yadot Nedarim: Ve-Hu Be'ur Maspiq 'al Kol ke-Lomar asher be-Ferush Rashi uva-Ran ... uvi-She'ar Meqomot ... shebe-Masekhet Nedarim. New York: Glass, 1956.
Sefer Yadot Nedarim, edited by Rabbi Eli'ezer Ze'ev Dvorets. Tel-Aviv: Defus ha-Po'el ha-Mizraḥi, 1956.

1958

Ale Ma'yses fun Eliyohu ha-Navi'. New York: S. Y. Meizlitz, 1958.

1960

Der Shpoler Zayde. Brooklyn: Yerushalayim, 1960.
Der Rambam. Jerusalem: n.p., 1960.

Sefer Refa'el ha-Mal'aḥ. Jerusalem: n.p., 1960.
Haggada shel Pesaḥ 'im Perush R. Yehuda Liva'. London: Ha-Ḥinukh, 1960.

1961

Nifla'os Maharal mit dem Goylem. Williamsburg: A. A. Kraus, 1961.

1962

Der Greiditser. Jerusalem: Di Ḥaredishe 'Idishe Bibliotek, 1962.

1963

Refa'el ha-Mal'aḥ. Tel-Aviv: Leon, 1963.

1964

Sefer Ḥokhmat Shlomo ha-Melekh. Jerusalem: S. Monson, 5724 (1964).
Sefer Eliyahu ha-Navi': Mahadurah Ḥadashah u-Metuqenet. Tel-Aviv: Leon, 1964.
Haggada shel Pesaḥ 'im Perush R. Yehuda Liva'. Jerusalem: Defus 'Erez, 1964.

1965

Sefer Refael ha-Mal'aḥ. Jerusalem: n.p., 1965.
Sefer Goral ha-'Assiriyot, edited by Me'ir ben Yitsḥaq Bakal. Jerusalem: Bakal, 1965)

1966

Sefer Refael ha-Mal'aḥ. Jerusalem[?]: n.p., 1966[?].
Ale Ma'yses fun Eliyohu ha-Navi'. Jerusalem: Even Yisra'el, 1966[?].

1967

Zohar Torah, 3 volumes. Jerusalem: 'Am 'Olam, 1967.
Sefer Nifla'ot ha-Zohar. Jerusalem: Pninei Even, 1967.
Refu'at ha-Nefesh u-Refu'at ha-Guf. Williamsburg, Brooklyn: A. A. Kraus, 1967.
Refa'el ha-Mal'aḥ. Jerusalem[?]: n.p., 1967.

1968

Sefer Nifla'ot Maharal. Jerusalem: n.p., 1968.
Der Rambam. New York: Tif'eret Ya'aqov, 1968.
Sefer Nifla'ot ha-Zohar. Jerusalem: Pninei Even, 1968.

1969

Tif'eret Mahar'el mi-Shpole. Jerusalem[?]: n.p., 1969.
Nifl'aot ha-Zohar. Brooklyn: Emunah, 1969.

1970

Zohar Torah, 3 volumes. New York: 'Otsar ha-Sefarim, 1970.

1971

Haggada shel Pesaḥ 'im Perush R. Yehuda Liva'. Jerusalem: n.p., 1971.

1972

Di Geshikhte Nifloes Maharal mit dem Goylem. Williamsburg, Brooklyn: Shmiress Shabes, 1972.
Sefer Refa'el ha-Mal'aḥ. Brooklyn: A. A. Kraus, 1972.

1974

Eliyahu ha-Navi' Zaḥur la-Tov. Jerusalem: Bakal, 1974.

1975

Sefer Tif'eret Mahar'el mi-Shpole. New York: 'Ateret, 1975.
Sefer Eliyahu ha-Navi'. Jerusalem: Bakal, 1975.
Sefer Ḥoshen ha-Mishpat. Union City, NJ: Gross Brothers, 1975.

1976

Sefer Refa'el ha-Mal'aḥ. Bnei Brak: Mesorah, 1976.

1980

The Golem of Prague: A New Adaption of the Documented Stories of the Golem of Prague with an Introductory Overview by Gershon Winkler; illustrated by Yochanan Jones. New York: Judaica Press, 1980. This is an English translation and adaptation of *Sefer Nifla'ot Maharal mi-Prag 'im ha-Golem*.

Sefer Divrei ha-Yamim asher le-Shlomo ha-Melekh. Jerusalem: Siaḥ Yisrael, 1980.

1982

Sefer Divre ha-Yamim asher li-Shelomoh ha-Melekh. Ashdod: 'Amos Hakohen, 1982.

1984

Sefer Refa'el ha-Mal'aḥ. New York: Beit Hillel, 1984.

Haggada shel Pesaḥ 'im Perush R. Yehuda Liva'. Jerusalem: Sefarim Toraniim, 1984.

1985

Sefer Ḥoshen ha-Mishpat shel ha-Kohen ha-Gadol. Brooklyn: 'A. Shanoyiṭsh, 1985.

Sefer Divre ha-Yamim asher li-Shelomoh ha-Melekh. Brooklyn: Beit Hillel, 1985.

Sefer Eliyahu ha-Navi'. Brooklyn: Beit Hillel, 1985.

1986

Yadot Nedarim: Ve-Hu Be'ur Maspiq 'al Kol ke-Lomar asher be-Ferush Rashi uva-Ran … uvi-She'ar Meqomot … shebe-Masekhet Nedarim. Jerusalem: n.p., 5746.

'Al Masekhet Nedarim: Tosafot Yeshanim. Jerusalem: n.p., 1986. This edition *Yadot Nedarim*.

Sefer Eliyahu ha-Navi'. Tifrah: M. Velman, 1986. Also published in Yiddish as *Ale Ma'yses fun Eliyohu ha-Navi'*. Brooklyn: Beit Hillel, 1986.

Der Rambam. Brooklyn: Beit Hillel, 1986.

Sefer Refa'el ha-Mal'aḥ. Jerusalem: Bakal, 1986. Also published in Yiddish as *Der Mal'aḥ Refa'el*. Jerusalem: Bakal, 1986.

Sefer Nifla'ot ha-Zohar. Brooklyn: Beit Hillel, 1986.

1987

Nifla'ot ha-Maharal: Ve-Hu 'Inyene ha-Golem mi-Prag. Jerusalem: n.p., 1987.

Der Shpoler Zayde. Brooklyn: Beit Hillel, 1987.

Der Rambam. Brooklyn: Beit Hillel, 1987.

1988

Qovets Ma'amar Yehudah, edited by Baruch Rosenberg. Toronto: Baruch Rosenberg, 1988. This edition includes a *Discourse on Tefillin* by Rabbi Yudel Rosenberg from an unpublished manuscript.

'Ets Yehudah: Ve-Hu kol Kitve Yehudah Yudl Rozenberg, edited by Baruch Rosenberg. Toronto: Baruch Rosenberg 1988.

Der Greiditser. Brooklyn: Beit Hillel, 1988.

Sefer Nifla'ot ha-Zohar [Yiddish], translated by Rabbi Benjamin Greenberg. Jerusalem: n.p., 1988.

1989

Agadot ha-Zohar, edited by M. Ts. Parush. Tel Aviv: Moriyah, 1989.

Qovets Ma'amar Yehuda: Collected Discourses of Rabbi Yehuda Yudel Rosenberg Zt"l, part 2: *Commentary on the Book of Jonah According to the Zohar,* edited by Baruch Rosenberg. Toronto: Eitz Yehuda Publishing Society, 1989.

Haggada shel Pesaḥ 'im Perush R. Yehuda Liva'. Brooklyn: Beit Hillel, 1989.

1990

Me'or ha-Ḥashmal. New York: n.p., 1990[?].

Sefer Zohar Torah, 3 volumes. Tel-Aviv: Mif'alei Sefarim le-Yitsu, 1990.

1991

Sefer Zohar: Tiqqunim Ḥadashim. Jerusalem: Ben-Shai, 1991. This edition also includes writings of Moshe Ḥayyim Luzzatto.

Peri Yehuda: Ḥidushim Perushim 'al Ḥamishah Ḥumshe Torah 'al pi Pardes. Brooklyn: Katz Bookbinding, 1991.

Ha-Golem mi-Prag u-Ma'asim Nifla'im Aḥerim, edited with an introduction by Eli Yassif. Jerusalem: Mossad Bialik, 1991.

1992

Kol Torah. Kiryat Yoel, Monroe, NY: n.p., 1992.

1994

Der Ḥoshen Mishpat. Jerusalem: M. Mandel, 1994.

1995

Sefer Goral ha-'Assiriyot. Jerusalem: Me'ir ben Yitsḥaq Bakal, 1995. Yudel Rosenberg is not mentioned in connection with this edition.

1996

Yabi'a Omer: Ḥamishim Derushim 'al Kol ha-Mo'adim ve-Shabbatot ha-Meyuhasin ve-'al kol Me'orot ha-Mitragshot la-Vo' le-Kehillot Yisra'el. Jerusalem: Hotsa'ah Meyuḥedet le-Nisu'e ben Nino, 1996–2005. This is a photo-offset edition from the original page-proofs dated Piotrków, 1934.

Rachel Friedman. *Le Maharal de Prague: Rabbi Yéhouda Liva Fils de Rabbi Betsalel de Prague,* translated and edited by Ḥanokh ben Moché. Jerusalem[?]: Ḥedva, 1996[?]. As indicated in this book, its stories are based on "*Niflaoth Maharal* ... composed by Youdel Rozenberg."

Sefer Refa'el ha-Mal'aḥ. Jerusalem: A. Klein, 1996.

Tif'eret Maharal mi-Shpoli: Ha-Qar'ui Der Shpoler Zayde. Jerusalem: Mekor ha-Sefarim, 1996.

Seder Haqqafot le-Shmini Atseret ule-Simḥat Torah. ... Kemo she-Ne'emru be-Veyt Midrasho shel ... Pinḥas mi-Korets. In *Qovets Siftei Tsaddiqim: Me'asef le-Torat ha-Ḥasidut Pirsum Geniza ve-Ḥeqer Toldoteha* 8 (Adar, 5756). Jerusalem: Merkaz Torani "Ohev Yisrael," 1996.

1997

Tiferet Mahar'el: Tales about R. Aryeh Leib of Spola [Hebrew], edited and with an introduction by Gedalyah Nigal. Jerusalem: Karmel, 1997.

2000

Sefer Refa'el ha-Mal'aḥ. Jerusalem: Yerid ha-Sefarim, 2000.

2001

Dinei Prozbul, edited and with additional notes by Meir Yehoshua Ben Meir. Jerusalem[?]:Meir Yehoshua Ben-Me'ir, 2001.

2004

Qeri'ah ha-Qedoshah: Ve-Hu Shulḥan 'Arukh 'al Hilkhot u-Minhagim shel Qeri'at ha-Torah, edited and with additional notes by Meir Yehoshua Ben Meir. Jerusalem: Me'ir Yehoshu'a ben Me'ir, 2004. Special edition to celebrate the enagagement of Navah Tehila and Avishai Sorek.

Seder Haqqafot. New York: Aharon Ary b. R. Yehudah Yudl Broida; Lakewood, NJ: Mekhon Be'er ha-Torah, 2004.

2005

Sefer Ḥokhmat ha-Yad veha-Partsuf. Jerusalem: Mosedot Or Yisrael, 2005. Includes Rosneberg's *Ziv ha-Zohar* commentary among others.

Seder Haqqafot. Jerusalem: Yeshivat Shevut Yisrael, 2005.

2007

Sefer Omer va-Da'at. Photocopy of 1934 page-proofs. Titlepage has added "By Ḥayyim 5767." http://www.hebrewbooks.org/5757.

The Golem and the Wondrous Deeds of the Maharal of Prague, translated, edited, and with an introduction and notes by Curt Leviant. New Haven: Yale University Press, 2007.

2008

Yadot Nedarim: Ve-Hu Be'ur Maspiq 'al Kol ke-Lomar asher be-Ferush Rashi uva-Ran ... uvi-She'ar Meqomot ... shebe-Masekhet Nedarim. Bnei Brak: Or ha-Ḥayyim, 2008.

Dinei Prozbul, with additional notes by Meir Yehoshua Ben-Meir. Efrat: Meir Yehoshua Ben-Meir, 2008.

2009

Ḥumash 'Otsar Midrashei ha-Zohar ha-Mevo'ar. Jerusalem: Makhon ha-Zohar ha-Mevo'ar she-'a"y Hatsalat ha-No'ar Tif'eret Baḥurim, 2009. Includes *Ziv ha-Zohar.*

2013

Zohar Torah, 7 volumes. Jerusalem: Makhon Bnei Moshe, 2013.

El gólem i els fets miraculosos del Maharal de Praga [Catalan]. Martorell: Adesiara, 2013.

2014

Mah Nokhal ba-Shana ha-Shevi'it. Efrat: Makhon le-Ḥeqer ule-Halakha she-'a"y Yeshivat Shevut Yisra'el, 2014. Includes Rosenberg's *Seder Prozbul* with additional notes by Meir Yehoshua Ben-Meir.

2015

Sefer Yadot Nedarim ha-Shalem. Jerusalem: Ha-Makhon le-Halakha u-Meḥqar she-ʿa"y Yeshivat Shevut Yisra'el, 2015. Includes excerpts from Rosenberg's *Kol Torah* (1908) as well as an undated manuscript sermon on "Kamtsa u-bar Kamtsa" including a photograph of the manuscript, 293–298.

2020

Omer va-Daʿat, 2 volumes. Jerusalem: Mossad ha-Rav Kook, 2020.

General Bibliography

I. ARCHIVAL DOCUMENTS

Jerusalem, Israel

Ben-Meir Family Archive

Schocken Library

- Rabbi Moshe Naḥum Yerusalimsky Papers

Montreal, Canada

Alex Dworkin Canadian Jewish Archives

- Jewish Community Council of Montreal
- P0073 Gordon, Rabbi Jacob

Archives de Montréal

- file on Municipal Bylaw 828, 1922–1924

Jewish Public Library, Jewish Canadiana Collection: Yehuda Rosenberg

- Anonymous, Memorandum [on the Rosenberg Family]
- Notebook

Jewish Public Library Archives

- *Ilan* Fonds 1399
- Reuben Brainin Papers

Quebec Ministry of Justice Archives, Montreal

- S.C. Montreal 3312 Getzel Laxer et al. vs. Jewish Butchers Society of Montreal et al.

Private Archive of Mr. Lionel Albert.

Cincinnati, USA

American Jewish Archives

- Simon Glazer Papers

New York, USA

YIVO Archives

- Circular on behalf of R. Hayyim Mendel Landau, a Candidate for the Łódź Rabbinate in 1912, RG28 Lodz#19.

Ottawa, Canada

Library and Archives Canada

- Microfilm Reel T-4801/ RG 76/ Item Number: 6302. http://www.bac-lac.gc.ca/eng/discover/immigration/immigration-records/passenger-lists/passenger-lists-1865-1922/Pages/item.aspx?IdNumber=6302&.
- Naturalization Lists. http://central.bac-lac.gc.ca/.item/?id=P20-21_541&op=pdf&app=naturalization19151936.

Savannah, USA

Rosenberg Family Archive[1]

Tel-Aviv, Israel

Arkhion Histori, Iriyat Tel-Aviv-Yaffo

- Rabbi Benzion Uziel Papers 8/1018

II. INTERVIEWS

Interview with Leah Rosenberg, January 28, 1987.

III. WEBSITES

il.bidspirit.com

- Bidspirit auction 3455, lot 130363. Letter of Yudel Rosenberg to Yosef Haim Sonnenfeld, 13 Tishrei, 5686 (October 1, 1925).
- Bidspirit auction 4180, lot 114694. Letter of Yudel Rosenberg to Yitsḥaq Gershenkorn, 5 Adar 5691 (February 22, 1931).

Historical Jewish Press. http://web.nli.org.il/sites/JPress/English/Pages/default.aspx.
Jewish Records Indexing—Poland https://jri-poland.org/jriplweb.htm.
The YIVO Encyclopedia of Jews in Eastern Europe. http://www.yivoencyclopedia.org/.

IV. SECONDARY SOURCES

Mayer S. Abramowitz, "Toronto Sages: Prominent Rabbis of Blessed Memory." http://www.bill-gladstone.ca/?p=10027. Accessed February 19, 2019.

H. J. Adler. "Some Halakhic Aspects of Electricity." In H. J. Adler, *The Blessing of Eliyahu*, 197–210. London: Bet ha-Midrash Golders Green, 1982.

---

1 This archive was consulted by the author in the 1990s when it was located in the home of the widow of Rabbi Abraham Isaac Rosenberg, Rabbi Yudel Rosenberg's youngest son in Savannah, Georgia. Photocopies of these documents are in the possession of the author.

Aaron Ze'ev Aescoly. *Hasidism in Poland* [Hebrew]. Jerusalem: Magnes Press, 1998.

Yitzhak Alfasi. *Glimpses of Jewish Warsaw*, translated and edited by Avraham Yaakov Finkel. New York and Jerusalem: CIS, 1992.

Meir Amsel. *Encyclopedia Hamaor.* Brooklyn, NY: Hamaor, 1986.

David Assaf. "Ḥasidut Polin be Me'ah ha-19: Matsav ha-Meḥqar u-Sekira Bibliografit." In *Hasidism in Poland*, edited by Raḥel Elior, Yisrael Bartal, and Chone Shmeruk, 357–379. Jerusalem: Bialik Institute, 1994.

——. "Hebetim Historiim ve-Ḥevratimim be-Ḥeker ha-Ḥasidut." In *Tsaddiq and Devotees: Historical and Sociological Aspects of Hasidism* [Hebrew], edited by David Assaf. Jerusalem: Zalman Shazar Center for Jewish History, 2001.

Shlomo Zalman Auerbach. *Ḥiddushim 'al Shev Shemateta.* Jerusalem: Yeshiva Sha'ar ha-Shamayim, 1990.

——. *Sefer Me'orei 'Esh/Kollel Ḥiqrei Halakhot Hiddushim u-Bi'urim be-'Inyanim Shonim ha-Nog'im le-'Inyan Me'or ha-'Elektria be-Shabbat ve-Yom Tov.* Jerusalem: Defus Salomon, 1934. Reprinted Jerusalem: Moriyah, 1980.

——. *Minḥat Shlomo*, 3 volumes. Jerusalem: Mekhon Sha'arei Ziv, 1986–1989.

Ira Axelrod. *Seventy-Five Years of Chassidic Life in America: The Story of the Bostoner Rebbes, an Authorized History.* Brookline, MA: New England Chassidic Center, 1990[?].

Yossi Azose. "The Use of Municipal City Water for a Mikveh and a Case Study of the Seattle Rabbinate in the 1950s." https://merrimackvalleyhavurah.files.wordpress.com/2017/08/municipal-city-tap-water-for-a-mikveh-rabbi-yossi-azose.pdf. Accessed February 17, 2019.

Gershon C. Bacon. "Birthpangs of the Messiah: The Reflections of Two Polish Rabbis on Their Era." In *Jews and Messianism in the Modern Era: Mataphor and Meaning. Studies in Contemporary Judaism, an Annual* 7 (1991): 86–99.

——. "Enduring Prestige, Eroding Authority: The Warsaw Rabbinate in the Interwar Period." In *Warsaw. The Jewish Metropolis: Essays in Honor of the 75th Birthday of Professor Antony Polonsky*, edited by Glenn Dynner and François Guesnet, 347–369. Leiden: Brill, 2015.

——. "Ha-Ḥevra ha-Mesoratit be-Temurot ha-'Itim: Hebetim be-Toldot ha-Yahadut ha-Ortodoqsit be-Polin uve-Rusya, 1850–1939." In *Kiyum va-Shever: Yehudei Polin le-Dorotehem*, edited by Israel Bartal and Yisrael Gutman, vol. 2, 453–491. Jerusalem: Merkaz Zalman Shazar, 2001.

——."Perlmutter, Abraham Tsevi." *YIVO Encyclopedia of Jews in Eastern Europe.* http://www.yivoencyclopedia.org/article.aspx/Perlmutter_Avraham_Tsevi. Accessed May 19, 2015.

——. *The Politics of Tradition: Agudat Yisrael in Poland, 1916–1939.* Jerusalem: Magnes Press, 1996.

——. "Warsaw-Radom-Vilna: Three Disputes Over Rabbinical Posts in Interwar Poland." *Jewish History* 13 (1999): 103–126.

Meir Bar-Ilan. "The Miracles of R. Yehuda Yudel Rozenberg" [Hebrew]. *'Alei Sefer* 19 (2001): 173–184.

Haya Bar-Itzhak. *Jewish Poland: Legends of Origin.* Detroit: Wayne State University Press, 2001.

Wladysław Bartoszewski and Antony Polonsky. *The Jews in Warsaw: A History.* Oxford: Blackwell, 1991.

Maya Barzilai. *Golem: Modern Wars and Their Monsters.* New York: New York University Press, 2016.

Ela Bauer. "In Warsaw and Beyond: The Contribution of Hayim Zelig Slonimski to Jewish Modernization." In *Warsaw. The Jewish Metropolis: Essays in Honor of the 75th Birthday of Professor Antony Polonsky*, edited by Glenn Dynner and Francois Guesnet, 70–90. Leiden and Boston: Brill, 2015.

N. Baumeil. "Ha-Rav R. Yehuda (Yudel) Rosenberg." In *Talmud Torah "Eitz Chaim" Jubilee Book*, 104–119. Toronto: n.p., 1943.

Eliezer Baumgarten, Uri Safrai, and J. S. Chajes. "'He Saw the Entire World Resembling a Ladder': Rabbi Yehoshua ben Rabbi David of Kurdistan's Kabbalistic Tree" [Hebrew]. In *Meir Benayahu Memorial Volume*, edited by Moshe Bar-Asher, Yehuda Liebes, Moshe Assis, and Yosef Kaplan, vol. 2, 843–871. Jerusalem: Yad ha-Rav Nissim, 2019.

Yehoshua Ben-Meir, "ha-Rav Yehuda Yudel Rosenberg zts"l veha-Haggada she Pesaḥ shel ha-Maharal," *ha-Me'ayen* 61, 2, no. 236 Tevet, 5781 [2021]: 105–111.

David Ben-Naeh. "R. Ḥayyim Ḥizkia Medini: Posek u-Meḥanekh Sefardi be-'Idan shel Temurot." In David Ben-Naeh, *Mayim mi-Dalyo*, 209–221. Jerusalem: Mikhlelet Lipshitz, 1996.

Guy Ben-Porat. *Between State and Synagogue: The Secularization of Contemporary Israel*. Cambridge: Cambridge University Press, 2013.

Mordecai Ben Yehezkel. "Sefer 'va-Yehe ha-Yom.'" In *Byalik: Yetsirato le-Sugeha bi-Re'i ha-Biqoret: Antologyah*, edited by Gershon Shaked, 337–372. Jerusalem: Mossad Bialik, 1974.

Abraham Benedict. "Hagadat Maharal o Aggadat Maharal?" *Moriah* 14, nos. 3–4 (1985): 102–113.

Jay R. Berkovitz. "The Persona of a Poseq: Law and Self-Fashioning in Seventeenth-Century Ashkenaz." *Modern Judaism* 32, no. 3 (October 2012): 251–269.

David Biale, David Assaf, Benjamin Brown, Uriel Gellman, Samuel Heilman, Moshe Rosman, Gadi Sagiv, Marcin Wodziński, and Arthur Green. *Hasidism: A New History*. Princeton: Princeton University Press, 2018.

Yoram Bilu. "Refu'a Mesoratit be-Qerev Yotse'i Maroko." In *Jews of the Middle East: Anthropological Perspectives on Past and Present*, edited by Shlomo Deshen and Moshe Shokeid, 166–175. Tel-Aviv: Schocken, 1984.

Menahem Blondheim, "Vela-Shom'im Yin'am: Ha-Derasha ha-Ortodoqsit be-Artsot ha-Berit beyn Ḥeyza Rabanit le-Bikush 'Amami." In *Ha-Tarbut ha-'Amami: Qovets Ma'amarim*, edited by B. Z. Kedar, 277–304. Jerusalem: Merkaz Zalman Shazar, 1996.

———. "Ha-Rabanut ha-Ortodoqsit Megale et Amerika: Ha-Geografia shel ha-Ruaḥ be-Mitavim shel Tiqshoret." In *Be-'Iqvot Kolumbus: Amerika, 1492–1992*, edited by M. Eliav-Feldon, 483–511. Jerusalem: Merkaz Zalman Shazar, 1997.

Gideon Bohak. "How Jewish Magic Survived the Disenchantment of the World." *Aries—Journal for the Study of Western Esotericism* 19 (2009): 7–37.

Yosef M. Boimel. "In Memoriam." In Yehoshua M. Boimel, *A Blaze in the Darkening Gloom: The Life of Rav Meir Shapiro*, xxi. Jerusalem: Feldheim, 1994.

Gerrit Bos. "Hayyim Vital's 'Practical Kabbalah and Alchemy': A 17th-Century Book of Secrets." *Journal of Jewish Thought and Philosophy* 4, no. 1 (1995): 55–112.

William G. Braude and Israel J. Kapstein. *Tanna Debe Eliyyahu: The Lore of the School of Elijah*. Philadelphia: Jewish Publication Society, 1981.

Mordecai Breuer. "Tradition and Change in European Yeshivot: 17th-19th Centuries." Paper delivered at Harvard Conference on "Tradition and Crisis," 1988.

———. "*Vikkuḥo shel Maharal mi-Prag 'im ha-Notsrim: Mabat Ḥadash 'al Sefer Be'er ha-Gola.*" *Tarbiz* 55 (1986): 253–260.

Alan Brill. *Thinking God: The Mysticism of Rabbi Zadok HaKohen of Lublin.* Hoboken, NJ: Ktav/ Yeshiva University Press, 2002.

Edward J. Bristow. *Prostitution and Prejudice: The Jewish Fight against White Slavery, 1870–1939.* New York: Schocken Books, 1983.

Jeffrey Brooks. *When Russia Learned to Read: Literacy and Popular Literature, 1861–1917.* Princeton: Princeton University Press, 1985.

Abraham Brosh. "Mikhtav 'Maqor' shel ha-Maharal mi-Prag." *Ha-Modi'a,* 20 Nisan 5750 (April 15, 1990).

Benjamin Brown. "'Ha-Ba'al Bayit: R. Yisrael Meir ha-Kohen, 'ha-Ḥafets Ḥayyim.'" In *The Gedoilim: Leaders Who Shaped the Israeli Haredi Society,* edited by Binyamin Brown and Nissim Leon, 105–151. Jerusalem: Magnes Press, 2017.

——. "Substitutes for Mysticism: a General Model for the Theological Development of Hasidism in the Nineteenth Century." *History of Religions* 56, no. 3 (February 2017): 247–287.

Michael Brown. *Jew or Juif? Jews, French Canadians, and Anglo-Canadians, 1759–1914.* Philadelphia: Jewish Publication Society, 1987.

Michael Broyde and Howard Jachter. "Electricity on Shabbat and Yom Tov." *Journal of Halacha and Contemporary Society* 21 (Spring 1991): 4–47. http://daat.co.il/daat/english/journal/broyde_1.htm.

Yael Buchman and Zohar Amar. *Practical Medicine of Rabbi Hayyim Vital (1543–1620): Healer in the Land of Israel and Vicinity.* Ramat-Gan: Bar-Ilan University, 2006.

Richard L. and Claudia L. Bushman. "The Early History of Cleanliness in America." *Journal of American History* 74, no. 4 (March 1988): 1213–1238.

Abraham Cahan. *The Rise of David Levinsky.* New York: Grosset and Dunlap, 1917.

Kimmy Caplan. "The Concerns of an Immigrant Rabbi: The Life and Sermons of Rabbi Moshe Shimon Sivitz." *Polin* 11 (1998): 192–215.

——. *Orthodoxy in the New World: Immigrant Rabbis and Preaching in America* [Hebrew]. Jerusalem: Zalman Shazar Center for Jewish History, 2002.

——. "Rabbi Isaac Margolis: From Eastern Europe to America" [Hebrew]. *Zion* 58, no. 2 (1993): 225–240.

J. H. Chajes. "Duchgelässige Grenzen: Die Visualierung Gottes zwischen jüdischer und christlicher Kabbala bei Knorr von Rosenroth und van Helmont." *Morgen-Glanz: Zeitschrift der Christian Knorr von Rosenroth-Gesellschaft,* ed. Rosemarie Zeller 27 (2017): 99–147.

——. "Kabbalah Practices / Practical Kabbalah: The Magic of Kabbalistic Trees." *Aries—Journal for the Study of Western Esotericism* 19 (2019): 112–145.

——. "'Too Holy to Print: Taboo Anxiety and the Printing of Practical Hebrew Esoterica." *Jewish History* 26 (2012): 247–262.

J. H. Chajes and Eliezer Baumgarten. "About Faces: Kabbalistic Visualizations of the Divine Visage in the Gross Family Collection." In *Windows on Jewish Worlds: Essays in Honor of William Gross, Collector of Judaica,* edited by Emile Schrijver, 73–83. Uitgeverig: Walburg Pers B.V., 2019.

Alfred S. Cohen. "Pruzbul." *Journal of Halacha and Contemporary Society* 28 (1994): 17–29.

Asher Cohen and Aaron Kampinsky. "Religious Leadership in Israel's Religious Zionism: The Board of Rabbis." *Jewish Political Studies Review* 18, nos. 3–4 (2006). http://jcpa.org/article/

religious-leadership-in-israel%E2%80%99s-religious-zionism-the-case-of-the-board-of-rabbis-2/.

Judah M. Cohen. "Trading Freedoms? Exploring Jewish Colonial Jewish Merchanthood between Europe and the Caribbean." In *American Jewry: Transcending the European Experience?*, edited by Christian Wiese and Cornelia Wilhelm, 47–63. London: Bloomsbury, 2017.

Nathan Cohen. "Distributing Knowledge: Warsaw as a Center of Jewish Publishing, 1850–1914." In *Warsaw. The Jewish Metropolis: Essays in Honor of the 75th Birthday of Professor Antony Polonsky*, edited by Glenn Dynner and Francois Guesnet, 180–206. Leiden and Boston: Brill, 2015.

Zvi Cohen, ed. *Sefer ha-Zikkaron le-Ḥag Yovel ha-Shiv'im shel ... R. Yehuda Rosenberg / Souvenir Dedicated to Rabbi Jehuda Rosenberg ... on the Occasion of His Seventieth Anniversary Jubilee.* Montreal: Keneder Adler Drukerei, 1931.

Levi Cooper. "D.I.Y. Mikveh: The Challenge of Encouraging Commitment." *Jewish Educational Leadership* 9, no. 2 (Winter 2011): 58–63.

——. "'Neged Zarmei ha-Mayim ha-Zedonim': Ha-Admor mi-Munkatsh R. Ḥayyim Elazar Shapira." In *The Gedoilim: Leaders Who Shaped the Israeli Haredi Society*, edited by Binyamin Brown and Nissim Leon, 259–291. Jerusalem: Magnes Press, 2017.

Arlette Corcos. *Montréal, les Juifs et l'École.* Sillery, QC: Septentrion, 1997.

Moses Cordovero. *Elimah Rabbati*, photo-offset of Brody, 1881 edition, edited by David ha-Kohen. Jerusalem, 1984.

Neil M. and Ruth Schwartz Cowan. *Our Parents' Lives: The Americanization of Eastern European Jews.* New York: Basic Books, 1989.

Yosef Dan. "The Beginnings of Hebrew Hagiographic Literature" [Hebrew]. *Jerusalem Studies in Jewish Folklore* 1 (1981): 82–101.

——. "A Bow to Frumkinian Hasidism." *Modern Judaism* 11 (1991): 175–193.

——. *Ha-Sippur ha-Ḥasidi.* Jerusalem: Keter, 1975.

——. *The Teachings of Hasidism.* New York: Behrman House, 1983.

Avraham David. "The Involvement of the Maharal of Prague in a Jewish-Christian Debate" [Hebrew]. *Kiryat Sefer* 64 (1992–1993): 1433–1434.

Marni Davis. *Jews and Booze: Becoming American in the Age of Prohibition.* New York: New York University Press, 2012.

Edan Dekel and David Gantt Gurley. "How the Golem Came to Prague." *Jewish Quarterly Review* 103, no. 2 (2013): 214–258.

——. "Kafka's Golem." *Jewish Quarterly Review* 107, no. 4 (Fall 2017): 531–556.

Nathaniel Deutsch. *The Jewish Dark Continent: Life and Death in the Russian Pale of Settlement.* Cambridge, MA: Harvard University Press, 2011.

Jacob I. Dienstag. "Maimonides in Yiddish Literature." *Yiddish* 7 (1987): 79–100.

Chaim Zalman Dimitrovsky. "On the Pilpulistic Method." In *Salo Wittmayer Baron Jubilee Volume on the Occasion of His Eightieth Birthday*, edited by Saul Lieberman and Arthur Hyman, vol. 3, 111–182. Jerusalem: American Academy for Jewish Research; New York: Columbia University Press, 1974.

Hasia Diner. *Roads Taken: The Great Jewish Migrations to the New World and the Peddlers Who Forged the Way.* New Haven: Yale University Press, 2015.

Simon Dubnow. *History of the Jews in Russia and Poland,* 3 volumes. Philadelphia: Jewish Publication Society, 1916–1920.

Deborah Dwork. "Immigrant Jews on the Lower East Side of New York, 1880–1914." In *The American Jewish Experience,* edited by Jonathan D. Sarna, 102–120. New York and London: Holmes and Meier, 1986.

Glenn Dynner. "The Garment of Torah: Clothing Decrees and the Warsaw Career of the First Gerrer Rebbe." In *Warsaw. The Jewish Metropolis: Essays in Honor of the 75th Birthday of Professor Antony Polonsky,* edited by Glenn Dynner and Francois Guesnet, 91–127. Leiden and Boston: Brill, 2015.

——. "Hasidism and Habitat: Managing the Jewish-Christian Encounter in the Kingdom of Poland." In *Holy Dissent: Jewish and Christian Mysitcs in Eastern Europe,* edited by Glenn Dynner, 104–131. Detroit: Wayne State University Press, 2011.

——. *Men of Silk: The Hasidic Conquest of Polish Jewish Society.* Oxford: Oxford University Press, 2006.

——. "Replenishing the 'Fountain of Judaism': Traditionalist Jewish Education in Interwar Poland." *Jewish History* 31, nos. 3–4 (2018): 229–261.

——. *Yankel's Tavern: Jews, Liquor, and Life in the Kingdom of Poland.* Oxford: Oxford University Press, 2014.

Emmanuel Eckstein. *Sefer Yetsira.* Marmorosszighet, 1910.

Azriel Eisenberg. *The Bar Mitzvah Treasury.* New York: Behrman, 1952.

Ben-Zion Eisenstadt. *Dorot ha-Aḥaronim,* part 3. New York: Rosenberg, 1915.

David Ellenson. "Rabbi Haim Hirschensohn: An Orthodox Rabbi Reponds to the Balfour Declaration." *American Jewish History* 101, no. 3 (July 2017): 247–269.

Yaakov Elman. "Rav Isaac Hutner's *Paḥad Yitzḥak*: A Torah Map of the Human Mind and Psyche in Changing Times." In *Books of the People: Revisiting Classic Works of Jewish Thought,* edited by Stuart W. Halpern, 303–343. New York: Maggid Books, 2017.

Menachem Elon. *Jewish Law: History, Sources, Principles,* 3 volumes. Philadelphia: Jewish Publication Society of America, 1994.

Lisa Epstein. "Caring for the Soul's House: The Jews of Russia and Health Care, 1860–1914." PhD diss., Yale University, 1995.

Immanuel Etkes, "Between Torah Scholarship and Rabbinate in Nineteenth-Century Lithuania" [Hebrew]. *Zion* 53 (1988): 385–403.

——. "Family and Torah Study in the Circles of *Lomdim* in Nineteenth-Century Lithuania" [Hebrew]. *Zion* 51 (1989): 87–106.

——. *The Gaon of Vilna: The Man and His Image.* Berkeley: University of California Press, 2002.

——. *Rabbi Israel Salanter and the Mussar Movement: Seeking the Torah of Truth.* Philadelphia: Jewish Publication Society, 1993.

——. "Talmudic Scholarship and the Rabbinate in Lithuanian Jewry during the Nineteenth Century." In *Scholars and Scholarship: The Interaction between Judaism and Other Cultures,* edited by Leo Landman, 107–132. New York: Yeshiva University Press, 1990.

——. "A Shtetl with a Yeshiva: The Case of Volozhin." In *The Shtetl: New Evaluations,* edited by Steven Katz, 39–52. New York: New York University Press, 2007.

Morris Faierstein. "Gershom Scholem and Hasidism." *Journal of Jewish Studies* 38, no. 2 (1987): 221–233.

Oscar Z. Fasman. "Trends in the American Yeshiva Today." *Tradition* 9, no. 3 (1967): 48–64.

Shmuel Feiner. *Haskalah and History: The Emergence of a Modern Jewish Historical Consciousness.* Oxford: Littman Library of Jewish Civilization, 2002.

Samuel Fine. *Yalkut Shmuel.* St. Louis: Salz and Gellman Publishing, 1935. http://www.hebrewbooks.org/pdf/yalkutshmuel.pdf. Accessed April 13, 2008.

Steven Fine. *The Menorah: From the Bible to Modern Israel.* Cambridge, MA: Harvard University Press, 2017.

Shim'on Fogel. "Pe'ilato ha-Safrutit shel R. Gershon Ḥanokh Henikh Leiner mi-Radzin." *Da'at* 68–69 (2010): 149–185.

Chaim Leib Fox, *100 Years of Hebrew and Yiddish Literature in Canada* [Yiddish]. Montreal: Adler, 1979).

——. "From the Poem 'Montreal'" [Yiddish]. *'Idisher Kempfer* (Pesaḥ 5740 [Spring 1980]).

Isser Frankel. *Rabi Meir Yeḥiel mi-Ostrovtsa: Ḥayyav, Shitato, ve-Torato.* Tel-Aviv: Netsaḥ, 1953.

Yeḥezkel Frankel, ed. *Sefer Imrei Pinḥas ha-Shalem.* Bnai Brak, 1988.

David Fraser. "The Blood Libel in North America: Jews, Law, and Citizenship in the Early 20th Century." *Law & Literature* 28, no. 1 (2016): 1–53.

——. *Honorary Protestants: The Jewish School Question in Montreal, 1867–1997.* Toronto: University of Toronto Press, 2015.

ChaeRan Y. Freeze. *Jewish Marriage and Divorce in Imperial Russia.* Hanover: University Press of New England, 2002.

Miri J. Freud-Kandel. *Orthodox Judaism in Britain since 1913: An Ideology Forgotten.* London: Valentine Mitchell, 2006.

Ḥaim Dov Friedberg. *Toledot ha-Defus ha-'Ivri be-Polania,* second edition. Tel-Aviv: Barukh Friedberg, 1950.

Menachem Friedman. "Haredim Confront the Modern City." *Studies in Contemporary Jewry* 2 (1986): 74–96.

——. *Ḥevrah va-Dat: ha-Ortodoqsia ha-lo' Tsionit be-Erets Yisra'el, 1918–1936.* Jerusalem: Yad Yitsḥaq Ben Zvi, 1977.

Susanne Galley. "Holy Men in Their Infancy: The Childhood of *Tsakidim* in Hasidic Legends." *Polin* 15 (2002): 169–186.

Jonathan Garb. *The Chosen Will Become Herds: Studies in Twentieth-Century Kabbalah* [Hebrew]. Jerusalem: Karmel, 2005.

——. *Kabbalist in the Heart of the Storm: R. Moshe Hayyim Luzzatto* [Hebrew]. Tel-Aviv: Ḥaim Rubin Tel Aviv University Press, 2014.

——. *Yearnings of the Soul: Psychological Thought in Modern Kabbala.* Chicago: University of Chicago Press, 2015.

Lloyd Gartner. *History of the Jews of Cleveland.* Cleveland: Western Reserve Historical Society and the Jewish Theological Seminary of America, 1978.

Harold Gastwirt. *Fraud, Corruption and Holiness: The Controversy over the Supervision of Jewish Dietary Practice in New York City 1881–1940.* Port Washington, NY: Kennikat Press, 1974.

Cathy S. Gelbin. *The Golem Returns: From German Romantic Literature to Global Jewish Culture, 1808–2008.* Ann Arbor: University of Michigan Press, 2011.

Moses Gelernter. *Sefer Tehilim.* Brooklyn: Samet, 1980.

Uriel Gellman. "An Author's Guide: Authorship of Hasidic Compendia" [Hebrew]. *Zutot* 9 (2012): 85–96.

——. "Stories." in *Studying Hasidism: Sources, Methods, Perspectives,* edited by Marcin Wodziński, 60–74. New Brunswick: Rutgers University Press, 2019.

Haim Gertner. *The Rabbi and the City; the Rabbinate in Galicia and Its Encounter with Modernity, 1815–1867* [Hebrew]. Jerusalem: Zalman Shazar Center, 2013.

Menuḥah Gilbo'a. *Leksikon ha-'Itonut ha-'Ivrit ba-Me'ot ha-Shemoneh 'Esreh veha-Tesha' 'Esreh.* Tel Aviv: Mossad Bialik, 1992.

Louis Ginzberg. *Students, Scholars and Saints.* Philadelphia: Jewish Publication Society, 1928.

Bill Gladstone. "History Scrapbook: Beth Jacob Congregation." December 15, 2011. http://www.billgladstone.ca/?p=3890. Accessed January 19, 2016.

Rod Glogauer. "The Impact of the American Experience upon Responsa Literature." *American Jewish History* 69 (1979): 257–269.

Ben-Zion Gold. "Religious Education in Poland: A Personal Perspective." In *The Jews of Poland Between Two World Wars,* edited by Yisrael Gutman, Ezra Mendelsohn, Jehuda Reinharz, and Chone Shmeruk, 272–282. Hanover, NH: Brandeis University Press, 1989.

Arnold Goldsmith. *The Golem Remembered, 1909–1980.* Detroit: Wayne State University Press, 1981.

Yosef Goldman. *Hebrew Printing in America, 1735–1926,* 2 volumes. Brooklyn: YG Books, 2006.

Arthur A. Goren. *New York Jews and the Quest for Community: The Kehillah Experiment 1908–1922.* New York: Columbia University Press, 1970.

Heinrich Graetz. *Geschichte der Juden,* vol. 7. Leipzig, 1863.

Anthony Grafton. *Forgers and Critics: Creativity and Duplicity in Western Scholarship* Princeton: Princeton University Press, 1990.

Arthur Green. "Introduction" to Yehudah Leib Alter, *The Language of Truth: The Torah Commentary of the Sefat Emet,* xv–lviii. Philadelphia: Jewish Publication Society, 1998.

——. *A Guide to the Zohar.* Stanford: Stanford University Press, 2004.

——. "Three Warsaw Mystics." In *Kolot Rabbim: Essays in Memory of Rivka Shatz-Uffenheimer,* edited by Rachel Elior, 1–58. Jerusalem: Magnes Press, 1997.

——. *Tormented Master.* Alabama: University of Alabama Press, 1978.

Gershon Greenberg. "'Da'at Torah neged 'Amalek': R. Elhanan Wasserman." In *The Gedoilim: Leaders Who Shaped the Israeli Haredi Society,* edited by Binyamin Brown and Nissim Leon, 209–233. Jerusalem: Magnes Press, 2017.

Zeev Gries. *The Book in the Jewish World 1700–1900.* Oxford and Portland: Littman Library of Jewish Civilization, 2007.

Ḥayyim Ozer Grodzinsky. *Sh'elot u-Teshuvot Ahi'ezer.* Jerusalem, 1960.

François Guesnet. "Frenk, Azriel Natan." In YIVO Encyclopedia of Jews in Eastern Europe. http://www.yivoencyclopedia.org/article.aspx/Frenk_Azriel_Natan. Accessed August 10, 2016.

——. *Polnische Juden im 19. Jahrhundert: Lebensbedingungen, Rechtsnormen und Organisation im Wandel.* Köln, Wiemar, Wien: Böhlau Verlag, 1998.

Alessandro Guetta. *Philosophy and Kabbalah: Elijah Benmozegh and the Reconciliation of Western Thought and Jewish Esoterism.* Albany: SUNY Press, 2009.

Jeffrey Gurock. "Resisters and Accomodators: Varieties of Orthodox Rabbis in America, 1886–1983." *American Jewish Archives* 35 (1983): 100–187.

——. "The Winnowing of American Orthodoxy." In *Approaches to Modern Judaism*, edited by Marc L. Raphael, 41–53, 106–110. Chico, CA: Scholars' Press, 1984.

Mordecai Halperin. "The Laws of Saving Lives: The Teachings of Rabbi S.Z. Auerbach." *Medicine, Ethics, and Jewish Law* 2 (1996): 15–24.

Salomon Alter Halpern. *The Prisoner and Other Tales of Faith*. Jerusalem and New York: Feldheim, 1981.

Raya Haran. "Ḥerut be-Tokh Emuna: Ha-Hatafa le-Limud ha-Nigleh veha-Nistar be-Hagut ha-Tsaddiqim le-Veyt Ziditschov-Komarna." In *Sefer Zikkaron le-Gershom Sholem: Bi-Mel'ot 'Esrim ve-Ḥamesh Shanim li-Fetirato*, edited by Yosef Dan, 305–352. Jerusalem: Makhon le-Mada'ei ha-Yahadut, 2007.

Yuval Harari. "Three Charms for Killing Adolf Hitler: Practical Kabbala in WW2." *Aries—Journal for the Study of Western Esotericism* 17 (2017): 171–214.

Andrew R. Heinze. *Adapting to Abundance: Jewish Immigrants, Mass Consumption, and the Search for American Identity*. New York: Columbia University Press, 1990.

Shim'on Aharon Hershkovitz. *Di Gneive in Britishen Muzeum fun Maharal mi-Prag*. Bnei Brak: Der Heyliger Kval, 1950.

——. *Dem Maharals Droshe: A Mayse*. Bnei Brak: Der Heyliger Kval, 1950.

Brad Sabin Hill. "Early Hebrew Printing in Canada." *Studia Rosenthaliana* 38/39 (2005/2006): 306–347.

Elliot Horowitz. *Reckless Rites: Purim and the Legacy of Jewish Violence*. Princeton and Oxford: Princeton University Press, 2006.

Irving Howe. *World of Our Father*. New York: Harcourt, Brace Jovanovich, 1976.

R. Po-Chia Hsia. *The Myth of Ritual Murder: Jews and Magic in Reformation Germany*. New Haven: Yale University Press, 1988.

Shim'on Huberband. *Kiddush Hashem: Jewish Religious and Cultural Life in Poland during the Holocaust*, translated David Fishman. Hoboken, NJ: Ktav, 1987.

Gershon David Hundert. "Jewish Popular Spirituality in the Eighteenth Century." *Polin* 15 (2002): 93–103.

——. *Jews in Poland-Lithuania in the Eighteenth Century: A Genealogy of Modernity*. Berkeley: University of California Press, 2004.

Boaz Huss. "Admiration and Disgust: The Ambivalent Re-Canonization of the Zohar in the Modern Period." In *Study and Knowledge in Jewish Thought*, edited by Howard Kreisel, 203–237. Beersheva: Ben-Gurion University, 2006.

——. "'Authorized Guardians': The Polemics of Academic Scholars of Jewish Mysticism Against Kabbalah Practitioners." In *Polemical Encounters: Esoteric Discourse and Its Others*, edited by Kocku von Stuckrad and Olav Hammer, 81–103. Leiden: Brill, 2007.

——. *Like the Radiance of the Sky: Chapters in the Reception History of the Zohar and the Construction of its Symbolic Value* [Hebrew]. Jerusalem: Bialik Institute and Ben-Zvi Institute, 2008.

——. "Komunizm Altruisti: Ha-Qabbala ha-Modernistit shel ha-Rav Ashlag." *'Iyunim bi-Tekumat Yisrael: Me'asef li-Ve'ayot ha-Tsionut, ha-Yishuv u-Medinat Yisra'el* 16 (2006): 109–130.

——. "The Translations of the Zohar" [Hebrew]. In *New Developments in Zohar Studies*, ed. Ronit Meroz, 33–107. Tel Aviv: Tel Aviv University Press, 2007.

———. "Translations of the Zohar: Historical Contexts and Ideological Frameworks." *Correspondences* 4 (2016): 81–128.

Moshe Idel. *Golem: Jewish Magical and Mystical Traditions on the Artificial Anthropoid.* Albany: SUNY Press, 1990.

———. "The Golem in Jewish Magic and Mysticism." In Emily D. Bilski, *Golem! Danger, Deliverance, and Art*, 15–35. New York: Jewish Museum, 1988.

———. "Maimonides and Kabbalah." In *Studies in Maimonides*, edited by Isadore Twersky, 31–81. Cambridge, MA: Harvard University Press, 1990.

Motti Inbari. "Messianic Expectations in Hungarian Orthodox Theology Before and During the Second World War: a Comparative Study." *Jewish Quarterly Review* 107, no. 4 (2017): 506–530.

Joseph Jacobs. *The Jews of Angevin England.* London: D. Nutt, 1893.

Louis Jacobs. *Hasidic Thought.* New York: Behrman House, 1976.

Jenna Weissman Joselit. *New York's Jewish Jews.* Bloomington: Indiana University Press, 1990.

———. 'What Happened to New York's Jewish Jews." *American Jewish History* 73 (1983): 163–172.

———. *The Wonders of America: Reinventing Jewish Culture 1880–1950.* New York: Hill and Wang, 1994.

Norma Joseph. "Ritual, Law, and Praxis: An American Response/a to Bat Mitsva Celebrations." *Modern Judaism* 22, no. 3 (2002): 234–260.

Yo'ets Kim Kadish of Przytyk, ed. *Siaḥ Sarfei Qodesh*, part 5. http://www.daat.ac.il/daat/vl/sarfeikodesh/sarfeikodesh23.pdf. Accessed September 2, 2019.

Nathan M. Kaganoff. "An Orthodox Jewish Rabbinate in the South." *American Jewish History* 73 (1983): 56–70.

Yedida Sharona Kanfer. "Lodz: Industry, Religion, and Nationalism in Russian Poland, 1880–1914." PhD diss., Yale University, 2011.

Aryeh Kaplan. *Mediation and Kabbala.* York Beach, ME: Samuel Weiser, 1982.

Nahum Karlinsky. "The Dawn of Hasidic-Haredi Historiography." *Modern Judaism* 27, no. 1 (February 2007): 20–46.

Abraham J. Karp. "New York Chooses a Chief Rabbi." *Proceedings of the American Jewish Historical Society* 44 (1954): 129–198.

———. "The Ridwas, Rabbi Jacob David Wilowsky, 1845–1913." In *Perspectives on Jews and Judaism: Essays in Honor of Wolfe Kelman*, edited by Arthur A. Chiel, 215–237. New York: Rabbinical Assembly, 1978.

Don Karr, "Which Lurianic Kabbalah?" https://www.academia.edu/30928619/Which_Lurianic_Kabbalah. Accessed November 3, 2019.

Samuel D. Kassow. "Community and Identity in the Interwar Shtetl.", In *The Jews of Poland Between Two World Wars*, edited by Yisrael Gutman, Ezra Mendelsohn, Jehuda Reinharz, and Chone Shmeruk, 198–220. Hanover, NH: Brandeis University Press, 1989.

Jacob Katz. *Divine Law in Human Hands: Case Studies in Halakhic Flexibility.* Jerusalem: Magnes Press, 1998.

———. *The "Shabbes Goy": A Study in Halakhic Flexibility.* Philadelphia: Jewish Publication Society, 1989.

Martin Kaufman. *Homeopathy in America: The Rise and Fall of a Medical Heresy.* Baltimore: Johns Hopkins University Press, 1974.

Menachem Keren-Kratz. "Mishmeret le-Moshmeret: R. Yosef Tsvi (Maharits) Dushinsky." In *The Gedoilim: Leaders Who Shaped the Israeli Haredi Society*, edited by Binyamin Brown and Nissim Leon, 337–367. Jerusalem: Magnes Press, 2017.

Zvi Hirsch Khotsh. *Naḥalat Tsvi*. Frankfurt, 1711.

Hillel Kieval. *Languages of Community: The Jewish Experience in the Czech Lands*. Berkeley: University of California Press, 2000.

——. "Pursuing the Golem of Prague: Jewish Culture and the Invention of a Tradition." *Modern Judaism* 17, no. 1 (1997): 1–23.

Yosef Klausner. *Historia shel ha-Sifrut ha-'Ivrit ha-Ḥadasha*. Jerusalem: Aḥiasaf, 1952.

Jonathan Klawans. "Deceptive Intentions: Forgeries, Falsehoods, and the Study of Ancient Judaism." *Jewish Quarterly Review* 108, no. 4 (Fall 2018): 489–501.

Heszel Klepfisz. *Culture of Compassion: The Spirit of Polish Jewry from Hasidism to the Holocaust*, translated by Curt Leviant. New York: Ktav, 1983.

Abraham Isaac Kook. *Igrot ha-Raiy'a*, vol. 4. Jerusalem: Zvi Yehuda Kook Foundation, 1984.

George Kranzler. *Williamsburg: a Jewish Community in Transition*. New York: Feldheim, 1961.

Valerie Knowles. *Strangers at Our Gates: Canadian Immigration and Immigration Policy, 1540–1997*. Toronto: Dundurn Press, 1997.

Israel Meir ha-Kohen. *Nidḥei Yisrael*. Warsaw, 1894.

William Kolbrener. *The Last Rabbi: Joseph Soloveitchik and the Talmudic Tradition*. Bloomington: Indiana University Press, 2016.

Alexander Kotok. "The History of Homeopathy in the Russian Empire until World War I, as Compared with other European Countries and the USA: Similarities and Discrepancies." http://homeoint.org/books4/kotok/index.htm.

——. "Homeopathy and the Russian Orthodox Clergy: Russian Homeopathy in Search of Allies in the Second Part of the 19th and Beginning of the 20th Centuries." *Medizin, Gesellschaft und Geschichte* 16 (1997): 171–193.

Reinhold Kramer. *Mordecai Richler: Leaving St Urbain*. Montreal and Kingston: McGill-Queen's University Press, 2008.

Jonathan B. Krasner. *The Benderly Boys and American Jewish Education*. Waltham: Brandeis University Press, 2011.

Hartley Lachter. "Kabbalah, Philosophy, and the Jewish-Christian Debate: Reconsidering the Early Works of Joseph Gikatilla." *Journal of Jewish Thought and Philosophy* 16, no. 1 (2008): 1–58.

Jiri Langer. *Nine Gates to the Hasidic Mysteries*. New York: David McKay, 1961.

Y. Tzvi Langermann and Robert G. Morrison. "Introduction." In *Texts in Transit in the Medieval Mediterranean*, edited by Y. Tzvi Langermann and Robert G. Morrison. University Park, PA: Penn State University Press, 2016. http://www.psupress.org/books/SampleChapters/978-0-271-07109-1sc.html. Accessed October 30, 2016.

Eli Lederhandler. *Jewish Responses to Modernity: New Voices in America and Eastern Europe*. New York: New York University Press, 1994.

——. "Modernity without Emancipation or Assimilation? The Case of Russian Jewry." In *Assimilation and Community: The Jews in Nineteenth Century Europe*, edited by Jonathan Frankel and Steven J. Zipperstein, 324–343. Cambridge: Cambridge University Press, 1992.

Shnayer Z. Leiman. "The Adventure of the Maharal of Prague in London: R. Yudl Rosenberg and the Golem of Prague." *Tradition* 36, no. 1 (2002): 26–58.

——. "From the Pages of Tradition: Montague Lawrence Marks in a Jewish Bookstore." *Tradition* 25, no. 1 (Fall 1989): 59–69.

Eve Lerner. "Making and Breaking Bread in Jewish Montreal, 1920–1940." MA thesis, Concordia University, 2002.

Ze'ev Lev. "Electricity and Shabbat." *Crossroads (Alon Shvut)* 2 (1988): 7–28.

Amnon Levi. "Anglo-Saxon Haredim: Can They Serve as a Bridge Between Haredim and Non-Religious." In *Religious and Secular: Conflict and Accomodation Between Jews in Israel*, edited by Charles Liebman, 1–20. Jerusalem: Keter, 1990.

Leo Levi. *Torah and Science: Their Interplay in the World Scheme*. New York: Association of Orthodox Jewish Scientists, 1983.

Shalom Duber Levin. *Toldois Chabad B'Artzois Ha'Bris*. Brooklyn: Kehot, 1988.

Jason Jaron Lewis. *Imagining Holiness: Classic Hasidic Tales in Modern Times*. Montreal and Kingston: McGill-Queen's University Press, 2009.

Yehuda Liebes, "*Ha-Mashiaḥ shel ha-Zohar*," in Yehuda Liebes and Yair Zakovits, eds., *The Messianic Idea in Jewish Thought* (Jerusalem: ha-Akademia ha-Leumit ha-Yisraelit la-Mada'im, 1982, 87–236.

Yehuda Liebes. *Studies in the Zohar*. Albany: State University of New York Press, 1993.

Max A. Lipschitz. *The Faith of a Hassid*. New York: Jonathan David, 1967.

Robert P. Lockwood. "Convent Horror Stories." *Catholic Answers Magazine* 19, no. 3 (March 2008). http://www.catholic.com/magazine/articles/convent-horror-stories. Accessed March 28, 2016.

Steven Lowenstein. "Ashkenazic Jewry and the European Marriage Pattern: A Preliminary Survey of Jewish Marriage Age." *Jewish History* 8, nos. 1–2 (1994): 155–175.

Ehud Luz. *Parallels Meet: Religion and Nationalism in the Early Zionist Movement (1882–1904)*. Philadelphia: Jewish Publication Society, 1988.

Shaul Magid. "Folk Narratives." in *Studying Hasidism: Sources, Methods, Perspectives*, edited by Marcin Wodziński, 127–143. New Brunswick, NJ: Rutgers University Press, 2019.

——. *Hasidism on the Margin: Reconciliation, Antinomianism, and Messianism in Izbica/Radzin Hasidism*. Madison: University of Wisconsin Press, 2003.

——. "The Metaphysics of *Malkhut*: *Malkhut* as *Eyn Sof* in the Writings of Ya'akov Koppel of Mezritch." *Kabbalah: Journal for the Study of Jewish Mystical Texts* 27 (2012): 245–267.

Raphael Mahler. *Hasidism and the Jewish Enlightenment: Their Confrontation in Galicia and Poland in the First Half of the Nineteenth Century*. Philadelphia: Jewish Publication Society, 1985.

Raphael Mahler. *A History of the Jewish People in Modern Times* [Hebrew]. Merḥavia: Sifriat Po'alim, 1962.

——. *A History of Modern Jewry, 1780–1815*. London: Vallentine, Mitchell, 1971.

Rachel Manekin. "Gaming the System: The Jewish Community Council, the Temple, and the Struggle over the Rabbinate in Mid-Nineteenth-Century Lemberg." *Jewish Quarterly Review* 106, no. 3 (2016): 352–382.

David Margalit. "Gedolei ha-Ḥasidut ke-Rof'im." *Qor'ot* 7 (1976): 81–88.

Michael Marmur. *Abraham Joshua Heschel and the Sources of Wonder*. Toronto: University of Toronto Press, 2016.

Jacob Marshak. *Sefer Divrei Moshe.* Warsaw, 1885.

Israel Medres. *Tsvishn Tsvei Velt Milkhomes.* Montreal: Keneder Adler, 1964.

Jonatan Meir, "Gilui ve-Gilui be-Hester: 'al Mamshikhei ha-R. Y. L. Ashlag, ha-Hitnagdut Lahem ve-Hafatsat Sifrut ha-Sod." *Kabbalah* 16 (2007): 151–258.

——. "Giluyyim Ḥadashim 'al R. Yehuda Leib Ashlag." *Kabbalah* 20 (2009): 345–368.

——. "Haskala and Esotericism: The Strange Case of Elyakim Getzel Hamilzahagi (1780–1854)." *Aries—Journal for the Study of Western Esotericism* 18 (2018): 153–187.

——. "Hithavuto ve-Gilgulav shel Mif'al Targum u-Be'ur Sefer ha-Zohar le-Hillel Tseitlin." *Kabbalah* 10 (2004): 119–157.

——. "The Imagined Decline of Kabbalah: The Kabbalistic Yeshiva Shaar ha-Shamayim and Kabbalah in Jerusalem in the Beginning of the Twentieth Century." In *Kabbalah and Modernity: Interpretations, Transformations, Adaptations,* edited by Boaz Huss, Marco Pasi, and Kocku von Stuckrad, 195–220. Leiden: Brill, 2010.

——. *Kabbalistic Circles in Jerusalem (1896–1948).* Leiden and Boston: Brill, 2016.

——. *Literary Hasidism: The Life and Works of Michael Levi Rodkinson.* Syracuse: Syracuse University Press, 2016.

——. "Michael Levi Rodkinson: Beyn Ḥasidut le-Haskala." *Kabbalah* 18 (2008): 229–286.

——. "Naftulei Sod: Hillel Zeitlin, ha-Rav Y. Ashlag, veha-Qabbala be-Erets Yisra'el." In *Yahadut: Sugyot, Qeta'im, Panim, Zehuyot: Sefer Rivqah,* edited by Haviva Pedaya and Ephraim Meir, 585–647. Beersheva: Ben-Gurion University, 2007.

Bernard J. Meislin. *Jewish Law in American Tribunals.* New York: Ktav, 1976.

Ezra Mendelsohn. *Zionism in Poland: The Formative Years, 1915–1926.* New Haven: Yale University Press, 1981.

Ronit Meroz. "The Archaeology of the Zohar: *Sifra Ditseni'uta* as a Sample Text." *Da'at* 82 (2016): ix–lxxxv.

Michael A. Meyer. "History of Hebrew Union College." in *Hebrew Union College-Jewish Institute of Religion at One Hundred Years,* edited by Samuel E. Karff, 7–283. Cincinnati: Hebrew Union College, 1976.

——. "New Waters in an Old Vessel: A History of Mikveh in Modern Judaism." In *Between Jewish Tradition and Modernity: Rethinking an Old Opposition, Essays in Honor of David Ellenson,* edited by Michael A. Meyer and David N. Myers, 142–158. Detroit: Wayne State University Press, 2014.

——. *The Origins of the Modern Jew.* Detroit: Wayne State University Press, 1967.

P. Minc (Alexander). *Lodz in Mayn Zikoron.* Buenos Aires: IDBUJ, 1958.

Adam Mintz. *Halakhah in America: The History of City Eruvin, 1894–1962.* PhD diss., New York University, 2011. http://www.rabbimintz.com/wp-content/uploads/Mintz-Dissertation-Final.pdf. Accessed May 18, 2015.

——. "Guenzberg, Lilienblum, and Haskala Autobiography." *AJS Review* 4 (1979): 71–110.

Jerome Mintz. *Hasidic People: A Place in the New World.* Cambridge, MA: Harvard University Press, 1993.

——. *Legends of the Hasidim: An Introduction to Hasidic Culture and Oral Tradition in the New World.* Chicago: PUBLISHER, 1968.

Dan Miron. "Folklore and Antifolklore in the Yiddish Fiction of the Haskala." In *Studies in Jewish Folklore,* edited by Frank Talmage, 219–249. Cambridge, MA: n.p., 1980.

——. *The Image of the Shtetl and Other Studies of Modern Jewish Literary Imagination.* Syracuse, NY: Syracuse University Press, 2000.

Basil Mitchell. *Language Politics and Language Survival: Yiddish among the Haredim in Post-War Britain.* Louvain: Peeters, 2006.

Yehuda Moraly. "Representations of the Maharal in Theater and Film." In *Maharal: Overtures, Biography, Doctrine, Influence* [Hebrew], edited by Elchanan Reiner, 567–588. Jerusalem: Zalman Shazar Center for Jewish History, 2015.

Aryeh Morgenstern. *Messianism and the Settlement of the Land of Israel* [Hebrew]. Jerusalem: Yad Ben-Zvi, 1985.

Nicola Morris. *The Golem in Jewish American Literature.* New York: Peter Lang, 2007.

Kenneth B. Moss. "Negotiating Jewish Nationalism in Interwar Warsaw." in *Warsaw. The Jewish Metropolis: Essays in Honor of the 75th Birthday of Professor Anony Polonsky*, edited by Glenn Dynner and François Guesnet, 390–434. Leiden: Brill, 2015.

——. Review of Joshua Shanes, *Diaspora Nationalism and Jewish Identity in Habsburg Galicia. AJS Review* 39 (2015): 433–437.

Allan Nadler, *The Faith of the Mithnagdim: Rabbinic Responses to Hasidic Rapture.* Baltimore: Johns Hopkins University Press, 1997.

——. "The War on Modernity of R. Hayyim Elazar Shapira of Munkacz." *Modern Judaism* 14 (1994): 233–264.

Joachim Neugroschel. *Yenne Velt: The Great Works of Jewish Fantasy and Occult.* New York: Pocket Books, 1976.

Nifla'ot Qedushat Levi. Bilgoraj, 1910/1.

Gedalyahu Nigal. *The Hasidic Tale: Its History and Topics.* Jerusalem: ha-Makhon le-ḥeqer ha-sifrut ha-Ḥasidit, 1981.

Shlomo Barukh Nissenboim. *Le-Qor'ot ha-Yehudim be-Lublin.* Lublin, 1900.

Iris Parush. *Reading Jewish Women: Marginality and Modernization in Nineteenth-Century Eastern European Jewish Society.* Waltham: Brandeis University Press, 2004.

Rachel S. A. Pear. "Differences Over Darwinism: American Orthodox Jewish Responses to Evolution in the 1920s." *Aleph: Historical Studies in Science and Judaism* 15, no. 2 (2015): 343–387.

Yohanan Petrovsky-Shtern. "Hasidei De'ar'a and Hasidei Dekokhvaya': Two Trends in Modern Jewish Historiography." *AJS Review* 32, no. 1 (2008): 141–167.

——. "'You Will Find It in the Pharmacy': Practical Kabbalah and Natural Medicine in the Polish-Lithuanian Commonwealth, 1690–1750." in *Holy Dissent: Jewish and Christian Mystics in Eastern Europe*, edited by Glen Dynner, 13–54. Detroit: Wayne State University Press, 2011.

Michael Pitkowsky. "Modernity as Seen Through the Responsa of Rabbi Yehuda Leib Zirelson." *G'vanim: The Journal of the Academy of Jewish Religion* 7, no. 1 (2011): 34–48.

Solomon Poll. *The Hasidic Community of Williamsburg: A Study in the Sociology of Religion.* New York: Schocken, 1962.

Antony Polonsky. *The Jews in Poland and Russia*, 3 volumes. Oxford and Portland, OR: Littman Library of Jewish Civilization, 2009–2012.

Harry M. Rabinowicz. *Chassidic Rebbes: From the Baal Shem Tov to Modern Times.* Southfield, MI and Spring Valley, NY: Feldheim, 1989.

——. *Hasidism: The Movement and Its Masters.* Northvale, NJ: Jason Aronson, 1988.
——. *The World of Hasidism.* Hartford: Hartmore House, 1970.
Ada Rapoport-Albert. "Hagiography with Footnotes: Edifying Tales and the Writing of History in Hasidism." *History and Theory* 27, no. 4: *Essays in Jewish Historiography* (December 1988): 119–159.
"The Rebbe's Progeny." *Jewish Standard,* January 15–31, 1983, 5.
B. Re'em. "Semukhim le-'Ad ule-'Olam," *Ha-Modi'a,* December 7, 1990, 10.
Elchanan Reiner. "Transformations in the Polish and Ashkenazic Yeshivot During the Sixteenth and Seventeenth Centires and the Dispute Over Pilpul" [Hebrew]. In *Ke-Minhag Ashkenaz ve-Polin: Sefer Yovel le Khone Shmeruk,* edited by Israel Bartal, Chava Turniansky, and Ezra Mendelsohn, 9–80. Jerusalem: Merkaz Zalman Shazar, 1989.
Zalman Reizin. *Leksikon fun der Yiddisher Literatur, Presse un Filologie,* vol. 4. Vilna: Kletzkin, 1929.
Immanuel Hai Ricchi. *Mishnat Ḥasidim.* Brooklyn, 1975.
Mordecai Richler. *This Year in Jerusalem.* Toronto: Knopf, 1994.
Caterina Rigo. "*Dux Neutrorum* and the Jewish Tradition." In *Maimonides' Guide of the Perplexed in Translation: a History From the Thirteenth Century to the Twentieth,* edited by Josef Stern, James T. Robinson, and Yonatan Shemesh, 81–139. Chicago: University of Chicago Press, 2019.
Moses Rischin. *The Promised City.* New York: Harper and Row, 1970.
W. H. R. Rivers. *Medicine, Magic, and Religion: The Fitzpatrick Lectures Delivered before the Royal College of Physicians of London in 1915 and 1916.* London and New York: Routledge, 2001.
Isaac Rivkind. *Bar Mitzvah: a Study in Jewish Cultural History* [Hebrew]. New York: Bloch, 1942.
Ira Robinson, "Abraham ben Eliezer Halevi: Kabbalist and Messianic Visionary of the Early Sixteenth Century." PhD diss., Harvard University, 1980.
——. "Because of Our Many Sins: The Contemporary Jewish World as Reflected in the Responsa of Moses Feinstein." *Judaism* 35 (1986): 35–46.
——, ed. *Cyrus Adler: Selected Letters,* 2 volumes. Philadelphia: Jewish Publication Society, 1985.
——. "David Rome as an Historian of Canadian Jewry." *Canadian Jewish Studies* 3 (1995): 1–10.
——. "The Education of an American Orthodox Rabbi: Mayer Joshua Rosenberg Comes to Holyoke, Massachusetts." *Judaism* 40 (1991): 543–551.
——. "The First Hasidic Rabbis in North America." *American Jewish Archives Journal* 44 (1992): 501–515.
——. "Hayyim Selig Slonimski and the Diffusion of Science among Russian Jewry in the Nineteenth Century." In *The Interaction between Scientific and Jewish Cultures,* edited by Yakov Rabkin and Ira Robinson, 49–65. Lewiston, Queenston, and Lampeter: Edwin Mellen Press, 1994.
——. *A History of Antisemitism in Canada.* Waterloo: Wilfrid Laurier University Press, 2015.
——. "Kabbala and Science in *Sefer ha-Berit*: A Modernization Strategy for Orthodox Jews." *Modern Judaism* 9 (1989): 275–288.
——. "Kabbalist and Communal Leader: Rabbi Yudel Rosenberg and the Canadian Jewish Community." *Canadian Jewish Studies* 1 (1993): 41–58.
——. "The Kosher Meat War and the Jewish Community Council of Montreal, 1922–1925." *Canadian Ethnic Studies* 22, no. 2 (1990): 41–53.

——. "A Letter From the Sabbath Queen: Rabbi Yudel Rosenberg Addresses Montreal Jewry." In *An Everyday Miracle: Yiddish Culture in Montreal*, edited by Ira Robinson, Pierre Anctil, and Mervin Butovsky, 101–114. Montreal: Vehicule Press, 1990.

——. "Literary Forgery and Hasidic Judaism: The Case of Rabbi Yudel Rosenberg." *Judaism* 40 (1991): 61–78.

——. *Rabbis and Their Community: Studies in the Immigrant Orthodox Rabbinate in Montreal, 1896–1930*. Calgary: University of Calgary Press, 2007.

——. "Reviving the Study of the Zohar in the First Half of the 20th Century: A Consideration of the Roles of Gershom Scholem, Yudel Rosenberg, and Yehuda Ashlag." In *From Something to Nothing: Jewish Mysticism in Contemporary Canadian Jewish Studies*, edited by Harry Fox, Daniel Maoz, and Tirzah Meacham, 41–50. Newcastle upon Tyne: Cambridge Scholars Publishing, 2019.

——. "The Tarler Rebbe of Łódź and His Medical Practice: Towards a History of Hasidic Life in Pre-First World War Poland." *Polin* 11 (1998): 53–61.

——. "Torah and Halakha in Medieval Judaism." *Studies in Religion* 13 (1984).

——. "Toward a History of Kashrut in Montreal: The Fight over Municipal Bylaw 828 (1922–1924)." In *Renewing Our Days: Montreal Jews in the Twentieth Century*, edited by Ira Robinson and Mervin Butovsky, 30–41. Montreal: Vehicule Press, 1995.

——. "The Uses of the Hasidic Story: Rabbi Yudel Rosenberg and His Tales of the Greiditzer Rabbi." *Journal of the Society of Rabbis in Academia* 1, nos. 1–2 (1991): 17–24.

Ira Robinson and Simcha Fishbane. "Ketavim Ḥadashim shel ha-Rav Yitsḥak Nissenbaum mi-Geniza Russit." In *Turim: Studies in Jewish History and Literature Presented to Dr. Bernard Lander*, edited by Michael Shmidman, vol. 2, Hebrew pagination, 97–129. New York: Touro College Press, 2008.

David Rome. *A Selected Bibliography of Jewish Canadiana*. Montreal: Canadian Jewish Congress and Jewish Public Library, 1959.

Aaron Elimelekh Rosenberg. *Liqqutei Beit Aharon*. Montreal: Friedman, 1954.

Judah ben Alexander Rosenberg, ed. *Qovetz Ma'asei Yedei Ge'onim Qadmonim*. Berlin, 1856.

——. *She'elot u-Teshuvot Maharah Or Zaru'a*. Leipzig, 1860.

——. *Zikhron Yehuda*. Berlin, 1846.

Leah Rosenberg. *The Errand Runner: Reflections of a Rabbi's Daughter*. Toronto: Wiley, 1981.

Meir Joshua Rosenberg. *Kur ha-Mivḥan*. Jerusalem: Agudat Yad le-Yisrael, 1968.

Suzanne Rosenberg. *A Soviet Odyssey*. Toronto: Oxford University Press, 1988.

David Roskies. "The Medium and the Message of the Maskilic Chapbook." *Jewish Social Studies* 41, nos. 3–4 (Summer–Autumn 1979): 275–290.

——. "S. Ansky and the Paradigm of Return." In *The Uses of Tradition: Jewish Continuity in the Modern Era*, edited by Jack Wertheimer, 243–260. New York and Jerusalem: Jewish Theological Seminary of America, 1992.

Moshe Rosman. *Founder of Hasidism: A Quest for the Historical Ba'al Shem Tov*. Berkeley, CA: University of California Press, 1996.

——. "Miedzyboz and Rabbi Israel Baal Shem Tov." In *Essential Papers on Hasidism*, edited by Gershon Hundert, 209–225. New York: New York University Press, 1991.

Joshua Rothenberg. "Demythologizing the Shtetl." *Midstream* 27, no. 3 (March 1981): 25–31.

Aaron Rothkoff. "The American Sojourns of Ridbaz: Religious Problems within the Immigrant Community." *American Jewish Historical Society Quarterly* 57 (1968): 557–572.

Aaron Rothkoff-Rakefet. *The Silver Era in American Orthodoxy*. Jerusalem and New York: Feldheim, 1981.

David B. Ruderman. *A Best-Selling Hebrew Book of the Modern Era: The Book of the Covenant of Pinḥas Hurwitz and its Remarkable Legacy*. Seattle: University of Washington Press, 2015.

——. *Jewish Thought and Scientific Discovery in Early Modern Europe*. New Haven: Yale University Press, 1995.

——. "Medicine and Scientific Thought: The World of Tobias Cohen." In *The Jews of Early Modern Venice*, edited by Robert C. Davis and Benjamin Ravid, 191–210. Baltimore: Johns Hopkins University Press, 2001.

Brad Sabin Hill, ed. *Incunabula, Hebraica & Judaica*. Ottawa: National Library of Canada, 1981.

Dov Sadan. *A Vort Bashteit*. Tel-Aviv: Farlag Y. L. Perets, 1978.

Vladimir Sadek. "Stories of the Golem and Their Relation to the Work of Rabbi Löw of Prague." *Judaica Bohemiae* 23, no. 2 (1987): 85–91.

Bezalel Safran. "Maharal and Early Hasidism." In *Hasidism: Continuity or Innovation*, edited by Bezalel Safran, 47–144. Cambridge: Harvard University Press, 1988.

Yosef Salmon, "R. Naftali Zvi Horovits mi-Ropshitz—Qavvim Biografiim." In *Hasidism in Poland*, edited by Raḥel Elior, Yisrael Bartal, and Chone Shmeruk, 321–342. Jerusalem: Bialik Institute, 1994.

Moshe Samet. *That Which Is New Is Prohibited by the Torah: Episodes in the History of Orthodoxy* [Hebrew]. Jerusalem: Dinur Center for Research in Jewish History, 2005.

Marc Saperstein. *Jewish Preaching, 1200–1800*. New Haven: Yale University Press, 1980.

——. *Your Voice Like a Ram's Horn: Themes and Texts in Traditional Jewish Preaching* Cincinnati: Hebrew Union College Press, 1996.

Jonathan Sarna. "The Myth of No Return: Jewish Return Migration to Eastern Europe, 1881–1914." *American Jewish History* (1981): 256–268.

——. *People Walk on Their Heads: Moses Weinberger's Jews and Judaism in New York*. New York and London: Holmes & Meier, 1981.

Deborah F. Sawyer. "Heterodoxy and Censorship: Some Critical Remarks on Wertheimer's Edition of Midrash Aleph-Beth." *Journal of Jewish Studies* 42 (1991): 115–121.

Jacob J. Schacter. "Haskalah, Secular Studies and the Close of the Yeshiva in Volozhin in 1892." *Torah u-Madda Journal* 2, no. 2 (1990): 76–133.

Solomon Schechter. *Seminary Addresses and Other Papers*. Cincinnati: Ark, 1915.

——. *Studies in Judaism*, first series. Philadelphia, Jewish Publication Society, 1896.

Joseph I. Schneersohn. *Lubavicher Rebbe's Memoirs*, 2 volumes. Brooklyn: Otsar Hachassidim, 1956–1960.

Sholom DovBer Schneerson. "The Foundation of Education" [*Ḥanokh la-Na'ar*], translated by Eliezer Danziger. www.chabad.org/library/article_cdo/aid/150276/jewish/The-Foundation-of-Education.htm.

Azriel Schochat. *The "Crown Rabbinate" in Russia: A Chapter in the Cultural Struggle between Orthodox Jews and Maskilim* [Hebrew]. Haifa: University of Haifa, 1975.

Gershom Scholem. *Elements in the Kabbalah and Its Symbolism* [Hebrew]. Jerusalem: Mossad Bialik, 1980.

——. *Kabbalah.* New York: Meridian, 1974.

——. *Major Trends in Jewish Mysticism.* New York: Schocken Books, 1941.

——. *The Messianic Idea in Judaism.* New York: Schocken Books, 1971.

——. *On the Kabbalah and Its Symbolism.* New York: Schocken Books, 1965.

——. *Sabbatai Sevi: The Mystical Messiah.* Princeton: Princeton University Press, 1973.

——. "Review of Chaim Bloch, Kovets Mikhtavim Mekoriim meha-Besht ve-Talmidav." *Kiryat Sefer* 1 (1924/5): 104–106.

Ismar Schorsch, *From Text to Context: The Turn to History in Modern Judaism.* Hanover, NH: Brandeis University Press, 1994.

Dafna Schreiber. "Melekh Yisrael: R. Avraham Mordecai mi-Gur, ha-'Imrei Emet.'" In *The Gedoilim: Leaders Who Shaped the Israeli Haredi Society,* edited by Binyamin Brown and Nissim Leon, 234–258. Jerusalem: Magnes Press, 2017.

B. Schwartz. *Artsot ha-Ḥayyim.* Brooklyn, 1992.

Simon Schwarzfuchs. *A Concise History of the Rabbinate.* Oxford: Blackwell, 1993.

Eliezer Schweid, *Democracy and Halakha.* Lanham: University Press of America, 1994.

——. *Orthodoxy and Religious Humanism* [Hebrew]. Jerusalem: Van Leer Institute, 1977.

David Sclar. "Adoption and Acceptance: Moses Hayim Luzzatto's Sojourn in Amsterdam among Portuguese Jews." *AJS Review* 40, no. 2 (2016): 335–358.

Sefer Refu'ot. Vienna, 1927.

Gershon Shaked, ed. *Melukhat Sha'ul.* Jerusalem, 1968.

Dan Shapira. "On Firkowicz, Forgeries, and Forging Jewish Identities." In *Manufacturing a Past for the Present: Forgery and Authenticity in Medievalist Texts and Objects in Nineteenth-Century Europe,* edited by János M. Bak, Patrick J. Geary, and Gábor Klaniczay, 156–169. Leiden, Brill, 2015.

Tsvi Hirsh Shapira. *Tif'eret Banim.* Jerusalem: Emet, 2000.

Kalonymus Kalman Shapiro. *A Student's Obligation,* translated by Micha Odenheimer. Northvale, NJ: Jason Aaronson, 1991.

Marc B. Shapiro, *Changing the Immutable: How Judaism Rewrites Its History.* Oxford: Oxford University Press, 2015.

——. "Concerning the Zohar and Other Matters." The Seforim Blog, August 29, 2012. http://seforim2.rssing.com/chan-9044709/all_p1.html. Accessed September 2, 2019.

——. Review of David Zohar, *Jewish Commitment in a Modern World: Rabbi Hayyim Hirschenson and His Attitude to Modernity* [Hebrew]. *The Edah Journal* 5, no. 1 (Tammuz 5765): 2. http://www.edah.org/backend/journalarticle/5_1_shapiro.pdf. Accessed March 25, 2016.

Robert M. Shapiro. "Jewish Self-Government in Lodz, 1914–1939." PhD diss., Columbia University, 1987.

Shmuel Meyer Shapiro. *The Rise of the Toronto Jewish Community.* Toronto: Now and Then Books, 2010.

Jacob Shatzky. *The History of the Jews in Warsaw* [Yiddish]. New York: YIVO, 1953.

Naḥman Shemen. *Lublin: City of Torah, Rabbinism, and Piety* [Yiddish]. Toronto: Gershon Pomerantz, 1951.

——. "Ortodoxie." *Der 'Idisher Journal: Yubiley Oisgabe.* Toronto, 1950.

Nahman Shemen and Y. Y. Wohlgelernter, "Entstehung un Antwicklung fun Talmud Torah 'Ets Ḥayyim." In *Talmud Torah "Eitz Chaim" Jubilee Book.* Toronto: n.p., 1943.

Byron Sherwin. *In Partnership with God: Contemporary Jewish Law and Ethics.* Syracuse: Syracuse University Press, 1990.

Efraim Shmueli. *With the Last Generation of Jews in Poland* [Hebrew]. Tel-Aviv: Aleph, 1986.

Raphael Shuchat. "*Qabbalat Lita' ke-Zerem 'Atsma'i be-Sifrut ha-Qabbala.*" *Kabbalah* 10 (2004): 181–206.

Aaron Benzion Shurin. "Ha-Rov R. Shlomo-Zalman Auerbach N"E: Zu Zayn 10-n Yortsayt." *Forward*, February 25, 2005, 8–9.

Gershon Silberberg, Meir Shimon Geshuri, eds. "Ostrowiec: A Monument on the Ruins of an Annihilated Jewish Community." https://www.jewishgen.org/yizkor/ostrowiec/oste111.html, English section. Accessed February 14, 2019.

Isaac Bashevis Singer. *In My Father's Court.* New York: Farrar, Straus and Giroux, 1962.

——. *Love and Exile: a Memoir.* Garden City, NY: Doubleday, 1984.

——. *More Stories From My Father's Court.* New York: Farrar, Straus and Giroux, 2000.

Israel Joshua Singer. *Of a World that is No More.* New York: Vanguard Press, 1970.

D. Sofer. "Rav Shlomo Zalman Auerbach ZT"L." http://www.tzemachdovid.org/gedolim/ravauerbach.html.

Norman Solomon. "The Analytic Movement in Rabbinic Jurisprudence: A Study of One Aspect of the Counter Emancipation in Lithuanian and White Russian Jewry from 1873 Onwards." PhD diss., University of Manchester, 1966.

——. *The Analytic Movement: Hayyim Soloveitchik and His Circle.* Atlanta: Scholars Press, 1993.

Haym Soloveitchik. *Collected Essays*, vol. 1. Oxford: Littman Library of Jewish Civilization, 2013.

David Sorotzkin, "'Geula shel Ḥoshekh va-Afela': R. Yoel Teitelbaum ha-Rabi mi-Satmar." In *The Gedoilim: Leaders Who Shaped the Israeli Haredi Society*, edited by Binyamin Brown and Nissim Leon, 371–401. Jerusalem: Magnes Press, 2017.

——. *Orthodoxy and Modern Disciplination: The Production of the Jewish Tradition in Europe in Modern Times* [Hebrew]. Tel-Aviv: Hakibbuts Hameuḥad, 2011.

Stephen A. Speisman. *The Jews of Toronto: A History to 1937.* Toronto: McClelland and Stewart, 1979.

——. "St. John's Shtetl: The Ward in 1911." In *Gathering Place: Peoples and Neighbourhoods of Toronto, 1834–1945*, Robert F. Harney, 107–120. Toronto: Multicultural History Society of Ontario, 1985.

Shaul Stampfer. *Families, Rabbis and Education: Traditional Jewish Society in Nineteenth-Century Eastern Europe.* Oxford: Littman Library of Jewish Civilization, 2010.

——. "An Unhappy Community and an Even Unhappier Rabbi." In *Warsaw. The Jewish Metropolis: Essays in Honor of the 75th Birthday of Professor Anony Polonsky*, edited Glenn Dynner and François Guesnet, 154–179. Leiden: Brill, 2015.

——. *Ha-Yeshiva ha-Lita'it be-Hithavutah ba-Me'ah ha-Tesha'-'Esreh.* Jerusalem: Merkaz Zalman Shazar, 1995.

——."Marital Patterns in Interwar Poland." In *The Jews of Poland Between Two World Wars*, edited by Yisrael Gutman, Ezra Mendelsohn, Jehuda Reinharz, and Chone Shmeruk, 173–197. Hanover, NH: Brandeis University Press, 1989.

Michael Stanislowski. *A Murder in Lemberg: Politics, Religion and Violence in Modern Jewish History.* Princeton: Princeton University Press, 2007.

——. *For Whom do I Toil?: Judah Leib Gordon and the Crisis of Russian Jewry.* New York: Oxford University Press, 1988.

——. "Reflections on the Russian Rabbinate." In *Jewish Religious Leadership: Image and Reality,* edited by Jack Wertheimer, vol. 2, 429–446. New York: Jewish Theological Seminary, 2004.

——. "The Transformation of Traditional Authority in Russian Jewry: The First Stage." In *The Legacy of Jewish Migration: 1881 and Its Impact,* edited by David Berger, 9–30. New York: Brooklyn College Press, 1983.

——. *Tsar Nicholas I and the Jews: The Transformation of Jewish Society in Russia, 1825–1855.* Philadelphia: Jewish Publication Society, 1983.

Sh. Stein, ed. *Radom.* Tel-Aviv: 'Irgunei Yots'ei Radom be-Yisrael uva-Tefutsot, 1961.

Avraham Steinberg. "Medical-Halachic Decisions of Rabbi Shlomo Zalman Auerbach (1910–1995)." *Assia* 3, no. 1 (1997): 30–43.

——. "Rabbi Shlomo Zalman Auerbach (1910–1995)." In *Pioneers in Jewish Medical Ethics,* edited by Fred Rosner, 99–126. Northvale, NJ: Jason Aronson, 1997.

Moritz Steinschneider. *Der Siddur des Saadia Gaon (als Manuscript gedruckt).* Berlin: Friedländer, March 28, 1856.

Adin Steinsaltz. *The Thirteen-Petalled Rose.* New York: Basic Books, 1980.

David Stern and Mark J. Mirsky. *Rabbinic Fantasies: Imaginative Narratives from Classical Rabbinic Literature.* New Haven: Yale University Press, 1990.

Eliyahu Stern. *Jewish Materialism: The Intellectual Revolution of the 1870s.* New Haven: Yale University Press, 2018.

——. Review of David B. Ruderman, *A Best-Selling Hebrew Book of the Modern Era: The Book of the Covenant of Pinḥas Hurwitz and Its Remarkable Legacy. AJS Review* 40, no. 2 (2016): 431–433.

Israel Ta-Shma, "On the History of the Jews in Twelfth-Thirteenth Century Poland." *Polin* 10 (1997): 287–317.

——. "le-Toledot ha-Yehudim be-Polin be Me'ot ha-12 veha-13." *Zion* 53 (1988): 347–369.

——. "Yediot Ḥadashot le-Toledot ha-Yehudim be-Polin be Me'ot ha-12 veha-13." *Zion* 54 (1989): 208.

Hanoch Teller. *The Bostoner: Stories and Recollections from the Colorful Chassidic Court of the Bostoner Rebbe, Rabbi Levi I. Horowitz.* Jerusalem and New York: Feldheim, 1990.

Shabtai Teveth. *Ben-Gurion: The Burning Ground, 1886–1948.* Boston: Houghton Mifflin, 1987.

Frederic Thieburger. *The Great Rabbi Loew of Prague.* London: East & West Library, 1954.

Tif'eret ha-Yehudi. Piotrkow, 1912.

Isaiah Tishby. "Beyn Shabta'ut le-Ḥassidut: Shabta'uto shel ha-Mequbal R. Yaakov Koppel Lipschitz mi-Mezrich." In Isaiah Tishby, *Netivei Emuna u-Minut.* Ramat-Gan: Makor, 1964.

——. *Mishnat ha-Zohar.* Jerusalem: Mossad Bialik, 1982.

Gerald Tulchinsky. "De Sola, Clarence." In *Dictionary of Canadian Biography,* http://www.biographi.ca/en/bio/de_sola_clarence_isaac_14E.html. Accessed August 21, 2016.

——. *Taking Root: The Origins of the Canadian Jewish Community.* Toronto: Lester Publishing, 1992.

Isadore Twersky. *Introduction to the Code of Maimonides.* New Haven: Yale University Press, 1980.

Efraim Urbach. "The History of Polish Jews after World War I As Reflected in the Traditional Literature." In *The Jews of Poland between Two World Wars,* edited by Yisrael Gutman, Ezra

Mendelsohn, Jehuda Reinharz, and Chone Shmeruk. Hanover, NH: Brandeis University Press, 1989.

Scott Ury. *Barricades and Banners: The Revolution of 1905 and the Transformation of Warsaw Jewry.* Stanford: Stanford University Press, 2012.

Gabriele von Glasenapp. "'Wie eine schaurige Sage der Vorzeit': Die Ritualmordbeschuldigung in der Jüdischen literatur des frühen 20. Jahrhunderts." In *Integration und Ausgrenzung*, edited by Mark H. Gelber, Jacob Hessing and Robert Jütte, 193–205. Tübingen: Niemeyer, 2009.

Elḥanan Wasserman. *Ma'amar Ikvete de-Meshiḥa.* New York, 1937.

Chaim I. Waxman. "Toward a Sociology of Psak." *Tradition* 25, no. 3 (Spring 1991): 12–25.

Sydney Stahl Weinberg. *The World of Our Mothers: The Lives of Jewish Immigrant Women.* Chapel Hill, University of North Carolina Press, 1988..

Aharon Wertheim. *Halakhot ve-Halikhot ba-Ḥassidut.* Jerusalem: Mossad ha-Rav Kook, 1960.

Jack Wertheimer, ed. *The Uses of Tradition: Jewish Continuity in the Modern Era.* New York and Jerusalem: Jewish Theological Seminary, 1992.

Elie Wiesel. *Sages and Dreamers: Biblical, Talmudic, and Hasidic Portraits and Legends.* New York: Summit Books, 1991.

Gershon Winkler, *The Golem of Prague.* New York: Judaica Press, 1980.

Isaac Mayer Wise. *Reminiscences.* New York: Arno, 1973.

Marcin Wodziński. *Hasidism and Politics: The Kingdom of Poland 1815–1864.* Oxford: Littman Library, 2013.

——. "War and Religion; or, How the First World War Changed Hasidism." *Jewish Quarterly Review* 106, no. 3 (2016): 283–312.

Hirsch Wolofsky. *Oyf Eybiken Kvall: Gedanken un Batrachtungen fun dem Hayntigen 'Idishen Leben un Shtreben, in Likht fun Unzer Alter un Eybig-Nayer Tora, Eingeteylt Loyt di Parshiyos fun der Vokh.* Montreal: Eagle Publishing Company, 1930.

Piotr Wrobel. "Jewish Warsaw before the First World War." In *The Jews in Warsaw: A History*, edited by Wladyslaw Bartoszewski and Antony Polonsky, 156–187. Oxford: Blackwell, 1991.

Eli Yassif, ed. *The Golem of Prague and Other Tales of Wonder* [Hebrew]. Jerusalem, Mossad Bialik, 1991.

——. *The Legend of Safed: Life and Fantasy in the City of Kabbalah.* Detroit: Wayne State University Press, 2019.

Ovadia Yosef. *She'elot u-Teshuvot Yabia' Omer*, part 2, *Oraḥ Ḥayyim.* Jerusalem: Mossad ha-Rav Kuk, 1954.

Isaac Yudlov. "Maharal of Prague and His Writings." In *Maharal: Overtures, Biography, Doctrine, Influence* [Hebrew], edited by Elchanan Reiner, 51–74. Jerusalem: Zalman Shazar Center for Jewish History, 2015.

Mordechai Zalkin, *Rabbi and Community in the Pale* [Hebrew] (Jerusalem, Magnes Press, 2017).

R. M. Zalmanovitz. *Derashot le-Bar Mitsva*, edited by M. Stern. New York: Hebrew Publishing Company, 1935.

G. Zelikovits. *Bar Mitsva Redes.* New York: Hebrew Publishing Company, 1925.

——. *Collection of Writings, Prose and Poetry* [Yiddish]. New York: Zelikovitsh Yibileum Komite, 1913.

H. J. Zimmels. *Magicians, Theologians and Doctors: Studies in Folk-Medicine and Folk-Lore as Reflected in the Rabbinical Responsa (12th–19th Centuries).* London: Goldston, 1952.

Israel Zinberg. *A History of Jewish Literature,* edited and translated by Bernard Martin, vol. 6. Cincinnati: Hebrew Union College, 1975.

Steven Zipperstein. *Elusive Prophet: Ahad Ha'am and the Origins of Zionism.* Berkeley: University of California Press, 1993.

——. *The Jews of Odessa: a Cultural History, 1794–1881.* Stanford, CA: Stanford University Press, 1985.

——. "Russian Maskilim and the City." In *The Legacy of Jewish Migration: 1881 and Its Impact,* edited by David Berger, 31–45. New York: Brooklyn College Press, 1983.

David Zohar. Jewish *Commitment in a Modern World: Rabbi Ḥayyim Hirschenson and His Attitude to Modernity* [Hebrew]. Jerusalem: Shalom Hartman Institute, 2003.

Oran Zweiter. "Turning a Church into a Synagogue: Jewish Law Meets Communal Politics on New York's Lower East Side." *American Jewish Archives Journal* 71, no. 1 (2019): 1–17.

Zalman Zylbercweig. "Israel Rosenberg II." In *Lives in the Yiddish Theatre: Short Biographies of Those Involved in the Yiddish Theatre as Described in Zalmen Zylbercweig's "Leksikon fun Yidishn Teater, 1931–1969."* http://www.museumoffamilyhistory.com/yt/lex/R/rosenberg-israel-II.htm. Accessed February 20, 2019.

Index

1905 Russian Revolution, 120

Abraham ibn Ezra
 Iggeret ha-Shabbat, 173–174
Adler, Cyrus, 176n10, 240
Aframovitz, Nathan Nata, 107, 110–111
Agudat Yisrael, 7
Albert, Lionel of Montreal, 17n1
Alemanno, Yohanan
 Ḥesheq Shlomo, 170n168
 Sefer ha-Yalkut, 170
Alexander II, 18
Alexandrov, Samuel, 214
Alfasi, Isaac, 238
Alter, Abraham Mordecai, 144n10, 147
Alter, Arye Leib, 42n17
Alter, Yizhak Meir of Ger, 199n52
An-ski, Solomon, 165
anti-Semitism, 156, 180
anti-Zionism, 72n76
Arye Leib of Shpole, 163–164
Asch, Sholom, 66
Asher of Toledo, 143
Asheri, Judah, 145
Ashlag, Yehuda Leib, 150n49, 214–215, 217n55, 221n69, 225, 227, 241, 244
Assaf, David, 9–10
Assaf, Simḥa
 Le-Kor'ot ha-Rabanut, 5–6
assimilation, 7, 66, 180–181
Auerbach, Chaim Yehuda Leib, 137, 240–241
Auerbach, Zalman of Jerusalem, 130–131, 133–139
 Me'orei Esh, 131, 133

Bacon, Gershon, 6–7
Balfour Declaration, 70–71
Barashi, Benjamin of Kotsk, 222
Barukh of Shklov, 196
Barzilay, Maya, 157
Baumritter, Ephraim, 51
Ben Gurion, Micha
 Meqor Yehuda, 158
Ben Yehezkel, Mordecai, 169
Benmozegh, Elijah, 226
Bercovitch, Peter, 79
Berger, Yosef David, 107, 110–111
Berkovitz, Jay, 3
Berlin, Ḥayyim of Elizavetgrad, 231
Berlin, Naftali Zvi Yehuda, 42n17
Berlin, Saul *Besamim Ro'sh*, 143
Bernardini, Paolo, 11
Bernhard, Ḥayyim David, 190
Berossus the Chaldean
 History of Kush and the Land of Abyssinia, 170
Biale, David, 3–4, 10, 55n78
 Hasidism: A New History, 10
Bialik, Ḥayyim Naḥman, 245
Bible
 Genesis, 54n70, 188n58, 203–204, 223, 231, 233
 Exodus, 233n140, 237

Leviticus, 233, 246
Numbers, 182, 223, 233n140
Deuteronomy, 233
Judges, 53
Zechariah, 182–183
Psalms, 35, 54n70, 185, 217, 224, 231, 234, 240
Proverbs, 54n70, 136, 144, 182, 184, 218, 224n85, 233
Song of Songs, 54n70, 224, 231, 234
Lamentations, 121
Ecclesiastes, 54n70, 218, 224n85, 233–234
Bleitrakh, Moshe, 240
Blistreich, Moshe, 55n77, 63n20, 192n16
Bloch, Chaim, 158–159
blood libel, 154, 156–157, 164
Blumenthal, Aaron Simḥa, 222
Bohak, Gideon, 199
Borukhov, Abba Yaakov ha-Kohen, 133
Brown, Benjamin, 10
Brown, Michael, 72
Buzaglo, Shalom
Hadrat Melekh, 232

Cahan, Abraham
The Rise of David Levinsky, 11
Canadian Jewish Chronicle, 102–103, 107
Caplan, Kimmy, 12n47, 202
Chajes, J.H., 223
Christianity, 1, 18, 154, 156–158, 170, 175
Catholic, 168
Orthodox, 193
Protestant, 180n31, 186
Coderre, Louis, 95
Cohen, Hirsch of Montreal, 68n46, 74–78, 80–89, 93–94, 96–97, 99–100, 107–109, 111–112, 114
Cohen, Tobias
Ma'aseh Toviya, 197
Columbus, Christopher, 204
Conan Doyle, Arthur, 166–167, 247
Cooper, Levi, 125
Copernicus, Nicholas, 204–205
Cordovero, Moses
Elimah Rabbati, 146–147
Pardes Rimmonim, 221–222, 232

Dan, Yosef, 153–154, 164n132, 236
Darwin, Charles, 152n58, 205–206
Davar, 245
Defoe, Daniel
Robinson Crusoe, 164
Deutsch, Ḥannania Yom Tov Lippa, 19n9
Diner, Hasia, 63
Drazin, A., 110
Dubitsky, Abraham Samuel, 78n16, 97, 107, 111
Dumas, Alexander
The Count of Monte Cristo, 164
Dunsky, Shimshon, 237–239
Dushinsky, Yosef Zvi of Jerusalem, 131n74
Dynner, Glenn, 1–2

Eckstein, Emmanuel, 159
Eger, Abraham, 40–41, 46–47, 51–52, 230–231
Eger, David, 41
Eger, Yehuda Leib, 38, 40, 210
Eichenstein, Tsvi Hirsh of Zhidachov, 209
Eisenstadt, Ben Zion,
Dorot ha-Aḥaronim, 17–18
Eliashiv, Shlomo, 216, 244
Elijah ben Solomon Zalman (Vilna Gaon), 144, 182, 225, 238
Elon, Menahem, 8
Emden, Jacob, 24n30, 127, 246–247
Ephraim ha-Kohen of Vilna, 127
Epstein, Baruch, 97

Epstein, Ḥayyim Fishel of St. Louis, 91
Epstein, Yeḥiel Mikhl ha-Levi, 119, 131, 135
'Arukh ha-Shulḥan, 119, 131
Etkes, Emmanuel, 29–30
Eybeschutz, Jonathan, 24n30
Ezra, Nissim Elias Benjamin, 240

Faitlovich, Jacques, 170n170
Falk, Joshua ha-Kohen, 31n63
Pnei Yehoshua, 31n63
Feigenbaum, Isaac ha-Kohen, 51, 54n70, 117, 152, 214–215, 230
Fine, Samuel of Detroit, 178
Yalkut Shmuel, 178
Fine, Steven, 66n38
Fox, Chaim Leib, 56–57, 120n18, 243
Fradkin, Shneur Zalman, 40
Frank, Adolphe, 205n92
Frank, Tsvi Pesaḥ, 133
Frekel, Y.
Der Hoyz Doctor, 196
Frenk, Azriel Natan
Aggadot ha-Zohar, 235
Friedlaender, Solomon
Yerushalmi, 143
Friedman, Israel of Ruzhyn, 31

Gabbai, Meir, 240
Garb, Jonathan, 214
Garber, Simcha, 76n8, 81
Gelbin, Cathy, 157
Gellman, Uriel, 10
Gerondi, Nissim ben Reuben (Ran), 50
Gershtenkorn, Yitsḥak, 234
Gikatilla, Joseph
Sha'arei Orakh, 221, 227
Ginzberg, Louis, 23
Glass, Shlomo Ze'ev Yosef, 58–59
Glazer, Simon, 75–76
Goldschmidt, Lazarus
Baraita de-Ma'aseh Bere'shit, 143
Goldsmith, Arnold, 157, 159n102, 166n147
Gordon, Jacob, 68, 70, 72, 80
Gordon, Judah Leib, 42
Gotlib, Meir
Zayt Gezunt, 196
Grafton, Anthony, 150
Graubart, Yehuda Leib, 91
Great Depression, 98, 100, 106, 242
Green, Arthur, 1, 10, 22n22, 244
Greenberg, Sarah, 113
Grimm, Jacob and Wilhelm, 157
Grodzinsky, Ḥayyim Ozer, 78, 132–133
Guttmacher, Elijah (Greiditser Rabbi), 167–168

Hadler, Moshe, 65
ha-Efrati, Yosef of Tropplowitz
Melukhat Sha'ul, 22–23, 27
Hahnemann, Samuel, 192–193
Halberstam, Ḥayyim of Sanz, 213
Halberstam, Yeḥezkel Shraga of Sieniawa, 213
ha-Levanon, 121–122
Haller, Albrecht von, 27
Halmilzahagi, Elyakim Getzel, 219
Halpern, Salomon Alter, 247
Halstok, Meir Yeḥiel ha-Levi (Ostrovtser Rebbe), 40, 42, 46, 49, 51, 53, 60–61, 214, 230–231
Halstok, Yeḥezkel, 42
ha-Maggid, 153n59
Harkavy, Alexander, 151n51, 231
Hasidism, 3, 9–11, 14–16, 19–20, 22–23, 26–31, 36–38, 40, 46–47, 49–50, 55–58, 60–63, 67, 81, 126, 143–145, 147–150, 160, 162–164, 167, 169, 171–173, 190–191, 193, 195, 197–198, 209, 212–214, 230

Haskalah, 2, 10–11, 22–23, 26–28, 33–35, 38, 43, 46, 57, 116, 123, 143–145, 185–186, 212, 232, 239
Ha-Tesefira, 25, 57
Hayyim ben Isaac
    Or Zaru'a, 145
Ḥayyim Dov of Piotrków, 191
Ḥazan, Leizerke of Lodz, 44
Hebrew Journal, 66, 68–70, 73, 104
Heilman, Samuel, 10
Hendel, Manoaḥ, 165
Herod, 156
Herschorn, Sheea (Joshua ha-Levi), 50n54, 81, 83–86, 90–91, 94, 96–98, 107–108, 111, 114
Hershkovitz, Shim'on Aharon
    Di Gneive, 167
Heschel, Abraham Joshua of Apt, 213
Hill, Brad Sabin, 65
Hillman, David Zvi, 219
Hinshparg, Moshe, 140
Hirschenson, Ḥayyim, 130
Hopstein, Israel (Maggid of Koznits), 213
Hornblass, Petaḥia, 51, 58n88, 64n32, 122–123, 152
Horodetsky, Samuel Abba, 236
Horowitz, Isaiah, 24n30, 119, 218
    Shlah, 218–219
Horowitz, Yaakov Yitzhak ha-Levi (Seer of Lublin), 190
Hundert, Gershon, 1
Hurwitz, Pinḥas Elijah, 24–26
    Sefer ha-Berit, 24–25

Idra Rabba, 237
Idra Zuta, 237
Ignatof, David
    Ma'asiyot fun Altn Prag, 158
Islam, 1, 175
Israel ben Eliezer (Baal Shem Tov), 172, 190, 215n47
Isserles, Moses, 119
Itche, Leizer, 42

Jacob ibn Habib
    Eyn Ya'aqov, 226
Jacobs, Leon V., 79
Jaffe, Mordecai, 218–219
    Levush, 218–219
Jesus Christ, 156
Joseph, Jacob, 16
Judah Loewe of Prague (Maharal), 19n7, 152–160, 163–167, 196n39, 221n69, 244–247
    Gevurot ha-Shem, 153
    Ḥiddushei Aggadot, 154
Judah the Patriarch, 19
Judah the Pietist (*he-Ḥasid*), 18–19, 164n132
    Sefer Ḥasidim, 19
Judaism
    Conservative, 13n52
    Orthodox, 2–5, 8–14, 25–28, 39, 59, 61, 63–70, 72, 74–75, 78, 80, 83, 86, 91, 100, 109–111, 113, 116, 121, 125, 127–131, 139–145, 147–149, 168, 171–172, 174, 177–178, 185–189, 202, 207–208, 211, 215, 218, 227–228, 231, 236, 240, 244–249
    Reform, 2, 13n52, 124, 176, 180
    ultra-Orthodox, 6, 217n56, 246
Jung, Leo, 240
Jung, Maier, 74n92

Kabbalah, 16, 19–20, 24–26, 53–54, 56, 71, 126, 142, 144n10, 151, 153, 156–157, 159, 168, 174, 193, 199, 203–218, 220–228, 230–232, 236–238, 240–241, 243–244, 248–249
Kagan, Israel Meir ha-Kohen, 15, 78

Ḥafets Ḥayyim, 15, 78, 118
Nidḥe Yisra'el, 15
Kahana, Solomon David, 51
Kaplan, Aryeh, 249
Karaites, 144, 151
Karlinsky, Nahum, 10, 143
Karo, Joseph
Shulḥan 'Arukh, 126–127, 140
kashrut (kosher), 13, 15, 57, 67–70, 72, 74–78, 80–86, 88–90, 92–97, 100–110, 112, 118, 122, 124, 187–188, 233
Katz, Bertsche of Siedlkov, 160
Katz, Isaac, 152–154
Keneder Adler, 66, 76–82, 85, 87–88, 90–91, 93–96, 99, 105–108, 110, 112, 114, 237
Kishinev Pogrom, 66, 140
Klepfisz, Heszel, 21–22, 26
Klepfisz, Samuel Zanvil of Warsaw, 38n88, 48, 52
Kol Torah, 117–118, 133, 140
Kook, Abraham Isaac, 92, 111–112, 133, 137, 139, 214, 239
Koppel Lipschitz, Jacob, 19–20
Sha'arei Gan Eden, 19
Kotok, Alexander, 193
Kranzler, George, 63
Kromer, Aaron Mordecai, 163–164

Landau, Samuel of Prague, 213
Langer, Jiri, 172
Langermann, Y. Tzvi, 4
Laxer, Getsel, 84, 87, 91, 96–98, 104–106
Lederhandler, Eli, 1
Lefin, Mendel, 196
Leiman, Shnayer, 245
Leiman, Sid, 158
Leiner, Gershon Henokh of Radzyn, 145n16, 190–191
Leiner, Mordecai Joseph El'azar (Radziner Rebbe), 230–231
Leiner, Mordechai Yosef of Izbica, 38
Leivick, H.
Der Goylem, 158
Leon, Moses de, 211, 224–225, 238
Levi Isaac of Berdichev, 162
Leviant, Curt, 246
Levinthal, Bernard of Philadelphia, 91
Levy, Meir Tsvi, 68, 70
Lewis, Justin, 118
Lilienblum, Moses Leib, 2, 34–35
Lipkin, Israel, 116
Litwin, A., 157
Livshits, Hillel Aryeh Leib, 51
Lobo, Jeronimo
Voyage historique d'Abissinie, 170
Lorberbaum, Jacob of Lissa, 127
Luria, Isaac, 24–25, 126, 144n10, 151, 204, 209, 212, 220–223, 232
Luria, Solomon, 19n7
Luzzatto, Moses Ḥayyim
La-Yesharim Tehilla, 22, 26

Magid, Shaul, 148
Mahler, Raphael, 9, 27
Maimonides, Moses, 19, 129, 135, 146, 174–175, 180n31, 201–202, 206
Mishneh Torah, 201
Margaliot, Ephraim Zalman
Mateh Ephraim, 152
Margolis, Gavriel Ze'ev, 89
Markuse, Moses, 196
Marshak, Jacob of Polotsk
Sefer Divrei Moshe, 51n59, 146
Martin, Mederic, 94
Mazeh, Jacob of Moscow, 231
Medini, Ḥayyim Hezekiah, 219–220, 229–230, 238
Sdei Ḥemed, 219
Meir ben Hertskes, 28

Meir of Opatow (Apt), 20
Meir, Golda, 123–124
Meir, Jonatan, 209
Meisels, Eliyahu Ḥaim, 42
Meltzer, Isser Zalman, 133, 137–138
Menaḥem Mendel of Vitebsk, 23
messianism, 5, 19, 26, 71, 125, 152, 188–189, 208–209, 212, 215, 226n93, 228–229
Michelson, Tsvi Yeḥezkel, 146
Midrash, 20, 117, 160–161, 169, 179, 223, 238–239
    Mishlei Rabbati, 169
    Tadshe, 161
    Tanna de-Be Eliyahu, 160–161
    va-Yosha', 161
Miesel, Elijah Ḥayyim of Lodz, 231
Mikhelson, Tsvi Yeḥezkel, 164
Miller, David of Oakland, 125
    Sefer Miqveh Yisra'el, 125
Mintz, Jerome, 14, 22n23
Mishnah, 19–20, 161, 226
mitnagdim, 9, 11, 15, 36, 63, 212
Mohilever, Samuel, 146
Montreal Star, 87
Morgen Journal, 99
Morgenstern, Yitsḥak Zelig of Sokolow, 191
Morrison, G., 4
Moss, Kenneth, 9

Naḥman of Bratslav, 155, 163–164, 172
nationalism, 71, 175
Neugroschel, Joachim, 153n65, 245
Nifla'ot Qedushat Levi, 162
Nigal, Gedaliahu, 164
Nissenboim, Yitzhak, 27–28

Or Torah, 246
Orner, Jacob of Nasielsk, 51
Orwell, George
    Animal Farm, 247

Perets, Isaac Leyb, 155
Perl, Joseph
    Megalleh Temirin, 143
Perlmutter, Abraham Zvi, 44
Petaya, Yehuda, 244
Phillipson, David, 124
Pinḥas of Korets, 159–160, 190
Poll, Solomon, 16, 56
Poppers, Meir, 151, 223

Rabinovitch, Israel, 96, 109–110
Rabinowicz, Shlomo Hakohen, 191
Rankin, Oliver Shaw, 244
Rapoport-Albert, Ada, 171
Rashi (Solomon ben Isaac), 50, 224
Rawidowicz, Simon, 235
Reizin, Zalman, 59n91, 158
Richler, Mordecai, 243
Rischin, Moses
    The Promised City, 12
Robinson, Ira
    Rabbis and Their Community, 13
Rodkinson, Michael
    Sefer Urim ve-Tumin ha-Ḥadash, 149n40
Rosenberg family
    Aaron Elimelekh, 30, 80, 176, 193, 243
        Likkutei Beit Aharon, 243–244
    Abraham Isaac, 49, 111, 113–114
    Baruch, 193n21, 235n149, 243
        Kovets Ma'amar Yehudah, 243n8
    Ḥaya Hava, 28, 30–32
    Israel, 79–80
    Meir Joshua, 30–31, 58, 57, 80–81, 83, 114, 149–150, 195, 235, 240, 243
        Kur ha-Mivḥan, 31n63, 149n40
    Leah, 49, 66n39, 75, 86, 243
    Sara Gitl, 31–32, 49

Rosenberg, Judah ben Alexander, 145
Rosenberg, Yudel
- *'Ateret Tif'eret*, 139n104, 177–178
- *Brivele*, 128, 173
- *Darsha Tsemer u-Fishtim*, 120
- *Der Greiditser*, 157n86, 167–169
- *Der Krizis fun Łódź Varshe*, 23n24, 121
- *Der Shpoler Zeyde*, 163–165, 167n151, 245
- *Derekh Erets*, 24, 50, 148n33
- *Haggada shel Pesaḥ*, 152
- *Haqqafot*, 55n72, 160, 233
- *ha-Qeri'ah ha-Qedosha*, 65, 125n49, 243n9
- *Ḥokhmat Maharal*, 158
- *Homeopatia*, 193–194
- *Ḥoshen*, 165, 247
- *Me'or ha-Hashmal*, 131
- *Midrash Zuta*, 64n31
- *Miqveh Yehuda*, 58n88, 64–65, 122, 125
- *Nifla'ot Maharal mi-Prag 'im ha-Golem*, 153, 155n75, 157–159
- *Omer*, 21n19, 120n19, 149n43, 182n36, 185, 242
- *Or Tsaḥ*, 232
- *Peri Yehuda*, 185–186, 222
- *Refu'at ha-Nefesh u-Refu'at ha-Guf*, 201
- *Seder ha-Prozbul*, 119–120, 243n9
- *Sefer Divrei ha-Yamim le-Shlomo ha-Melekh*, 169
- *Sefer Eliyahu ha-Navi'*, 160
- *Sefer Goral ha-'Assiriyot*, 149, 151–152
- *Sefer Refa'el ha-Mal'akh*, 192, 195–198, 200, 245
- *Sha'arei Zohar Ktuvim*, 54n70
- *Sha'arei Zohar Torah*, 19n7, 54n70, 214–216, 219–220, 223, 229–237, 239, 243, 246
- *Tif'eret Mahar'el mi-Shpole*, 163
- *Yadot Nedarim*, 37n88, 48, 50–54, 116, 149, 210–211, 230
- *Yeḥeveḥ Da'at*, 54, 139–140, 185

Roskies, David, 27, 146n24, 149
Rosman, Moshe, 10, 145
Rothenberg, Joshua, 3
Rotlev, Tuvia ha-Kohen, 51

Saadia Gaon, 146
Sabbatai Tsvi, 20n11, 212
Sagiv, Gadi, 10
Saperstein, Marc, 176
Schacter, Jacob, 42n17
Schechter, Solomon, 144–145
Schischa, Abraham, 160
Schneersohn, Menaḥem Mendel of Lubavitch, 198
Schneersohn, Shalom Dov Baer (Lubavicher Rebbe), 15
Scholem, Gershom, 24n29, 159, 164n136, 236, 241, 248
Schorsch, Ismar, 5
Schwadron, Mordecai ha-Kohen of Berezhany, 230–231
Schweid, Eliezer, 9
secularism, 6, 10, 13, 24n29, 43, 72, 95n109, 121, 147–148, 168, 171–172, 180, 182, 188, 207, 245
Sefer ha-Temuna, 204
Sefer Razi'el, 197
Segal Etinga, Abraham of Dukla, 164
Sha'arei Torah, 54n70, 117, 215
Sha'arei Tsion, 131–132
Shakespeare, William, 108
Shapiro, Kalonymous Kalman, 191
Shapiro, Marc, 219, 247
Sharfstein, Ḥayyim, 150–153, 165
Sheftel, Shabetai ben Akiva ha-Levi of Prague
- *Shefa Tal*, 232

Shifrin, David, 15
Shim'on bar Yoḥai (Rashbi), 54n70, 203n77, 211, 221, 224–225, 234–235, 238
Shivḥei ha-Besht, 164
Shneur Zalman of Liadi, 127, 232
    Siddur, 232
Sholom Aleykhem, 155
Shternberg, Yitzḥak, 107–108, 110–111
Simḥa Bunem of Przysucha, 190
Singer, Isaac Bashevis, 36n82, 42, 229n120
Singer, Israel Joshua, 36n82, 42
Singer, Pinḥas Mendel, 36n82, 42–43, 48n43
Sirkis, Joel, 119, 225
Sitruk, Madroche, 240
Slonimsky, Ḥayyim Selig, 25–26
    Ma'amarei Ḥokhma, 23, 25
Smolenskin, Perets, 3
Sofer, Yaakov Ḥayyim, 219
Sola, Clarence de, 79
Solomon, Norman, 28, 143
Sonnenfeld, Yosef Haim, 241n173
Spector, Isaac Elḥanan of Kovno, 15
Spinoza, Baruch, 152n58, 181
Stanislawski, Michael, 6–7
Steinsaltz, Adin, 249
Steinschneider, Moritz, 146
Stern, Eliahu, 6
Stern, Harry, 176n12
Stern, Henry Aaron
    Wanderings among the Falashas in Abyssinia, 170n165
Sylvester, Jan, 157–158

Tageblatt, 233, 236
Talmud
    Babylonian
        Pesaḥim, 132, 136
        Yevamot, 136
        Ketubot, 161n110
        Nedarim, 50
        Sotah, 99
        Horayot, 132
    Palestinian, 144n10, 231n130
Teitelbaum, Joshua of Warsaw, 162
Temkin, 91, 97
Tevuna, 116
Tiqqunei Zohar, 231–232
Tishby, Isaiah, 20n11, 24n29, 236
Tosafot, 51
Trunk, Y.Y., 191
    Letste Ḥasidishe Folks Mayses, 158
Tsadoq ha-Kohen, 38, 41, 147, 210
Tsuker, Yearḥmiel Gedalia, 63
Tsvi ha-Kohen, 237
Tsvi Ze'ev of Ladysmith, 140
Tursh, Dovberish, 158
Twersky, Abraham of Trisk, 197
Twersky, Isadore, 22

Ullman, Shalom, 216
Uziel, Benzion, 71n69, 113, 139, 239–240

Valdenburg, Eliezer, 139
Vital, Ḥayyim, 144n10, 199
    Sha'ar ha-Qedusha, 24–25
    Sha'ar ha-Yiḥudim, 210

Wachtfogel, Moshe Yom Tov, 97–98, 101, 107–108, 110–112
Wajnberg, Szloma, 234, 242
Wasserman, Elḥanan, 215
Weinryb, Yosef, 68–70
Wertheimer, Jack, 3
Wertheimer, Solomon Aaron, 162
Wesley, John
    Primitive Physick, 196
Willowsky, David, 15
Wilowsky, Jacob David (Slutsker Rav), 39, 42, 231n130

Wilson, Woodrow, 166–167
Winchevsky, Morris, 3
Wissenschaft des Judentums, 142, 144
Wodzinski, Marcin, 10
Wolofsky, Hirsch, 77, 82–83, 89, 114, 181n32
World War I, 27, 55, 60, 113, 120, 171
World War II, 12, 14, 56, 171

Yassif, Eli, 35n76, 59n91, 158n95, 160n109, 169, 245–246
Yehuda Leib ben Ze'ev
    Talmud L'shon 'Ivri, 22–23
Yeraḥmiel Yisroel Yitsḥak (Aleksander Rebbe), 191
Yerusalimsky, Moshe Naḥum of Kamenka, 44–47, 53–54, 64n32, 213, 230–231
Yissakhar Baer of Kremnits, 218–219
    Imrei Bina, 218
    Meqor Ḥokhma, 219
Yoreh De'ah, 39
Yosef, Ovadia, 139

Zagorodsky, Israel Hayyim, 201
Zalmanovitz, Aaron, 107, 111–112
Zeitlin, Hillel, 214, 235–236
Zionism, 57, 70–72, 79, 123, 148n33, 183
Zipperstein, Steven, 7, 10–11
Zlotnick, Yehuda Leib, 97
Zohar, 54, 89, 113, 137, 146–147, 151n51, 162, 167, 173, 186, 203–206, 208–221, 223–241, 243–244–245, 248
Zucker, Leibush, 28

www.ingramcontent.com/pod-product-compliance
Lightning Source LLC
Chambersburg PA
CBHW071402300426
44114CB00016B/2151
* 9 7 9 8 8 8 7 1 9 4 4 4 8 *